Dancing with Mosquitoes

Dancing with Mosquitoes

To Liberate the Mind from Humanism—
A Way to Green the Mind

Theo Grutter

VANTAGE PRESS
New York

Published by Vantage Press, Inc.
516 West 34th Street, New York, New York 10001

Manufactured in the United States of America
ISBN: 0-533-12977-X

Library of Congress Catalog Card No.: 98-90895

0 9 8 7 6 5 4 3 2

*How can I love the wildness of life if I cannot love this
wildness deep inside myself?*

Contents

Note

Thirty years ago, after a brief business career in Europe, I spent some years as a vagabond, turning inside, writing and questioning myself. I printed some notes I called "Anger and Gentleness" and gave copies to those for whom I felt it was right. I was more angry than gentle because the Creator does not stick to the morals I learned. Nonetheless, this tumult of emotions onto paper started a fortunate change for me. Since then I have been migrating with Clara and our five children between the coast of Alaska in the spring, and a tropical fishing village in the fall. The children went to school here and there and are now grown up. In the South and the North I fish independently and alone. We lead a simple life which has been good to us, certainly better than I was told to expect. What a bargain to be alive!

During these thirty years, I have spent half of my days and half of the nights alone, on northern waters or on the tropical sea or in swamps and lagoons, fishing and hunting in the woods, and more often in the taiga, in the countryside, or up in the Sierra Madre just curiously loafing around, sometimes smiling or mumbling to myself.

When alone I still patiently try to heal myself of that anger pestering me, thinking that maybe all is wonderfully right and simply waits to be seen. I have learned that there is a world beyond pity and beyond hate that is not monstrous. I have learned that earnest helping is something different from the comforting so sacred to us. This discovery still shakes me.

In my writing you will find me in my serene moments and also in moments when I struggle at the foot of my mountain to heaven throwing up, still purging myself of sickening slogans and sour plums. It is good so. I like to see my writing as a quest toward health, an organic event, that recombines itself time and again like a sprouting bean to show itself stronger each morning. It's my mental survival course.

This writing is also the net of thoughts I have hung to catch that shamelessly efficient fisherman in me, my "guardian angel," so to speak; I have my personal sins to tend.

These thoughts do me good. They make me come alive—they green my mind. They do for my mind what breaking through the pupa does to a butterfly. I cannot think of a healthier or a more amusing thing I have done for myself. Slowly these visual thoughts turn into physical pain and joy that are friendly to me.

I must especially emphasize that this is not a packaged mental tour. I let the forms of the ideas become difficult or incomplete as they are naturally. I resisted to classify and whitewash the thoughts for simplicity and convenient clarity. Such forced clarity usually feels quite unnourishing and sterile to me and has often misled me. "Break the stare on a subject," I told myself, "so wisdom may run loose to do its unfocused thinking."

I have poured out my share of kindness as well as my share of meanness and so have become an easy target for those who only argue to win, but there are others who can share with me the thrill when I ride a crest of goodness not always obvious to me, and I follow a mysterious attraction blindly holding onto faith. I have found more people than I expected who are excited to come down from safe ground and become cheerfully puzzled or even lost as wanderers in wonderland. I like to share these thoughts with those wanderers. They may be crude chunks of fertilizer to them who enjoy jumping from one level of knowledge to another while we liberate our minds of humanism and will make use of the paradoxes that occur. Learning to think outside of humanism is as extraordinary to me as for a fish to learn to fly.

These thoughts are not meant to be engraved in stone; they are meant to be alive and put the reader in a pregnant mood. Watch out! I didn't kill them by framing them in a conclusion. They might bite! A dandelion in your mind might start to green again to flower its gold! I leave blanks, expecting the reader to contribute. For those who are more grounded and self-assured than I, it is best we do not meet. Misunderstanding is too easy and the harsh feelings it breeds make losers of us all.

Adding to Galileo's mischief, I accept that I and the whole clan of man are also not at the center, but turn around life. I may now dance with mosquitoes, hence the title. I may now hug a tree and look for good news also through its eyes. With this simple acceptance, badness is never certain anymore.

I declared a part of my time and of my mind a wildlife refuge for my own delight to discover what grows in this piece of unplowed inner landscape. There is a different order of things allowed there, another discipline, other rules for being a friend. There are no paved roads for thought, no furrows and yellow lines, no ordinary traffic signs, no supermarkets for neatly butchered thoughts with shelves for hate or love, or for ecology, cut flowers, or for the prime ribs of the beast. Accepting this refuge's principle of uncertainty, one remains humble, nicely puzzled and wondering. I allowed myself the freedom in which thoughts bubble up that may be ridiculously right or wrong. I resisted the trend of breaking down the pattern of life into compartments, and instead enjoyed a mental vagabondage acceptable to few. My instinct for likenesses had a feast. I love to sneak away from our paradigms to breathtaking viewpoints that may not yet be socially acceptable and to try myself out without being reinforced by a crowd. And so, for that less biased view, I trot along a little to the side of the herd and its net. My sweetest trips came from trespassing into land the puritans had told me was forbidden.

When my mind lives outside, away from people, soon I am surrounded by a thousand helpers telling me, "Quit moaning about the ways of men. Look what we can do with what you bemoan." But first I had to find out that it is by these "prohibited" trespassings that a person reaches a supercritical state, cracks his old form with his breakthrough into a green philosophy and molts to wholly reengineer his attitude.

Such a non-scholarly, eclectic piece of writing, which has turned quite unplanned into some rather unconventional research into the roots of ecology meant to be more than a confrontation, requires from the reader an extraordinary tolerance for apparent contradictions. To sift for this tolerance, let me say bluntly that all my income to support our family for my last 35 years has come from a few years logging and then from fishing. It has been slow for me to bring my activity at sea into harmony with my thoughts.

I should warn you that I am at my best when my thoughts are rather more spicy than sweet. These notes are not meant to be read in one long sitting. They might even be poisonous when swallowed in one gulp. I expect the reader rather to read here and there. A sip of weirdness a day may keep the monotony away. Some of you might be better off to start in the middle. Most are not practical thoughts, some are koans. They are, however, an account of an ordinary man; no shadows come to life, no magic herbs fire the mind. I cannot even juggle three apples with one hand. But at times I have perfumed my ideas with a little poetry.

I wrote this in a language I learned late. This may be good for the reader since there is less temptation for me to play with words, but I do use words in unfashionable ways. This writing is also my "egg tooth" that helps me to hatch from humanism: some thoughts have been upsetting for me and most probably will be so for others who have grasped the implications. I was not at all anxious to please myself or others at once. May I ask you to be patient when you initially note a trespass or offense in my ideas. I have found that once the unusual becomes anticipated and is given a chance, many of the thoughts with broken ends may gradually fall into place. Some ideas, though, only make sense when one becomes accustomed to stepping out of the bewitching circle humanism draws around itself. I wish I could in the past have better overcome my arrogance.

These are the few things I wanted to say in preparing you. It will feel good when after reading these sketches you can at times think kindly of me.

—T.G.

Dancing with Mosquitoes

1

I wish myself the luck to get over my anger when I talk and write. I wish myself the luck to discover my love for the listener and the reader. These gifts still play hide and seek with me.

When I hop down from the pedestal of safe high ground to be with the person or critter who has to anger or pester me, I find I can look at their mischief from above and below, from left, from right, even from five generations ahead. I can look through their eyes and even sometimes conclude: wow—how wonderful! I then can guess that we are partners after all who may have never before been allowed to meet yet are nonetheless handcuffed together on this trek. To climb over the fence of the personality game to where there is no loser, no winner, and to where my missteps are your missteps and your victories are also my victories, what a treat! I can surface for a happy hour from the underworld of victory and defeat. Mean aggression may turn into stimulation and smile.

When so taking on different identities soon my anger may lose its sting and become simply a riddle in which I can switch on a lamp. Anger makes me so physical, so uninspired and blind, simply blackmail, a gun aimed at a stranger who has to prostrate himself or be shot. Such cocky self-defense has helped me in my adolescence to cut my second umbilical cord, but now that I am trying to put everything to good use of what a day brings me, it is not the time to simply chase my opponents away. So much good luck was sent yet I wailed and whimpered instead of welcoming it.

When angrily I struck my C flat, your C flat string was ready to resonate to my angry tune. But you, you were a great potter with a dream—your relationships: your pile of clay. You arranged the incoming pitch of my fit and you made of my gooey clay a pot.

"Theo, why should you get angry with the Mountain you climb? Let him simply be your dear puzzling challenge, he will be more fun," I tell myself.

I feel ripe to hatch from the cocky pride that protected my tender incubation years. I feel ripe to hatch from that intellectual power game in which we only aspire to snatch attention, to shock, to intimidate, to ambush, to come out on top. Now I look forward to letting myself think, talk, question and before all look and listen shamelessly naked and be a full moon. Behind our gaudy fashion shows, where we compete for the best-dressed minds, we seem to know each other astonishingly well. Out in that freer world, I am simply a mountain climber in cheerful dialogue with the mountain he climbs.

2

When I look down from high upon a kite, an outlaw's life looks more intriguing and less offensive than when watched from across the road.

It can't be that everyone is favored with easy chores that bring their rewards soon. Not everybody has the luck to squeeze a sore and then be given time to see the splinter come out. Life seems to have little respect for the bookkeeping that one person or one generation sums up to judge its deeds.

You, I, she, like all cells, we must be tied up to a function. The Creator says: You heal, she ferments, it will grow to my fingernail, in my needle this lad is the hole! The Creator also decrees: Here are your tools, your skills, your appetite for doing so, spotlighting our memories here and there. And there goes my dream for wholeness, for perfection, and for independence.

And why should a gentle man over his many lifetimes not also be asked to serve as a storm, an earthquake, an ice age, an experiment, a misty October day that happily rots and sweeps the fading feast of summer away? Why should he be spared from pulling for one term the plow of meanness over the earth? Such thoughts make me think respectfully of pagan tribes that expect their gods to have a good man be reborn as a bad man in his next life. In the climate of a people's long life, the sun, the rain, the hail all have their turn to be king for the day. Slowly, I get hints that it is within this amazing profusion of creative mutations, crimes, oozes, sins, paradoxes, perversions and April fools that life tells me its most fantastic creation tales. Sinners, inventors, mutagens might so come close to being synonymies. All are experimenters; most end up in life's compost pile.

And so, some of us take off into ecstasy when the early autumn frost explodes a maple wood into a jubilant firework of decay in golden yellow, red and blue; in such a September mood, we sense new expectations flying our way. What a relief to see that our own calendar also has room for those difficult acts that guarantee us the great gift of birth and the great gift of death—the thawing winds; the hails; the greedy, youthful May; the breeding noons; the month of hay and of baskets heaped with giveaways; the spells of mean, crisp cold that wash the air and plow the soil.

3

In the hierarchy of societies, some step up its ladder, others step down.

Ancient China had a saying: "No good deed goes unpunished." I note that our parents' good deeds have let us become frighteningly numerous across the face of the earth. I also note that we are now triggered by the Creator to enhance a climate that is unfavorable for our children to become caring and productive moms and dads. The present inclination for abortion, for sterility enhancement, a society stepping down into a career in egotism; are these such corrective "punishments" for our parents' good deeds?

To join the wealthy club of the first world I must switch off to long distance calls. It demands my good-bye to the great four-dimensional society beyond common sense and larger than man that has been our psychic home for so long. That great, mixed and outrageously permissive society I am to leave is composed of storms, of sunshine and rain, of animals and trees, of women and of men, and is many generations tall. Individuals who stand up by themselves and do without a shepherd, a middleman to God and a fence in their mind, step up to this inter-species club. There we seem primarily steered by faith in the voice of the Earth and secondarily by an anchor of stern rationality our egos cautiously drag behind.

Why does life want mankind to unionize just by itself and become raisins in a bag? I would think it likes us better dotting its cake. Ah! If I could more clearly visualize life's universal organism with its universal healing system. This would be a comforting arm around Theo the whiner and rebel. Here begins the science I am excited about. Imagine what comfort the awareness of such a great togetherness could bring. Maybe the Great Society does not have to be invented. I suspect it to be waiting cash in the hand, right in front of my eyes, maybe too fantastic and socially still unacceptable to be fearlessly seen, maybe too large to be caught with any net made of "abc's." In that great union absolutely nothing may need changing—no fences go down, no crime is abolished, no blood is mixed— but is simply formed by enlarging my vision. When I snoop around I see bits of this grandiose script for grandiose loving acted out by pollinating insects, by bushes cooking their berries for any straggler in need of a seed scattering job, by the great family of earthworms, by every "behaved" and "misbehaved" organism in the sea and on the prairie, even by our own intuitive grunts and smiles. To be triggered by the present crisis alert of our population explosion to temporarily clam up into an adult commune. This love in house arrest enhancing a climate that is unfavorable for our children to become caring and productive moms and dads may turn out to be one of life's high level cures. Much of my criticism may be naive barking at leaves rustling in the wind. Finding hidden rhymes in the Great Riddle—that's yummy ice cream for my soul.

I also note that, supplementary to Darwin's Theory, every speck of protoplasm seems not only to blindly lust for its own best, but to be the best lover of all. I see the "Fitter-Gardener-Principle" at work. When I can hang-glide on my soul, I get glimpses of such a promising view and my confidence soars. And I am still Lazarus happy with just crumbs of serenity. In such triumphs of my senses I am guest of scenic viewpoints, looking down on that enormous stage where trillions of actors act out God's play.

Is it not ultimately to this poetic togetherness, still playing hide and seek with me, that all scientists in the art of ecstasy dedicate the mandalas they paint, write, trumpet, and theorize about?

4

For many people, there is still nothing quite like becoming a soul brother to Albert Schweitzer to command instant respect.

I am encouraged to stand in line for the "noble" jobs—the work that instantly lights up on credit all the smiles that were meant to shine on a hundred years. Here the handshakes, affectionate company, prompt promotions, honors, and the punishment of fame are secure. Still the laborers of the Great Spirit who do the work too dirty for high-bred minds have their lobbyists in me. When I curiously wander off from my safe intellectual routine, these unpopular daimons jump on their chance and sneak behind my dogmas nifty question marks. They might even lobby me to do my share in their demolition crew.

A tall mind may see together with a "noble" deed's spectacular instant success also its more discreet side effects rippling through time that can produce all kinds of debts and sores in the forests, the land and in our own neighboring three generations up the hill. Who knows, the author of that old Oriental saying, "No good deed goes unmended," may have left us more than an exotic play of words. Perhaps he wanted to remind us that such a deed remains a pure and blameless spinster who never loved a man. And with the lightning of his insight he shook the earth. Yet to think about the dark side of goodness remains for most of us too hot.

Even in our meanness-breeding crowdedness saving a failing man from death we still like to see as a virtue—maybe because we like to be treated the same later on. But how can it be? From the scenic viewpoints of all the hundred generations surrounding us this must look like an addiction—a roadblock on life's ballad.

I wonder whether the ideal is not here, tirelessly teasing my intellect: "Let me light you up if you dare." Beyond our protective sciences of thinking out ever better harvesters and whips, smarter genes, rounder wheels and more kilowatts to whip Mother Earth to give us more, are we not invited to also rest our thinking—to unlock the mind, to become aware so our creativity, our capacity to be enlightened, can pitch and polish its mirror dish? We can listen to the dream of the Earth. Here no judgment, no conclusions are needed. Each simply presents his questions and may be granted to see the answer somewhere on that huge stage acted out. We can patiently wait for a provocative act to show off its meaning, resist impatiently intervening, resist the conventional solution of swiftly dragging that shadowy act from our curiosity and condemning it as a crime sending for the technicians. And we realize that to be shown its hidden rhyme is the cure! Who knows? Out of the shade of that shady lady an undisclosed kindness might step out into the light. Imagine, if you can, nature laying before us all its mountain of good intentions behind its "brutal" justice and strength which shine with apparent idiocies. Surprise, surprise! Our heroes might dim a little and may have performed the glamorous chores of the blossom chosen by the thorn bush to hand out its yummy-fruits when ripe. Yet we may not be eternally cursed to be semi-blind and forced to condemn the shady businesses of the roots, of the fermenters, the grindstones and composters, but be granted leisure time with radar eyes. We then can follow that blossom's stem down to the dark business of its sucker roots, listen to the song of putrefaction, marvel at the "dirty" work the roots do.

5

When my soul is in the comfortable, the practical and hooked on common sense, it is a fish landed on a pier leaping out of tune.

My moments worth living have not been the prize of comfort and safety. They didn't come from sitting down. I found that it was those cussed hardships and curled roads one is out to abolish that sparked the few triumphs of living still serving me well. They came from eruptions that shattered the husk in which I nicely curled up my love and my mind. They came from unpopular goals given to me that I have finally taken on, from the terror of change which I did not let turn me back, but which I turned into a "let's try me out." They came from being a brave little tern circling its own white circles high above an immense indigo sea of "thou shalt not"s, and I set out on my own assuming a man's worth amounts to what's unique in him. I discovered that acts which do not comfort, but animate, are our best seeds—and are serenaded by all the emotions of pregnancy.

When I remain curious instead of whining, I may make out the gift wrapped in a hindrance that life has planted in my way. My soul thrives on the witty, the mischievous, the curly, anything that's not neatly balanced and straight. My soul conspires with the wild and likes to dance with the mosquitoes, the paradoxes and the wolf. I am reluctant to become a professional rationalist and to dedicate myself to the "better behaved" world so widely advertised, because I fear that in it the faint capacity for ecstasy will never awaken in me.

I live on the few things in a day that I do not clench in my weak little logic but give up to the heart to decide. My reason is definitely a non-swimmer. Why let the artists serve me the ocean experience cup by cup? Take off your seven coats, Theo, dive in!

6

We are engrossed by physical solutions. Are we going to turn into a generation of elephant-men?

Why this addiction to physical solutions? Consider the naive answer to our terrible male aggression: simply provide shelters for women.

Is our enormously increasing energy consumption not a symptom of the increased friction that our mentality causes? Are we becoming such bad cooks, we wear down a knife every day for not knowing the joints? We now awkwardly bulldoze through life, fumbling for our joys, with an equivalent of a continuous ten kilowatts per man. We have become so physical. In biological terms this state might well be called a monstrosity. Yet does not a spirited man aim at getting more results with less, turning streamlining, yielding, efficiency into his highest art? Considering nuclear energy, before I worry about its polluting powers, I first wonder: do we really need to become so enormously physical and so brutal with the earth? Do we want to persuade nature of our goodwill with ever fewer carrots and gifts while clobbering her into submission with a zillion kilowatts?

It might well be this spectacular psychic meltdown of all our mysterious subtleties into a public show of power that sets the dominant civilizations apart from the countries of ecstasies. Ah! There is knowing and knowing. And only one kind can be bragged about, gives kilowatts, or can be sold. We certainly know how to be big! Slowly we begin to ask ourselves whether our short-term gain from melting down our spirituality into brute digital reasoning will not soon be eclipsed by the long-term losses such a mental fission can cause.

Some now start to hesitate to use the terms "Third World" and "underdeveloped" countries for we do not want to remain prisoners of our pedestals. Soon some travel agents will advertise with the catch words, "Come to the spiritual power spots; sip from the wisdom of wilderness."

7

Mr. Black-and-White in seminar.

Feeling compelled to demonstrate to my skeptical Mr. Black-and-White that the same act can for one man be a "sin" and then "well done" for another, I made up the story of two exhausted wanderers in endless dunes—two men tired beyond dragging themselves further. Meric and Deric were so tired they even let their last water jugs slip from them. Meric felt guilty about leaving his jug behind. Deric seemed relieved and even began to lightly hum. Deric knew there was an oasis waiting behind the nearest dune.

8

Is it human to work? Is it horse-like to pull a plow?

I was slow to freely serve myself in the unbelievable market of goodies we were provided with when most of us decided to become components in a few world-wide assembly lines. And I become more pensive and slower now that I can better see how with armies of workers we slowly, incessantly, chew out the face of mother earth to fatten us with candies and wealth. Why am I so pressed to participate? Why are there so few who scold me for working and fishing so shamelessly hard? Heroically cultivating fatter warts on the face of the earth gives me bad dreams.

I love the free outdoor life as much as I love my wife. One thing I know: I need now four Sundays a week as never before. How to free my mind again from forced labor and thinking in circles about how this earth—good beyond imagination—can be simplified into one giant udder for us so our race may become even more obese?

When singing has become work, when loving, hugging, dancing, gathering, caring, storytelling, raising kids, when all our natural acts have been reoriented into work—is it this achievement we call a thriving economy? When I become so grounded and a professional rationalist and worker, do I not have to divorce many of my capacities? Again and again I need to shut up unwanted spirits who linger around, pestering me to be heard, used, beautified and loved. This is a world of a zillion hints to which a person dreaming of becoming successful in town must first blindfold himself. No cure seems foreseen for the pain when I deny my mind its wings, but a profusion of mental and physical sports are suggested to orderly phase out my poetic life. How masturbation in all its elegant forms is becoming needed! One's mind is fitted tightly into a uniform. Much bravery in thinking and dreaming is lost. Few remain shameless thinkers without clothes on. An addiction to technology seems to bring about a sort of lip-bit peace, gluing us together within the commodity-market whether we are in love with each other or not. And I note that the relations between First and Third "rate" nations seem now often to become the relationship between an addict and a new convert who also got hooked.

I still do not know how to bring the above thoughts in step with my thrill when from the furnace of our psychological complexes, space shuttles finally take off to the moon. Then I also note that the history of evolution has been thriving nicely on our neuroses for a very long time.

I am puzzled when the Holy Spirit blinds and stuns the souls of billions of us and it discreetly lays a cuckoo's egg into our minds. Should I protest or should I applaud when new Boeing birds flap proudly from our nest? How thoughtful of the Creator to wrap a towel around an inventor's soul so he sees and knows few neighbors—so this daredevil may not spend his life asking around for approval for what he wants to improve in the world. Dear egotism seems to be the inventors' patron-saint.

At times I envy those with reckless souls who never flinch, but are curious kids on fairgrounds—rushing from scene to scene of science's thrillers without the worries of those souls who are, like all good moms, always late and dragging behind for some untrained child or far off reasons.

Slowly, messily, we are just learning to manage our success and to not transgress the law of moderation in evolution. We still seem kids who erred into a candy store.

9

I could become immune to many tears.

With the numbing repetitions of work I might well form such a callous around my mind that I become a clam; I become impenetrable then to many unfamiliar foes and friends as a beaver becomes quite untouchable holed up in his winter den. I could win a kind of mini-freedom there, burrowing in my working den. I could become free from the nagging whispers from the outside world that loves to rub all kinds of love lotions, itches, bugs and question marks into my skin. I could remain asleep when each spring in roots, seeds and minds a zillion fires break out and new follies are added to the celebration. I could tie up to the banks of that unruly torrent of pristine life and safely experience Lady Nature as a peephole show.

10

Thanks for those weird gifts; thanks again.

Now that I feel brave—quick, let a presumptuous thought be heard. Is it not wonderful to find one's doubts, weaknesses and the cracks in determination? They are my invitations to dare on the ladder one step up. A view to other worlds opens up, a longing is born, trails and freshly baked adventures lie ahead, another peak teases, "Come on up!" When I get kicked out of my routine and things are getting tough, I place an encouraging arm around my own sagging shoulders and kindly ask,

"Theo, why moan, when excitement, a chance to break camp, thrills to leave are in sight?"

11

I learned from the snail and gave my mind a shell.

When my intellect has no ladder to reach up to a great woman or man I am tempted to belittle these awesome giants in my mind and pull them down. When life is a storm, a searing sun, a wilderness, an overpowering man I must shun, I retreat into the armor of my pride. Under this umbrella all provocative suns, all in and outgoing love, all teasings to question, to wonder and to outgrow, all seeds and seductive ladies are repelled. Safely and chastely I ride out the storm in the capsule of my pride.

And so, as my body so my mind has become less and less a riding Hun. My mind needs its architecture, its roof and abode for fear to sleep under a wide open sky that's wild with awesome ghosts and question marks. It likes its comfy living rooms, its servants, its credos and patios to feel protected and warm. Yet when the heart wins, my mind still likes to come out of this self-imposed confinement and try itself out in the four winds. Yet, also pride might be one of the Creator's nifty tools to kick me off the good old merry-go-round that cranks out its song, "let's do it again." Go diversify! On this lonely island of pride slowly a new kind of clover starts to evolve.

12

It seems to be for its enormous foresight and hindsight that the society of wilderness has become out of step with us and that its laws, when expressed in words, have become so bewildering to most.

An organic society is an undertaking many generations tall. It is not a crowd of contemporary women and men who huddle lovingly together in a mutual insurance company of some "ism."

That legendary Unity, perhaps integrating every name you know, seems not a relationship we have to invent and proselytize to the world. It has nothing to do with peace, with neighborly love and a better world. As I see it, it's here for those who can see. It's the show that has been acted out for three billions years. To peek into that ecstatic land, where the countless opponents are united in amicable tags of war, we invent for our minds many kinds of stilts.

I get hints for the riddle of this peaceful war from the song of a meadow which has not been plowed and is free to celebrate its springs and falls with all its teeth, sucker roots, stingers, pollen-blues, perfumes and claws. It's the song so baggy and so long that it has room for a thousand hues of poppy reds and lupine blues, for the snails and the snail eating crows. It plays every leaf, sways the grasses and drones with insect wings. It thunders from the flash of lightning and storms of hail. It murmurs with rivers, loafers and lovers. It perfumes itself with summer noons full of boiling berries, sap and honeydew and adds to its Octoberfest the aromas of all the beers and the fermenters of its autumn brew. It's absolutely outrageous. Even the tricks of our outlaws and exiled seem welcomed by the creator of this club. Yet its company gives me more a sense of being provided for than do our joint ventures where quite legally, quite righteously, we share our orderly fields of sugar beets, our high-yield farms of trees, our surplus wheat, telecommunications and databanks; and we labor so hard to rearrange the world to suit our impatient egos. Listening to the September song, I am in awe of that cosmic conspiracy so divinely drunk it seems to simply wish all things well.

In this Great Society the squirrel scampers the seeds of the spruce to the juiciest flats—up valley, down valley and over hills, busily picking and chucking cones. But this is how the spruce himself becomes a fast-legged vagabond striding a mile per thousand years and gladly grows for the squirrel some extra cones. So when next time you draw a spruce don't forget to draw his legs!

I understand that North American Indians saw themselves as members of that society much larger than mankind or the United Nations. This perception stood in their way of quickly becoming great technologists and engineers. One has to be all and only human to feel entirely free to hack without a tear through ecstatic land an Interstate No. 3. Not to undo this world but to live with the anxiety its grandiose rules may cause without being crippled by that anxiety—this is a goal I respect.

This wilderness society proves to be my medicine-land—always cheering me to plunge in, always ready to bathe my dirty mind. This land wakes me up from crisis alert and from my dream in rationality. My attention becomes so luxuriant and relaxed that soon a million storytellers are surrounding me—and my own memory is my only storyteller no more. To be lured into such sensitivity is to me "becoming aware." I know of no better laundromat for my mind than washing in the wild. Who is more patient to teach me wisdom than this shady "worthless" land? I never look deeper into generosity than when I look into wilderness. In this land more qualities of God can be seen than in our sacred books or in our potato fields. Ladies and gentlemen, don't be late, the show has begun.

13
The wilderness therapy.

The therapeutic ability to discover likenesses in seemingly divergent phenomena and to open our eyes to the myriad parables nature acts out remained a gift prudishly kept in its box through my years in school. I find now that this gift is the eighth day in Genesis and is still waiting for me.

That "lilies-of-the-field" therapy concocts metaphors that can melt away my fears, bellyaches, gloom and greed. It can pacify my angers that load the gun in me. It even builds up some immunity against my old archenemy, hate. It makes fun of that rascal by showing me that somewhere else and under different names, nature uses those same behaviors, phenomena and acts I hate and gets results to which we stamp and shout applause. We are given the ability to produce thought pictures which are "don't worry" drugs that beat the antidepression drug Prozac. Should our curriculum miss that chance?

14
My mind is a hen. That land called wilderness is the cock. Without it who would fertilize my eggs?

My civilization discreetly taught me to deal with most fellow life forms as Hitler dealt with the Gypsies and the Jews—burn them, blow them under—and have one pure race, the human species, with the slave labor of a few "chosen" plants and animals sullenly trailing behind. From the crib on, I was reared for leadership and slavemaking in all of life's kingdoms. My civilization left me retarded in conversing with the fauna and flora. It left many of us blind and insensitive toward the tears and joys of this wondrous world. This break in communication is curled up in a nameless neurosis and loneliness that pesters us now from deep in our collective mind. I share a handicap with many. For fifteen years I have been bred in vitro into a practical man while mostly confined to sitting on my buttocks. My eyes became narrowly focused. No wonder I can now barely make you out one lifetime long. Now isn't that seeing barely one inch of a man? I became a man who lost his gusto for all but the most obvious things. In this shift in my spectrum of knowledge toward a brilliant shortsightedness, I became retarded in my grasp for the intuitive world. I became a frog that fell in a well. I am now offered a desperate cure. I am to comfortably settle in the well and to forget. I am to help erase the sights that could stir memories of the lost home of my native intellect which are still haunting me. I should surrender heroically to rationality and depart with the troops to whitewash the world.

The fist on the table—silence!—and the proof that we are in the right to do our thing the practical way will be invented once more. It is here I sense an obscure motive behind "rescue" programs for the underdeveloped, the amaterialists and amateurs, the modest and the poetic countries, the poor, the illiterates, the singers and the dancers and the general practitioners. Are our glory missions to help anyone still lingering in the garden of unplowed profusion secretly meant to lure the last general practitioners out of this garden and to stop them from stirring up doubts and forgotten shame in our minds? For the "troops," the sight of personal courage and nonconformity and the jubilant forces of spontaneity are better rooted.

How obsessed we have become with committing our curiosity to schemes of war eclipsing Attila's furious zest. With chainsaws, pesticides, vaccines, bulldozers, with our sciences and databanks, with walls of fishing webs and harnessing genes, we spend now more time on the war path against the other residents of the earth than any society has done before. How much longer should we applaud our sciences for enlarging our monstrous tooth to munch up even more fellow life more speedily than before? Did you ever wonder why the lion takes six Sundays in the week and reserves but one day for such wars? Should every waterfall be pipelined and put to work? Should life's whole world population be conquered, unionized, and submitted to the empire of man? Is that the wish of the Western God? All life that has not been baptized—man, beasts, even the inoffensive moss humbly nesting on granite—they could become our enemies who have to be forced into line in such a haughty scheme.

I now find that it is the godly profusion of organisms which we evict that offers me the feasts for my wonderlust. What a spectacle of inventiveness. Do we really want to bring down a world so generously composed that in it each of us can confidently play his wonderfully unequal part: saints, sinners, bums, hunchbacks, hoboes, sirens, experts and all? It cooks medicine for any imaginable sore. It has a lantern ready for the longest nights. It gives assurance that a child buried by a slide is provided for and that the caribou has its hidden way to bounce on the wolf. And it can keep our angers tender and our laughters warm. Shouldn't we be very very reluctant when we have to blow under such a spirited menagerie to simply grow an energy crop instead?

A psychotherapy that no longer takes my delusion of grandeur for granted can light a lamp above my guilt feelings for Earth abuse. I need light on the shaded side of my soul.

Do I stir up a nest of guilt so tightly covered up in the Western mind that it might still be taboo to think loudly about it? Yet to think it out might shed light on why it was easier to first sell a chainsaw to a Christian than to persons of other faiths. Christianity narrowed down my native compassion that loves to mingle also with God's creepies, crawlies, mini flyers and his fleets of clouds. It neglected teaching me to draw wisdom from observing the animals, the plants, the elements, nature's phenomena, and the heavenly bodies. Hence our low opinion of the natural and our obsession with technology to change it. Be practical and neighborly—keep your love on a leash!

To remain sane, a mind needs its daily glimpse of wilderness; it needs its vitamins. How fat a mind grows on practical thoughts alone, when it lives on its daily white bread, so to speak, on thoughts reduced to calories. There is so much a media-made mind has never experienced. A person free to quietly see, smell, touch, hear and read wilderness is triggered to produce different neurochemicals, different sensibility and behavior patterns from someone leaving those 999 worlds to live off the information

15

bowels of mankind. His neurons connect in different forms. He may become more of a poet and less of a mole. The curves of the woman pray for sperms and the whole chemistry of the male responds. Thoughts are triggered by the environment of the mind. And do I not become what I see?

If we do not let the land be a little wild and rejuvenate, psychotherapy might soon be cursed and not be the opener of eyes anymore but the surgeon for mental amputation and inducer of lasting forgetfulness. What good is it to stir up a hunger where there will be no table set? What good to rekindle in a man the adventurer where the lime trees would stand in endless rows north and south? One wants to go gently about it when one needs to graft into a youngster some moral of mathematics, some bookkeeper's virginal sense of justice, and to blindfold him with the "ABCs." It might breed in him the docile psyche of an ox, or make of him an amnesiac.

Clara, there is a sky you look into every evening and you start to glow and that sky was empty for me. There were so many apparent wastelands and idiocies around me. There are so many wonderful things nobody else taught me to see. And there is this trail of dance and music, of yummy raspberries and warm feelings you have been leaving behind for sixty years—what a treat!

15
Paid to perform as a Wailing Wall.

When a man starves for warmth, when he is in fire with a fever to pollinate, and has no mate, he may well have to make do with a prostitute who soothes the storm whipping up his blood, who bares herself for a while for him and gives herself up for brandy, a good laugh or a check. When my thoughts get lovesick from house arrest behind humanism's garden fence, they also run a fever. I am then invited to go to someone for counsel who prostitutes his soul. That person may love me an hour without my mask on. He himself may go wild and naked and let his mental guard down for this while. He may let me have a peek at the naked motives and passions of his own unfenced soul and may become himself a mirror for my obscured wants. For that moment, he may be my mate, making me feel hugged and understood.

What a dilemma for many priests, whores, shamans and psychotherapists alike when, losing control over their souls, they become more than showmen who perform a lover's act. What happens when the bell rings at the end of the round and compassion has made them drunk?

Somewhere around these oldest kinds of professions, most of us have settled and built our towns—some to rent out a corner of their minds; others to sell their peanuts or their busy-bee hands.

In rare happy moments when I need not compete but can simply wish others well, I also can share this wonderful dilemma with those first professionals among us. Three times thanks for the gift when I am allowed to do an act not for pay but simply for its own yummy joy.

16

Still snorting I slowly begin to approve a little more of God even when He sends us droughts and perversions which may dry out in many the delight to have a child and so cull the thicket of men.

When in our crammed world life confuses in many the desire to procreate, when it lures our passions away from a family and tries them out on new projects, my older feelings rebel in a terror of change. Yet I also feel it is a benediction when I can finally accept that others are now meant for a different kind of health than mine. Obviously there are now more pressing ways to give oneself than in my own romantic old-fashioned way of preparing five children for this world.

I tell myself, "Remain an apprentice with the eyes of a hawk and the ears of a hare. Watch life's healing process to cure our runaway growth and learn. Be unafraid when life turns virtues into droughts and sharpens purposeful meanness to cut off excess."

I also notice that Mother Nature seems to seduce many among us to do in our way what a runaway population of lemmings does and provides them with a psyche that makes them willing sacrifices to the goddess of fertility. I have a hunch that the Spirit of Life means well doing so. This corruption of passions can lead to more than Friday night fun. Brave young people illustrate this. So many creatures outside our fence now need a Mother Teresa, a nurse, a friend.

It is because of my outdated routine to expect others to react sexually in a traditional way that I often feel resentment toward a rather neutered breed of women and men. I like to learn how to relate well to them, although, at first sight, they seem not to fit into my world. This is truly an extraordinary time when traditionally quite similar people are going such different ways. Now so many need also to belong more closely to a shepherd and a flock. Do we, in our own ways, live through the trauma of the termites and bees—when nature has guided them through the invention of social hormones and worker castes, lavishly decorating some to be adored, groomed and fanned as queens, others to be sunk safely into the gray function of bowels?

I feel made for another kind of progress; a step into a clearing flooded with light where I see more and need to curse less and need no middleman to God. I feel lame and ashamed from so much taming and standardizing; from weeding, sterilizing, straightening, from too much clothing.

Born into possibilities beyond imagination, are we not meant to add picture to picture, mate answer with answer, hook up loose connections, integrate new relationships into our inner forms? Clearly it's not so much what I physically see that counts but what pictures I can add to what I see, my eye the catalyst. I feel invited on a fantastic sightseeing tour—new vistas, other orgasms, many more star cities twinkling in the night, brighter loves beyond our families rise into sight. Here is progress that does not turn a single stone. We are born so strong. We can take off time to wonder about everything that happens in the cosmos. This is a lucky fate.

17

To age, to happily give, to wrinkle and dry out well, as a seed potato does among its young . . .

When I am lazy at work and at war, voices bubble up that make me think about the dilemma we put young people in. Preoccupied with longevity, we seem to spend much of our courage and our love begetting industries that are obedient, and reliable maids ordered to stand at our bedsides and in our defense, for the time when we will be ripe for the season when the erections do not come anymore on command but turn into gifts, and when the leaves turn gold. Are we getting dull in our universal mind? Why should I break my soul with its magic eyes that, when I am ripe, turn me into a happy fool so the forward storming vitality of children can make good use of me and take over my wealth and health? Why should I wear out my life with the old stag games: pitting bank account against bank account, locking horns and minds, impressing with my bigger load of fish, bluffing competitors with the most authoritative pose? As a plum, so a man; they become sweeter for the same reason when they mature. They want to be eaten. Why should I want to make of my sweet golden season, dedicated to generosity and giveaways, a berry preserve for myself? I do not want this quiet season of wisdom distorted to a sickness that has to be feared, fought and healed.

Did you notice how courageous, open and curious our children are before we graft usefulness on them? How they are born more scientists than later they ever will be? Drunk with enthusiasm, they barely ever look back. Yet how tempting it becomes to lure them into a kind of education that castrates their minds, that bends backwards their courage, thoughts and sight, that makes them nurse us for pay when we are old. Are we going to be sour spinsters who order them to tiptoe through the landscapes that our overcautious adult commune laid out for itself? Do we want to draft our kids to work on seedless science, a medicine and a law that should abolish the beautiful gifts of danger and death and allow us to fail our tests and still hang on? Why does apoptosis on the level of our species frighten us so much? Have we completely forgotten how important it can be that people die? This tragic mutation in our inherited memory equals the tragic mutation in a tumor cell that makes its suicide genes forget how and when to kill itself. I fear we become excessively harsh with our grandchildren and excessively soft with ourselves.

One should never ridicule and exorcise the native emotions in a growing child. These emotions are the sex organs of the mind. I might yet become wise to the slide show of suggestions that God projects onto my screen, selling me in youth the thrill to grab, smile and run, and then charming me with the pleasure to be fearlessly generous later on. Watch-

19

ing this gradual reversal of love in a maturing woman and man, it dawns on me how a system of "one justice for all" misleads and can pervert good relations between the generations. And I see how we may have erected a gap of mistrust between the adult community and the young. God willing, I may still learn that fabulous trick to always come out with a profit, even when I give.

To age, to happily give, to dry out well, like a seed potato in fall—this is the happiness of a mother finding her yummy pies all eaten and gone. She is content with just the mischievous smiles of her young that are sweeter to her than her rightful piece of the pie. Is there another happiness as harmless and as wonderfully unjust as Mom's?

18

When I do not stray far from my faith in the good spirit of nine billion names, when I do not bulldoze with blinders for goals my little ego tries to impose, I am amazed. The nine billion helpers soon fall in step with me. Astonishingly helpful things start happening to me.

Why is it that when full and content by a good season's catch, I should suspiciously take my boat out again and pound it into an October gale to secure my family with safety for years? I discovered that to work simply piling up my pile with no partner who waits for a meal, to hoard sunshine and smartly say, "It might run out"; to mistrust life to be a good mom to us—all this means double work for my body and blisters on my soul. Prudence is a drag. She requires an endless workout from me. This dame wants to make me run through a soaking rain when not even a donkey goes out. She steals my free time—no happy hour for greetings, storytelling, laughs, thanks and walk-abouts. Endlessly she hands me out some honey-do job or storage problem to keep me from taking off. Ah, but when the freezer is empty and they will tiptoe at home to see from afar whether I shoulder a deer, I am a cheerful deer hunter—and I barely ever grit my teeth or curse when I bag a boot full of muskeg. What sparkle, what feelings. Here is a privilege reserved for the poor. I am never better spirited and helped than when I am lean and am God's fool and talk and walk from my soul, without being smart, heavily guarded, insured, motivated and armed. When my whole being jubilates in harmony, "Let's do it!" I lose ten heavy pounds.

Ah! to let life sway me to its rhymes, to wake up in the morning to its: Welcome, Theo, here are your gifts—then unwrap them, one by one, over the day—and laugh, whatever mischief tumbles from this box of gifts.

How to again lasso that trust in my magical mind—this spirit that seems able to swiftly invoke every hand to help me out. And with this trust comes also the time off for my trips into creativity land. I now learn to dive timidly into every new minute, never quite sure what gifts it brings, and whether I can swim. Timidly, I also learn to leave it to Mother Grace to bail me out. Have patience. Here comes a second-hand apprentice already itching with many dubious needs and goals, a consumer society rubbed under his skin.

19

To crack open a window in our dome of rationality, do we not do the most impractical things?

To let spontaneity flavor my routine, to let it lure my mind away from its trodden down traffic lanes of all my fishing days, to invite for a treat the company of lively unbleached thoughts that idle now unattended in my shade, to take my mind into the bushes thought-picking, these are all ways I trick myself into a receptive mood. Memories may thaw that I have only known in dreams, memories that can sneak a happy face between my gloomy moods. I can learn beyond the "ABCs" and beyond the laws that limit us to being good girls and good boys. To stir up my settled mind, I need a big long spoon.

Some of us were so pestered by our curiosity idling in safe-keeping that we awkwardly broke finally our own good strong legs, so to speak. Drowsy with comfort, we needed pain, feelings, danger so badly. Others forcibly changed their routine of digestion, of breathing, or the beating of their hearts. They went without food or sex for weeks. They tried any deviation from safe morals for a promise of help to escape from their play- and work-pen. Some sit cross-legged on top of a pole; others change into a pair of striped Sunday pants to shake off the sleep and mildew creeping over them. When drugged into mild insanity by too much rationality, we antidote that tyrant in our minds.

Others are more desperate. In our present marathon into high socialization tremendous stress and beatings of self-esteem occur. A man's natural opioids may simply burn out. Terrorized he may have to take drugs artificially to compensate. Nicely forgetful, for a treat, of the grim earthly needs and ego trips, he hopes he can unfold wings and flutter for a happy hour out of his career into dazzling heights. He risks much to step so close to the edge of death, burning for a look down into God's purse of gifts. He may slip over the edge and fly off into dream-worlds for good.

Any sudden curve can take a tyrannic reason aback and become medicine for a hyper-rational attack. Any overly persistent monotony that sways us and makes us dizzy, be it a prayerwheel, a mantra, music that strokes us and makes us hum and purr, a litany or rosary, or a long and mesmerizing "om"—a beat that rocks us back and forth—they can become gentle knockout tools and the "open sesame" that releases the three locks behind which our reason safely locked us up. And then we are free for an ecstatic daydreaming tour! Eureka! We thus are kids that skip school, standing at the entrance of other worlds and hurrah! our guards are rocked asleep. Here I see the healing power of all the impractical, the apparently senseless, the waste of useful time, the amoral and the experimental beyond health, the pomp of rites and glitters that can take a square head by surprise. And here I see also how a religion that adjusts to the practical and the bare can fail to make us fly.

What a fatal health it is that does not make me sick of a goodness monotonously ticking away. What good is health that never breaks its rule or opens a window, that does not risk and never says to an enemy, a north wind, a daddy longlegs: be my guest—welcome in? Who, after all, aspires to remain forever a healthy worm? Risking, one might err closer to that divine goodwill so many cubic light years big and so outrageously patient as to appear foolish, unjust, and full of crimes to a grounded mind. Just think of the surprises which our prodigious capacity to sidestep, mutate, blunder, sin and get lost in wonderland can bring. Would we not be a monotonous world if we were not enriched by visiting comets and the shattering impact of meteors, by trespassings into wild harmonies of our souls, by vagaries and sins?

And what good would a man have done to himself, had he dragged through his whole life the same burdensome notion of good and evil?

Good people do not risk and explore. Misbehaving people may.

20

Slowly I see shimmers of light in the puzzling wisdom of some eastern tribes who expect their saints to be reborn as rascals—that a stout eraser may earn himself a term as a gentle hero in generations to come.

I suspect that every man contains all the seasons that surge and ebb through evolving life. And maybe he has little say in what script he will be triggered to act. Every man seems to have his gentleness and his meanness, his spring and his fall, his earthquakes, his thawing winds, his power to putrefy and his battering storms. He has frosts in store to test others, to grind, plow, chisel, polish and pry open what is curled up asleep in another soul. He can be water probing for cracks and holes. A man knows the tenderness of a woman that softly sings a child to sleep. He can caress another man's storm until that storm turns into a breeze. When needed a woman can bring out her memory of a man. A fogged-in man may turn kind when the sun is warming him. In every tyrant who might be asked to pull a mighty evil plow, that healing warmth of Mother Theresa waits for its turn. And this seems to work the other way around—as reliable as spring is the baby girl of fall. I missed this point because I was taught that after each individual life or after each of a people's generations life is cut off, the merits added up, the monuments and seats in hell allocated and the count started anew.

Oftentimes a woman seems allowed to pass on her share of killing, cunning and storming to a man and so makes a more fierce provider of him while she is triggered to remember tenderness for her home. A man may be commanded to hoe the ground in unpopular ways, so weed trees can grow again and so gold finches may sing and feed upon them. He might be told to drop his anger and hail it over contemporary mankind and by so doing, maybe he benefits a generation of life I do not know. One can only forgive such a person if one is able to so greatly stretch one's imagination that one can perhaps share the mischievous smiles of the finches and the woods when the loggers are fuming on strike. But how would a one floor thinker make such a mental jump?

Generations who lived truest to Darwin's model and fortified, multiplied, and glorified themselves at the expense of all fellow life seem to finally produce their own power of self-bleeding. We naturally produce all kinds of dispersing agents to scatter the cyclone of the *Wirtschaftswunder* we become when we pool all our cunning. With custom-made homicides, boredom, self-satisfactions, meanness, drugs, with a love for lies, with many people asked to remain pleasurely curled up in the egg for life and never to hatch from such an ego trip, with the juveniles' angry "fuck you's," with a general loss of vision, excessive vitality will be starved away. I do not know of another species whose members spend now more energy to politely fool and mislead each other than us. And an over-crowded mankind which is not allowed to fall in old fashioned love any-more—doesn't it need to produce their substitute drugs for love? How readily success turns into a pest!

Let me follow an idea that might profit from the above string of thoughts about closing books on each individual lifespan alone. Do not practical religions rather see and judge a man from below—by individual lifespans alone? They invent morals that protect, guide, reward, or roast him in hell for punishment after they framed him this way. Yet might such ethics not ultimately mislead a man to fight his multigenerational soul? When I see that timeless soul pulsating between a man and woman, a seed, a child, time and again (as other species metamorphose, like, for instance, the acorns to the oaks pulsing back and forth)—from an individualistic point of view, no matter how I look, it seems always ill-behaved and full of apparent idiocies. And so when distributing our praise we mostly prefer a person good to her neighbors, maybe even good to mankind. A person good to life is probably out of favors.

When I invent, plunge into science, find cures to improve mankind's lot and distribute my good deeds, the planet's whole rowdy crowd of residents looks over my shoulders. There is inside me a meeting hall that's crowded with their voices. The dandelions, the evangelists and politicians,

Alice in Wonderland, the kinglets in the hedges three generations away—they each have their case and all comment on what I do. Maybe it is to the wisps and puffs of this global murmur that our inclinations, neurochemicals and karma bend. To become tuned in to this universal murmur: this, to me, is to become aware. Or do you think that in your soul "accidents" do not occur which end you up as a wrecker or a saint?

21

When I think about progress, I also realize that my dearest moments came to me when I abandoned the lifestyle of just rational progress, of the practical, chasing safety and comfort and being plugged into our own round-the-clock news.

My happy hours began when I left our freeways of the land and of the mind, the store-bought meat, the printed science of nature, the supermarketed psychology, the convenience of sipping knowledge nicely processed into alphabet soup. These glorious moments blessed me when I did not buy artificial love fantasies that do not need caring nor produce love sickness, when I passed up fast answers of mass-produced religion for busy minds and I covered my ears to Madame Economy's siren songs. Wriggling out of the five coats that a town life protectingly wraps around my body and my soul, I entered the bushes of my mind and the bushes at the end of our fields with the barest, homespun defenses. And it seems that it was such wonderful trusting in my own resources that created the climate for the few triumphs of living I could claim. But I also found that the progress of comfort stood in my way.

Naked to the waist, I left Interstate Number One and Information Freeway Channel two to dig into my own resources, fighting bugs, moods and question marks, and I fell into a surprise. Edging into regions not yet plowed, I confronted a beauty in and around me which touched unnamed musical strings in me so powerful that at times they took away my breath. I found superb ideas—some a hundred generations long, others a hundred species wide, lying around by the bucketful. I thought: in such a wonderland it is a waste of options and time to cruise at sixty mph. I had one more happy find when I realized that whenever we are not acting the noblemen of some clique or town and for a treat become happy emperors with no clothes on, we know each other quite well. Out there my mind enters the liveliest colloquiums. I find myself with more severe yet kinder teachers than in a classroom. This land teaches me the unteachable things.

Dreaming in the moss, with open sky above, is a good way to fish for complimentary answers that sink to the bottom of my soul. Out there my mind at times also hops, whistles and chatters in a way that may well sound like a thanksgiving dance to you.

In this separate reality every animal, every herb, even a fleet of clouds, each has its personal fable to tell; it has its soul, its psychology, its architecture, its problems to solve with neighbors. It has to deal with population control. Each owns a series of inventions and secrets no other species knows. This world has misty mornings full of worried spiders because a heavy morning dew betrays their webs. Here the sea becomes my formidable mistress in indigo-blue who lavishly sets my table. And she takes me on rides on all her many winds, giving me a seminar on how to put to good use every imaginable temperament. She also bathes me in solitude; and so heals many of my inner sores. She stretches my wits with tests more wholesome than a round with a bull. And I—I didn't know any better but to rape this mistress time and again. Why was I not initiated into the secrets of a mutually pleasing relationship? Why was I cheered for courting her in cold, calculating blood and encouraged just to think to fish, fish, kill more of her fish?

Now as I slowly recover my senses, it hurts me again when I don't make love rightly with this world—with the hibiscus and its friends, the darting hummingbirds, who for long now have made my breakfasts gay; with the sharks, the snappers, the sting rays, the cows, palms, shrimps, oysters and deer of which I ask so many gifts day after day; with the grave digger, my neighbor, and with madame of the whorehouse around the corner; with all creatures. They all turn out to be great mystery books, adventure books, maybe comic books.

Outside of town, a mind may softly sink into that cosmic poem so rich in symbiotic rhymes one may lose interest for awhile in poems confined to books.

Earlier I was puffed up with pride about our standard of living; I come now to think that the highest culture is probably rather invisible, completely unsellable and incomputable. I think about a progress that does not necessarily cultivate exciting gismos and bank accounts but lasting and exciting relationships with all residents of the earth. How badly our species needs some social skills. Maybe to light streetlights in the dark of this legendary symbiosis is what great progress is about.

22

For swiftness and speed of mind, there is nothing like being a Hun. This mind does not wear a fashionable dress and does not like to settle down. This mind does not ask to have what it lives on ornamented or cooked. This mind has not much use for a chair or an idol and needs no roads. It feels trapped under a roof and thrives under the open sky. It is a lean mind always in the saddle ready to move.

How can I capture again the courage to be poor—lean, light, available in body and mind and ready to join when life passes flashing an invitation, teasing me, "Let's try it; let's think it through!" I envy the swiftness of those so ingeniously streamlined that they can carry most of their belongings in their bellies and their souls. Possessions immobilize my mind with compromises. Possessions make such huge targets of me. What blindness strikes the crazed squirrel that keeps him hoarding enough pine cones for ten years, as if there would never again be bluebells of spring ringing, only endless snow?

When we inaugurated agriculture, we inaugurated the take-over that has tied us mentally and physically down as no other ballast did. In the garden of grace, we became the slave hunters; we caught each useful plant, meadow and stand of trees and tied it to an owner. Can you imagine the agony in all the families of life when we divided them? Angry with their indiscriminate generosity, we have forced each plant into a man's yard for caretaking, so its fruits can be snatched before other critters get a taste. No other burden we have assumed has been causing us more imprisonment and sweat. This declaration of war against the planet's life seems now to make the earth into one great killing field from pole to pole. To justify our biological crusade, we invented the possessive philosophy of humanism and made it our idol. Yet humanism has proven a distorted diving mask for exploring the depth of life. It is a mind hiding behind a thousand shamans' masks that make us look different and the chosen folks. Those masks are blurred with many assumptions, ornaments and credos. They also keep our wildly daring minds behind three locks.

Confused with mistrust in life's goodwill, one can barely move. Loaded down with possessions that should guarantee success for an expedition through Darwin's unfriendly land to personal fitness and success, one seems too hopelessly busy with the cargo to lift eyes from the ground, to scan God's menagerie for reasons to be less possessive and more trusting.

Entangled in a thousand little, "I hate this and that too's," one barely moves. A boring dog tied himself to a stake close to his food bowl. A boring woman never leaves her beautiful garden. If you want to know my worth, ask what fears I turned into invitations, what hates into mountain climbs.

Stonewalling with philosophic catch phrases, German shepherds and barbed wire, credos and symphonies, bodyguards and credit cards, with friendships, with vows of politeness, with lawyers, with social security checks, with weed and pest and birth controls, with notarized deeds, with our pledge of mental allegiance to humanity before all, and God knows how many kinds of fences, we build the Great Wall. What barricades and hates, what taboos, what compromises! With such a pack how could my mind remain free? Everyone of my possessions is recruiting and points an "I want you" finger at my thinking. When my free thinking gets entangled in my obsessive love-affair with fishing it soon grinds in friction.

Do I really need six overcoats around my soul? Do I really want to go underground into impenetrable, well-stocked fortresses and plunge with others into the grim and consuming sciences that install us there—plunge into a technology that provides even deadlier hooks and ammunition for our species of poachers? I made myself a promise to try myself outside— away from that nice mental lifestyle that gives me peace of mind under a geodesic dome of beautifully rhymed thoughts. I can chisel on my needs so more of the high time is at hand when there is nothing needed.

28

When I look up to the frigate birds sailing thermal drafts, I am shown how poverty for the right reasons can make us soar.

23
Is there a better eye-opener than sickness—the slayer of routine?

It seems to me that a creative person should be less inclined to whine about his health. Isn't he a man who at times may even willfully blind himself— maybe for the sheer excitement of watching what new eye nature will bud in him, maybe to steer away from our good old sun in the quest of new sources of light, perhaps to see what only can be seen in the night. In his homeland of plenty he may fast from food or from biochemical love, sending these hungers off into unexplored regions to look for alternatives. Excitedly, he might invent a new fire when he is pushed out into the wind and his mind turns cold. Is she not a new breed of woman, who in reaction to a crowded world, says no to her own body in pleading heat to be fertilized and to duplicate itself, but instead lets her energy overflow into a caring nobody thought to care about? I am not so brave. I am quite happy when I can cheerfully welcome the little boo-boos, scratches, tests and changes of course that tomorrow bestows on me.

It seems to be the break with the comfortably known or a triumph over the terror to molt from outdated rites or an instinctive contempt for safety and common sense that lifts a mind into unused worlds where many of our complimentary twins and great soul food gardens can be found. While old defenses and immunities give way, new worlds and unexpected help from the jungle of eclipsed memories become visible through the crack and test the old.

Blessed by nature to be sick, awkward, vulnerable, maybe just to be a weirdo, a mutant, a dare-devil fool, and to follow a course to the edge of madness and physical bankruptcy, neurochemicals may be activated to trigger a person's system of perception to broaden the focus of its lenses, and his view becomes less human and more universal. He might invent a new style of survival. She comes up with new resources. A new situation creates new vision. He adds a new step to the dance of the lamb with the wolf. He is not granted the healthy state of harmonious repetitions. She becomes knowledgeable where she is troubled and hurt. Perhaps a bad temper or a wart in pride wants to steer us into careers like Columbus' and Scott's. Some explorers overcome; others do not.

I have a hunch that diseases are not failures of nature, but provide the landscapes for triumphs of insight. And so a mankind without sicknesses might well be worse off. What a mishap for a sculptor to lose his chisels; for a species to lose its pathogens.

24

We can meet as the firestones we are and light up the world with our sparks. Or should we veil ourselves in politeness and miss that chance?

Relationships that wrap me with comfort and cottonwood, that provide a safe den to hibernate in peace do not sparkle my eyes. You can also be my courageous friend who bugs me out of my routine, who makes all kinds of buds in me break open and become green. You can be a brave woman who walks straight into my center, ignoring my twitter and veil of politeness, a woman who launches an enterprise to make of a boy a man, and teases the poet out of him. You can be my strong catalyst and refuse to meet me as one of the nice people all dressed up in a masquerade of courtesies and denials. Jumping fences, you are the adventurer who takes me out for a stroll through our intimate minds where we are dangerously more than just men. Together we explore our braver worlds where life is an eternally young woman dancing charmingly out into the twilight and back into the shade, teasing, "Grab me if you dare!"

Disregarding the common rules for denial, such brave friends court my secret longings, sparkling with dangers, which I learned to keep under lock. When I open their letters, my hand trembles a little with a terror of change. To break his enamored stare at his own shadow on the wall of his cave, to provoke her to look out and become hit by the heat wave of a thousand other lives, to become a contagion of vitality and a thawing wind for him; Do you know a more generous gift?

I have never been encouraged to socialize this way and told: "You are the potter, here are your relationships, here is your clay." I am trained to play it safe and be a seedless grape. Maybe this inflammation of the spirit is a gift that can only be received by those whose prayers ask for a daily hunger rather than for bread.

To be given the talent of compassionate criticism and play well with fire around a frozen man whose mind is full with tenderness and loaded guns, I would gladly walk a hundred miles for this gift.

25

Even if given a magic scepter, I know of few improvements I would like to make on the earth.

On the one side: Zillions of ways how to criticize, zillions of options to mess up the world, censoring the Creator with my "good" deeds.
On the other side: I can stop all my quarrels with God, become indestructibly patient, become all ears, and go for serenity. I search for the Creator's right answers among the haystack of the zillion blind alleys. The answers that gave me a world so fabulously rich may be rarer finds than a $E = mC^2$. No wonder I am fluent in criticizing. No wonder I stutter when translating a glimpse of life's wisdom.

I feel less and less competent to give lessons to Mother Earth. Beyond my short-tempered complaining at the Creator's high court, I realize: this world is a mountain of excitement and I am invited to climb her. This world has become the best world for me. I don't wish to live in another time. I have been born into a tremendous mental weather front and that is fine. I can only pray for lots of light so I can love this mountain life where those who do not work hard to come down to trodden ground seem to be few and far apart. I can only pray that slowly my anger, my fear and my stupid hatred may soon learn from the fiddler crab and also develop eyes that can see all around.

Still, the wiser a theory becomes, the more scary to my common sense it becomes. Wisdom is still quite frightening to me. If there were a woman or man with so much breath in their mind that they could blow a great clearing into my overcast sky, would I recognize and love these saints?

26

A fashion show for the best-dressed minds.

Much of our intellectual effort seems ultimately not a search for higher truth but for better garments, for a warmer credo, for beliefs that do not wear out over night and that protect us from mosquito bites—thoughts that are sunglasses protecting us from enlightenment so intense it is said to have knocked down the famous Roman soldier Saul and changed him into Paul. For healing anxiety, few can dive on their own for true metaphors; most have to make do with beautifully ornamented mental placebos we may call credos.

When one ridicules a person's or a people's beliefs, one tears and smears the dress they have knitted around their souls; one leaves them shivering in the cold—hence the terrible outcry when left naked on the road. How easily truthfulness without the gentleness of poetry turns into rape.

Garment-making for the mind has grown to a much bigger industry than mentioned in the monthly report of the GNP. Underneath a permissive bikini we now permanently wear an armored mental uniform that we rarely take off but in the presence of a confessor, a psychotherapist or when we are heavenly drunk with love.

It is said that once upon a time we were less split in two, and needed less to dress our shivering minds in all kinds of tough, poetic or flashy philosophies; we were less caught in the middle of mental weather fronts.

27

Are they not mostly champions of some kind of deformity or excess in a talent or of one of the seven old capital sins, those who—for the ventures of a technological society—are most in demand?

When I am pushed to withdraw from the great society of all the zillion things alive to specialize my love and to socialize with our species alone, helping to make man an even more muscular team, I am also warned by my obscure doubts. Yet these doubts are of another logic and, glared by the obvious benefits I am offered, have difficulty withstanding reason.

It appears to me that it is my own disharmonies, the excesses, the holes in my soul, my missing corners or tumors in my loving, a brain lobe usefullized by some steroid or serotonin enhancer, even my cowardice, that are the raw material asked for to make a technological society prosper. It appears that in such a society, women and men with integrity, robust health and the ability to stand alone, in brief, general practitioners in loving, are the least desirable of all. The GNP miracle does not thrive on the serene but flourishes on unbalanced character traits, on neuroses, on wounds to tap the blood, on the manure of decomposed souls, on all of our thousand little short- and long-comings and sins. Such a society celebrates a man who grows one of his talents into a great tumor disharmonizing himself while being useful to them. It celebrates a man of whom it made just one pair of super-legs—a man with no arms, no head, no soul—in short, a pair of sprinter legs so dominant, smart and powerful it can outrace in the Olympic games any man or woman who carry also their head and soul through the race. Yet will such a man not terribly limp through life if ever again left to live by his own body and soul?

Misers, great swindlers, the suicide candidates, the hunch-minds and tender-hearted and brute, men blessed somewhere with an intellectual surplus—the more possessive the growth the better—all of these disproportioned traits are put to good use. A petty maniac can receive a license for perpetual destruction; he can bulldoze a highway bed through the greens of the Amazon and get his fill for good pay. Theo, the obsessed fish killer, can get his fill on the ocean and expect applause. A heart bleeding uncontrolled with pity finds employment and relief and a heart tempered with hatred can spearhead full-time through enemy land. Cowards are favored soldiers for never doing and thinking anything on their own. Anybody who took a bite of a particular love too big to swallow by himself becomes precious and eligible to join. Are you personally bankrupt? For some exotic treasure buried under your rubble that is quite trivial to you, you might be bailed out, given a new chance and a home.

There is work for me. The more outstanding my excess, the better the pay. Then who in a healthy state of vigor and joy may want to rent himself out? What slide obstructed the merry gossiping flow of her desires; what dam of damnations, what imprint of shame or curse that our activated

33

guilt feeling shouted at her, what perfume of praise deviated her from exploring anywhere to settle down as a precise and high-paid worker! What kind of desperation, what broken wing, what uncontrolled usefulness has brought the flying mustang down from the highland to pull a plow?

In this society a spirited nerd that lacks stout health and strength can find happiness walking arm in arm with a docile muscle man. This brave new society can produce health for a man who has lost his self-defenses. It gives a credo and a goal to those who lost the vision and do not know where to go. For the depressed it provides cheers; to those feeling too short it offers a chance to become tall celebrities or heroes. It produces cadres of whiz-men, giants in reason not hampered by an authoritative soul, miracle workers with a capacity for self-denial astonishing to me—some to monopolize planning, those more timid to specialize in the functions of the bowls. Its cultural environment quenches the respect for our bodies, for our emotions, for our nature. It favors those to survive that have a bent for technological solutions. And so in the hierarchy of societies I can step one step down into more safety and become partner in a symbiosis that seems soon to work with an ingeniously computerized bureaucracy as its middleman to God. It may be the way the Spirit of Nature makes a success from my thousand little defeats, making fun of the purist in me.

In spite of my many sessions to learn the pride in this kind of social success, there clings to me a quiet admiration for the lonesome man who is not free to socialize just among mankind. He prefers his own multigenerational soul to the Environmental Protection Agency for advise on how he should live; and he likes to settle across the fence from our booming businesses where we cultivate our vices and our charities separately. And he seems alive, content and with less broken-off ends. Capable to keep his social circle wide open, he might be a new kind of savage, a poetic savage with the shield of a new mental immunity against the slogans of our sectarianism at his side. No education has quite succeeded to confound these archetypical road signs in me. And so I still doubt that I should drill into my soul just one single, huge hole so my merry flute would play just the one and deepest sound.

A need to be uncommitted in the mind for awhile seduces now many of us to make our yearly pilgrimages to shrines of youth and innocence or to sacred groves where we can wash and refresh our minds in a greater society than that of man. We are hurriedly putting anything not yet subdued by the empire of man on tapes or into parks. We fill our libraries with books and cassettes preserving the endangered subspecies of the human soul as if they were our own memories that may fade forever away. We realize that our active memory is only a small part of our memory.

Technology itself seems still quite an adolescent with much arrogance and strong maniacal tendencies. Behind its cheerful front hide perhaps many unhappy actors and prostitutes who need a tamer, whitewashed world to survive. I need a special sun hour a day to figure out that problem child. Who knows, that offspring might turn out to be an exciting daughter to all earthlings—men, snails, ferns and all—when given a soul.

28

My Christian upbringing has made me a rather dull stranger in barefooted nature's celebrations.

How different from my impatient pity, in which I am trained, I find nature's welfare in her no-man's land; how mind-boggling to me is her compassion, her ten commandments, her help. Slowly I realize that there I am faced with a shockingly far-sighted goodness. No wonder that my love, which is trained to be neighborly and not to stray far from our generation and our homes, often impatiently mistakes her grandiose generosity as a show of force by an apparently idiotic brute. This loss of vision seems to be at the root of my intellectual unrest and the angry protests I send off to God. I need reading glasses to see reactions only five generations away. Most world religions were too practical to accommodate and glorify the intellectually so messy business of on-going evolution in their creation myths and their moral teachings. They conveniently glorify a pure, unmutable state of goodness at rest from a time of innocence, of old, of before the fall, of a static harmony. Hence, the preoccupation with perversion, sin, badness, and hotter coal for their hells. Hence their grave problems of mental waste and pollution. Yet evolving life never tires to teach me that its goodness is much more exciting than a merry-go-round.

Under the black cloud forecasting an ecological cataclysm, other sicknesses have become trifles that for now I want to forget about. I need a philosophy with a deeper more serious approach to ecology that is closer to my religious instinct. A vision that lights up my kinship with all life and greens my mind again could serve me well. I feel that it is in this respect that my Christian upbringing has left me in the dark. The dull remedy to socialize horizontally and herd together ever more, just among man, each time tragedy occurs, leaving our other neighbors, the swallows, the diatoms, the trees, further out in the cold, saddens my religious instinct. Why was I taught morals that made me abandon so many capacities and critters of this wonderful place? Slowly this sick mentality seems to sicken the whole living earth. The voice of a freer world, though, which educators so effectively jammed in me, likes to treat me as a member of a society so vast, that it has telecommunication to all creatures of all times. This spirit keeps triggering a behavior in me as if I were to live a thousand years. And so a Christian drinks wine at great risk. So much of his soul he has silenced and made into demons jailed in his chest. Then the first crime of wine is truthfulness.

It does not seem that the fathers of our western soul revolution and of our ten commandments had the time to ponder much about what subtle daily side-effects the new rules of their miracle-love would have on our fellow life. Yet, also here, the principle of complementary powers seems helpfully at work and starts punching holes into the balloon of our success which we keep on pumping up—Theo, spray paint it on your ceiling: The wild is a system unspeakably more compassionate and refined than any moral system our different cultures proudly parade. The logic of wilderness is the potent center of the onion. Our reasoning is its outer layers. None of the new ideologies we perform made us yet to better behave in the family of life. They are the first clumsy steps when autonomous creatures learn the line dance of a new and highly social structure. And we step still on every paw, root and toe. Yet not a moment I think that life does such expensive experiments in vain. Didn't she start the wings with deformed bones? We are now that promising hump on that bone.

When I think that the Navajos held nine-day song festivals to preserve their integrity with the cosmos, I recognize how crude my education in relationships remains.

29

When you fight your personal fights, do you ever
wonder whether my eager offer to help may perhaps
be just one more siren luring you with a siren-song out
of your privacy into a dependence on me?

When I am allowed to sit down and pass on to somebody else the test I
may fail, I sense the discreet dislike a man may feel for a helping hand and
I uncomfortably smile my defeat away. When helped out of a bind, I sometimes feel an inner reproach which seems to know that when I take a test, I
should not cheat and lightly dodge that chance to find out how much I can
take. These good-natured cheatings make uneasy bonds that no ceremony
has ever quite been able to hold together for long—because the heart
knows differently. One might get insight into that troubled pact when, in a
generous moment, one can quietly watch a child who, amid the circle of a
hundred hands eager to help, keeps stubbornly to its unique way of doing
things, kingly minding its own wits.

It is this same inner pride that intrigues me—when I think of animals
who are so devoted to their individual colors and fates that they resist
domestication with an inexplicable ferocity, missing out on an ever full
feed lot with beds made for them and maid service every day. To keep their
own tails and flags upright, they risk injury, even death, and raise under
great risk and rather alone litters of ten young instead of living practically
with social health care and settling for two. This stubbornness might be
more than foolishness. It takes only a few mental steps to notice that a people over-indulging in helpfulness does not leave its coming generation a
clean start, but much temporary mending and filth.

We put braces, we support, we rescue with sacks of flour, with tanks
or new dams—yet we simply end up shifting the slide somewhere else—
mostly to our kids. The global power law of Yin and Yang stays the same.

Here I face again my many requests for help—my lack of courage so
to speak. A person can miss his chance when he sneaks away from a
unique invitation to completely mobilize himself for once. That gift might
never come again. I can miss my chance to take on a battle single-heartedly
and to find once and for all my awesome self and strengths. Whining
unashamedly for help, I may cheat myself of my one great day when I can

drum out and mobilize a full army of resources and risk my neck to bring them under my command.

When you let me help you, did you ever think of what you are giving up? Did you ever consider that it is the giver that may want to thank the one he helps? Each time I can help you, I live a little more—and you live a little less. What a strange way to make war!

I heard an unaccustomed point of view on help: the help of the fox to the ailing hare is most times a total help—he swallows the whole hare. Our help is more partial, and more gentle. We nibble on an unfortunate fellow man; hair by hair, responsibility by responsibility, capacity by capacity, we take over more subtly than the fox when he steps into the life of a hare.

I wish myself the strength that in moments I am tempted to yield to pity, I do not seduce others to hang onto me, get them down from the high of danger and cheat them lightly out of their hair-raising, heart-rising chance!

Take Odysseus' advice. Rope yourself to the mast so you will not lightly plunge toward my whining siren-song, so you may not leave our next ten generations tangled in a mess of faint-heartedness, of temporary fixes, of cures that were postponed.

30

In spite of our public show of solidarity, it seems we still secretly confide to each other that we really love only those "cruel" lovers who give us our freedoms— the freedom to possess our joys and the freedom to possess our sorrows; the freedom to live or to die fully on our own inner terms, day after day.

If we impose on ourselves a peace simply by becoming too dependent on each other for remaining healthy opponents, this is a forced peace to me. International addiction to consumerism can oblige nations to this kind of pact. It is more a tense truce. Such peace comes from enmeshing us with pipe lines, the flow of credit, the health industry, fiber optics, loans, insurances, satellites, data banks, common markets and celebrities, the dependence on each other's narrow expertise, the tunnel under the channel, the

Net. Much is not said or given up to huddle together in this communal bed. We live a pact of brotherhood, fighting in a crowded loneliness a silenced contempt that ferments between an addict to seedless love and his convert to this addiction. We could become partners in a plural dictatorship, united in a holy war against all creatures who do not venerate mankind as their God.

In the face of all my strong talk, I do not want to forget the *Shirley B* that came plowing through a mad sea full-board for my life when my boat exploded and sank in front of Icy Point. I was badly burned and on the brink of being frozen and drowned. What bugs me is my learned willingness, even eagerness, to fall back on a last resort and to thoughtlessly and without shame give up at the slightest sigh of pain a piece of my life into the public lap. Do we not cultivate pride in being able to do just that? There are now so many helping hands that tempt.

Why is it that we now try harder than ever to collectively bail out any individual who has spent his own resources and is coming to an end— when we could nicely exchange her for a freshly baked child? In a world so full of us that we often have to step on each other's heart, why is it that we fight death moving among us so fiercely? Death seems to me such a wise and invigorating population control. Does not also the health and life span extension industries producing personal eternity need themselves now some "birth control"?

31

When life prescribed for me a spell of laziness, it made me a difficult gift. At first glance I wanted to send this upsetting "stop working" sign right back.

"Laziness is the mother of all sins." Many such prudish old sayings made laziness in me the villain which cooks up all kinds of devilment. These unimaginative sayings also soiled the brave, noble reasons for my instinctive reluctance to shamelessly sink into work. Is it not in the silence of inactivity pregnant with question marks, suggestions and advice, where eye-openers, illuminating trespassings and the creativity of daydreaming start?

For a long while I did not realize what a fantastic eye-opener my periodic inclinations for laziness were meant to be. This misunderstood and battered talent might turn out to be the poet in me when patiently heard out.

Sometimes a lack of zest might also be the fulfilled prayers of the zillion creatures on earth who agonize now under our exaggerated activity. Think of a crazy lion who would kill every day of the week! Laziness is fast becoming the most therapeutic gift we can offer to life at large after, drunk with our success, we transgress the law of moderation.

Even the armies of driver ants have to deal with this law and devote half their lives to camp, to do who-knows-what.

32

My thanks to a daydreamer, three times my thanks.

It's generous of him not to drill, intervene, scheme or kill. He lets his thoughts wander and wonder in the garden radiating unlimited learning and rarely rents them out. A true vagabond, his ears shameless, his eyes without a leash, following the path of life's hottest gossip, he risks being a sore to a generation deeply in love with harvesters, level-mindedness, hospitals, hammers and megabytes. He might be sweet music to the zillion creatures who shiver with fear when we, the good boys and girls, are very seriously at work to multiply our stake. The big blue-stem grasses, the forests, the mumble-creeks might be out of their minds with joy when a man walks about just making friends, shaking paws and hands, simply distributing our thanks. Such women and men may well be the best PR people to grease our relations with the earth.

I was raised by proud masters of controlled imagination—no side steps, no high steps, guaranteed. I was to be a predictable man born into only one predictable world. I learned to focus my thoughts with a sharpshooter's precision. I learned to hold my lively thoughts by the throat, pointing them strictly at the grim needs and serious problems to keep my body tuned and our fuel tanks filled. I learned to pan every shade, every tremor, every scent and nook in foe and friend just for their usefulness to me and to my clan. I was equipped with mental filters so fine my whole being was transformed into a deadly efficient provider tool. How could I see far while I was busy staring just into my bag of memories and thinking so hard? And so I forgot all about the art of how to freely dream with the dream of the earth.

Maybe some of those mental vagabonds loaf closer to the holy spirit than I do. Maybe they are meant to be our guardian angels so that we do not go down in life's history as the kings of poachers and parasites.

33

How I became more thoroughly trapped in the belly of the whale than Jonah himself.

My imagination is still trained to miss so much. A man risks being left handicapped in wisdom after he sat through a sixteen-year session of herding his thoughts into a one-way street, purposely castrating questions and answers that wander curiously off into the foreign lands of no-man's thoughts. He misses the chance to wonder about things which are just fun to wonder about, yet might be too great to ever pay off his short ego. For sixteen of my jubilant years of spring, itching me with dare devils, curiosity, the sweet follies of May, I was transformed into a grainship moored under a "loading bridge." My curiosity was narrowly focused on speakers gushing information that often prepares for a career in transforming the jungle of life into a playground for an adult commune. This is how I became more permanently installed in the belly of the whale than Jonah himself.

Retarded in the wise world of emotions that still begs to inspire me with the curiosity of a child, I was continuously reminded of my privilege to be cultivated and made a superbly trained soldier for the Church of Rationality. Look at the bulging muscles of the digital part of that mind! Is that not how we often become our parents' pride? Still, a mind is primarily a mirror dish and should not be degraded into a formidable tank or super-chip. A university should not compete with Silicon Valley to produce in us simply models and megabytes. A school can become more than just a center for breeding usefulness for our world economy. It can do better than stonewall our peace of mind with tyrannical assumptions. A school can do better than recite formulas for personal success and heroic myths. It can become a seminar in which wise women and men kindle the imagination of their young and animate them not to imitate but to look and think leaving their teachers behind. A university should not be allowed to sink so low that it becomes an engineer of monstrous cleverness—whose physical counterpart would make us shiver with fear. Do you know of a more challenging occupation than to make of a child a woman or man and to tease the poet out of them?

There will be great joy all over the earth when our schools kick the habit of conspiring with the consumer society's appetites and make daily lessons in convivial living and comfy relationships their principal seminar. In this era of achievement, do you know of any science as equally beneficial as the art of breathing into each other fascination for exploring our relationship with all life? It will feel good to glow with confidence, to become spectators with our mouths agape, shouting applause to the Creator, giving our thanks.

I suspect that, in a still obscure way, every organism is medicine to all others and ultimately survives only for its better fitness in this capacity. To decode life's poem being acted out by the universal symbiosis mostly beyond our awareness-horizon: do you know of an adventure in learning that would round up more friends? After all, is there not under the crust of our consciousness the infinite magma of other worlds waiting to be drawn up and seeded, a whole mental cosmos to be probed and lit up, a billion and one Arabian Nights still to be told, so much water to be parted? A fertile mind can synthesize from our fears, weeds, phantoms, sins, refuse and compost piles new companions it can gossip with and care about. It can alchemize sins into virtues, rascals into saviors, lead into gold. It can make new stars swim into sight. It can synthesize thoughts to counter hatred. It can wash off the stigma of a cursed creature or act. It can scavenge in hell for all kinds of usable things. Experts in serenity have found that for everyone of my anguishes, fits, fears, depressions and hates—with which my weak imagination often awkwardly reacts—there is also a perfect thought picture acted out somewhere in the jungle of life that is an antidote for such sick attitudes. When tamed and visualized such metaphoric pictures rub out that anguish, fear, fit, the notion of enemies, and miserable hate; they undo constipation in our love affairs and can take ten pounds of aching. There waits in us an alchemist who takes all plants and animals as base materials to transmute them into one single undividable sight. We have barely started the eighth evolutionary day in our awareness game. Maybe all evil turns out to be somebody's daily bread.

We could encourage one another not to simply keep on cloning the good girls and good boys in our schools with their meager and so wasteful goodness. Why is it that education from man to man should be so much stricter, harsher and more boring than the one mother nature kindly dispenses to her pupils. She does not stuff us with comments on comments, and information on information but lets us sip wisdom from the source. She does not make us sit tight-lipped at attention, but is rather an educational clown. She teases us onto the stage. She likes to dive with us for sunken memories. She frees our thoughts from work to race through many lifetimes without stopping them at the borders of birthdays or when leaves whine and decay.

34

You should not fuss and sob when I have to go. I am often not worried when people die! And I don't want to even argue with life about which of the many ways she may choose for renewing us.

There is something I need to shout to myself. It seems to me that a woman or a man who have their own children cheerfully nibbling on them should have little worry about their personal mortality. And thinking about all the young people who wait hard-pressed for a little homestead on this planet should also lessen the worry about the mortality of others. I think it is a fine sight and a fine time in a man's life when, after he has given of himself in his days and he is in his last hours, he is surrounded by his children and by all the things he has cared about and wishes them farewell.

When death comes to us, I try not to take any part in the conspiracy to lower our voices and pretend a disaster has happened. I feel I ought to have more courage in this respect so that I will be better prepared when it is my turn to generously go. Sometimes I feel relieved when people depart. It is hard not to, after we had to castrate the thoughts and the vitality of our children so much for lack of space for their hearts to gesticulate. I can see neither wisdom nor compassion for life in many efforts to invent a magic for hanging on a few more years in full sight of all the youth around us who meanwhile have to lay low. I cannot join with my trumpet in the praise when a man talks proudly about saving lives. Has it not become obvious for any but the blindest minds that our obsession with furiously saving failing human lives has openly turned into an ecocide?

Deep down I hear that shy yet universal plea: "For our children's sake, please stop saving more bankrupt lives; allow also the forests, the butterflies, the lily ponds ample elbow room to bloom."

35

Two urgent questions: Are we inaugurating an eugenically stratified society to breed a caste of neuter and disposable careerists who are relieved of the worries of what happens past their own term? Are we begetting a new kind of gentlewomen and gentlemen who enjoy reorienting their love into the more pressing parental needs of mother earth than into tending more of our own seeds?

I notice a powerful new caste which is branching from our society. They seem to observe other morals, other dimensions, other role models and rules for peace of mind; they seem to explore a new asexual form of love. A need not to beget more children appears to neuter the psyche and the body of many now. Slowly that old spicy drug that makes us fall in lust might evolve there into a social hormone, a magic cement that glues us more horizontally together and gratifies us with a new, cleaner kind of tenderness. In this new union there is no need for male nor female names nor for the emotions' moody reds and blues. Stress-induced neurochemicals triggered by careerism are helping toward this needed infertility. (In wasp societies parasite-induced stress helps to neuter females metamorphosing them into a devoted altruistic career caste.)

Would people so metamorphosed not need their own codes, their own education, entertainment, fiestas and musky songs, their own soap operas, prayers and heroes? It will be my test of tolerance to find a code of respect that accommodates such different chores.

At first I felt irritated to find these new citizens so different from myself. I felt awkward in their company. My barefooted feelings seemed to offend. And I had the wrong blinders to see what they see, to see their sky. I thought I was regarded by them as a retarded mind, left behind, hopelessly in love with a picnic place that is too much of a wonderland for me to want to move on. I missed the chords needed to vibrate with them and play my fiddle in their triumphs.

Do I see nature's first steps to making true a recent commandment to focus our love on our neighbor when it tentatively confuses in some the old heterosexual urges and moves them toward a world of unilove? Who else, after all, could be freer to love neighborly than a person with a holistic kind of homosexual love, a love slowly released from our old flower games advertising and attracting pollination among ourselves? Who would be genetically better predisposed to the sisterly love needed in the kind of society that Christ was teaching us than those with that rare tenderness which does not beget a child? Maybe out of that old flower game nature concocts for some of us a new gift behind her back that will be also a kind of star-twinkling and tender-holding-hands-tinkling but this time not to glue us together as sexual partners but to gratify us when we gently rub against each other doing our new asexual social functions.

It seems that the great feasts of cultures—from old Greece to Rome to Saint Francis' brotherhood were often woven on a new horizontal loom with love that reasons when it falls in the other's arms.

36
How to handle a chainsaw and become a saint?

I have two ladies with me who are still learning to get along. When Miss Technology presents me with her circus show, I am thrilled, awed, tickled and proud. I also love to walk with barefooted Mother Nature and listen to what this wise old mama says. Why should I want to be rude to her and drive her away? She has been around for a few billion years. She knows a few things. I like to accommodate the ladies so that they may get along. It is for this reason that, in the glorious march of progress, I drag behind and dance to two different rhythms, wondering whether our clever shortcuts will not put our grandchildren in a bind.

Progress that finally takes root seems to have little to do with break-throughs bragged about in the morning news. Instead, it appears to me to be the precious residue of wounds, disasters, delusions, fears and broken loves that over generations we have slowly learned to heal. It might be the victories in our battles against the shadows, foggy goggles, assumptions and hatred. Such triumphs come about a little like our immune system perfects itself. This kind of progress takes a long time because every new gismo and tool, every new advice or social order, even the new tears and victories our politicians invent for us, all need to be questioned by every organism in the world and given its go ahead. The furious inventiveness of a technology that naively wants to humanize the whole globe often fails this test. When we plant a new idea, a miracle-tree, a seed we genetically engineered, a new sadness or a brand new rhyme that fits myopic eyes, when we come up with a life extension or better crutches for a failing man, doesn't every organism in the world have to scoot over a bit and make room? And contrary to what I was told, it seems not to be the strongest idea but the idea that makes the most friends that ultimately is welcomed to stay.

Maybe technology doesn't always need to be taken so seriously and is more like a circus tent with the wildest magicians and clowns. It is the playground for our phenomenal capacity for monkey business.

Still, I stand back to remain whole, round and low and not to volunteer as a martyr. It seems to be this act in the divine comedy I am to perform. Should I do my exploring as an expert and be carried on a throne, who knows, I might wake up one morning welded to the shoulders of the men of burden who carry me around.

Great organizers of the human hive make me shy. I do not like the land to be ingeniously simplified into one giant udder just for man. The growth of this science seems now to transgress the law of moderation and has turned malignant for life. Here an illustration: fishing technology has turned the long line fleet into such a deadly tool it rivals the nuclear bomb. You would turn us loose for ten full days and half the halibut population would be gone. Did we progress into a tooth bigger than the mouth?

When the six billion "dams" of six billion individuals break—each having sustained a sub-ecosystem of its own—what could resist the flood of power we so become by giving up each his uniqueness? When all women and men withdraw from the kinship with all things alive and regress into one united mankind, will we not be united in enmity against all that grows and loves on earth but cannot be profitably sold? When we all so solemnly contract into one huge clam, do you think our souls are better off? Social betterment seems to me not so much denying one's lively nature, but a matter of clearer sight.

When I think about progress in our standard of living, I do not necessarily think about a home with three baths or a fabulous chainsaw that fells three trees in one swift scream. I may think about a better capacity to enter a lasting relationship that is no tease but ripens our berries through summer and brightens our colors in fall. I think about earning the fabulous gift of never being shocked by what Mother Nature, or you, will do. I think of us being able to enthusiastically wait for every new day—to be each morning an impatient child who excitedly fingers that gift still wrapped in its box. I imagine that in a person's priorities, delivering some of one's dormant capacity might be higher up than climbing the consumer ladder to the top. I wish our applied science the good luck to become less of a whore and more of a friend who will give us five Sundays a week, good luck also to my faint ability to excitedly welcome whatever happens to me. When I manage to talk my dear reason out of having fits, stubbornly rebelling and shouting "unfair!" when my course is changed, I can use that turbulence to soar—and I start to wonder: why should I long for a paradise? I like it here.

37

What do you think is progress to a river that is a good mother to all?

For millions of years this river has been good to the watercress, the antelopes, the water striders, the gold diggers and the lovers and poets who came to listen to her song. She was a good wise mother to them all. Nobody wanted a fence. It was in this peaceful noon that a troubled man stepped out on her bank; and soon this practical man studiously stayed up long nights to drive his mind at the question: how can he steal the mighty, lusty river and harness that good mother for himself and for himself alone?

It was much work and sweat to chase all other partners away, to pull out the roots, dams and bridges of the other tenants in this lively meeting place, to connect his sewer pipes, to pour her banks in cement. But slowly he got good at it and, in an unclaimed moment, could sit back breathing in proud contentment over the progress his technology had made. It was a progress toward a new order of things, to fit our species that had locked up its love and swallowed the key.

His river is a docile river now, neatly bundled into a mighty team of horsepower, pulling on our generators, pushing our manure downstream; and only in the rare moments of our negligence has she been allowed to enjoy herself. Yet this river now has been rediscovered by many of us as one of the first of nature's wonders in which we start to remember and love again the wild; and this psychic discovery has started us on a unique campaign to give standing in our minds to such wonders.

And aren't our great wild streams of thought, in which our whole inner menagerie of spirits is dependent and at home, such endangered wonders, needing our love and protection—and to be included in our earth psychology's green campaign?

38
A closing out sale on all that is mysterious in a man.

When I was very young and a bundle of innocent trust, I was hurriedly made a child of the church that kindles rational goodness among us. Here I found merchants of love organizing their markets to give and to be given love when in need. Here things were offered which I was astonished to find for sale.

The time reserved to sing our children to sleep has a "For Sale" sign out, along with the tears, broken hearts, the wanderlust, the whole world of emotions and unknowables, the fertility, testicles, dreams, siesta time, ecstasies, our spells of weirdness and our great gusto for danger, the jungle world of paradoxes and hunches and mountains of treasures that have never yet been opened by those who sell. Even the fragile high of unemployment and of a woman playing with her child is tagged with a price. Impractical treasures, pregnant moods, times to loaf and to wonder, our nostalgias, all these exotic gifts can profitably be sold. Unfathomed dimensions still sealed in their boxes, antique dreams of a serenity buried in a soul, pangs of love and pain, any love that is not due to ripen in our life span or too big to fit in a theory's box are welcome to be pawned or melted down for fast power or a ticket to instant fun. Could all this auction be some exclusive reward for those whose lives are not to be renewed in order to heal our overcrowded race? No doubt people with such a tight blindfold should be compensated with the privilege to use up the joy of all their thousand springs in a feast of spending and having fun.

Yet those among us who remain in love with the winds, the cold, the paradoxes and the wild and open sun, those among us who hesitate to leave the contradictions of a shady soul that seems a thousand unknown generations tall—we question this well-lit heaven of orgies and fast obvious goodness and we wonder how we might resist also being sucked into this spending spree which could plunge our planet's life into a holocaust? We do not want to conveniently erase the remaining living memories that remind us of the tragic loss many suffered in the wake of their moving sale when leaving a million-year plan for a five-year plan. And we side with this brave new breed of young warriors who defend that memorable earth—too permissive, too long-range for most of us—some with gentle persuasion, others with disobedience and homemade monkey wrenching.

I wonder how this brave new community, those who undergo a change of mind and free themselves from the "Cosa Nostra of Man," presumed emperors of the world, can take a better hold on me. How courageous it is to make a promise not only to the Red Cross but to our planet's health. There are few officers, few lawyers, hardly a written law. Each is left alone with just his timid self-made thoughts as his judge that spank him when he flunks. It may be from people like the EarthFirst! family that the seed crystals for the new Earth-sociology may come.

Here an idea bubbles up that might switch on a lamp. Do you know what delays the conspiracy for a united mankind that promises miraculous profits? I suspect it is our hidden love, still rather unknown to psychology, for all other life which stands stubbornly between us. It is our inborn shame to hold hands just among ourselves and leave out the trees, our mistress the sea, the whole lively crowd that homesteads with us the sky, the oceans, the land. And I will never trade this shame.

Did you consider that our unschooled egoism, at times so outrageously presumptuous or humble in its demands, might be a love of a holistic co-existence as big and puzzling as all the known and unknown worlds? Although a "man only" union seems to offer us a Faustian loan, there are countless quivering hearts out there in the bushes praying that this human cyclone never forms. Anguished I realize that a world with ten billion people who are healthy, vigorously working, and in our way wealthy, is a monstrous wish. And so, may the Creator save me from an invention that can feed another billion of us.

39

Rebelling, snorting in the civilized corner of my mind, I begin to realize that to be heroic might well be a chauvinistic state of mind.

Every bird in the tree chirps to me the wish that I enlarge the models of my mythological hero-dreams, encouraging me to model my part so inclusively and baggy that my angels, my heroes, my Batmen, Rambos and Theo the hero ultimately do not have much to angrily fight against anymore. To out-think the old heroes with their clans of men who shout their praise; to out-think the darlings of our merry generation in which we tiptoe arrogantly in a hundred years of solitude; to crane my vision and see beyond the rather Judaic inward vision of those who won the West but never quite learned how to accommodate the flora and fauna within their mythology—these are thoughts that do me good.

How can one become a hero in a "motherland" so great, it has room for both the human tribes and the many other tribes? Are we not all offsprings of this primordial soup blessed with a dream not to remain a soup? Look at the colors of a meadow for what this love-dream can do.

More and more critters of the fourth world can be promoted to spirited neighbors, inventors, teachers, patent holders so they need not tremble for fear anymore that I am some man-god's hero, willing to battle just for the empire of man. One can dream of heroes who now know better things to do than to be saviors of human lives and simply add another million to our hacking, trampling troops. For this I retire now in my mind the myth of St. George fighting nature the "brute."

I like to listen to the North American Indian's stories of once-upon-a-time, in which the whole of God's menagerie is invited to supply the heroes. When diving deeper and deeper into our mind, do we not hit a depth where there seems less need for favors and heroically taking sides?

40

When I noticed that God had no clothes on, I was shocked.

In my sarcastic moments, I see no end to our beautiful philosophical mumbo jumbo with which we mask our intellect and hypnotize ourselves into the trance of rationality. It seems to be with this kind of shaman's mask and drapings that we separate ourselves from the crowd to make ourselves the Grand Clan of demi-gods, politicians, and sorcerers of all species. Is this not how we charm and beguile all life into grandiosely maintaining us? To many of us this seems our best survival kit.

When I was still a lad and played with beetles and Samanta, my rat, I was helped to knot such lofty thoughts into a hammock. In it I could swing high among that Grand Clan which choose to be seen as the darling of God. From that pure and lofty height I could look down on all else; and without getting a dirty mind, I could command the lowly bunch of critters that could not even walk erect.

Soon the mischievous boy in me got bored and looked for the pretentious string of myths that held me with that poetic net of thoughts all lonely in the sky. Soon the boy fond other thoughts even more fit and sharp than those venerable myths and whack!, with them he hacked those stringers in two. And Theo fell down into the Navajo's Pollen Path. "Oh, beauty before me; beauty behind me; beauty to the left and the right, above and below."

Look, I fell right on that wonderful Pollen Path! I understand that the ancient Chinese called this path "The Way."

41

So many actresses have so much going on out here; there is no need to dial-a-porn.

When my traps or baited hooks on longline gear don't soak and put my mind to work, when I don't let myself be prejudiced by books, when I can wriggle out of people to the left, the right, above, below, triggering in me greed, the not-enough-for-all-to-go around syndrome, I sigh and feel free. I can do what I all along have been dreaming of doing: nothing, no single itch, no need to scratch. I can be all lazy and all easy. I can let life be an uninterrupted gift. I can look out from my wheelhouse onto this northern coast not as a fisherman this time but as a man. Such laziness is Sunday for me.

Here, far away from the common sense of the crowd and alone on my boat, anchored in this forsaken bay of Alaska's coast, I steal a little solitude. Here life seems to chatter to itself in the language beyond our models and our abc's. Here ideas are not only spoken of but acted out. I can be simply host for awhile to all those wonderful critters that accompany me on our trek to "who knows where." I see myself surrounded by fantastic happenings and I am awed. Wow, but this is God's country, no doubt! This no-man's land gave me the gift to fall in love with it. This is my second falling in love; this time with that nifty Gaia woman who lies in wait for her man in every creature peopling the world. And is there a happier event? My mind bows. Many thanks for that gift of enthusiasm! What a community of inventors, what a circus, what a seminar. Here my mind can take off its mask, open wide its arms, soak in the wisdom this land has cooked and distilled for billions of years. I can explore e.g. what it came up with from the idea of combustion for locomotion and compare it with Ford's model T idea including our latest additions. I can hear "predators" and "prey" wonder: *why be so unimaginative and label animals with such boring and unnecessary chores?* Intelligence radiates from every speck of protoplasm here. My mind plunges into innocence. My thinking becomes more original. My confused thoughts recover strength and confidence.

This land wants to drag me out of my ignorance and light me up with its epics. It erects the hunch in me that we all behave much better than we think. In its company it's simply impossible to remain grim. I look around. I am surrounded by the history of my long memory all laid out to be read and seen—my memory for when I was a mineral, a leaf of grass, a cave man, a man at sea.

I am surrounded by a glorious story of successful co-existence, wisdom not yet fathomed. I realize that to keep such a progressive unity among minorities for so long, even the seaweed must be so social-minded that it can give a lesson in social science to me. Here, long ago, a communication explosion was realized and I know practically nothing about it. Imagine that each of the zillion molecules in the cosmos sends out its signals. The universe is made of messengers!

This bewildering land exorcises the spell that humanistic civilization has cast over my mind. It is the catalyst to long range thinking. My reason, so used to only lightly touching on a small part of a thing loses its filters. I see every cubic inch packed with a zillion pieces of information. In the company of a tidal pool I gather fresher news than from Newsweek. And this place washes the blood of my mind when it has served too much simply as a slaughterhouse.

In town I rapidly become deadly sober with rationality and my communications are bundled and leveled out. There I am overwhelmed by the informative interchange confined within the bowels of our Hive. That information has been censored beforehand, chewed and prejudiced so that it becomes useful and digestible for the "lords" of the world. In that crowd I am endlessly encouraged to induce my deeper mind to throw up my useful knowledge into my consciousness and to empty it into our communal web of databanks. What productivity, what fame such explosions can bring!

No, the explosion of data exchange has not made us more communicative. It has made us more communicative among ourselves by focusing the loose dialogue each man kept up with the whole of God's zoo peopling with us the earth. The information explosion means fewer and fewer different sounds but many more trillions of echoes. It makes each of us less of an original thinker. No wonder the enormous commotion of the mass-media storm, the fights for the public opinion, the forests of telephone poles, and mail boxes that overflow. No wonder the air is so sluggishly thick with the flood of our communications where we trade our models made from our trillion yes's and no's.

The shortcomings of the telephone: it can only connect me with other women and men—never with lady loon, never with a family of trees, never with a future generation, never with the moon. In me original things seem to better mature when I can hold tight in solitude. Why then would I want a telephone that every ten minutes makes me leak? I feel it important that I keep up my system of unfocused long distance calls—not necessarily with some alien E.T. worlds we try to contact, but with the spirits of our future and our past. I like to correspond with the advocates of every creature of the earth. I like to exchange ideas with the spirit of the oceans, of pine cones, of the cities of stars, and to keep in touch with my own acts which zoom away from me by asking of them how they will do five generations from now.

I am on the Ark, so to speak, here in this bay untouched by man. Everything around me talks to me or acts out its ideas at the same time. I am besieged by one great identification hum while the whole lively world wraps around me. My mind feels warm. At first I see quite a merry turmoil; at the second glance everybody seems busy with things that seem vital to my health. Everybody on the Ark also looks worried, a little like during the reign of the Nazis, whether some world improver of the supreme lords will shoot another undesired guest. My deeper mind has a field day, all busy to respond and shake paws and hands and I become much more than a Christian for this little while. Is that not a neat Sabbath for the mind?

No, you need not worry for Theo who is not so well connected to the flatlanders' communication system in town—he is not a lonely man.

42

I see a relation between how overcrowdedly we live and how rational we become. Uncontrolled rationality might well be a mild state of panic when seen from a lookout in evolutionary time.

Take a bull and neuter it and you have a hard working, predictable and docile ox. Take knowledge and neuter it and you have docile rationality—

a tool highly suitable for work.

In the bowels of a city I often feel herded and in other people's way. I live and think there in a rather permanent state of crisis alert and emergencies. This environment encircles and overwhelms me with our own slogans and commands, and imposes a curfew on my thoughts. There my mind lives on "candy bars," of yes and no, on instant calories. Crowded by too many of us into an unnamed state of hostility that compels me to quick and short-sighted actions, my state of mind often becomes that of a caged animal fighting with an egoism of barest survival, mothballing in a kind of mental autotomy the long-range concerns, its soul. My mind misses the land of plenty and mystery which could keep me in a yeasty, trusty, unhurried and fertile mood. My mind is battered by the media management and its advertisement storms. It is twisted, whirled around, confused and neutered by the mind altering machine. My mind in stress becomes drunk with adrenaline—the drug that induces egotism in me. Every wolf in me is called out to help me stand the ground. I become superbly competitive. Submerged in our own cloud of noise, I become information-poor. This harsh mental climate seems to slowly provoke an ice-age in which my soul hibernates and my rationality takes control of my mind and my bodily functions. And I see our voracious communication systems rapidly eating up my last places of solitude!

To be safely taken down into the bowels of humanity, and be permanently "online," is that the salvation one should be praying for? I have found that my multiple viewpoints soon get obstructed there. I have found that in cloisters of rationality, one loses the capacity to love life at large. Many become zombies and insiders ideal for great careers whose souls are soon replaced by the environmental protection agency's laws. I wonder how other animals fared when evolution switched them from solitary creatures to highly social beings.

A humanistic mind feels good in town. It has found its ideal home. Things are aesthetically pleasing there. Isn't a city a monoculture in which everything is about, for, or from man? Wild and beasty ideas are driven out. Yet outside its gates that mind can be a lonely tourist of a foreign tongue and painfully insecure in the presence of that awesome Goddess whose necklace is not necessarily made of rubies, charities, Ferraris, miracle rice and bank accounts, but of more refined and precious things like beetles, grasses, butterflies, earthquakes, sicknesses, worms—and of us, the "lords." To live with the wild fills a highly cultivated person with anxiety she has never learned to deal with. This anxiety can mentally disable her—hence her obsession to undo the wild world.

I feel the whole earth quivering now with hope that humanism finally starts to hatch, that I will come to a peace between the "towns" I build in my mind and the mindscapes that remained poetic uncultivated mystery land. I can learn to love an organism first for its large portfolio of relationships and for its inventiveness and second for the calories and manure it can produce for us. I can become better at listening to the wonderful "Bible stories" of nature, such as the inconspicuous slime mold of the woods, is trying to tell us. For in this amazing biological happening we recently discovered, every autumn innumerable free-wheeling microbic organisms of the woods join to reproduce—forming for this phase one body, one brilliant flower, one soul. Who would have thought that the Christian message had been acted out by nature long before Christ? Such heart raising discoveries slowly will fill that glorious eighth day in the Genesis of my mind.

No, we needn't be condemned to forever asking aesthetic arts to wrap untamed and awesome beauty into all kinds of embroidered veils or to simplify it in indoor beauties like classic music.

And thanks to this wonderful, oozy and wildly permissive earth out there, the belly of my mind always gets filled.

43

I did not plot when I did my best, but risked being called an idiot.

After all my trouble to behave smartly, there are still just my few strong illogic acts of faith scattered through my life that paid me simply with their delicious taste which I can now remember and feel warm. I was good to myself then. Those hearty acts of an apparent fool have never cheated me. I like to recapture that faith in my guardian spirits that I chased away, mistakenly calling them names.

Nonetheless, we may have all been stung by the Holy Spirit when she laid that mischievous egg of reasoning in our minds. It seems a sly cat in a box eager to try all kinds of new hat-tricks that my heart has heard nothing about or never dared. Now I try to take this fussy new friend down into my more intimate mind. We sit together on the same bench, just a little apart, with few words, trying not to be too serious and not to fight. We just sit tight on our prejudiced hands. We make little grimaces to break the ice. We scoot closer—and a little closer. We both hope that later we will have something to celebrate.

44
Of ugly ducklings and toads.

Thanks for my spells of weirdness and craziness: three times thanks for these little peepholes in the box of my routine. Are the anomalies not the chances given to a man to come out of his clamshell and to look at himself through the eyes of a flower or an owl? Better still, are they not his shuttles to other worlds?

This capacity to not conform is probably the most generous, most daring gift nature gives to its players. And no other species seems to be as gifted with little crazinesses as we are—nature's lords of the weirdoes, dreamers, sinners and clowns. Yet in a mass education that likes to teach some kind of mental square dancing, this capacity becomes an unwanted child. It needs protection from our practical mind which can be so rude with this curious and "useless" child.

These stirring spells seem vital to a balanced mental health and promise a person that, if loved, they will never let her become dull. Yet this capacity to play a rhapsody can maybe not be taught but only kept alive. And is it not in these ugly ducklings that the genius of a woman or a man may hide?

When a people will design loopholes for unusual living under its laws, does it not draw itself an ace? That chance, perhaps even an invitation—to live a courageous lifestyle on a curly road that does not lead to Washington can produce the salt that is as precious to a society as their darlings who keep their aim, their hair, their walks and thoughts straight. Maybe a piece of driftwood has a better story to tell than a good useful two-by-four nailed into a wall. Maybe the vitality and creativity of a people can best be measured by how few laws it needs to nail itself down. Remember, Theo, only when life becomes "illegal" does excitement start. Trying itself out in excesses it inflicts creative injuries to the status quo. And does our species not honestly earn the gold medal in excesses? The question: How much of an excess can I bite off and swallow?

When a community protects its hermits, its weirdoes, its beggars, surfers, hippies and nerds, its extraordinary women and men with a trespassing permit, it also protects all that is deeper and higher than its laws; it does not plug its source of charismatic leadership. And the bran of the society might ferment into poets and become the people's wine. It might be about these "ugly" persons that the fables of the princess with the toad and the ugly duckling are talking. Or was it each man's troublesome and ugly character-traits that the wise author expected to turn beautiful when loved?

45
I have never learned well how another's freedom is preserved.

It is said that when I choose a companion, a sorrow shared becomes half a sorrow, that a vice shared seems to be half a vice, and that to sit in each other's laps becomes a formidable temptation for the two of us. Maybe this simply says that a man is never quite as responsible, sharp and universal as when he is on his own, that even in a togetherness of two a seed of mass hysteria may sneak in. Hence the respect our forebearers had for their hermits.

When a thousand similar catch-thoughts mill and bump into each other forming a crowd, I want to watch out; such a mass gathering can soon invoke a false feeling of higher truth and strength. In a crowd I am surrounded with so much sameness that rocks me back and forth—soon I start to imitate and fall asleep.

When I asked my companion, "Please understand my world and follow me to my goal," I asked much of her. Did I have in mind to just strip-mine some useful commodity in the meadows of her heart or trade the goods I need on banker's terms? Did I want to level her garden, in which she grows her dreams, her raspberries, her joys, and make of it a parking lot to nightly rest my greed? No, it does not feel good when we simply drain each other's sap in a frivolous trading spree. When we pull down our wonderfully unprofitable moods alive with exotic pregnancies and build with them a penthouse for our egos, might we not end up with a nest of boredom instead? How easily we now slip in our great native careers to understand and act and become instead partners glued together by a mutual addiction for self-pleasures and solitary games that overshout a nostalgia of our souls.

I will be truly damned if I enter her unplowed mindscape that made her glow in a thousand yellows and blues and use my land-developer's mind to bulldoze into it my own profitable roads. I will be damned if I plow my motivated goodness into her ground. I find we are more electrifying partners the less we have to domesticate each other's world. I find that when we help each other not to buckle under to the other's whining, that affectionate friction makes us glow.

How thrilling can be the prize from a compassionate relationship that needs not be diffused by the fig leaves of niceness and politeness in order to endure its seasons. There, during a spell of innocent laziness, I can stand back and watch her own wonderland, close to which I was allowed to settle. I can marvel, wow! I never guessed how much is hiding in a soul. I start to tiptoe instead of just trample and mess around. Maybe I should just try to rake away some of those fig leaves in which an overcautious civilization has buried her. It will feel good just to watch her glow, tan and grow. Her sunrises and her sunsets will brighten my days. I can learn to see her dreams, her raspberries ripen, the stars in her sky. Maybe this equals the great artist's chiseling his rock to make it come alive and talk. Courting her, little by little, my mind dares to take off some of its clothes, some of its politeness, its credos, its school knowledge, some of its slogans, the sunglasses, the pride, the mask of reputation and let her peek into my own jungleland. And I get to know her wants below her wellspoken advertisement and cover-ups. These animal likings that seldom are called by their name form nonetheless the magnetic field that swings our compass around. Becoming so intimately naked and friendly we get in each other's presence all excited and tanned. And then, when she is not here, she leaves the lights turned on in me.

Under such a sky our naked passions will not come down as harshly as a calculated fertilizer spray does on a field of Brussels sprouts. Our passions will do better than hate, pity or flirting. They will pour down as a searing sun. They will settle on each other with the gentleness of a settling dew. They will soak us in torrents of vitality on which mighty joy and sadness can thrive.

Clara, you have been that deep soil for me, so rich with uncertainties, mysteries, paradoxes, yummy impurities; I have been thriving on this humus, puzzled and lit up by it for thirty-five years. Thank you for having been resisting to become farmland for sixty years.

And then when we luckily stumble into a clearing and bask in all our rhapsodic thoughts, we may realize that we really love only those lovers who ignore our whining, but made us free and strong to stand on our own in the sun and in the rain.

46
About molting and controlling—about positive and negative "sins."

When the mind molts, when it sheds the shell, a model or philosophy into which it securely wriggled and boxed itself—and starts to form a new ring of growth, is that not the time when a wider vision fights to take possession of a woman or man? New longings meet a chorus of protests when they are born. One becomes out of step with common convictions while pursuing further goals. There will be other commandments. Old tears, answers, friendships and slippers might have to go. I worry then and reflect on how vulnerable I could become in such openness and how alone. A terror of change rattles my mind.

"Cling to the safeways, lay low," I shyly try to persuade myself. "Fall back on solid ground." Still, the sting of new desires and the new wings will not retreat. An old virginity is lost for good. With your strange new idea you seeded a dilemma in my mind—your writings changed me more lasting than would cocaine. After the fever and sweat while confusing and testing in me the old, your gift started to tip the scale. Surprise! These terrible gifts from our positive sins, the trespassings that come from a passion for inner growth, become, little by little, kinder. Enemies start to turn into helpers. What was yesterday in the spotlight starts to blend in. Who, with just a glimpse of goodness could resist and remain a "good boy" and stay home?

I think I know why dreams can be so illuminating. In our dreams we are emboldened to meet ourselves beyond our egos where each is a divine critter a thousand monsters and saints great. We are encouraged not to be meek. There is so much elbowroom and no "No Trespassing" signs in the world of dreams, and much forgiveness for being a fool. Do you know a more gentle drug for us than the sleep that gives us dreams?

When a troubled man leaves the "United Tribes of Life" and retreats into humanity to profitably cultivate his goodness and compassion just within its fence, when a failing person retraces and evolves downward, joining a herd of men to save himself—doesn't he suffer in his descent from his negative sins? When stepping down to be one of them, it becomes a crime for him to be self-confident, to be generous and brave, to think erect, to be his own judge, to daydream, to not forget. To look deep inside and recall pictures of freer times is punished here with a sunstroke in the mind. Lotions are recommended against wisdom that is too hot for tender minds. Here it is commanded that we degrade ourselves and prostrate our minds to the "virtue" of facilitating life, to dulling it, filing down its teeth, smothering its ecstasies, believing this is the way to sugarland. Here no seeds that sprout simply for the birds or beyond our time or on the shaded side of the moon are allowed.

When our passions tangle, spark and violently mix their truths, we must become swiftly proper and veil ourselves in clothes and in clouds; we are not allowed to promenade our souls without an umbrella of politeness and other "half-lies" that are to control our adrenaline. Into the minds of all those born to live in such protective caves the commandment is branded: "Thou shalt not self-confidently stroll out into this treacherous beauty without a hat, without a credo, without a shepherd and a coat around your soul, for unbearable harm and confusion may come to you and to your fellow men from such openness." To fight nostalgia one might be given anti-insight drugs, sleeping pills for the soul such as Prozac.

Down in that safer world, Miss Prudence, the mother of all boredom, is not the spoiler or sinner anymore but the hero in the economy's educational TV shows. Yet in spite of the low self-trust the peddlers of safety and the consumer animators spread among us, do we not also produce the most amazing firewalkers this planet has ever known. And do their great stories not begin one step beyond our safety-loving crowd, where our terror of change keeps us laying low?

I like to remain an apprentice all my life. I wish myself the luck to become blind to the temptations to settle as a mastermind. It's when I press myself for completion and conclusions that I stumble and blunder the most. Why kill the "animal" for inspection and frame it? I will take it as a privilege if I can hold out and remain a curious child and can find myself to be wrong again and again.

47

When you kindle a kinder lifestyle in me, when you sharpen my eyes, and show me how to live lean, so I can better tiptoe my needs and greeds less messily through this beautiful, lively earth, and become Theo in Wonderland, you make me a good gift. That gift also rewards you with happy faces from every tribe of critters on earth.

When people try to break out of our rude consumer world and we make fun of them, don't we miss a great chance? When these shy explorers shrug off our common sense and live materialistically leaner to build their own comfy homes more with mental solutions, like homes made of friendly relationships, and less with the physical solutions of the GNP, aren't they lanterns in the dark? They become disciples of their own paradoxical voices and risk becoming bugs in our cherished models. They dare to doubt the wisdom of begging God for a second bathroom for their homes. They stop being a warehouse. A bouquet of bright relationships seems sweeter wealth to them.

These modern adventurers barely have anybody to imitate. There are no TV preachers to support their cause, few politicians, few parents, no Henry Fords. Yet are they not timely explorers? And although they may at times seem unsure, hostile, and awkwardly arrogant and with only a shoestring or a monkey wrench to hold onto, this might just come from a new adolescence they are trying to outgrow. In a society that added an eleventh commandment: "Thou shalt consume and produce jobs to please our God." and for this purpose tied all kinds of rattling pots, phantoms, empty fears, cans, and expectations, rotten trust and foul herring onto our backsides, it is high adventure to try to minimally disturb and consume and to go for wealth in diversity and a home of good relationships. They can count on a patriarchal contempt when they try to wriggle their needs slick as eels through our planet's life and make our dear GNP whine and lose weight.

When I think about our children experimenting with new lifestyles and our lack of tolerance, the little dandelion puts me to shame. That brave little researcher frees its seeds to hitch a ride on any wind, to land and try itself out anywhere, on a dung heap, maybe in a gutter, perhaps on an immaculate golf course lawn. Remember how we swiftly buried our flower children in ridicule when they started to explore new ways to live. Yet, from some of such spirited young, who choose to be as lightweight as kites, a new, more poetic breed of high-rising economists may emerge.

48

Don't let this man stand in the blazing sun. Give him a straw hat; give him a good hat woven with freshly picked lies. Let him decide for himself when it is a gentle day of May to leave his hat at home.

I am amazed how much lying in all its raw and mannerly forms is a vital part of life. I will feel relieved to discover good intent, even beauty, in these mischievous tricks of which nature is so fond. I snoop around for clues and catch myself admiring the halibut for changing its colors into a pattern of its surrounding gravel or sand to mislead its prey, telling it flatly: "I am a rock." I watch that inconspicuous pebble, and oh!—it's a seed; it's a million secrets in hiding. I think of my illiterate friends fishing alongside me between the mangroves in the lagoons, who when cornered with a rational argument often can only defend their hidden truth with paradoxes or with beautifully ornated lies. I think of young untested people who are still untrained in the arms of self-defense. Would you blame them for keeping their freshly planted world behind a fence of arrogance and other little lies? Even the actor in his role as professional pretender and imitator seems a refreshment for us. We love him for luring us away from our stale repetitious days. When a woman is pregnant she is also rather possessed by a warm illogic, a shady truthfulness too tall for me that may laugh at me and laugh at her, yet seems to serve the child in her.

The deeper purpose and beauty of the lie may well be rooted in a puzzling commandment the good spirit has scribbled deep down in our genes. We seem to be asked to each preserve some vital secrets and pass them forward as gifts in the generations' relay run. Doesn't diversity come from withheld information—a law that may shame our Internet? Who wants the fireweed to auction off the password to its fiesta in purple and blue for a momentary gain? It might end up in a pot of stew on the commodity market and turn grey.

Are we women and men meant to stand erect on our own or are we bums, leaners and beggars, ever ready to ask questions begging for answers for which a brave person does not beg? Are we imitators ever ready to plunder somebody's heart? To bare oneself to others and to trade one's truth with them as if all truths were giveaways as apples and pears, seems to me often the "privilege" of a chaste brotherhood that likes to hold hands only in a circle. When you ask a person for truthfulness, do you realize that it may be a forbidden favor you ask of her?

In the case for withheld information, think about the kingfisher along the creek and the kinglet in the bushes that are close to 99% similar, the trimmings that make them strikingly different may biologically amount to one percent. Nature decrees for them not to be a blabbermouth so that this one percent truth may remain secret and withheld. Think on the other side of the lie in all its mannerly forms of politeness and self-denials as the most important lubricant of any society. Without that friction relief, wouldn't a society soon squeak and grind to a halt? The good of lying seems ultimately always a question of degree and not one of yes or no.

How nicely motivated openness could calm the storm of life for us. Yet do you want the clam to leave its shell agape, a man to burst open and to spill his mental guts? Can we, so addicted to the charities of the mind and self-denial, still dimly understand a forward storming soul that forbids its man to brag about what he knows and to proudly make of it a public give-away in front of his house while his disinherited children are looking on? An unfriendly world, you may say. It is true, for a super-rational man whose world has shrunk to one life span alone.

I know now there are "pregnancies" that just have to hold tight. You may have to stuff my curiosity with a lie so you may not deliver them prematurely. There are your lies that seem to protect your most vital seeds not ready yet to sprout. There are ideas still packed in hunches that are so explosive they become monsters if prematurely made conscious and known. There are intimacies so fragile I am never quite sure that I can be so discreet as to witness them without breaking them up.

To fight my addiction for the hefty bribes I get for being an informer, I like to think of all those women and men, animals and plants who remain brave messengers. Some let themselves be skinned alive, so important it is for them not to spill on the way what secrets they feel they are asked to carry through a fire line, to another generation, another place, maybe to a far off home. With this in mind, my sour mod cheers up when a man cannot striptease his mind for me.

Please do not tempt me to argue with you about what I feel called to do. For I have no obvious arguments to defend what is great, what is secret, what is sacred to me. My deepest compassion lies beyond any size of rationality. Likewise, a woman that is more than a comrade I cannot figure her out. She might be just God's fingernail yet nonetheless fathomless as the beholder itself. Please do not charm me out of my faith.

So we sing our songs and write our poems to applaud the golden beauty of decay in fall, after we have cheated the corn field of its ears of corn and we harvested the bees' honey for which they worked so hard.

Isn't a two-dimensional lie just another skin holding the roaring winds out and our precious little warmth in? These welcome umbrellas and shelters have little to do with our terrible lies with which we barricade ourselves against our children, against our inner voices and the heavens, against our own daring souls. What a degradation in nature it is when a father has to drive with his lie a wedge between himself and his son.

The wonderfully mischievous law of division that seduces us to lie and that mushrooms life into profuse diversity, gives headaches to theologists and moralists.

And so the wine's biggest crime is truthfulness.

49

Remember: It's the fir that gets axed first that is most anxious to fetch the loggers' prize for the straightest, tallest log, ignoring its cones, needles and neighbors and declining to be stubby and lean into the wind.

When one offers to organize a better world for just men, women and the few useful beasts and greens smoothly socialized, there is a Catch-22 that's nagging me. Invitingly, the good shepherds stretch out their arms, "Look at our great herd! It's wonderful medicine!" The holes, the shortcomings, the humps, anything overdone or missing in your character, even cracks in courage—they are appreciated talents somewhere in our enterprise. You will feel new strength from the smooth companionship of a million other followers, softly swaying together with you to our command: "Do come in!"

Yet in the individual of higher insect societies I notice an awkwardness close to stupidity when left on its own. And watch a hero when he is alone and the grotesque side of his personality that he let wither in neglect is not supported and groomed by a crowd.

I know of no bigger temptation for a man than his outstanding talents. His pride and his reasoning, the society he belongs to, the chamber of commerce and his proud parents are all after him to force-feed and commercialize this spectacular growth in his personality at the expense of what is shy in him and to sell the product for cash and fame. These talents in a woman and man may also be sleeping cancers. When allowed to take over the personality, these dominant gifts can soon become tyrants and corrupt a person's wisdom. Her capacity of enjoying solitude may die.

Intuitively I blush when I sell out to a spectacular one-sidedness of a cash-crop mentality. I have seen what cash crops repeatedly planted on highly suitable land can do to that land. And I feel more at peace when I am a good mama and guardian in this respect and first care for my timid talents instead and whip up my stragglers.

50

I will closely watch our mellow season of the leaves turning yellow and dancing to the ground. I might learn something about a compassionate meanness that can serve me well. I expect it will be quite a scandalous change of mind when I turn my own share of meanness into a friend.

Grumbling, I realize that to compensate my one-sidedness, life may have to answer my feasts of clever and premeditated good deeds with a good dose of destruction, with frosts, tests, blackouts, lame erections and pests, with all kinds of unpopular antidotes. Maybe it has to delegate a young man to become a champion in being mean and pitiless. My acts of mercy that love to stand in the limelight of the show can produce much fat. Nature may counter these binges with a diet of meanness, a little like making the partners dance together in the two-particle system of zero spin. I belong to an age of saints and criminals, of virtue existing divorced from vice, an age of specialists—a smooth clean hand that spreads seeds and only seeds; a callused fist numb to tears at the plow that loves to plow and plow under again; eager workers with souls still split by ignorance and yelling at each other, yet handcuffed together by a commanding interdependence in which each would still rather swear by his own kind of God.

To compensate for our soft ethic that drowns the earth in a flood of too much man, we leave it up to our kids to spend equal time inventing and administering sterility and sickness—to deliver us from our possessive self-consciousness with drugs and dreaming, to bleed our aggression enslaving the Earth with welfaring, tripping out and riding the surf, to get their victories in games of "deadly combat," to spill their sap on exercise machines, to promote death "in utero," to sabotage our runaway-success. We are leaving our kids with many thorns, splinters, plugs, nails and plows to be pulled and many switches to be turned off. They are asked to say so many painful "no's" which we postponed, to catch up with so many tests we discreetly put off. They are to be the wicked kids who make us sweat away our population's fat, who make a racket to wake us up, who pull the plug on our big board games for which we cut down whatever is needed to win, who are to pull the triggers of nature's guns to reduce the flood of our six billion and mushrooming troops. They are in a stupor from an excess of rationality we cultivated in them and experiment with mind-altering medicines and dreaming to liberate themselves from the tyranny of self-consciousness.

When I visualize this imminent explosion of our biomass produced by a philosophical mumbo-jumbo commercializing our philanthropy, when I preview its shock wave through the woods, the land, the sea, through the rain forests of our minds, I wonder: Should we not blush to have left the young with all those naughty chores to make us once again less numerous, less cunning, less armed, less powerful and more giving?

The day when a "good man" stops dead in his tracks, while a "bad boy or girl" crosses his path, and in a lightning of insight he wonders: What dirty work is this untouchable fulfilling that I, an all spic and span man, have left undone? That day his mental health jubilates. He may realize that, unfit to take the whining, he has monopolized cuddling, comforting, nursing for their instantly and obviously rewarding smile; and he is a spoiled brat of an idealistic indoor love fit only for healing and for spring. It might dawn on him that his constructive lifestyle was simply dedicated to construct even more manpower and guns to round up this beautiful Earth, and that he may have so triggered his daughter or son to become his opposite who, in defense of the Earth, will pull the plow of meanness and thin out those hordes of men. Astonished, he might have to conclude that crime, parasites, witch-weeds, God's thinning and wrecking crews, composters and tempests of fall also have their lobbyists in our souls.

When in ignorant enthusiasm I help just our generation and clan, abusing nature's kindness for us, another man or woman seems to be called out to return to the earth what was not meant just for us. We have never been allowed to keep our goodness conveniently in house arrest for long. The center of my soul is not my mind—it is not even mankind. The soul seems to be an outrageously permissive super-communication system to which every tree, every hacker, every flea is welcomed to break in, leave a message or take advice. For this we may sometimes be triggered into behaviors that do not benefit the individual, a generation, or even mankind, but benefits life. There is compassion coded into my genes that may be a moral as tall as the tall tale of life.

And so it may well be the hare who knows how to fertilize his meadow's soil with nitric compost that becomes the fittest hare and gardener. Or do you think a hare can remain completely blind to the needs of, and the help from, his neighboring life; and does he not adopt his table manners, his procreation, his aggression accordingly? I am thinking here about the evolutionary roots of compassion.

In life's stupendous inventiveness, a man's life starts out as a hat full of options and tricks, yet may be triggered to specialize in enzymes happily breaking down excess.

The immaculate goodness western soul-doctors promote as a role model is suspect to me. Who knows what comeback a mischievous ghost exiled into a man's underworld will scheme. Its uncomfortably posing dead might be a dammed stream holding back, ready to burst and jubilate, maybe in another man, in another generation. Maybe it's a ghost of a broom locked in a closet anxiously waiting his turn to cleaning house.

It seems the Holy Spirit gives to everyone a custom-made role to act out, together with the tools, the obsessions, the joys, the costume needed for whatever chores entrusted. And he listens to our advice in morality for amusement.

Life tells me that we are again and again being saved by the mysterious chemistry of our own genes below our cultural coding which had us civilized and scientized. Our genes are the most loyal wildlife we have in us. Therefore I expect our healing to be mostly mysterious, and misunderstood for calamities, that have to be fought.

In cataclysmic moments in which all the fog lifts I have seen it devastatingly clear; the fisher that lies to me and the one that does not, the fish buyer that cheats me and the one that does not, they are all equally my friends. And this creative infection of my old credo has never quite healed. The glimpse of this outrageous idea has become the catalyst to a new and vaster logic in me. My bewildered mind safely hiding behind our "Good boy-bad boy" model has been found out and harshly confronted with a more realistic world.

Maybe I should more respect a man simply for his joyfulness regardless of whether he builds or pulls down. I may learn to love her for accepting her turn in God's wrecking crew and to vigorously bang making gravel out of rocks.

51

Here is a free thought, gone with the wind; it doesn't mind trespassing, yet also follows a discipline.

When I remember the face of a radiant woman I met in the Sierra Madre, I fill with a nostalgia for all I left behind because of being too complex to make me an "instant success." This woman's mind was not yet divorced but quite whole, as a free landscape is, which also is a good mother to its virtues and sweet fruits, to its rascals, spoilers, weirdoes, storms and sucker-roots. In that face I saw plenty of room for thundering rivers in the seasons of rain and for the gentle times of dew and hay. I saw fierce passions that seemed to be wings firmly attached to mysterious, saintly visions reaching beyond my purity, beyond the aura of humanistic behavior with which I often make humbler friends in nature cry. I met a beauty that can make a meek mind feel all hot and solemnly hide behind a tirade of holy accusations and cross itself. I thought that in this face virtues and vices were rhymed and woven into an intensely provocative health.

It seems again the same healthy goodwill which a wise old oak acts out for me to see, when this venerable brother lavishly grows year after year thousands of acorns for the squirrels, the mice, the caterpillars, the grasses to feast upon, yet keeps in his lifetime maybe but one acorn for himself to rejuvenate again. When this tree finally lies down, he has given himself so completely that he does not even claim a cross so we would remember his loss. Such is the wisdom one gets from watching girls and trees.

To be an inspired leader for oneself and to not be led has become an endangered wholeness among us. Many of us now suffer the trauma from a tyrannical reason that would not submit anymore to our soul, hence the disputes between the soul, my oracle, and its chauffeur. When I squeeze my mind into a tight career, so to become the best in that niche, and get drunk on applause, I may mistake myself for being wise and I become a misleader for others and for myself.

When we protect unplowed land with "keep off" signs for our sick greed, do we not protect our girl- and tree-watching—the catalyst for poetic women and men so they may translate for us the wisdom this mystic land grows and become streetlights along our road?

In that world of grandiose goodwill, one can take lessons in generosity. Here critters have been educated for two billion years. One can applaud the frigate bird's superb aeronautics as it dives onto the plumage of a gulping booby, pecking its neck, pulling up its tail—harassing this great gulper into giving up a meal. We can admire an expert at work whose mastery rivals the skill of the foxiest lawyer in town. In that wise world the lazy and the freeloaders are celebrated for their reluctance to kill; the obsessed fisherman, the great farmer and gulper are welcomed for letting themselves be abused so as not to sink from an overload of apples or fish. There the bee's sexual perversions have flowered into marvelous languages of dances and pheromones and I am invited to a colloquium of the latest in social sciences. These busy-bees have cracked the secret of the elixir of life and feed larvae they decide to become their future queens with a royal panacea that makes them last many years. Ant societies became so successful and high-rising, they domesticated some 5,000 animal species, some to be their guests and pets, just to freely nibble and live off them, some simply to provide necessary entertainment or ballast. In this world, insect civilizations have given status to their kind of Mafia millions of years ago to be their legitimate pain and memory killer, the administrators of anesthesia, of self-satisfactions and distractions, the soothers of nostalgia when needed. There is much these little folks had to forget and give up when these long-ago individuals squeezed into their great society's overalls.

On this level in the hierarchy of knowledge, a jammed river fulfills her unpopular task as a patient miser. She is respected for holding back and hoarding the laughing waters, damming them high onto her banks to finally let them burst over dusty sad-lands that a "well-behaved" river has never before fertilized. In this separate reality I am safe from virtue and vice; spitfires and fire fighters are equally welcomed. Here pity and hate are interchangeable as a train seen from here is arriving, seen from there is leaving. It is the open space where I can chase a thought long enough to end up in any science—no gun in my back forces me to selective attention. In such mental cross-pollination between species and between phenomena, great thoughts for forgiveness are combined. Reasons to be optimistic and forgiving come to light—judge and accused wonder who is who or whether such dull roles are needed.

On this level I am faced with that unnervingly patient goodness that seems often to defy the lesson of the good Samaritan—symbol of our modern western religions—a vision which proved sadly insensitive to and neglectful of the flora and fauna, putting these creatures at our mercy as outcasts or slaves; a vision that, it seems, made us rather free to ask any sacrifice from our fellow life in order to again pull up those of us who failed their personality test. This vision seems to gradually have become more hostile to anything in and around us that is not human and that does not bow to our rational minds. Its philosophical theorem has allowed man to become the most egotistic species among all organisms that populate the earth. Its religions helped unknowingly to create the climate in which we could hammer our the miracle of technology from a pagan landscape without a need to blush. Consider—here a great religion with its ten powerful commandments and seven cardinal sins, yet there is barely a hint how we should behave toward our fellow life. We are now haunted by the long-range side effects of the miracle love we spread. Its well-meant pity turned behind its back to a hateful pesticide that now also slowly kills the grower himself.

This vision now yearns to hatch and expand beyond the humanistic sphere, so that we do not breed a Cosa Nostra in our minds, so we may never become a *Reichsmacht* in the garden of unlimited wonders, so that we succeed in adding the needs of our habitat to our prayers for daily bread. Our ecological pains seem to be rooted in our most sacred beliefs. And so trying to storm heaven with our technical, chemical and moral highs by ourselves alone could well become our mortal sin.

In our culture that has for many become a mental torture, more of us now make an effort to initiate our intellect into a larger welfare so we need not be the center and the mastermind of all life anymore. We hope such new openness will also show us better reasons to forgive ourselves.

52

I start to realize that my intuitive world is the biggest grace that has come my way.

In my intuitive animal soul I am encoded with predictions that deal with results over many generations including marigolds, sparrows and rice. It draws from a knowledge in relationships that started to gather even before the blue algae peopled the earth. In my educated mind I am more modest. I am programmed with models that have only the success of myself and my closest kin and neighbors in mind. There my vision and my knowledge became limited by what I was taught to see. And so my soul is obsessed with relationships, my ego with armament and defenses.

Uncreative moralists taught me to look for a clean and level field inside when appreciating myself. When I saw my thistles, my boulders, my marigolds, my rice and my sparrows and grasshoppers happily nibbling on it, I started reforming myself.

When tyrannized by my reason I look in a mirror, I also see a face that has become whitewashed, impenetrable, hardened and cold. Panicked by too many of us, this helpful bodyguard in me often cuts my communications with the wild land. One by one the lights then go out in all that's mysterious in me. My own deadly sober look then frightens me. Left to the mercy of this servant I simply whirl around my or, at best, mankind's little world and I become one of the most common drunks: the drunkards delirious with rationality. You probably watch my drama then as you watch a loose leaf fumble and tumble, when it is left to its own strength to fight the winds. When I am so possessed, even a friend crawls under a blanket of politeness so not to ice up in my presence.

More women now also become sanitized, straighten out, stiffen, level and are engulfed by this golden cloud of humanistic macho-pride, egoistic justice and the notion of one clean rational logic fitting all. No, I do not want to fight for such equal rights. Why should one lure even more of us into naively divorcing what is too deep in their souls to be mined or rented out? Why put even more of us under the plow and make of our economy a kind of universal masturbation open to all? Then the gallons of unpractical tears I have in the process learned not to shed, they never dried out. My inside is swollen and still cries out to be drained. My personal memory, even mankind's memory, that's now filed in the Net, they are a very small place we call common sense. On its diet my day-dreaming loses every day a pound. Friend, break my stare on that narrow place!

The intuitive world is my stove. It is my woman and muse. It is my deeper sense of orientation. It is there where I risk dreaming up ideas from the frontier of my mind. It is my energy gusher Number One. Its sciences seem quiet fluent in many theories of relativity. It gives to each of us a mirror dish so wide, it might even catch the ripples of every thought in the cosmos—of every wish. It gives me my multi-generational thinking that practical school knowledge so often blurs.

I like to play more often with that peripheral space-time vision which lets me be a curious merry child. Emotions do not hurriedly work with dead models and dummies made of the few things of the Earth we consciously know. They can draw from previous experience to which the active memory of my aggressive ego fortunately does not have unlimited access. This makes their science more tolerant, more patient, more feminine and wise.

With incredible flexibility our emotions dive into our logic, a booby swooping down and under for a fish and up to soar again, out of the reach of the surface skimmers and the ocean's fishy logic.

A young child kept out of school and from knowing to read and from T.V. viewing long enough to grow its emotions from the very source to health and dominant strength—will it not enjoy the privilege of having this kind of universal guardian spirit for its mind for the rest of its life? No wonder Einstein did not speak until he was over four years old. Maybe it was then that he missed our road signs and stumbled into $E = mC^2$.

53

Frequent exposures to the undomesticated mind in and around me seem to be the only pill that can save me from sinking into the Faustian conspiracy where we become evolution's highest paid martyrs.

I am still fascinated by all that has been missed by our heroes, by the Billy Grahams and earlier crusaders, by the Peace Corps, the green revolution, good shepherds and patent holders, by the World Bank delegates and the sundry corporations working toward a "tamer" world. Nature's picture writings still untouched by man, which we now shyly start to protect from our virulent success, have remained my most helpful and sacred book. In these free, poetic lands, a Divine Comedy is acted out that appears to me more forgiving and less arrogant and wasteful and much more amusing than the one Dante has composed.

It seems in each man there is an assembly of spirits lobbying from his depth—a universal twitter and compassion that is larger than man and that reckons with a life expectancy of a billion years. It forms that protective membrane between you and me and a chestnut tree, keeping you and me from snowballing into a Faustian conspiracy.

In that fashionable Faustian pact we conspire to become the magicians among the species and to perform the miracle of our economy. We experiment with a cannibalistic economy in which we feast upon our children and their world. We do the "impossible" and our success seems miraculous. Mephistopheles, God's expert in seduction, perversion and evolution becomes our patron saint. We draw a magic circle around ourselves within which we are permitting ourselves to experiment for a limited time with the most extravagant tricks, tricks, shortcuts and ruses of living on credit which in the old proven wisdom of Nature's economy are seldom allowed. We become that historic generation of ghost busters that cuts off all its long distance connections to become superbly free to do whatever is superbly practical within our circle. We do not mind the footnotes of our contract predicting that outside that circle of time our power will burn out in some kind of hell.

To share knowledge about how to produce a more wonderful monoculture or a nourishing wart on the face of mother Earth we may call a miracle economy produces a bigger, more wonderful wart. To share knowledge about how to abuse nature in a joint abusing venture can produce great pesticides and genetic engineers, fantastic inventions, delirious comfort, the deepest mines and highest dams and holocausts for whole species. I see a science at work that discreetly empties water buckets into a flood and gets paid for it. Sharing our logistic on the Net we cultivate our communications in a superb monoculture. There no wind talks to us in his September song; no "ugly" toad serenades us from his mud hole when we celebrate spring. No heron cusses us for evicting her from her home. I see a science that has "healed" our whining egos of many hardships that are vital for our species' health.

To share wisdom on how well we are nested in that bushy tree of life and how amazingly well we are being cared for, reduces the need for physical solutions: for dynamite, for herbicides, for energy, barbed wire, concrete, RPMs, pulp for hate campaigns, shelters for women and for being angry with God. This kind of sharing does not produce new gismos, yet can build a thousand floating bridges in our minds. And are not guests with impressive portfolios from every tribe of life waiting in front of our minds to be welcomed in?

Why always rebel and invent? There is so much to learn and see. Digging into that wisdom we unearth unexpected feedback systems at work; a nightingale in us starts to sing: Life, what a bargain! Greed turns into trust. Confidence soars. Try it; this mental activity may become your sweetest hobby. Mr. Nobel, could you spare a prize for serenity?

I feel at home with those unknown women and men who prefer to be just big cheerful brothers and sisters in the family of life rather than becoming great warriors for the glory of man. Most of what the Great Spirit created seems to them admirably good and in no need of repair; and that's probably how they can remain unspectacular, laissez-faire, and exalted give thanks rather than make a big fuss about what is not obviously just and round.

And thanks to the inexhaustible playground of all the unknown my mind eager to play Columbus never runs out of new Americas.

54
Of Noah's Arks and refugees for anti-slogan thoughts.

Worries that our ever-rising success will turn us into another Great Flood have triggered again an old urge in us to build a fleet of Noah's Arks. In the absence of any man-made system of coexistence in which we really trust, we set aside refuges for a system of thought older than we are. We secretly trust that wilderness is our medicine land. We put such land aside in which we can wash our minds, lands which we hope can produce the anti-thoughts for times when we are down with doomsday fever and foul trust. We like that some soil is not cash cropped but left free to cook the wisdom for our menus. And we try to keep a hole in our minds open that's big enough for catching it.

We consecrate land to be our Noah's barges. We stonewall it against our victories we do not yet trust. A slowly stirring mistrust in the glory of our enormous rational growth, in which we start to see malignant traits, sparks in us an obsession of "do-not-touch." We run ourselves out of sections of land. We declare these refuges for remedial thoughts off-limits for our success. We let them be islands of paradise. We ask for time to better synthesize our two hundred primal-ideas into an organic point of view that cares for as many springs as the dandelions include in their thoughts.

If a child were raised in an environment of numbers and words, of asphalt, traffic signs, aesthetic arts, video games, and Mickey Mouse—with no surf, no nettles, no morning dew, no blooming marshes humming their song in a hundred hues of oranges, greens and blues—would she not soon develop a kind of scurvy of the mind? A child would miss the chance to learn thinking in likenesses. Her curious intellect becomes tranquilized with the sweetest junk-thought-food, losing her intellectual immune system and counter thought-pictures for fighting fear, hate, loneliness, arrogance and gloom. She becomes easy pray for malevolent slogans. Psycho-immunology is hinting how the side effects of such clean education can lower the body's capacity to defend itself.

To enrich my man-made, irradiated intelligence, my mind needs earthy, fibrous, living thoughts. Under a highly civilized and highly protected adult mind lurks an acquired immune deficiency syndrome that may become more menacing to our long-range mental health than the more physical AIDS. Some cancers may well have such psychic roots.

We were the first to become immune against smallpox. When crowded by the overcrowd, we can be the first to become immune against hyper rational attacks! I see brave new minds which arm themselves with anti-thoughts for sick courage, for addictions to safety, pity, unification, for dubious wealth, for fear of death. Those who climb after those forbidding thoughts are the Spiderwomen and Batmen to me.

55

To make peace with one's shadow is to me no ghost hunt. It is my work of art, simple and naked, behind the curtains of art's dazzling fashion shows.

I suspect that a person on the way to making peace with the four seasons of his soul will have less and less shadows lurking in him—and even through all his turmoils he might begin to steadily glow. This adventurer ventures into the shaded side of his moons to hang a lamp. He learns to like in himself what I do not like. He climbs unauthorized viewpoints which I am still scared to take on and draws in aspects I conveniently keep under a hat. He invites his daimons to advocate perspectives to which I do not yet dare listen. When he is yelled at he is not simply logical and rational and yells back, but follows a different reasoning one step higher up. He makes his raw power to kick over to cooperate with his gentleness. He fits friends and opponents together into one cozy quilt. He is an apprentice to become a merry saint with the unbreakable humor of a man who can laugh about himself.

For most of us this wholeness is still in bits and pieces of all imaginable shapes and hues and is scattered between the ornery beasts and eager helpers, between my sunny side and my weather fronts I do not like. Specializing, we have divided among ourselves the many characteristics needed by our weedy, seedy flower fields of the soul. You may have run off with a gem in the Goddess's necklace—the beauty of which is obvious to a fool; I may have ended up with the love affair of one of her broody October moods where She is so unnervingly patient, She buries seeds—to let them dream another hundred years.

Most of the time, it seems, we are each triggered to remember a different plot and a different month in the memory-land. Each is engulfed by the noise-cloud of his own thoughts that blots out the sun on this or that other region in his deeper mind. Each has his barriers in understanding. Each navigates by the stars that are made visible to him. Take a virtue, a law, a truth, take any anger or joy—all standpoints have their own logic. My bowels have their logic; an individual, a family, a town, a nation, a religion, life itself—all have their own logic. I will never see what you see. And so one lies under the spell of the law that decrees for each a different ordinance. What an orchestra!

But when each of us is thoroughly drunk with pride, completely in his right with his logic according to what he can see, completely firm, unique and alone, it happens that there is a soft, hearty fool among us who is greater than himself. Think of a man who became bigger than a man and broke out of his "I"—and slowly he became also you and me. He steps forward, offers the other cheek to be slapped and breaks the spell of our argument's vicious circle—and not because he would not be clever and strong enough to defend his ego's point-of-view. That wise Galilean knew and tried to teach me such magic tricks.

After long navigating under an overcast sky, I tremble a little in fear that when a courageous friend appears and blows a clearing in my sky, the North Star might twinkle where I suspect the south. When I am so surprised, I may panic and plug this mischievous opening in my sky with a tirade of cussing, so much it hurts to realize that I had worked up a sweat, simply running away from sunny days. There are things I rapidly swallowed again after I had them halfway said, so disturbing can an image clearly formulated in words become.

Still, if you light another star in my sky, I will navigate better after I soothe my terror of changing course.

56
When religion is no social worker but the noble art of becoming high . . .

To grab me, to shake me violently—throw me in the air and down—to break my glazed stare at my own tight little memory full of gurgling and mumbling with what has been written in it at school and to get every string in me to wake up and play to the universal memory, has that not been the most sacred art since our legendary fall? Many kinds of step-ladders to climb the Wall and leap over the horizon have been perfected by religions dedicated to the art of highs. When so winged and cruising high, one may be rendered speechless realizing how well we are taken care of, and how good it can feel to be alive and to fly.

Nietzsche was so right to call religions the opium of the folks. But did he miss the point? Why his contempt, when religion can beat the quality of any chemical drug to give a mind grounded in routine a lasting high, get it in tune and make it fly? Today, though, religions like to drive out the shamans and the mind-altering procedures and they turn to the welfare nurses, the practical and the banal.

Every critter seems to have its biography carved into the living earth which might well turn out to be one single memory bank. It might be from this data bank our intuitive minds get advice. There seems no pebble, no insect wing, no gene, no sting I haven't met in my journey of evolution. Everything alive may prove worthwhile to be cheerfully loved, listened to and its inventions praised. Listen! This Earth hums with delightful laughter and advice.

Now also our advanced physics find that every creature is a star that continuously twinkles, talks and that cannot be thought of without changing it. In your presence, I change, a deer, a grass, an atom changes. We are all heavenly bodies. Each receives a zillion times more information than what he is served by his five senses. After all, every molecule in the cosmic ballroom is musician and dancer. Every molecule sends out its signals to which no other molecule can resist. On hidden membranes we seem able to listen to the chatter of the world's infinite collection of megabytes communicating among all living things. There I listen to stories so fantastic I forget about our own comic books.

"Theo, stop endlessly staring inside your own shopping bag of memories and spinning your own thoughts. Be a window, an antenna, a seismograph. Look outside! The whole living world is your memory bank that wants to fill you in!"

57

When I finally nibbled myself free from the humanistic cocoon, I stepped into a circus that has trained its acts for two billions years. Its magicians and acrobats have since been treating me to every imaginable trick.

In a cultivated delusion of grandeur, my mind settled on a throne. Up there nobody bothered to learn the language of the animals, the trees, the mountains, the clouds, and so I had little company to gossip with. I mumble-bumbled often to myself and felt alone. In that yawning nest of elegance no friendly wind sang through pines, carrying scents of berries cooking in the sun; no lizard rustled through the leaves. Around this refined community tripping on high heels and grand self-esteem, many of life's most exciting actors seemed in need of being sprayed, battered into line, pitied, sheltered, kept off-stage, confined to reform schools, exiled into parks, poisoned or damned. There I was constantly reminded to use fig leaves and condoms and not to make noise. Was it for such indoctrination that devotees of man-centered religions in the west became the supreme drillmasters of nature, the champions of technology, the great organizers of the armies of workers busy building higher the Wall, or busy inventing taller ladders to get over that Wall? Aren't we trained not to blush when we do a great job as slave-drivers in the garden of unlimited wonders?

Outside of this shelter, I breathe in relief, realizing how well I am being cared for, how little there is to worry about, or to be sprayed, changed or exiled. My ego's personal memory, so full of idealistic forms, like trees loaded with yummy fruits yet with no roots, is sobering up. Here, wise "prophets" older than man tell me of truer and taller tales than our sacred books recite. What amazing storytellers are entertaining me. I found none better in all of Marrakesh's squares. Here any place is a lively market where inspirations and genes are traded and broken feelings are mended. Here the best-dressed sea stars promenade on the tide flats and invite me to a fashion show. You can cuss the bluejay for spying on you. You see critters walk on water. You can listen to songs of raven wings playing the strings of the winds. What a festival of folk-lore when a whole meadow in ecstasy of courtship dresses up to dance in another spring. Leave the balcony to your mind open; soon some lively actress will be sneaking in.

58

Who knows what next in our sex lives Eros will ask us to fertilize, to give birth to, cuddle and nurse.

When in a people's history many women and men rather suddenly branch out into new and somewhat neutered careers, of which grandpa never even dreamed, doesn't it cause a storm of misgivings and sour feelings, if for them the same prayers, law books, language, mythology, heroes, jokes, wishes and songs are expected?

When a man suffered a mutation or a graft in his mind or a woman was transplanted onto a desk, it is kind not to stir up buried pictures of past adventures and tenderness that were unsuspiciously kindled in them not long ago but now are not welcome anymore. I wish my educated mind could stop insisting that a woman has to remain a biblical woman the rest of our evolutionary way.

It seems a slow, achy task, when nature makes some forget and takes us to other tasks and other homes, maybe making of us neuter experts in new chores that have nothing to do with being woman or man. Often the whole psyche has to be rearranged. This has become a time in which many need to forget, so that hang-ups in old outdated memories and loves can be switched off and do not spoil our merry world that likes to wear a fancy new dress every day.

Many now seem to be asked to take on a neutered life that is relieved of the pollination game. They are asked to give their best love in a career to erect one great well-ordered apartment house for the human hive. Home-made children may be bewildering animals from the jungle and strangers to them. Harmless sex games and fantasies may be recommended as aero-bics for a new health; perhaps to softly induce a later abstinence. Sex games seem also to become the most gentle form of birth control. Pan's war games played with inoffensive weapons and souls. This spicy lust in playful retirement has stubbornly remained a stranger to my inherited thoughts. I have trouble happily welcoming this reorientation in others. They are made to wear a mask that is sometimes terrifyingly different from mine. When engulfed by the merry high of a Friday night crowd enjoying their games, I cannot easily join in. Many other worlds too won-derful for me to let them go stand in my way.

I see now that much of my distrust in the new code for love comes from my obstinate misunderstanding patronized by Freud: that sex is mostly limited to the musky dance of sperms and eggs. I did not see the endless possibilities of making love when life continuously recomposes itself adding more and more dazzling structures of societies to its show.

59

I know of no health care as invigorating as life's jour-

ney cycling through birth and death. What a master-
stroke of inventiveness.

I wonder whether a surgeon is ultimately a healer of man when with his
team he transplants a heart. I am uncomfortable with the unconditional
fame his profession commands, making of itself a rather sacred cow. When
I visualize the burden merchants in human spare parts may load on the
vitality of all life, I am awed. Such mended lives often need to be permanently provided with an all-conditioned dome. I think also of the agonizing temptation for our confused minds when this profession shows off its
goodies in front of us. What a temptation to pawn one's patrimony and
buy those extra days—to pull down the sky, the trees, the vagabonds, the
wonderful ups and downs in our trails, to put up ever more stop signs and
traffic lights, to mortgage again the family home and leave our children
out and make them shut up and lay low. All of this so we may hang on past
our given time, to bestow on this world a few more grim hours of an
ungiving man who "heroically" fights his soul and keeps the children
waiting in the cold. This may become the ultimate in the glorious art of
egoism. Maybe I should simply include some of this profession's performers in life's circus show as great dare-devils, showmen, magicians and
before all experimenters who still need, for respecting our tender feelings,
to shroud themselves in an aura of healers. Seen in this light I can throw
my hat up in applause.

Yet how far away all this hectic rebellion against death is from the
peacefulness that must have come to the old Eskimo woman who walked
out into the cold to die when her heart had told her to. She was from a tribe
that accepts our cycling through death more easily than we do. In the
midst of that heroic "Albert Schweitzer syndrome" now "blessing" the
tropical world with more and more millions of us, one may begin to wonder: Was it the lack of good untempered imagination that made us so
unfriendly toward our brother death and so calling him Brother Calamity
instead?

Also in clinical medicine I see now the self-regulating effect of "the
better forest fire fighter principle" at work. Our approach increases the
"dry underbrush" and prepares for hotter, more devastating fires.

Why this compulsion to intervene up to the last resource when the "forest fires" are periodically cleaning us? Many such anguishing thoughts have been suppressed for too long from being visualized and talked about.

For long I have been intrigued by how peacefully other creatures seem to come and go, yet now I think I know the reason why. They don't kill each other. They make each other gifts. In a togetherness blurred to me, species seem to ask each other for gifts from their biomass—a kind of festive give-away in which species outdo each other to produce the most gifts without being sunk by their generosity. They teach me that only species who can bleed for and remain generous to others survive for long.

Ultimately we might find that the ant-eater is a kind inspector and that there is no hate but only love between the spirit of the ants and him. Has not their marriage endured a long, long time? Ultimately we might find that the gift of pathogens and the gift of death are more beneficial to us than gold. And so the swollen berries with their sweetest perfume boiling up want to be eaten to pay the birds for a flight ticket to carry the seeds of the berry bushes to other homes. Could such hints explain why other creatures seem rather peaceful and forgiving when they die, making me ashamed of our own often quite scandalous giving in?

60

And to the horror of the common sense in him and in his friends, he hopped off the comfort-express and became again a happy fool.

When my energies stumble over each other, when my ranks of longings get mixed up and become a knot of fighting dogs, when my whole body throws itself finally to the ground, worn out from inner disputes, when my curious mind is bogged down in safety belts and in cotton-wool, when all these quarrels slowly break up my march into personal glory, I once again slam my fist onto the table—Quiet! And good common sense invokes a new series of exercises. It commands the rebels, the doubters, the neurotics to once more step in line and relax, relax, breathe deep, relax and get drunk on oxygen.

More controls will be prescribed for remedy; controls of the breath, the beating of the heart, the daydreams, the erections, the cholesterol. What I say and what I do not say, my imagination, seeds, hunches and pregnancies, the sad or angry moods my emotions may boil up, the buttercups blooming again in my mind, the nagging whisper of my guardian spirits, all this I should learn to better police. I am to discipline my curiosity with meditation. I am to command my whole quarreling self to relax and become refreshed, to stop the cussing, to take a vacation—and become a healthier egoist and worker.

This, or an act of the heart—that sobering slap into the horrified face of that proud part of my mind that has been encoded to make me arrogantly humane. I admire a man who can resist taking painkillers for his rebelling soul, the self-hypnosis to relax, the beer, entertainment, Prozac, the rock or symphonies' credos, the repetitive beat of a good-boy-life, the exercises in happiness. I admire a woman who does not simply whip the rebels in her again into line but takes the heat of hearing them out.

I slowly learn to also hear my rebels out. I am ashamed of how long I aspired to join the troops and stand on my head to become a perfect worker. It's just hilarious, some of what I learned to wish! Is that not a brave woman or man who can say: Oh, let me be shaken, let me find out what is my biggest world? What is the limit of my strength to keep distance in solitude? Let all my unknown resources for once be shaken awake in one great roller coaster ride.

I wish myself the luck to excitedly accept the challenge to win that scary high, to stand at the edge of society and above its noisy clouds, to become more alive, maybe to tumble down in the vertigo of being alone.

61

There is a lot of sweat, cursing and squandering of free time when my team of oxen is no team but each ox pulls the opposite way.

I am soon fatigued when my right hand busily fumbles to pity and heal, to avoid, to painkill and forget, to stonewall, amputate and masturbate, to buy insurance, to sew up the volcanoes and to level the world so I can comfortably sit down; my other hand fights that glorious boredom, reinvents my adventures and sufferings, drills peepholes and escape tunnels into The Wall we built around ourselves. I can again intoxicate the part of my brain I yesterday patiently domesticated, purified and trained and I can make that good boy in me pose dead awhile. In my plenty I can reinvent famine for myself and fast. I can invoke horror, brainstorms, pushups, and marathons, many kinds of psychedelic pains. I can bring mind shattering loneliness upon myself and break down my hard-earned stereo sight. I can stone my super-rationality and be a merry fool with windows in my memory. After I killed my taboos and my shame I can again take a vacation from this freedom in a meditation center, and abstain from sex. I can at will play saint or wild. Others may pray for their daily bread, yet in their opulence they are so bored they starve themselves just for the sake of seeing how hunger activates their minds. Some ask to be defecated upon as an antidote to their whitewashed routine. With every imaginable privation and excess, with every virtue and vice we seem to counter the sullen comfort our work is earning us. To my ego's content such tricks seem how I finally could become that goldfish that is master of himself and his bowl.

Is this the way to harmony? Should I become my own God and make myself master of my own little world and goldfish bowl—with my gismos, my willpower, with my control of my body functions and with my smartness alone, with no faith, no grace, no lifeline, no higher home? Should I retire to the garden of my own creation and be the slave of Theo and his short rational goals?

Some among us do not dream of life as a job and an exercise machine and a package tour to Cancun. We dream of dangers as others dream of ice cream. We dream to take off on the adventure tours of our souls, competing to invent the slickest lifestyle of all. We are shy poets. We enjoy building floating bridges to other realities and worlds. We follow a hunch that there is a poverty which is exciting, ingenious and elegant. We are such confident fools.

62

When I risk and leap from the nest made of preconditioned views, I become free to ask around for the complementary side of offensive acts. I can make limping acts whole and dance again in my mind. Perhaps it is by this unheroic way that one can earn a morsel of serenity.

My mind is a crab pot that catches best when immersed into the wild ocean of life. Sometimes my mind gets seasick and I raise it above that wild and murky world. I ornate that trap with gold and rhymes and try to feel pride. Yet, meanwhile the water runs out of it. What ideas my beautiful, lofty trap then would fish?

When the banker outgrows his need for a shaman's mask of prestige to intimidate, he relaxes and he can widen his view. When I stop being a lifetime actor in some philosopher's play and when I do not cover up the politicians behind rituals of politics, in which they make us act out their credo, I cannot pretend to be a blind minor anymore. I become responsible for my acts beyond their written laws. The arrogance of humanism seems also such a convenient mask. It is a shield for the season of an intellectual adolescence. It lifted me and my kin onto a pedestal to keep us safely alone like eaglets nested high on their throne. But now that my mind has grown "feathers," it is time to hop from this nest, to dive with my questions into a depth that may not be safe, to soar where the air is thin.

In this grand opening it becomes secondary for our sciences to invent an even better nest for our egos. We want to enjoy the view first of all and perhaps shake hands and paws with the other actors, who seem such a menacing lot when seen from the safety of the nest. We start to invent vaccines for the mind that prevent it from curling and fogging up, from kicking, fuming and spitting dirty names around. We plunge into a science that deciphers nature's parables that can counter our worry, gloom, hatred, mental rape, boredom, rotten trust. We search nature for tumor suppressant thoughts that help us to fight carcinogenic beliefs. We are after medicine that may render us more serene.

Imagine, we can soar and learn with wide angle eyes from the anthropology of termites, from the science of the bees who are so keen that they invented miracle-food to give seven life-times to their queens. We can wonder about the biosonar of bats, who knew to use the Doppler shift a million years before we did. We can listen to the saga of the oceans, the aphids, the star cities and the atom cities. We can listen to the genes singing the poem of a tumbleweed. And think of how many problems that weed has solved since its emergence from the dreaming ooze. We can learn spontaneity from the wild waters that laugh foaming through the fern, the September sun, the golden maple trees. Worlds of complex societies formed at the birthdays of our archetypes are waiting to give advice in sociology. Out there, the woods, the clouds that wander the skies, the grasses and the tse-tse flies that guard the savannas from being overgrazed seem no minors anymore but begin to talk to more of us on equal terms. Out there is the chorus of all God's critters calling us with their trillion different twee-twee songs, flashlights and perfumes: "I have ideas a hundred generations tall; I trade in exotic genes; I am a scientist wrapped in bark; I have worked out a morsel of wisdom for you; do you want to hear forgiving thoughts? I parade a Nobel Prize for something rounder than the wheel. Look at me, remember me!" And we might start to consider how to more gently tiptoe through Graceland according to the rules of our poetic nature and we will get better at minding the impact of our acts. When I dare to lower my self-defense and I truly listen to somebody or something else: surprise! All creatures turn into prophets for me.

Freed at last from a system of castes that made him stand in rigid attention so long apart, he simply laid back into the chirping, sparkling morning grass. He dropped his arms and his thoughts still steaming from work between the chirpers and hoppers and the cool blades of grass. In this glorious moment memories that are balsams started to thaw in him. Slowly his sorrows and his joys fell into each other's arms.

63

I feel I'm missing the show by being on the sea simply as a feared man of prey.

Fishing on the sea has become more than killing fish to me. It has become a great activity in a great place to explore my own capacities. At school I have never learned well how to pick, harvest, kill and serve myself a meal and do it with a love for nature that is my host. How does one ask such a difficult favor from friends? This endless exchanging of gifts between the species seems such a vital part in the story of life. I have a hunch that there is a sunny state of mind in which this trade in biomass can turn into a beautiful dance and give an unclouded climax to those that remain God's fools. This continuous going back and forth of visitors between species, happily bringing gifts and happily taking other gifts home might well be one big potlatch among all tribes of life where we try to outdo each other in this art of generosity. I watch life's efficiency principle at work: to sell at the lowest price possible without going bankrupt. Is it not from this vigorous chiseling on each other's biomass that the whole living *oeuvre d'art* slowly stands up and walks?

How can one translate into our time the state of mind of ancient hunters, when they talked and made promises to the deer they stalked. It is said that some danced for forgiveness and thanks even before the hunt. These people seem to have known better than I how to enlighten their minds and how to make good when they needed to ask favors from their fellow life. Such a poetic state of mind is an even better guardian angel to protect the endangered separate reality of the wild than Greenpeace, the Sierra Club and other consumption fighters who also propagate a consumption-resistant mentality.

Some of us now like to be quiet, alone and away from the hypnotic beat of our TV shows. We want to press our ears against bare ground underneath the entrancing shimmer of our smartness and follow the roots of our mind. We want to let down our buckets deeper into our memories and fish for wisdom that has long been giving good advice to this wonderful Earth on how knowledge is best used. It's not so long ago our mind emerged from the minerals and the grass. We like to spend time in the wind, the sun and God's "bioglyphs" that all talk to us of a wisdom older than the one we learned at our formal schools. We gladly would walk a hundred miles for that enchanting sight that can keep our feelings warm when we deal, chainsaw, politic and fish—and when in the end we are the ones who are "fished" or battered and tested by a weather front. We are building stilts for our minds for a better view, so we needn't hurry to rake in our needs in blind cold blood anymore, but can be mellow and do so with excited reverence.

To love the flea under my pants and to love scratching I have to become a sculptor who loves his rock together with its grain from which he enjoys to chip chop chips.

64

Is it good to tease awake a man's adventurous dreams
of long ago, when such stout and individualistic
adventures are not welcome anymore?

In this time of overpopulation, in this time of much reorientation, of town
arrest, of forming great herds, in this time when many souls are made to
partially hibernate and live in metamorphosis, the healing of a pioneer
mind sobbing for losing his last frontier may be a dubious good. One
might open in a man a sealed bag of terribly lively memories and longing
that could begin to tumble out again. Is this planet plentiful, lush, sunny
enough to calm six billion women and men with the wanderlust of swallows and the courage of lions? Our age seems rather a time of winter, not
spring—a time of less kernels and more shells. Many dangerous memories
are lulled to curl up and nicely fall asleep—memories for which it is not
the season to stir and boil our blood. Forgetfulness is one of nature's wonderful tools for growth control. To function as an organic whole with a trillion partners, are the offspring of our primal cells not made to forget 99
percent of the hundreds of thousands of recipes for proteins they know—
each recipe leading to a specific power tool?

It requires a lot of forgetfulness, denial, contraction of vitality, many
acoustic tiles, soap operas, pulling elbows in and a mental monoculture so
that six billion of us can squeeze in between the profusion of all our fellow
life and might still somehow all survive. Six billion great adventures—
Captain Cooks, great mothers, pioneers that "won the West," six billion
individualists who wake up into spring to get up, start fires and think by
themselves—obviously is not what Mother Earth can bear.

I can thus appreciate that after twenty years the plumber is still
rumored to remain a cheerful plumber happy to sell us crooked pipes; that
the clerk remains a happy lifetime clerk who in the evening settles into his
slippers and TV shows; and a fisher keeps to his niche bragging simply
about fish. If each of us would remember all of his possibilities—what a
monstrous heap of action, what an excess of bravery and aggression, what

a holocaust! Are not cancerous cells those that are not made to forget in time what they can do? Thank God we are not all struck by an enlightening bolt and shown all we could do, but are content to curl up, live in neat furrows and settle in the nook of one trade, made to feel small and good. Don't we now mostly beg to be mentally "healed" so that we may still keep our old friends, our safety and insurance, our sports, suspenders, slippers, toys and cars, our sweet routines, a merrily painted fence for our souls?

How fashionable it has become to cultivate forgetfulness; it has become necessary to be banal and join the amnesiacs. Imagine the catastrophe in the fluffy, rooty soil under a field blooming with beans, poppies and maize if the armies of earthworms were to stop tunneling, become adventurous and grow eyes.

65

I have found that a lively thought is a squirrel who knows when I want to catch it for its pelt.

Most of the time, my mind is strictly focused and bogged down in the grim need for practical thoughts, thoughts that are beautiful soap bubbles or sheltering domes, thoughts that are hard rock or Bach fugues to bathe my awed reason in warm aesthetic justice when I am terror-stricken amidst life's hard-driving storms, thoughts that are chainsaws and bulldozers eager to make everything breathing around us become our docile underlings supporting us.

Yet my better thoughts are neither power tools nor poems in which I nicely dress up my mind shivering in confusion, but are simply wings, my unfocused mind in dream time. They can help me not to stumble over you. Even better, they show me tricks how to forgive and to visit you. My better thoughts come from wonderment; they are the lucky thoughts that I do not draft for the dull need to work and fill my belly. They do not die in wars.

I discover that thinking is a more delicate art than I imagined. Slowly I unlearn to just greedily pull down and butcher all thoughts for their meat. It is better to let some thoughts alone, to let them freely walk into my mind to socialize, to treat them like clouds that are better not hastened but allowed to come down when ripe.

When I enter the scene with a farmer's mind, with a fisherman's or businessman's mind, everything alive seems alarmed and runs, afraid to be butchered for its calories, its wool, for one of its qualities which happens to be in demand. Every one of my thoughts when I do not leash it to a goal, takes me on a safari through the wonders of jungleland where all sciences are free to interact.

So many incessantly computing brains are now out all hunting useful thoughts, for finer food, for fame, better tanks, mousetraps and walls. Many minds became as clever as a raven who lost one eye and so the depth perception, but trained his other eye to a superb flatland vision. We know how to focus our mind in a way no other species does.

Ah! A day with absolutely no trying; I will not try to please, to scheme, to have an erection, to turn my insides out and be truthful; I will not try to live up to my reputation, to be good and to please God pretending I know his wishes. I will just sit in my canoe drifting with bliss—no paddling—simply curiously looking around, floating and whistling my thanksgiving.

Innocent, unemployed thinking has such a wonderful prize. It delights in just sipping wisdom. It's the sabbatical for my mind. It plants seeds of adoration. It hangs lamps in the dark and bridges leading into enemy land. It's a luxury I like.

When on an especially friendly summer day you violated a taboo and courageously cracked a peephole into the shelter I put up with my beliefs, you made me a rather sour gift that grows better and better with the years as does wine.

When Theo goes idea-fishing I see him forgetting many serious things, making a big hole in his mind. Lazily he sits on a log on the bank of a merrily gossiping creek, away from the neon lights, and dips his hole into it. Soon, flip-flop, a fat juicy thought has fallen into it. Soon the smell of good cooking is making him smile.

How could a full mind catch a thought? Free lively ideas are shy fishes. They would not show up when Theo plays Rodin's *Le Penseur* and summons them to lay at his feet; but instead they would dive to the bottom of the creek. How could an empty mind remain empty when even a water bug is a whole treasure box of ideas?

66

It seems that the things that make us grow and glow most are not bartered, borrowed or paid for with checks. Rather they are given and sipped as bumblebees sip honeydew. And off they dart to pay for it, who knows where and when, who knows to whom.

I am not so offended anymore when at first thought someone appears unjust, taking and giving for reasons and to beneficiaries hidden to me. I have noted that when a woman is pregnant, she tends to value everything more deeply and with a different scale. She follows a logic I did not learn at school. Yet doesn't her unpaid labor makes her beautiful? Here is injustice at its best. An act, a man, a day, she then values them all more for their roots, for their genes, for their effects seven generations up the hill. She looks at me with her larger thoughts that roam beyond what adds up soon. A favor or anger, a compliment, an advice worth millions, a sweaty hour of a man hammering nails for her; they become then crumbs of soil that might or might not be of use to the tall world that grows through her; and in that world one has all of God's time to pay. In that world a favor that's paid back becomes vomit you lick again; a justice that's obvious is suspect; a debt justly settled between you and me may simply be the play of two mice chasing each others' tail. And does not also a man have his kind of pregnancies? Maybe our unpaid labors are the best we can do.

When so tuned into long-distance calls little good can come from flirtations that don't fit into the wave lengths of such a woman or man. Roses, fun, good checks, Ph.D.'s, sensible talk, practicalities, the frosting of the cake or common sense, or figures and justice that nicely add up today might then not hold up in her impact statement. But a piece of vagabondland, a black night soaked in rain, a talk radioactive with paradoxes, an uneducated advice might happen to fall in step with the tall song humming in her. For a soul that is so drunk with spirits, my temper on fire, your snores or lies, his lazy moods, an awkwardness, a flat tire or a flight that's late, an unpaid debt, her moody moods—they may simply appear as some of nature's puzzling vitamins which we, the sober people, cannot fit in. How, after all, could the greatness of man or beast fit into one life span alone?

And so to watch the river that seems to endlessly flow one way and to wonder where it finally turns uphill again is good exercise in figuring out justice that does not meet the eye. From the corner of that eye one might then see, ten springs ahead, a monsoon wind that's happily rushing opposite into the hills.

67

I wonder why the birds stopped chirping where the Messiah passed, the fish dove to the bottom and the trees looked frightened and many of them begin to die.

A sense of loss spoils my pride when another wildflower can be successfully improved with genetic engineering and then exploited as an ingredient for soups. Standing on my head to shake awake my sleepy routine, I see this victory as one more hump on a wart we rather proudly and thoughtlessly grow on the face of the living earth. How that spectacular growth has become malignant can now easily be seen from flight number 717.

It is for this afterthought that I feel a knot in my gut when way up in the Sierra Madre mountains I run into the missionaries of the green and cash crop revolution. With anguish I realize the fable of the apprentice calling out the sorcerer's broom is true. It takes ever more greatness of soul to make good the ever-increasing favors we ask nature on credit for our sumptuous lifestyles. Yet such pity for ourselves and favors asked make us ever more frail to settle such debts. How to be brave enough to stop that unstoppable broom, to stop a radical technology with a one way ticket to our benefits on a faster and faster track, and start paying back our debts? That wonder child we engendered by the prostitution of our minds, grows, grows, grows and the GNP slaps contentedly the belly while eating away the smiles of the Earth. When we start to watch the unrestricted breeding of our economy with the same dark preoccupation as we now watch the growth of our world population, our mentality will draw an ace.

I see now better what our high-yield miracle love of the West can do to the sea, to our grandchildren, and to the soil. I am dissatisfied with the efficient way I am encouraged to fish. Our ever smarter fishing methods have become sickening for the sea. Every new gismo for better fishing we now invent drills another hole into the Ark and makes it list more. I want to learn how to ask the sea more gently for its gifts so that we may be happy in each other's company.

With rather childless minds we have built "The Dam" across the stream of our love. We seem now to be using this windfall of love for our and our siblings' virginal goals. We pity ourselves greatly and think we are in love. Yet when one is very still, sharpening the ears, one can hear that our children's children way downstream do not like our dam and they rebel.

This puritan, virginal vision of the West that teaches us to love our neighbors more than the generations ahead starts to affect our bodies and minds. Could medicine and the priesthood of the western religions at long last meet to diagnose that ultimate neurosis which may well be rooted in our "man only" myth? Could their healers and theologians discuss a two-thousand-year-old doctrine that might have unsuspectingly worked to the benefit of that strange growth we have provoked on the face of Mother Earth? That doctrine also seems to encourage its believers to enslave all other worlds, making them serve mankind's overexpressed ego. Its authors invented a clean and practical goodness that is highly profitable for the contemporary egos. But life, that glorious revolt against purity, does not seem to like our humane goodness and counteracts.

In violation of the law of fair play among all species, Christianity taught to reorient the quality and population controlling aggression within our species toward the forest, the rivers, the oceans. Go fell another tree to make good with a neighbor who stole a log from you! Hence, the disharmony—the too many people and too few trees.

Eutrophication, the excess of nitric fertilizer we unwittingly wash into the sea turning into an explosive growth of algae has its likeness. Think of the terrible growth and bloom of humanity after we over fertilized the earth with the humane goodness of our Western ethics.

It seems to be mentally and physically the most restricted or handicapped society that has the best reasons to revolt against this wildly permissive world and to become highly technological and to iron it out. After the commandment to be superior, walk on high heels and become the species of shamans, half the wildly beautiful animal qualities a Christian is born with are cut off. The other half is dressed up and masked to look different. A shamelessly permissive mind is roped to a credo and cash cropped. How can I feel and touch barefooted nature while I am strapped into such a beautiful harness? It appears to be this ingenious mutilation, this shaman's initiation that made Christianity into the winning candidate to move the mountains, to flatten the earth, to conceive the minds that cruise on wheelchairs at sixty mph. Our bodies still ache performing this new experiment and rebel each day with a billion headaches.

So help me God, in spite of or because of its marvelous momentary success, I do not know of a more downgrading act lately against all nature across our fence than the implantation of our western religions. It seems also to be for that mentality's dispassion for plant and animal life and for the life of our future children that our narrow-hearted and seedless technology, so humiliating to all other creatures, could unhindered and with such zest and glory rise. This is a bitter thought for me. These religions have given me many instructive detours and are the native home of my cultivated mind. They have sneaked many pains and pebbles into my oyster which I had to turn into pearls. They have put up a dazzling show of technology never seen before. They have been geysers gushing amazing inventions serving and perpetuating our egos.

It might be because of this miracle love that, when the Messiah came through the towns and fields to teach and pray, the people flocked to him; yet the birds stopped chirping, the fishes dove and the fig trees bent the other way, offended. They appeared afraid of what the saint was teaching to his friends, or maybe they just felt neglected. Worries that this haughty credo could let us become the abusers of the planet's life might have clouded their thoughts. Certainly they didn't feel protected.

A spontaneous mind still observes such subtle and tragic connections and hesitates with its praise when in a neighborly love more and more men are saved from the season of death that wants to rejuvenate us. This mind also notes that as antidotes to each of these good-natured cheating in the personality tests, life makes our children one drop meaner, lamer, duller, and better liars; nothing like a spectacular invasion of demons from without, but simply this grain of extra friction and callus when a soul has to shrink itself to elbow its way through an ever-thicker thicket of men. A spontaneous mind discovers many historic side-effects in displaced or myopic pity. And it may even know a level of knowledge on which to save a failing individual life might be a crime.

This mind also sees nature saddened to have to supply more and more of her blood and to have more of her colorful feathers plucked to better cushion each of us against the hordes upon hordes of trampling fellow men. Excitedly, the child that caught the emperor without any clothes on realizes, but it is not mankind, it is the whole living world agonizing under the yoke of our arrogance who needs now a messiah.

With anguish, more of us now suspect that on Gaia's body we may have become the cancer. Our science is geared to spreading this terrible winner. Our foreign-aid grain ships spread it. Our population of gismos that all want to be painted, fed, housed, beautified and healed spread it. Our humanistic beliefs also do until that leap beyond a humanistic imagination is dared. From that breathtaking and still tabooed viewpoint, taking sides and intervening will be less needed. With this new input a mental immune system fighting cancerous thoughts can form. And the good news: exiled friends may come home; moral and political prisoners may come home; the persecuted flora and fauna may come home. My soul with wings broken by dualism may heal again and fly. Butterflies may flit and flutter again. Host and parasite merge into one. Thousands of forgotten continents come again into view, all happy to be explored and seen.

Our planet is not the heart of the world and our species is not the center of life anymore. Christianity is not the ocean; it is one of many ships on the sea of religious thought. Religions with their many diverse cultures become flowers, constellations, galaxies of the universal mind. In spite of our awesome power, we seem just one of the mighty waves in the ocean of light that come and go—all helpers, it seems, to chisel, think and computer for a more fantastic world. Who knows how many other stars have exploded into life-like bloom. There are no isolated systems anymore. All looks more and more equally connected to one single soul.

Now that with the new instruments of sight, every hidden spark of life, even the farthest pulsars, have become neighbors in our minds, the anthropocentric myths have done their service and I need to molt. This shield of arrogance was proper for my intellectual adolescence. I can think of no change of mind that equals in its consequences the one of a woman or a man who dare taking off the mask that made their minds humane.

68

There is a competition going on. Who, on the ladder of mentalities, is the fittest climber of all?

When at year's end my grocer questions his computer, the diviners of the *Wall Street Journal* and his mountain of paperwork, he hopes to predict his coming business year and to hammer out a strategy. When a people of ants, busy winterizing its town, takes a Sunday off and casts its own I Ching into a million years of its memoryscape, it hopes the oracle will foretell how freezing the coming winter will be.

When in an unemployed moment I can lay back into the clover, the buttercups and the grass, and I open up to the memories written all over the earth and the firmament; I also send my questions fishing. I cast my bait into a memory bank that may hold the saga of a lively three billion years. While I quieted down in the company of the clover, the chirpers and grasses, the Spirit of the Earth may quietly match my questions with the best answers from that humongous wisdom of the one living Internet, where my brain's domain seems just one other megabyte, just one more research project, or a wonderful fingernail. Subtle tides of unnamed galaxies made of invisible messages rush and clash in obscure battles, defending, attacking, competing on the merry battleground of creativeness—yet ultimately all grouping around one common attraction some call God. When I stay so quiet and wait, I may get a telegram from Mother Grace.

When not anchored in my own neat little pile of memories but dancing around the daisies, the rivers, the mosquitoes, the clouds, the unplowed land that remained billionaires in ideas, what a daring slingshot my soul becomes, shooting my mind into a thousand orbits at one time; shooting my mind 300 years away from my belly's merry-go-round. While riding on the back of such scenic orbits, every other creature seems to behave as if it also has a soul, a receiver-transmitter, with which it converses with the communication system of the whole motley crowd peopling the earth. And I might see order which some call chaos, an order which we didn't mutilate to squeeze it into the horizon of our common sense. Do you think a raindrop is not guided in its flight or budding aspen leaves can fill their space in whatever way they may choose? And so, when flying high, I do not even mind when you do not always act practical and immediately good, as civilized flatlanders may wish.

69
Is there a higher art than to know how much is enough?

We seem each made of a little flickering flame and of much wind. When I simply insist that this wind is bad and that wind is good, I find I am being lazy or a simpleton. I note that we are all fond of fanning each other into flame and turn up the lights. I learned that what is worthy is a question of degree and not one of "Yes" or "No." I know of no trickier art than to know how to vigorously fan without blowing the candle out; how to fan a friend into fire without making him run, hide behind three locks, and fume.

Take the need to kill and to make things grow or take a man's aggressive armament and his generous vulnerability, his spontaneity and his politeness, his cunning and his wisdom. Take any kind of taking and giving, winning and losing you know; they need harmony and not just "Yes" and "No." Look how carefully every species manages its reproduction, how it balances the gifts of its own biomass it makes to other species with the gifts of biomass it takes from others, careful not to trip on the tightrope of yin and yang. Note how Darwin's fighting-dog ordinance to become the fittest of all is ultimately overruled by an enough-is-enough law that orders the fighters home. We are to balance on the tightrope between giver and taker, virtue and crime, honesty and lies—and only a little treat is allowed of clowning with extremes.

I wish myself the gift to hit the bull's-eye of a friend's tolerance when taking from him or loading him down. When I do not wonder how much he can take, I am not his friend. When you give me too much of a bite of a truth, I might vomit it right back into your face. Ah! If I could aim my encounter, wishing you well, I could be an artist. Wondering, I could nibble, probe and chip and not simply break you and go for a kill.

We are all the chisel and the rock, the yin and the yang, the candle and the wind. And so, when a person can spontaneously visualize a loaded tree together with its sucker roots, he is helped to make friends with my dark side too.

I know of a violinist who played so powerfully with his bow that he sawed his instrument in two. I know of a supermind that did not bother to keep in touch with the creatures around him, but dreamed up such far-off stuff that the humbler folks could only laugh at him. When excitedly you spoke of strange, of deep, of unaccustomed things and you drilled holes into my systems, theorems and credos, I first angrily thought, *Oh, I am going to sink.*

You were also kind; and at the same time you held my hand; you kept open a bridge so I wouldn't be frightened, stumble and tumble on that abyss you opened in me. You didn't just walk off as victor and leave my world in shambles. Later when I looked at the mischief you did: surprise, I saw new peepholes into other worlds in my ship.

To remain a player in life's drama, it is not enough to be a supreme survivor. A player needs to be fit and strong enough to also be a good gardener investing in good relations to remain hired. He is to help God's zoo with his body, his perspiration, his breath, his songs, his shade, whining and genes, his excrement and color! To trim Eden's garden he may use his claws, his brain, his poisons, his beak or teeth. Even his breaking wind is to improve the world.

In life's play one is allowed to remain a player as long as one is neither loser nor winner and possesses the art of knowing how much is a bellyful, balancing the line between deficiency and cancer, that terrible winner, to be beautiful and dance close to the center. If one does not play compassionately, one is triggered to produce neurochemicals like hydrocortisone that warns with stress. If the warning is ignored that same warner kills the bad actor, eliminating him from the show.

I heard of a barefooted tribe of philosophers in jungleland who like to act out this law in a learning log race: with two equal teams they race two logs of quite unequal size to the village square. The team ahead keeps on racing back to help the other so that all might advance harmoniously and arrive together; thus, the feasting crowd may gasp in joyous agreement, "How beautiful is our race!"

70
The self seems to me a mighty flexible shopping bag.

When I quarreled with her about our being selfish or unselfish, when I reproached him egotism and he fumed, I wonder now whether these arguments were not simply quarrels about how baggy or how tight our inner-selves have become.

Maybe my dear self remained an infant ego just squawking for attention and milk. Perhaps the world you keep awake in you is assembled in a symphony for two that you blast so loud that all your more poetic worlds are overridden and they had to curl up in your dreams. Or did that self contract to a nation's five-year plan to cultivate spuds? In the jungle of life one might have prudently fenced off one's self together with some brotherhood of like-minded believers begging to be left alone to play Beethoven's *Missa Solemnis* or to act out the philosophy of some patriarch. Others enlarge the vision of their selves, joining the list of nobles and saints who chose their contemporary generation of men, perhaps even our whole species, for their egos.

Yet the self that fascinates me is the one that does not necessarily fit in my pants or in any tribe of man, a self with the bright, innocent laughter not clouded by a future's motives or by a learned past that loves to fly on the wings of all winds. In that self Theo is just one of the raisins in the cake. With that poetic self one moves to mighty tides as does the kelp. One breathes in and out the air together with the woods and together we keep the air good. Think of a motherly self with open arms as beamy and long as Noah's Ark cuddling a mind full of neighbors, exiles, eccentrics, strangers and loners, playing sweet music in many homes. The spirit of frogs, the manmade moons, the fishes, rivers, the air one breathes, the brains in gray and trees in green, the tax collectors and you and me, we all take refuge in this self roomy as the belly of God in which the Creator produces every imaginable joy and bellyache to keep his world on course. A man or woman with such a multiple self—what an orchestra!

In this belly of God progress is synthesized from innumerable kinds of inventive cells—in swollen berries hanging ripe, in the stems of leeks, from teams of Sitka spruce that work on outdoor tests, and from the gray of our monkey-business minds. And without much fuss, an inconspicuous thistle, or perhaps that team of Sitka spruce from the Iris Flats, can share a Nobel prize with us.

Aren't there as many heavens as there are minds, as many different Nobel prizes as there are selves, all products of individual sights that have specialized perhaps in myopic or telescopic sight, or from a viewpoint on top of a tall boulder, or from a space flight propelled by a super drug, or from a Christian's shoulders? Aren't all these selves the poems from thoughts that chose different angles of view, different sets of dimensions, other chunks of time? The heaven for my cleverness may be a different one from that of my intuitive mind. There may be a heaven for leaves and one for trees, a fancier heaven for the wood, each so different from the other in its definition of a saint. There are heavens for individuals, others for nations, for whole species maybe. There are demanding heavens that order a thousand generations to stand in one single line to be questioned for what they did good and in what they failed. What do I know? Maybe there is a holy state of mind in which every possible creature is seen as a welcomed child. On the level of the tree, the storm is the devil that raises hell and does evil. Yet on the level of the forest that same storm may be the patron-saint of all the tree surgeons trimming the woods. Isn't it in part for the storm's mighty doing that the wood, which was not made into a high yield tree farm but could remain free, looks ever so mysterious with divine diversity and in shape?

When a full moon lights up the mind, it might become clear that to every erring ant, the anteater is a hangman sent from hell. Yet to an ant-people's self that same visitor is welcome as a good old family doctor and invited in as a soft and careful broom that has always kept these little people healthy and in line. Just look how well these friends have done together.

Aren't we all pilgrims climbing somewhere up this timeless ladder minding our own inner and outer points of view? The farther apart we are, the more we have to gesticulate and to yell to make others understand, as each cherishes his own values and view and swears by the slice of what he can see. Communication becomes harder from further up or down. While these bewildered on the lower steps shake their heads, children and birds above may have merry talks and seem quite unconcerned.

When great mental energies build up a thunderstorm, lightning may flare up the darkened part of our brains where we think in forms that are completely different from trees, tables, numbers, and from whatever the alphabet can compose and where an elephant might be just one of the "elephant's" toes. I have a hunch that God does not at all know what an elephant is. This gray cluster of ideas we call elephant may just be one of our innumerable convenient little theorems.

We are born the rider—a thundering flash—and we wake up the rider, the horse and the prairie we are riding on. Another flash and that whole landscape riding and the other riders just generations ahead become one. I will not further expand. That form has already become too difficult to draw. Forms integrate into more general forms when the fog lifts.

71

If there were a giant who in his soul was so awesomely resourceful and forgiving that he could rhyme the doings of a great jungle doctor, an executioner, a blue sunny breeze and a battering storm into one awesome but beautiful song, would he be a monster in your eyes?

To comb God's unruly hair, I was harnessed to a rake for evil, a rake so rigid and fine, it endlessly got me hung up in all the crooked, unbehaved and wicked things that seem not to be serving our tribe. I worked so hard, sweat ran from my brows, yet I barely made a mile while getting buried in waste.

I wonder: is it not for a convenient simplicity in thought that I was taught to quickly wrinkle my nose at people whom life drafts for distant, dirty, thankless chores? Was I to remain an intellectual minor for life? Such mental blinders do make me a steadier worker. They also make me a limping dancer and blind to all kinds of ugly ducklings and toads that really are friends and swans whom our time horizon cut in half. I became dumbfounded, even offended, that a man who is asked to become a surfer, an executioner, a jackhammer in the Creator's demolition crew should also be rewarded with joys. Why, as a Christian, didn't I wonder what trophy awaits at the last judgment for God's hardest working rotters and wreckers? Conveniently, I was made to forget that later somebody has to mend my favorism. How, with such blinders, could I ever happily fall in step with a great October storm that drags his net through the thicket, fishing for the rotten and the slow and is all smiles after a job well done? Damned be that genius of malice, my elegant mind was about to curse. Now, however, after that cursed storm has rested awhile, its dreams at peace, happily showing off to my grandchildren his well-thinned, well-swept and fertilized plot, they seem happy about what they see and happy grandpa could not intervene. With my mind better trained to be less neighborly and more a generalist, I could have readily seen, when that storm was moving in, a kind giant hunchback loaded down with all the ungrateful labors fine people with their hands washed spic and span have left behind to be done by a caste of "dirty" men they did not want to know. My mind could have become a guest house to the world.

My upbringing handicapped me to mingle with people who do me the favor to become my opposite. I was constantly talked into being a good boy. I was counseled to be chicken and not to start fires in my mind. I learned to underestimate many people—and this still does me harm. Many things I carelessly discarded into hell turn out to be a great loss. Why was I not encouraged to become an astronaut and land on the shaded side of dubious acts? Why was I not cheered into becoming a fire walker and find out more about the persons I am supposed to condemn? No parable in our sacred books could have been more helpful than a fable about life's system of morals that is self-regulating, self-changing—a tool box for tolerance, a guide to forgiveness. It wouldn't have taken me so long to find out that nothing pays better than to explore God's argument in defense of weeds, offenses, spices, sins, thorns and crimes. Maybe a redeemer needs not to suffer for my sins but shows me there is no sin—washing my vision is his cure. Maybe the Creator can win the case and get a cheerful pardon for any client we are about to send to hell. Maybe there is absolutely nothing to pardon!

How easily I let my thoughts in defense of some outsider capitulate so I may swiftly side with the closest neighbor's hurrahs or whining; how easily I invoke slogan-thoughts as a kind of aspirin, killing new thoughts that give pain when born. Movies, prayers, most politicians and evangelists, baseball games, batmen, cartoons and most of what my civilization has philosophized about; too often they court my mental laziness, or my lowest self to take sides. They offer a refuge from where I can safely shake and fumble an angry fist against presumed devils or enemy land. Conveniently I capitulate when at first attempt my argument in defense of my deeper self fails. I go on my knees, ask to be punished, and I repent. Why lose time and whine? Be an apprentice, Theo, try again. Does the chemist repent when there is no result after the second experiment? So, don't let me get away with a picky, wasteful one-sidedness, as if the art of becoming aware were as easy as eating the same food and squeezing out the same pile of waste over and over again. Make me taste with my soul what I criticize. Who knows, the soul may have a stomach so big it can swallow the world and leave no waste.

I have a hunch that miracles and sins may be nearly synonyms. Both those presumed lawbreakers seem inventions of my awestricken mind to patch up my partial understanding of the divine order. When sinking in uncertainty, these cheatings help me swiftly to reach a conclusion. They are putty and cottonwool to caulk our leaky philosophical theorems, so on the ocean of infinite truths those "ships of the mind" will not sink. Still, the assumption that we can kick over the cosmic order feels presumptuous to me.

But now that life reveals itself so extraordinarily shameless to us, we ordinary people have to walk most times huddled under an umbrella of some approved semi-lies. Here are lotions against the burning rays of truth and mental fig leaves for shade. We need our credos, our tents standing in the howling, whistling thoughts and elements; but don't sew the doors closed!

I am dumbfounded: why should have God revealed to John all these terrible apocalyptic things? Why not an abracadabra for forgiveness or an $E=mC^2$.

105

72

Deep down a man is no cuckoo clock for he seems to feel better when in each of his seasons he ticks to a different moral and to a different justice and rights.

How much longer should we pester our seniors with equal duties and equal rights and have the economists whisper to them to keep on dancing to the cocky song of youth? Why do we keep them standing for so long in that blazing midday sun? Beneath the pride to remain authoritative and to play young, force-fed by consumer animators into their minds, I think I see older people quietly longing to bend each morning a little more to that overwhelming and illogical generosity of the season that indulges in giveaways.

A woman's or a man's life seems to have first its season in sap, mostly as sucker roots, taking more and giving less. Later on comes the great season of comfortable modesty, where it feels good to be used and "abused" and to freely wrinkle and unload oneself. One ripens into one big udder that longs to be sucked. Elders who follow another justice than trading on merely equal terms do not become old fools—they become merry fools. A woman then enjoys serving more and commanding less. Slowly a man then wants less to vote for himself but likes to be milked dry of what he has and what he knows, a little like the bulb that makes a tulip grow.

I have seen this golden wisdom bud just in time to rescue a man from his first October frost and spark in him that amazing heart warmer, to give and give again, a zest that at first try seems not to quite slip into Darwin's theory. Finally, lean to the bone and no longer tormented by youthful greed, he can ripen to a gentle breeze that settles an evening on him full of youngsters, honeybees, beggars, birds, butterflies, his brainchildren, who all merrily nibble on him. He will be a well-spent golden pumpkin vine surrounded by his pumpkins jubilant orange and in their prime.

It is this cheerful parting I have noted in well-matured women and men that makes me envious and curious. How different this victorious giving-in is compared to that grim last stand where, tortured by a feeling of being cheated and robbed, a graying man digs in his heels. His pack of watchdog-spirits still defending him never have learned when to stop barking at the nibblers and to let their master graciously disperse his wealth.

I suspect a person whose mind becomes a good grandparent to this world does not enjoy being nursed by society and allowed only to consume. I figure that one must be an eunuch in the soul to dream of a retirement in an adult commune.

It might be for the sake of our GNP that clients are being brainwashed to hold on to a teenage vision the rest of their lives and that mellowed homesick souls are again driven out into another vicious consumer storm. Think of all the fire that is lit again under empty pots. How this cruelty can spoil the cheerful song of a man sitting in his evening sun among the goodies he has amassed, ripening in his final success; to become generous, to indulge in giving away his hat-tricks, his goodies and tallest stories, his pride, his vote, his lies.

An organic society that is more that a mere brotherhood likes its generations to hold hands, not in a circle but in a relay race toward a luminous dawn. Yet when such a people contracts into an adult society, it seems to become obsessed with personal power trips and equal rights for its members to abuse whatever is not yet born or does not walk erect. It appears to be this preoccupation with constantly jockeying for career and status that finally opens the gap between the generations and makes us awkward, even unfit, to live with the young.

It is unfortunate that our society does not prepare us to become round, humble and less authoritative when getting wrinkly and gray so that we could find a niche with the young and become happy helpers to them. There are so many chores for a ripe woman and man who learned to put their rowdy pride in a gift box at the right time and send it to the young.

In less confused times we know the rules better—when to grab the torch and when to pass it on. Many seem now caught in the destiny of a prostitute, who, turned down by age and freed at last, might well be left in a hundred years of solitude with a constipated soul.

73

When I watch the leaves turn gently yellow . . .

When a dying animal surprises me with its peacefulness and puts my terror of death to shame; when I think of old wrinkly Ramon who used to fish alongside me in the jungle lagoons, how he now hands himself out to his heart's content, humbly, unreasonably generous and how he is surrounded by his clan nibbling noisily at his mellowed love as he still carpenters for them; when Clara talks affectionately of her grandpa swinging the jump rope for her, then our adult communities with their "Keep Off, Keep Out and Keep Quiet" signs become malformed organs of a society to me.

At sixty-five, many seniors are pushed, against their hearts, into a superficial life of discreet vices. When taken to the side, their inner voices have little to brag about their retired lives. This, in spite of politicians lavishly rubbing reassurance and pride into them. Our retired parents might well be the best kept junkyard our technological civilization has produced.

Have we not created a social system that condemns our seniors to a life as mistletoes with the right, for the time being, to hang on? We discreetly condemn them to be beggars and to a second time of nursing and to hold on to that one thread of our learned obligation to bake bread and cake for them and send them on a vacation in a mobile home. To hold on to that thin rope of a fading moral's promise as a sole support is a terrifying thought, threatening our retired people's peace of mind.

How undesirable I could become once I understep the breaking point of profitability in a production-crazy society when slowing down on the Common Market's assembly line where we try to produce a worse life for the animals and plants and a better life for man. Could I still fascinate them with the wisdom I learned from tall tales I lived so that they would love to shoulder grandpa around? Could I count on an abundance of cash and love that permits them the luxury of happily taking a storyteller along? I see so many grandparents cursed to simply whine and vote for their alms. Even the wealthy retiree is a beggar, yet a beggar with a policeman to enforce the alms at his side.

To let our elders participate in the dangers, the blisters, the hurrahs, the sweat and baking of cakes and not to let chauvinistic economists measure the profit of it, seems to me a more imaginative gift than settlement checks. I note that older people who do not fall for the slogans of economic growth but let their hearts prepare them to become great, merry fools, make a feast of their give away time and become quiet helpers and vote against themselves to vote for the young, remain a well for the young to dip in.

I note that when young we get our thrills when we win. Later, with the blinders of our golden season of fall, only to be happy losers makes us full—and we can start the only business that we may run for the rest of our lives at a loss and still come up with a profit of a million friends. And is there a more comfy wealth for a man than his relationships?

When nature gently metamorphoses us from one generation to the next, she is a good mother and no slut. She makes our horizon transparent when we get ripe. Our personal memory, that in our middle age becomes quite tyrannic, gets gently fogged in again. Names, words, numbers, all the short term smartness becomes again overridden by more unfocused forms that are many generations tall. Nature bubbles up in us a powerful and pleasurable need to give. For our smooth parting she even grows a field of opioids in our minds.

Please pass me up, you marketers of consumption and pride. Let me become completely helpful and sweet—no tricks from me anymore, just treats. Don't enchant me to remain a firm and sour plum to its sour end.

74

Are you going to be my friend? Are you going to drive me out of my nest of comforts with a stick and make a ranch duck fly?

Most of us settled and modestly use day after day the same trodden and safe valley of conventions to fish for our joys. We do not even blush anymore for being so pale. Its trails have been weeded, ironed, its Broadway legalized again and again and became our dear routine. Its meadows are plowed. Its slopes whitewashed spic and span. The salmonberry bushes, the droughts and floods, all nature's beggars and vagabonds that crept, breathed, sang, held a strange idea or an almbowl into our path have for our dear safety and hygiene been banned. Hence this latest phobia to all that's wild and mystic, to the daddy longlegs and the silence of the night, to the open windows and open credos. In that neat and narrow place my mind has also become narrow and precise.

With just a peephole in my eyes for our own news, I am trained to rush in a straight course daily to my kill. Lulled to sleep by imitation, I became a pebble among pebbles and was about to remain a pebble for life. But some feel now with me that this glorified state of comfort is canning us alive. A can opener, please, for Theo, who learned to keep his soul so canned and controlled it cannot even break wind. When by chance a quake opens a crack in my mind, I am dumbfounded how narrow my view of this great wild world has become; how far down I have sunk from the risky freedom of clear, chilly heights, where my eyeballs can excitedly swivel around to take on bold ideas advertised by every critter alive. Up there I can brace myself and stand in the middle of the weather fronts and be electrified. Up there I can breathe in divine understanding that is not blackened out with slogans and RPMs. I am in uneducated land that remains an eternal child—crisp with danger, laughter, mischief, and rewards. Up there I discovered that blue after all is blue. And I wonder: have I been an April fool?

What personal catastrophe, what drug, risk or quake explosive enough to invoke? What sickness, brainstorm or tragedy should I pray for to crack and collapse these shimmering walls enshrining me? What mud-slide in me should I welcome to fill in fox holes that my zealous logician and security guard made me dig with the forced labor of all my practical acts so I can hide from the temptress, Miss Diversity, who charms me to stick my mind and neck further and further out. In what danger should my mind sweat to open its pores?

In the great flood of discouragement, of ever more consumption, membership, insurance, consultation, we can encourage each other. We can be less accomplices and more radioactive friends—and quickly drive each other out of these nests with a stick and let Miss Prudence and jolly Mr. Routine fume about it. We might be stronger than we guessed and quite fit to stand up to the terror of a changing scenery. We can cheer each other into sidestepping the rational march to soft being, a safe harbor, diaper-land, metallic life and union; and dare each other to try more serious escapes than an occasional pilgrimage to Chartres or to a refuge for a pristine wonderland. It might just be that such infusions of courage are what great help is all about; and do you know a help that beats encouragement?

To step over the cliff, beyond practicality, and into the abyss of the immense wonderland and have impeccable faith that the soul can fly in it; might be the simple abracadabra that allows us to enter a separate reality. In such peak times where everywhere awesome possibilities rise higher and higher above us, I might have to battle with vertigo, fight panic, spirit away the temptation to let myself slide down from these obstacles onto solid trodden ground, and in this way become again a minor, a suckling on the Internet, turning my mind once more over to the credo of some mastermind. Up there I may better see the acts weaving themselves through the many levels of knowledge, swinging, hopping, dancing elegantly between yin and yang, between saintliness and crime. A trick to forgiveness may open to me.

75

Chiseling and hacking on my thoughts and needs, making of their turbulence a streamlined flow; inventing a simple, elegant lifestyle—here is growth in which something is chopped off every day, yet never declared missing.

I do not notice in our longings, motives and dreams where we differ so much but rather in the dressing up of our motives and in our friction when we tunnel, bulldoze, elbow, wriggle as slick and swift as we can to the source of light as does a vine. It's just unbelievable how much we lately have to spend to dress our motives up. When my ego gets fat with all that money can buy; when with an impressive load of possessions stuffed in my mind and in my pack I stumble ahead trying to catch up with my dreams, I constantly get in others' ways. The air becomes thick with the emotions and language typical to any traffic jam. With such a pack on my back, no other creature beats me in clumsiness and friction and leaves messier tracks. Is it not for a sick trust in life's goodness that a man freaks

111

out and stands in line to become rich and safely all wrapped up in wealth. He becomes one of the maniacs who the animals and plants fear most, for wealthy men's erratic joy rides cause many tears among them. Thus we had to refine the wolf's occasional pissing to mark and defend his property line to such an extent and elegance that we have to spend now half our activity for such pissing rounds.

I admire a man who knows how to be lean and does not need a whole log for a cane. I admire him for making do with ingeniously simple thoughts like $E = mC^2$. I envy him for using his mind for solutions instead of a pick, a kilowatt or a stick. His sight is not glued to the ground but remains unobstructed, liquid and free. I envy her for her impeccable trust that life is good and sees to it that she is given her daily love, excitement and bread so she doesn't have to groan under a heavy pack. Drunk with the spirit, she is pliable, not stiff with convictions. To me, the prize for living ingeniously poor is leisure time.

Now here comes also rolling along a nearsighted man who obviously needs more wealth for padding because he bangs into many things. He comes with a wide load of bank accounts and sunny days stockpiled to the rafters, with insurance policies, many kinds of diapers, convictions, hard-hats and a camper all wrapped around his myopic, stumble foot self. He comes blazing through a meadow in green and bloom that sways happily in the arms of a soft blue summer breeze.

Yet this man is also on the way toward the same sun as you, I and the white gulls sailing an indigo-blue sea. A formidable tank let loose that trails its flags of smoke, runs awkwardly down many smiles, owns stock with the oilers of Kuwait and plugs the sewer holes. What a tumbling boulder of mistrust one can rapidly become and how disoriented and alone when one has twenty-four hours of running water and running man-made information and advertisement in the home. Nonetheless, here comes the hero of billions, all brainwashed to believe they have to imitate that most common clown, endlessly worried to lose his pants.

Longing for wealth seems to come from a feeling of insecurity—an added show of how menacing and dangerous one can be—a refined version of the wolf's signal when he fixes his opponent with baring his teeths—an extension of horns.

Have our minds become dull knives? Look how much energy we need to cut off our needed slice of the pie we share with our fellow life. How messily those knives now cut! Take our pity and hate; take how we heal and abort; take our jerks between vacations and work, exercise and comfort. We accelerate like mad, we brake like mad and go into reverse more erratically than the hare population in the Arctic north. Do we compete for how powerful we can become, how much energy we can throw around and consume? We now need a continuous ten kilowatts per hour per man and aspire to become duller and more powerful.

I can make a pebble from a rock; render my turbulence into a streamlined flow; make my needs so polished, slick and light that you hardly see ripples when they have to cross your path. I can let the poet in myself wake up and move me in a way which leaves the slightest wisp of enmity behind, I could and become a true economist then.

How popular it becomes for an economist to turn into his opposite, planting thorn bushes in our hearts, selling raingear to the divers, making us carry water in a sieve. He becomes a chauvinist, whipping bigger and bigger ripples through the garden of life, stirring up demand for throw aways, consumption, jobs, profits that are mere figures in stockmarket games. Few become strong enough to willingly live with a light pack. Consumption promoters, though, have created billions of would-like-to-be-rich who are wretchedly unsuccessful at their bid.

I wonder whether that wise Galilean of two thousand years ago had in mind our whole materialistic civilization, which got enormously rich by worshipping the GNP and plunging the Earth's flora and fauna deep into poverty. Did he mean such a civilization is less likely to enter a state of grace than a camel to sneak through a needle's eye? When he counseled us to distribute the riches among the poor, did he mean the penguins, the condors, the butterflies, the spotted owls, the lilies of the fields, our wise old friends the trees, the native lands that all seem now among us to be the most miserably poor?

In spite of the nice nursery rhyme we like to make of it, that Bible story praising the lilies of the field might well be a primal idea of our native mind that one should think about seriously.

76

He resigned from the clan of emperors of all life's kingdoms and he sighed with relief.

I am trained to keep my goodwill on a short, tight leash. I heard it said a thousand times that it pays to reserve one's admiration and love for one's contemporary neighbors and not to waste it childishly on those non-payers far ahead in time or in the bushes where Jack-in-the-Green lives with the critters who do not even live in houses. As a result of the preaching of this pretentious discovery, we felt free to join in a worldwide union of the perfect egoists and to subdue all "unenlightened" citizens that go on bare paws or do not wear hats. We may now harvest together the Earth and soon pride ourselves by quite justly sharing among all of us the loot.

My winged spirits with eagle's eyes are not happy with this meek advice. And they are offended when I keep them grounded. They sabotage every day I do not let them fly to guide my action on the ground from above our traffic jams. These guardians like to scrutinize my good news, my fashionable heroes, celebrities and saints, for how many critters and generations their goodwill includes. They are my astronauts, keeping me informed about the needs of my other worlds in other generations of life. I learned to contemptibly call them wild for their mind boggling farsightedness in their impact statements.

With such training, my acts have become rather nice and are pleasing the crowd. Few care that they may also unwittingly stab our children in their backs. My pity has become of bad hearing, sided swiftly with the closest whiners, has turned into a sloppy broom and leaves my grandchildren in a mess.

It might be for such reasons that practical religions specializing in nearsighted and fast-paying love produce so much waste, so many exiled and damned that their prisons seem always overfilled and their hells are running out of coal. With such cultivated dislike for what is mysterious and unreasonably far, most of life's highly productive options get out of sight.

"Don't buy fig leaves, an imagination without clothes on is excitingly beautiful," I say encouraging myself. "Don't be afraid to get carried away and high, to race through seven generations in one thought; keep that door to unlimited options open in your mind." *Or does one think that every soul should be unionized, have a middle man to God, be told when to strike and what to fight for?*

To enter the reality beyond humanism, maybe my old heroes, saints, and monuments to bygone glorious deeds should be put to rest in museums of anthropology. A greener mythology can fire our children's imagination; heroes who may stand for an endangered pond with no fat carps but peopled with muskrats, watercress, dragonflies and thousands of unlicensed flyers and divers; a wise old pond and breeding ground of so many wonderful ideas, it can give me more helpful advice than our columnists; heroes that are different from modern versions of St. George fighting the dragon, Nature, in defense of fair Lady Humanity tripping on high heels; daring saints who can welcome back what has been exiled, damned, wasted and weeded out; and scientists who produce ice cream for our souls.

More of us now realize that it is after all the company of this persecuted, innocent, barefoot and incredibly versatile environment in and around us that can make us wise, rather than the neat places where we simply farm our useful knowledge and kraut. With nostalgia and hope I watch in us the tide of morals change. Old laws want to hatch out of their tablets. Did you notice that old sins are under consideration to be sanctified, that some terrible acts of old which take from man and make room for other more needy creatures than us are about to become acceptable, even blessed? Are we not beginning to unofficially recognize, even welcome, some pests, sicknesses, abortions, forest fires, and tragedies as remedies? There is much wisdom we know but do not yet publicly acknowledge. To make mankind lose weight some seem tricked into becoming "bad" boys and girls and to living on a diet of love with minimal calories. To better understand this change of season, one can listen to the mega-hits with which the young singers bewilder us. The foxgloves, the gold finches, the elms, people seven generations ahead might finally have something to celebrate. They love to see leeches put on our success on credit, on our number, on our strictly humane love. It dawns on many of us that every critter, even the dung beetle, is not only food for others. It may be an Edison, an omen, a psalm in the song of creation. Do we want these wondrous happenings to become extinct so that we have more room for human biomass? Maybe we are first of all meant to simply get high on the entrancing beauty of life at large.

Who of the apostles would have thought that their crusade for better goodness would turn into that harsh crusade for technology to remove suffering from man—and to burden our fellow life with it? Who would have guessed that it would inspire us to build this huge trap to catch nature, our mother and our neighbor?

Later, one may better see how we lived as puzzled witnesses to a cataclysmic time during whic'. that mighty philosophical theorem of the west, in which we tried ourselves out as the most egoistic and inventive species among all organisms, started to molt. We start to question our old answers we expressed in this enormous socio-biological experiment of Christianity that is changing us mentally and physically so much while it reorients our zest. We start to try our love out beyond humanism, our shield of arrogance, which our forbearers have beautified with some of our most enchanting rhythms and rhymes. And we do not even mind that this journey of our thinking will be littered with discarded ladders, ideas and picks, with shedded philosophies, models and beautifully ornated garments we outgrew.

When one thinks of it, each man is now pushed to crawl up the shore of this new continent we call consciousness, quite blind, often panicked, but giving his best gold for just a foothold and getting happily drunk on the most trivial success. He clings together with others for warmth, reassurance and rest, having no measure yet for how much is enough. Who knows? We might for the time being even pardon ourselves for our grotesque behavior on this new beachhead and forgive our dumbfounded selves for their awkwardness.

77

I wonder why God is so fond of growing hedges and putting distance between you, her and me.

We seem to have become the most prosperous traders in knowledge of all time. Systems of rejection are broken. Skins are slashed. Doors and shame are knocked down. Borders and other fire-breaks are given up. Freeways for information on cunning are humming day and night. The Internet is becoming our fabulous copy machine. While clearing us from the interference of the communication among all life forms, it inbreeds our self-serving knowledge, promoting an all man-made mind. Most of us have overcome our shame and feel quite free to cart away the personal secrets we pledged to guard, to the market square of the information merchants to trade for friendships, safety, life extensions or for the excitement of gossiping. Quietly the knowledge market has become the stoutest promoter of communism. This joint venture is also fast buying up all personal bankruptcies in autonomous thinking. Have we mentally started to build a space needle of Babel again?

It has been profitable to sit on one single plot in one's personality and breed it. While patiently sitting on these promising nests, astonishing memories may finally become conscious to the ego and available for sale. The cash crop of such plantations in our minds can be exchanged for bleached bread, GM trucks or fame. Yet I worry. Is a mind that becomes merely farmland not in danger of becoming plundered, information-poor or sold? Is a mind that becomes the sweetest, juiciest, thinnest-skinned orange not the first to end up in a press? Is our capacity to be each one unique not getting scarce? When I can remain in my thoughts self-sufficient and sour when needed, maybe by protecting my secrets with lies or thorns, do I not have a better chance to become myself a subspecies and king of my world? A mind seems never quite as sharp as when it wanders by itself.

The immense knowledge in an individual locked safely away from the ego can, byte by byte, be mined, made known to the ego so it can sell it to the communal data bank. Is not information to society what blood is to mosquitoes? Society must prey on the individual to grow. In our time of fierce competition between the individual and society more of the scientists are giving up to become shamans. They rent out as society's celebrated informers. When a secret is after great persuasion finally leaked to the ego and becomes conscious—the ego and the society it belongs to rub their hands pleased. One more information one can get hands on, control and put to work! For a long time I mistook becoming conscious and becoming aware for synonyms. Yet to become aware, does one not stop all scheming so from head to toe to become one big guitar, ready to be plucked by God's zillion fingers?

When a business-minded crowd presses a spirited man against a wall, his mind may become a genius on the one side where the light, the cheers and grants continuously converge on him. It seems to be these shortcuts our society counts on for producing the experts on instant success needed to become the highest power house on earth. But where that talented man is crowded against the wall and suffers shade and neglect, does he not risk growing mildew, becoming a dwarf, even a monster on that shaded side of his soul? For these side effects, I hesitate to let a trifle of my native intelligence be cultivated as profitable to my purse and fame and as devastating to my inner flora as we plow fields of our high yield sugar canes in lush and pristine wonderland.

I share a fear of the united and commercialized sciences with all those who still like to stand psychically on their own. We face the superb, superhuman capacity of the legions of collaborators who, hard-pressed, sold out to join the columns of our version of driver ants that prey on the practical knowledge locked in the individual. How not to go under in the computerized scientific commune of professional rationalists who produce aggressive science for pay? How to remain such a lucky, unfocused fool that one can dream up wisdom by oneself and remain one's own pope? In the present break up of the countless subspecies of the human race, tremendous rational powers are released among which an amateur of individuality may not remain competitive. Think of what the flood of the melt waters from six billion melting snow crystals can do.

Did you ever think carefully about what the wise man with his fable about the tower of Babel meant? Why should God have scrambled the language of the proud tower builder's union and made each builder talk in his very own color and tongue? Why did he curtail their side-talks and side-glances and scattered them and their tower between the savannas, the rivers, the palm trees and the generations? Why did he scatter life in a Big Bang as he did the stars? Maybe only a multi-species mind—so out of fashion now—can have access to the answers that can build an immunity to unionitis, which is perhaps our greatest sin.

Let's linger a little on this unfashionable thought and, to get a more picturesque point of view, visualize how all of the 8,000 kinds of birds frolicking on earth would kick one day at the law of diversity and at apartheid and unionize into one bird kind—one single immense flock of stout grey birds, unsurpassably efficient, ever-pecking and with one kind of appetite. One might then wonder how welcome in Graceland the undertaking of a United Nations and Common Market under one color, one police, one shared knowledge and mental uniform, and one soul might be.

When the Spaniards conquered the new world, they quickly melted down its artworks of a thousand years to brute ingots of gold. The Mayas, the Aztecs, the Incas lost their souls. When the economists go now on the warpath to conquer the Limeys, the Frenchies, the Krauts, maybe fifty cultures in all and make them to slave for their Common Market of Europe, how much more silently they go about it than Cortez. International corporations are melting down some fifty different cultures, flowers of the mind, into one enormous resource of raw physical and rational power, into police power, media power, potato power and manpower to win another round in the stockmarket game. They skin these nations alive. Think of an orange or apple without a peel. Think of the ethnic wars such skinning can provoke after a people's immune system has clicked in!

The subspecies of human culture have all evolved in relative isolation. Over time the local cultures have also worked out arms agreements with their land. As a man with a woman, so the corporate cash croppers with the land; many now seek less a lasting relationship with mutual benefits—a flirt, plunder her gift, take a bath, move on—alone. Succumbing to "unionists" we now can mix and recombine our virulence to a broader more effective and virulent technology to attack our host, the living Earth. Smuggling such arms secrets has become a virtue. This global recombining of our cunning is a dramatic new phenomenon in the history of our aggression that alters our relationship with life. This crossbreeding of our different strains of "mental" scorpion tails seems to be at the root of why we are fast becoming in global life that incredibly successful pathogene. Ask any pathologist what happens when we pull down borders and local strains of malaria or HIV join in international trafficking of their genetic tricks and forces. Wonderful things can only exist in separation with limited access. And that's why no organism is known to live without some kind of membrane.

There is a lilac blooming between you and me. There is a sparrow chirping for the evening sun, for his partner, for us, for the linden tree. There is a hedge of impenetrable wilderness guarding the distance between you and me preserving that precious moment when it is neither your turn nor the mass media's turn, but the turn of the whole of God's menagerie to communicate with me. That is privacy to me.

78

A man caught in the mental cyclone that whirls all our thinking around the destiny of man alone may break out of that terrible ring; a woman who strengthens herself and washes the slogans off her mind to visualize again many generations and species tall might be able to scatter her thoughts evenly over them.

I suspect that in the sketchbook of life, there is for every sorrow a counter-picture that when recognized, visualized, and applied to the sore spot, becomes a mental medicine and produces a long "ahh" of relief. One can compose visions for the lost at sea: shorebirds, debris, seaweeds and other tell-tale signs that tell us land is near. There are thoughts to be uncovered that make heating pads for a mental chill; or cold beer and a breeze for minds broiling in the desert of confusion. There are thought compositions that are more soothing than aspirin, that makes parts of my work unnecessary, that make of death a door, that are angels who can wing us out of a deep black well we fell in. One can create positive and negative visions that mend thoughts that have ends broken and make them rhyme; thoughts that are walking sticks for when we stumble and stagger while sweetly intoxicated by the slogans that lure us into a consumer spree; thoughts that relieve sickening pride. There is daily tree-watching which promises us that we will never get scurvy of the mind. There is river watching to make us harmonious again. Who knows? Perhaps there are mental pictures that make a man without arms and legs see himself as a healthy man or make a woman meeting death feel healthy and fine.

Maybe one should outgrow the old pioneer spirit and not sleep anymore with the ax in hand and the command to be a missionary in mind. Mental solutions can be found that do not need to violate the oceans, the trees, the great seas of the waving grasses, the butterflies, the minds of beautiful opponents, the seductive ghosts in us who sell us creative laziness and leisure time. Soon there will be less need to interfere.

79

Did you notice that the Divine Gardener discreetly implants among us desires for mutilation, abortion, lean diet, devotion to "chores of hell" and when needed pulling nails? She triggers hunger for drugs which can sing to sleep a tyrannic brainchild, our hyper rationality, and its malignant success. Watch how She changes around our active neurochemicals and hormones, our heroes, our attractors and magnetic North.

Many among us are daughters and sons of a religion that appointed itself to teach Mother Nature a lesson. Many of her laws we were told are throwaway laws to be dealt with as pests. We rolled up our sleeves and built great fires on her cloudy days. When it was our turn for the season of giveaways we started a revolt. We insisted on building our homes in an ambiance of eternal peace, opulence, sunshine and spring. We aspired to be forever cozily nested at the foot of the "Great Wall" we erected around our dear Babylon. It was a long, splendid, carefree noon. We took in more and more. We did not waste time to cook juicy berries for lady bird and brother raccoon on the other side of the wall. Nobody really cared to talk about the terms of credit that came with those preposterous loans of privileges that we took out from the bank of Mother Earth.

Oh no, we could not just walk away from the mess of the party and take to a more wholesome and beautiful living. Look at the monocultures in our minds and how many of our feelings are going extinct. Look at the oceans, the forests, the community of the pond behind your house, the erosion in our souls. Look at the huge trampling herd of men. There is nowhere to run away to, and nobody wants to join a thinning crew. Has not a debt come overdue? Has not a tough openness among us been kept under a cover for too long? Does that long litany of lamentation from our flora and fauna not make it clear that they are suing us? We have loved ourselves too much and have kept ourselves fat. Why didn't we wash our minds more often in dangers, waterfalls and droughts?

That world which our industries have too often plundered and pissed on is taking us to court. One now wonders what law of Nature will strike to cull us and bring us down again to a healthy, hardy stand; to have us give back some of our huge possessions and biomass. A restoration is asked so that we may never become so hopelessly arrogant and fat that the Great Spirit judges it better to simply sink us with the millstone of some terrible obsession tied to our necks.

Astonished, one notices that our ten commandments which promised us eternal spring are starting to wrinkle and fade; the wheel of morality and the wheel of medicine spin; frost and October gales are composting the perishable rhymes of our humanistic poem. Changes in morals, though, have their logic; they can be forecasted by those who have not turned into surface skimmers but nurtured their capacity to communicate with their deeper selves.

As in a developing cell so in a man it seems to be the environment that selects and triggers qualities of us into action while others are drugged to sleep. What's more, those same qualities can be oriented toward "virtue" or "crime" according to the need of clawbars or building blocks. So our behavior is not the property of our character but the property of our character in interaction with the environment.

When we overreach into a life of dominance and at the top—outrageous and obnoxious, high levels of androgens from stress sterilize us or make us less fertile. Such is the help we get to bring our estranged enterprise down again to the warm center.

"Theo, don't be chicken," I tell myself. "Listen to the warnings the spirit of our time is telling you. Think why the Divine Gardener makes of the playboy and playgirl cult and other diversions tools for birth control. Think why She deep freezes so much maternal love. This spirit also whispers about a need to better welcome death among us; although our anguish is still divided on how we should share death among our children to come, among our aged and among ourselves."

I also note that this spirit impregnates others with a religious zest to procreate themselves by advancing the sciences of nature beyond practicality. It organizes green-corps and Ark-builder unions all over the earth defending flora and fauna from the harsh demands of our practical world which endlessly squeaks and rusts and needs more barrels of oil and endless repair. Others it baits with the adventure to replace economic growth with economic refinement, bucking an unimaginative crowd of political gnomes that seems to still dwell in an underworld of ever more GNP, more waste and more work. These friends to all the earth might well be the first rays of an eighth day in the genesis that seems to never end. They give the Christian wisdom stars, leaves, roots, flowers and fins.

To me this has become a time of scientific renaissance in which a naive knowledge-hunt to simply press our planet for more advantages, more energy, clinical medicines and food to fatten mankind even more would not only become a chauvinistic and negative science but would involve a mortal misstep for us. How does one learn to resist becoming a sorcerer's apprentice which is still such a praised career? How to improve on an imagination that, without a whimper, can still happily plow under and enslave another thousand freedom loving acres for energy crops to fuel maybe a few more semis loaded with Toyota trucks? A chain of "better seeing institutes" might soon outdo the hamburger empires on the stock exchange.

Way below my naive lobbying for a better life for man I feel that all we invent and brag about—the space-flights, the symphonies, the heart transplants, the radar belts—are not meant for monuments to man but are rather contributions to a vaster venture to which even we, the Lords, might ultimately be sacrificed.

80

There is a proud, old Swiss saying, "United, the weak are strong and mighty."

I was conditioned to be a highly rational man and to be proud about that. My sight was lassoed and brought in from dreamtime. It was aimed, focused and ironed out. I became a ray in the most beautiful laser—the laser made of all our mental energy bundled and focus on the need of contemporary man. We found that when our thousand thoughts and two thousand arms are united and bundled into one single beam, a remote free-thinking village will shatter under our attack; it will disintegrate and capitulate. In the grip of our beam its lush fauna of loose thinkers, dreamers and drinkers, April fools, tree watchers and tinkers in all trades who brighten and perfume their homes with homemade folklore, saints, sausages and novel ways of doing things would melt down to maybe one more customer for chain saws, soft drinks or a chain selling fast food for our souls. And soon it will not be allowed to decorate its days with its own brand of tears and joys. It will be taught to grow a cash crop, to be bored in repetitive work, to buy more. That special little tribe will become one more sound that makes the stockmarket sing.

It is the tragedy of many indigenous people that their cultures do not fare better when hit by our consumerism than their immunity system and health fared when first confronted with T.B. or smallpox. I believed that through my education I was a privileged man. Yet is that so? Exposed to soulful people and ecstatic land, I now discover myself to be awkwardly one-sided and rude. I live now among people, many of whom never or barely went to formal school; I live now among the kind of people for whom a subtle disrespect was cultivated in me—and I learn from them! In the counsel of a wise old tree, I feel like a first-grader in a seminar on advanced love. At times I feel I belong to a new breed of cannibals. At other times I see myself as one of the million fluffy clouds of love all loosely peopling the skies, being sucked down into the mental hurricane where we start to center our thoughts just around the ego of mankind and became a trillion kilowatts strong.

When I was bred for producing strictly usable knowledge, my reality became corrupt. Most of my eyes' one hundred million nerve cells were pressed into the search for practicality. I learned a lot about loving the individual—the me, the he, the she and the tree and what can be caught in the net of the "ABCs." I learned little about loving the species of man. I became quite physically blind in regard to the unfocused forms and the mysterious—the life at large or the woods. That's how I became a retarded poet and a superb fisherman. Yet our species developed for its vision so many neurons, its needs not delegate all of them for shadow-effects and other practicalities of workaholic eyes. It can free some nerve cells for a poetic vision with its forms that make sense only on Sabbaths and Sundays, so one can readily see that a man is more than a man. This is acquiring good luxuries to me.

My mind has become obsessed with tool making. It wants now to carve a spoon out of everything it sees. Will I always have to simplify a great spruce to a pile of two-by-fours or a great variety of lifestyles to one mighty economy so that my eyes may shine? Wretched vision, that, among an endless profusion of wonders, can barely see how a handle fits a hammer. Wretched education that produces smooth seedless minds good only for work.

When I am aimed and have a goal am I not half blind? I may be a bleeding bull in the ring furiously going for a cape. My mind is straight. My mind is in a tunnel to that goal and unaware of options left and right.

I made myself a promise: I will scatter my neatly filed bundles of thoughts back into the black soil rich with rot and fluffy with worms.

81

When the wild leaves a man's life, he loses his wife.

Wisdom, the beautiful song of the wild, is hunted, clear-cut, dissected and its sellable knowledge is processed. Knowledge has become a hungry supermarket crowding out blue-blossom-land. What we sell there is "usefulized" and guaranteed not to sing, not to wriggle—i.e., to be perfectly dead. The pursuit of wisdom and falling in love with the muse, have they become luxuries to us?

I notice also a nostalgia gnawing at many old-fashioned minds that nobody before us has known. We mourn the end of the call from the wild. This may become for most the end of one great reality. After the church of reason has been everywhere to spread the good news of its miracle-love and wonder-rice, we are now the first people who are truly broken-hearted. We fear we are losing our roots for good. I wonder, do we do good to erase the playground of that archaic Robinson Crusoe dream from our land and minds?

This homesickness becomes a boulder that rocks heavier on many a spontaneous mind than other human sufferings and the fights among ourselves. How to calm that mute anger without another mantra than the "fuck you's" graffitied on the walls, when the young find themselves born into a high-tech feedlot without an outlet where they can wash and refresh their minds? I now hear in many popular songs that sad refrain: "My parents did their own thing; I am a kid of the insemination machine."

Does the crew of the National Geographic Society realize what may happen to the last secret places after it has soft-talked its way into them, pulling those rare and fragile souls on-stage to become an exhibition for the billion customers who are too afraid to make the trip on their own? When such intimacies are strip-teased, I barely can stand to look, and I often blush. There are intimacies that cannot survive my presence. Is it good that a man who stumbles onto such privacies should rush home to sell these secrets for a check or fame? The nights at the campfire, where we roll out our sleeping bags and spin yarns with no worry of barbed wires or an owner's flashlight to drive us on, should they be published and their secrets sold?

When a small band of people becomes immune to the great global drive for one human hive, when they find an effort toward a more self-provided, dangerous living and thinking, and toward an unspecialized learning system exciting and rewarding, could we not treat them to a bit of "foolish" generosity? Could we exempt from some of our laws those with the rare urge and courage to follow new trails and become general practitioners? We could cut those born vagabonds lose as living experiments— free them from the traffic laws that keep the busy people safely to one freeway system, one reality and one size of pants and logic for all. We need not be as unimaginative as our parents when they swiftly hassled and ridiculed the flower children out of existence. After all, the wealthiest in diversity may be among that motley gang of career-dodgers, non-conformists, down-steppers, kiters, and other specialists in sabbaticals. We could risk loving our ugly ducklings. We could make provisions in our regulations for God's tramps, hoboes and vagabonds. The weirdos could be scouts. We could let the hermits light obscured stars. We could decide: Amundsens and Scotts exploring new lifestyles are great gifts. With their other logic such madmen, clowns, and runaways could color our gray routine. Let them be a caste of outcasts by their own choosing, free to explore in their unaccustomed way. Let them have their unequal rights they need to function as an unofficial kind of C.I.A. Accommodating the non-con-

126

formists, drilling holes through our laws for these messengers could become another victory in life's saga of getting wildly diverse.

Theologians, moralists, legislators—a refuge, please, better than carnivals, for the endangered wildlife of our minds!

Thinking about this new sadness, how could one forget the trillion candles now burning in all the shrines of all the menaced creatures that suffer under the cartel of reasonable man; how could one be deaf to the trillion murmurs pleading to God to spare the living earth a scorching human super nova? How can one remain deaf to that global prayer for more death among us—for more births among the plants and animals so we become fewer and the animals and plants again more plentiful? And because you don't know their language don't think that crocodiles and trees do not call their neighbors by their names when telling them we are marching in with our saws and guns.

Looking down from a Caravelle's flight I lose some pride. From up there we look a little like smallpox. We leave so many scars. From up there I wonder: *will disappearing wilderness in its own way make true that futuristic fictitious story of a mob of men folk outdoing each other to lay with the last woman on earth?*

But today I got a treat. From where I look and wonder, it's a hundred miles around and no human sign in sight, none of our industrial excrements, no other man to count. Wise leaders have spared this free land little untouched by us and made of it a gift to our young. This is the Goddess' country without a doubt. Most may never have seen anything so agreeably composed—it is yellow cedar, crabapples, and spruce, it is a rhythmic beat of tidelands in all their perfumes, salmon, eagles, terns—fantastic towers of clouds. No, I would not advertise it here. If this should end; it would be a man losing his wife.

82

A challenge hovers over our lawmakers now, that will pick out those brave women and men who do not mind going for us out into the unexpected and the cold.

I feel that if the legislators—the composers of our laws—become visionaries, they can lift our justice out of its humanistic foundation, wholly reengineer it to replant it a step higher up in the hierarchy of laws; then such women and men will go down in history as having enriched our destiny more than all the Nobel Prize winners did. They will have done more for our well-being and long-range health than our medical industry did.

Gradually, our lawmakers will embrace in their frame of judicial logic a society of ever-increasing species and generations. Drilling loopholes and peepholes will become as important for them as the fences. They will crack and make our laws less strict, add to the rights of the minorities, meadows giving us no fodder and apples but growing luminous bunches of mental delights, giving us the gold of all the blooming dandelions and buttercups. They will give the people seven generations from now a vote. They will find ways to grant a hillside peopled with spruce and with a raven-folk representation in our legal system as we now provide for our minors. These future heroes will push their concept of justice beyond our present limits to also accommodate life's obscure tunnelers that, deaf to our whining, pass under generations before they surface again with gifts and justifications in hand. Patiently, inclusively, these artists will compose their part in a Pastorale so wildly great that Beethoven's Sixth Symphony becomes a merry drop of dew settling in the dancing sea. Their courage of mind will infect future generations long after the fame of the civil rights leaders now talked about has calmed down. Fortunately life everywhere seems more amused than impressed with our present judicial impatience.

In this judicial revolution we will slowly make all these wonderful things around us come alive in our minds, take on family names, talk intelligently back to us, exchange advice with us. Millipedes will be seen and remembered. A venerable Sitka Spruce with his team from the Iris Flats—all specialists in solar energy—will become neighbors and eligible for a Nobel Prize. There are other civilizations before us who cultivated their relationships likewise to show us the way. This grand opening will become for minds sheltered in humanism the spittle behind the "open your eyes and see!"

Yet there lingers something even more promising. Such legislators could finally give a vote to our own undomesticated spiritual heritage that grows its stupendous creation in the depth of our memoryscape which we now so carelessly spray, bulldoze, whitewash, missionize, cash crop and straighten out. Advanced psychology could rediscover that man's psyche is not a Noah but a Noah's ark. I can think of no invitation more challenging to a lawmaker's mind.

If you are accused, I wish you the luck not to be judged by a person who is addicted to the intellectually so comfortable classic justice which we indoctrinate and celebrate with beautiful art and classic music. This obvious logic, perhaps a refined offspring of the old Hebrew law of retaliation, an eye for an eye, a dollar for a dollar, a green for two reds, is a logic in a rush that has to make good maybe in an hour's spectacle of sound, perhaps in one short lifetime of a good boy. It gives the logician in me his aesthetic satisfaction. Listening to beautiful music soon got me addicted to the few most obvious and easiest to understand justices, rhythms and rhymes. Less obvious things started for me to squeak that before didn't squeak. Plants without visible use turned into weeds, puzzling acts into crimes. My options for how to love life and to pardon became narrowed. This man-made justice of simple retaliation made me mentally a spoiled brat and a stranger in life's stupendous celebration where all species, all generations, saints and rascals alike, are invited for its rhymes.

83
Health in life's generous wheelings and dealings seems to have little to do with a one-generation fix.

Despite their brilliant instant effects, our health-assisting businesses seem, on the long-range, not to purge mankind from our weaknesses, our unhealthy genes, our addictions, our sickening thoughts, from the sickness of overpopulation, epidemics of cowardice and from becoming fat. They rather do the contrary. They help our susceptibilities and the cuckoo's eggs to stay, and multiply. They seem fast breeders of inherited weaknesses and they multiply their clientele. They give us the explosion of our world population. And they breed superbly one-legged people who ultimately must socialize more and more to stand erect and who are not allowed in the ring alone any more to fight the bull. I like to follow this naughty thought because I myself am so used to ask at the slightest inconvenience for a fix.

It seems to me the more we arrange a man's disorders from outside, the more we relieve him of his inbuilt testing system that would allow him to heal, in the course of his generations, his disorders and to sift for an ever more sensitive and autonomous health. Impatiently we try to switch off this system of evolution and innovation built into him that leads him through the cycles of birth and death purifying, alchemizing him into a higher quality of life. Is such a man's health not fast becoming a spoiled brat? A tender brat so used to getting a fix, who starts to farm out, one by one, his immunities and his defenses. Slowly, over generations he may lose his tools for self-maintenance—and his capacity for personal freedom and living by his own worth is dying with it. Take infectious diseases. Haven't they been our natural brush and forest fires for a long time? Commercial antibiotics have become our overzealous fire fighters. From the result we learn now the wisdom to sometimes better let those forest fires take their course.

On the level of personal thought, all this is lofty talk from the moon. Here the wonderful instant success of such healthcare is such a stunningly beautiful seductress, it needs more than common sense to question her rights.

Autonomous health and independent strength obviously can be a nuisance to an authoritative society. It has for long been a sore spot in such a public's mind for a woman and a man to be wild, to independently reproduce, to care and think with their bare minds for themselves. Sometimes I think our society is afraid that our children could become healthy, happy, and poetic. Are we afraid our supply of inventors and technologists might run out?

An infant raised on medical welfare will be a better hooked citizen and less of a rebel in a system to which it owes and on which it depends for its life. Hence there is that public support to preserve disadvantaged lives and to collectively save the immaturely born, the dependent, the needy, the orphan, the drop-out, the suicide, the soft to mold, the one-eyed, the coward, and a readiness to abort the healthy, the stout and the wild that may be in a position to rebel. Think of what tyrannical societies have done to unsubmissive people of autonomous strength.

The new science of nativity is more than a high class entertainment for the TV crowd. It is also eugenics, pollination management and a gate to a new society's womb. In a technological society that needs to breed a supply of people that never grow up, it is the young science for breeding custom-made citizens for that tamer world. And note what happens to the battery chicken when usefulness is bred.

May I also nose here into the subject of how we might get unexpected help when we blunder in our dabbling in healthcare. The procession of mankind's moral climates has rhymes that are visible to multigenerational minds. Maybe the "Joseph Theory" of seven years of feasts and seven years of famine and bust can also here be applied. Maybe our moral behavior oscillates self-regulatingly. It has its feasts of exaggerated mutual help, neighbor-watch, and nursing, of multiplying ourselves and giving generous loans to bankrupt lives—sending death into exile.

And then that miracle love swings to a bust and a highly personal justice, splendid meanness, a compulsion for competition, excellence in egotism, love for analysis, for self defenses and karate, a loss of soul, and a dispassion for children, a dead-end vision. Knowledge gets abusive and inventive, spinning closer around the ego-boosters and defenses, the contemporary and practical. Science aims at anti-insight drugs: a pill suppressing bad conscience and shame for being an egoist, a pill killing unhappy guardian spirits pestering us, a pill that inhibits the outbursts of a saddened soul, psychotropic drugs to induce social peace, so that we may become smooth playboys and workers. Many are allowed to get disoriented and to gently, playfully abort themselves in a lifetime of work and spending sprees.

84

I must have something of an elephant in me. The older I get the more I like to leave the herd to enjoy a more assorted company.

Way down I feel urged with a fervor of life or death to resist the epidemic spread of a convenient, flat unification just among us. Yet how difficult it turns out to be to rationally justify this dangerous appeal. My education proves a worthless advocate for that hunch in me.

I see exciting worlds—of jungle lands, rivers, winds and of our grandchildren, standing between you and me. I feel these worlds will turn out to be as fulfilling and enjoyable to me as the world of our production centers. To harshly trespass with my practical thoughts those worlds for shortcuts to my neighbors Betsy and Bill angers many voices in me. With every horizontal union so many thoughts that are seeds, so many rhymes, possibilities, feelings and floating bridges into the future and the past are lost. Many avenues to forgive become blocked. Ends and insights that are over three generations long are broken off. I also watch the merry Andalusian hills being nicely shaved and combed into neat lines of uniformed olive trees standing at attention in front of us as far as I can see, now that these lively hills have joined the common market of Europe. I wonder what bills the aftereffects of such a biological cleansing will send.

Power may become a cancer when we binge on that legendary forbidden fruit of unashamed international cooperation in all the raw physics in disregard to the law that decrees a feast of diversity and to moderate the arms race between our species and life at large by respecting for now a Non-Proliferation Treaty. Fatal power may develop from the knowledge explosion of the information freeway system—our latest hall of mirrors—where we break the incest taboo that forbids a species to inbreed their self-serving knowledge and cunning. This taboo decrees that communications must remain an undertaking between all generations and species, so we remain plugged into wisdom and may never become that self-defeating porcupine with a warhead in every quill, and with the ability to run like hell. This taboo also decrees that health care may never become a one-sided pursuit of knowledge relating to the well-being of an individual or our species alone.

Diving deep, I find that it is rather for my fear of the passionate, bare-footed nature in and around me that I am constantly tempted to meekly lay those other awesome worlds down and just huddle together with my contemporaries in one great harmonious insurance company. Yet I am told by the grasses, the mountains and all the trees that the Divine Mother just wants to blend us in, keeping plenty of room for many other guests on our ark in space, so that with our presence we may just dot its grandiose epic like the daisies in a hay-meadow celebrating spring. To remain vulnerable

132

to other species is one of the first laws of nature.

How farsighted it is to allow the daring few, without clenching our fists to menace them, to slowly wean themselves of humanism; to let those on the outskirt of the herd, per chance, penetrate our conspiracy of huddling-together to keep warm, not with another pile of blankets but with an infectious fire from within to disperse and diversify our compassion.

I think I am on the brink of discovering a togetherness that is kinder and complimentary to the one Darwin figured out. After most is done, fishing, raising children, rebelling, who knows? One might be allowed a dessert of a little wisdom and serenity.

85

I have learned that an earnest helping hand is often something quite different from the comforting so sacred to us.

The Muse is a noble helper. She is a lively and demanding Lady but she is certainly no registered nurse. That spunky little lady sneaks up on me and snatches my dear blindfold, my pain killers, the list of convenient answers I bought yesterday. When I peacefully nap in forgetfulness she mischievously flips on the lights in me. Longingly, sedulously she turns on her heels and with a "catch me if you can," off she runs into the jungle land. Such is that brave Lady's help.

To be good to me and tease alive what's asleep in me, you may have to let me hang on struggling by myself onto a branch when I am in danger of being swept away or stand out in the cold all on my own. You may do me a favor to refuse me your own personal answer to my question that I am chicken enough to take on and to mold my own personal response. Why should I hang onto you?

In spite or for your refusal to lightly intervene, I am about to see a wonderful reason for our mutual esteem. I have started to discover the enormous goodness you follow, when you cling to your own sap and roots and you give me the chance to do the same. I have started to trail you on the huge mysterious loop of your native pity and find that we may be after all brothers at heart with an urge to hold together a colorful integrity that is larger than man. I suspect it is from there that our seemingly cruel refusal to conveniently lock arms originates. Who knows? The native compassion written into the script of our genes might be the most farsighted compassion of all.

Tomorrow when you leave me alone standing in the cold, in a mess, in the wind, or to pay back a loan, I will remember when my dad watched me toddle my first steps, just by myself, long ago, while he just deliriously looked on, so proud of me.

Yesterday I went to the moon. From up there I noticed how God often sends me, to conjure up my great ghosts, a gift so large my moonlit reasoning can't see its end and I mistake that favor for an evil. I curse; I shake my fist toward the sender; and I send that gift still wrapped in its box right back, including my anger. Likewise, when in danger and warned by inner voices, I also get blinded with a terror of change. What temptation then to simply painkill that guardian angel without hearing what this messenger has to say. Up there another view was also puzzling me: It is the tree of our dearest virtues on which those sweetly bewitching fruits grow that later cause our most persistent sores, diseases of repetitive stress and degeneration, debts and bellyaches—a flirting tree loaded with narcotic misunderstandings that I became hooked on when still very young. From up there, I was surprised to see how many of us huddle in naive good-naturedness safely under the umbrella of malice of a formidable man. Have you ever observed how shoals of gentle little anchovies swim in the wake of the "mean" whale shark to protect themselves by that giant's looks? There are many friendly people who would have been sunk by their unselfish niceness long ago were it not for their partners or leaders who have meanness or greed enough for both and to spare.

I can now see that by your deeper nature you are not quite free to nicely converse, help, love neighborly and grow just flat to your sides, that the harsh acts and thoughts you are asked may be your highest generation-leaps, jumping many a fence into our unborn children's land about which petty virtues seldom care. I realize that so much more than convenient friends are to be taken in before you can close your arms and say: "This is me!" When I give to you, you have always to make good—but not necessarily with me. When you can break away from that old stagnant Hebrew law of retaliation: "an eye for an eye," you turn a light on in me.

I suspect that in a justice as big as the mysterious mind of God, every man is just and helping and more so when his acts are not paying as obviously as in a Bach aria or in a tennis match or in a deal with a bearded God. That every man gives ultimately again away all he takes is a fact so obvious it nearly remains unseen. When those faithful thoughts prevail in me, a man who does not nicely pay back, but passes on my help to him sometimes beyond my awareness horizon, sometimes to jump-rope with critters well beyond humanity's garden fence, he can remain a just and helping man to me.

Niceness are the cheapest rags I can put on for your reception—and you should be offended. When friends meet we talk radioactive gifts to each other and buds burst into leaves.

86
Of constipated souls.

Am I of the last generations in which we can shamelessly dance the familiar dance of man, woman and child?

Living with a warm woman and raising five children are sheltered and cozy chores I picked out of the grab bag of luck. This simple way of spending myself and of being needed is a comfortable routine sweet to my old, natural bent. When in the evening a man can stretch out by a stove and listen to his family munch, discuss, play and show off their day, this can be an easy, cheerful way he can grow his "fruits" and give them away. Yet slowly this simple law has also become visible: each time an eager society comes to the "rescue" of the family, that society takes another bite out of the family life.

As our technological society stands confused over the graves of families it accidentally killed, this familiar dance is about to end for more women and men. One invents new ways to spend or exercise and burn off one's love so not to end up with a constipated soul. There, no children buzz around to take off with the giveaways that a man and a woman become loaded with in their summer days. For many, no wind that is a good old friend is shaking their "apples" down. They may never share our "foolish" thrill when children rush enthusiastically in, take from us, steal us blind and off they run, yet play better music in us than all the "thank you's" of that day.

How to cool that fever to give when one is still loaded but harvest time is gone? One can sink from such an overload. One can indeed! It can be all-sweat-no-fun when I have to pick my own apples to treadle them away on some exercise machine. When I have to finally hurl my give-aways in the empty sky or pile them on top of my grave, I miss the fun to see somebody happily packing them away.

To find relief from such a belly full of love some plunge into a crusade to refine a me-generation into an us-generation, spreading peace, neighborhood-watch, equal rights, good manners and hospitals among us, helping each other to rewarding and healthy self-satisfactions.

Others are still in doubt. We need to take a break. We listen and look with all our antennas out and make good our parents' numbing excess in work. We sit on overlooking beaches and benches from Guatemala to the Rhine, with our love often idle in our laps, waiting, looking for guidance in the creator's show, and we resist offering our gifts to those who whine closest and shamelessly loud for help. We feel that we are asked for just this creative unemployment, so important it has become to let our thoughts catch up with this change of course in our love.

An instinctive modesty to produce and reproduce becomes slowly dominant among our children. We feel all asked to calm our devastatingly efficient hands that learned to provide so deadly well but seldom inquire with just a touch. To simply ride the surf, to dream, to trip out on a guitar, to walk about and listen and touch, to be materialistically trim and put a fat economy on a diet: our ever busy hands, our sexual zest, our brute rationality are for a while ordered into house arrest. More of us now enjoy the simple gentle high of loafing, dreaming, recklessly looking, following Alice into a Wonderland that hums with ripening thoughts, with greens and pollinating bumblebees, which for once we need not harm. We like to go into the bushes thought-picking with an empty mind. In no time our containers are filled. Free as a dream, maybe we can make good after all the years we trampled hurriedly over our inner voices to kill more. How promising to find that life tends to trigger us to want to make up for our parents' sins.

Who knows? Nature may now love more a dope and dream grower

who grows moments of forgiveness, gentleness, tranquillity, dreams and a wholly passive vision than it does a good fisherman who supplies endurance and even more energy for all those callused hands on the plows, the machetes, the fish finders, our guns. Why should she be more fond of us when we invent an even better trap to trap her in, or an even faster chain saw to cut down the planets lungs? It seems to me that anyone who creates inactivity in our furious labor camps is now welcomed as a friend by all that is deep and green in us and in love with the Earth. And I start wondering to what degree is the crime of a man on a hard or soft trip considered a desertion from a consumer society.

The golden chance to have more creative unemployment and four Sundays a week instead of constantly being whipped on by the furious heat of one's seeds and greed might be the greatest thing that lately is happening to our race. No, these clearings in our furious activities should not be hurriedly stuffed by creating extra jobs. Instead of such vandalism by our enforcers of sobriety we could create openings and places where the young can, like some temporary Buddhist monks, retreat for a year or two. Away from careers, away from learning by imprinting, away from competitive examinations, they could dedicate themselves to sabbatical sciences and become poets for part of their lives. To become beggars and all passive to life for awhile, to become spectators and get drunk by its beauty in which we have the luck to live—here is a gift of luxury that makes our planet dance. No hammers and scalpels, no sports, no begetting of children but becoming one huge ear. "Stop hassling that curious tramp! I see a person who does the one best thing for us right now."

To make good will not be as easy as to extend our rights to arrogance to the Third World and to share our bank accounts so more can buy chain saws, secure careers or build three more dams. This would not make the oceans our friends. I know now that no priest can forgive me for my excesses, no man, no human God, but the eelgrass can and the mollusks, the fishes and streams of air out there that suffer me. A gift of my energy, of my mind, my time, my fertility, only a human sacrifice to the Mama, goddess of fertility, may bring down upon me that motherly forgiving advice: "Go in peace and hence forth talk with the ocean when you fish, learn from the wisdom acted out by the peoples of grasses, of the trees and by all the many peoples of life, so you will not need to pilfer these peoples' knowledge and write their merits down on man's side, so that you will not mistakenly congratulate yourself for standing closer to God." Red poppies have a patent on the chemical inventions they have contributed to the saga of life. When I just break in to loot knowledge I lose a friend who might have gladly made me a gift even better than the loot, if I had kindly asked for it.

After just shouting orders for so long at these wise, timid lands, some of us have stopped our yelling. We spend some of our energy in walkabouts just listening, looking, remembering, maybe stamping our feet in awe and joy of what we see. Here our minds perverted by too much man recover their originality and strength. And a few might ferment into poets with the gift to translate the mysterious ideas of this land into therapeutic pictures our minds can readily see.

87

I wonder why a human life should have no price.

I was trained to create my models, my philosophy, my systems and my code of ethics as I have learned to conveniently let the firmament turn around the North Star. Yet I find now with dismay that these and all fixed points are just snails among cheetahs and not fixed points at all. When I elegantly build my ideas around a fixed assumption, around macho pride, around a patriarch who says he is the darling of God, around a Newtonian law, around the well-being of our generations alone: when I weave my dogmas around what one great thinker has said, I forget that I still orient myself by a big pebble that merrily rocks and rolls with all other pebbles to the beat of a surf.

Most of my thinking is still tied to a fixed point somewhere close by within mankind. With such a straight mind, how could I follow life's crooked ideas when it bypasses my whining and harvests some of us to support others of its creatures who may be more in a bind than mankind? Yet below my cultivated whining and revolt when disaster strikes among us, my deeper mind quietly ignores my presumptuous fix, draws in forgotten or exiled ideas and instead may show me a healing process. A wisp of thankfulness may then mischievously mingle with my grief.

Hatching my mind from humanism, experiencing the terror of being born again into an even more fantastic world is adventure I like. That adolescent mentality had nicely nested my tender mind in an immense wealth of scientific, aesthetic and mythological poetry held together with rhymes that kept me from falling into the deep unknown. Yet I hear now every barefooted creature practically on its knees, pleading with me: "Fly and see; remember me!" Our pro-life movements must be besought to become of such a generous scope that we can feel quite confident when some of our huge biomass is sacrificed for other life forms that are more endangered than us and desperately beg for status and a homestead among us.

What is called sacred human life, that stands with its mind and motives elegantly dressed up on a pedestal proclaiming, "We are the North Star and The Great Attractor, see, we stand erect, can make grimaces, are wearing shoes and hats" is a carcinogenic idea. After I step down from that grandiose crowd, my mind becomes a happy goldfish that found the ocean again. I step down into an electrifying environment that courts my mind with the same intoxicating attraction that draws a man to a woman and a woman to a man. In this larger mentality it's all right for me to die for a mighty ceiba tree and for the ceiba to die for me.

I am a fisher and a pilgrim here. I still tremble in the morning at the prospects of what big fish I can catch. I tremble in the afternoon with awe and joy visiting this land that is a billionaire in ideas. One tiny piece of space/time in this holy land may cradle an incomputable diversity. I open my eyes, my arms, my code of ethics. I drill holes into my assumptions, so wisdom of this land may leak in—and I start sharing again nature's wish that a human body remains as degradable as plastic wrappers and fish.

88

To me your one-man show is the best help you can send.

I wonder what the lure or fear was that brought the dreamers and flying mustangs down from the highland to stand in line for jobs.

When one delegates one's soul; when one becomes a midget who hires himself out for some narrow function in a society's digestive tract, isn't one soon menaced by repetitive thinking that quickly can make a mind sterile?

How much I now need your acts of personal courage to inspire me after the many revolutions in and around me have seldom bled for a man's right to be master of his own joys, blunders, sorrows and the glowing irons waiting to be forged in his soul. When you hatch from being someone's member and you stand up to give a show of your own ideas, feathers and colors, you add your own square to "The Great Quilt." You also infect me with your courage to keep your distance. And this is the best help you can send. To live with the least of memberships so to remain surrounded by the wildest profusion of options for my thinking: this is anxiety I have learned to enjoy. Is not each "I-belong-to" also a fence and corral for my eyes, my courage, my thinking?

When an inconspicuous inky cap breaks with its amazing inner violence right through the blacktopped sidewalk to mushroom proudly its own world, this brave little mushroom lives a lesson in courage for me. It reminds me of my own inner violence—meant, in spite of the slogans of all the -isms, to push a world of my own out.

I am in a hall of mirrors when with people, even with my dearest partners. I am surrounded by approximate copies of myself. With this tight focus, how could I become more than a man? Solitude widens my focus. It breaks my stare on the precious little pile on what we do, what we know, and what we talk about. Less biased advisers such as storms, beetles, and trees come into view. A more general, more poetic vision prevails. Solitude is good medicine for me. It also takes the stage fright out of my thoughts. It saves me from my bragging. It makes me trusting, modest, sharp and a little more free.

89

More details for the case against a United States of Mankind.

We belong to a species of parasites that, thanks to its many different strains, which showed great courage for apartheid, has elegantly wriggled through disasters and pest controls. I am glad that in my native joys, fears and window-views I am wonderfully unequal to you. Your different clearings in your sky, your balcony from which you see another side of the moon than I, make me all impatient to visit you. This diversity in peepholes and blind spots seems a great gift to me. When my mind gets swept away by a mass hysteria that endlessly, naively chants for unity and makes me fight for equal rain, equal sun and genes, equal patches of blue in the sky for all; and when it demands the right to level this excitingly unjust and creative place, that mind should be scolded for vandalism and sent off for ten days into a wise old forest for a corrective seminar about living with the diversity of a thousand minorities.

How to exorcise the mass superstition that simply uniting among ourselves is the magic fix-it-all? This planet knows a man for every occasion; one for the plains; an acrobat for higher seasons, a sucker who needs to drink barrels of rain, a man who thrives merrily among cacti and sand, a woman whose happy day is filled with flowers all around, a short man who storms by in one short blazing summertime, a tall perennial man who lingers around a long while and another who thrives only on a season in danger and hell.

We move along a wide front in youthful times. With so many unequal hands, viewpoints and original minds, we are equipped with a great lifestyle pool to fight epidemics, catastrophes, boredom and to take on cataclysmic diversions from our love when needed. We know how to cook a fish a thousand different ways. We know how to enjoy sleep in a master bedroom or in hay. From our high-yield tree farms with trees of equal kind, genes, and trim, we learn how deadly numerous and how vulnerable we could also become should we decide everyone ought to share one kind of credo, ethics and rights, having the same recipe for loving and one size of overalls fitting all.

Yet no worry, Mother Grace seems to keep her own balance of withheld knowledge so that none of her troops gets too fat or runs too far ahead and out of sight. When a spot gets too crowded or too hot, she delegates a cloud or turns a hormone around. After we feasted for seven generations on raw knowledge, raking in the calories, the smartness, the kilowatts, just to ever more blow ourselves up as a scared puffer fish would do, and after we developed an appetite for short term gains, forgetting all about wisdom—oh!—that beautiful success turns discreetly into a pest! And as a remedy mother nature decrees seven generations of lame erections and schools, of oil shortage, laziness, of flat ambitions, antibiotics and tires, of exiters, welfarers, hermits, playboys, surfers, druggies and dreamers so some may ferment into mountaineers and poets who can give our flat souls a high vista again.

90
Should we be proud to be the best ghost-busters?

Backtracking historically all our bizarre efforts to see from above and over the fences beyond downtrodden trails, I thought of that lone marmot that also climbs on a boulder to higher ground to watch into afar and to stand guard for its marmot-town. I remembered ancient tribes that surrounded their territories with nests on poles to get high enough to see the horizon beyond their fifteen furrows of maize, beyond their own quarrels, their cattle fences and garbage piles. Up there, they saw their friends and enemies going and coming without warpaint on. Up there they also marveled at their enemy's fantastic ears of corn. Up there, they were a little more relaxed and their enemies seemed less menacing.

I like to add these old ceremonies to our own raisings of the inner eye which we celebrate in such a profusion of ways that, bewildered, we fight with each other over which is the best elevator for the mind. I like to add these recipes for highs to the book for the gentle and not-so-gentle knockouts of the rational Theo inside me, in case this zealous bodyguard becomes tyrannical and endlessly plugs my lines with local calls, fighting hordes of hurried fellowmen who step too often on my toes. I sometimes like to free my mind to fly at high altitudes. I like to shuttle between the levels of intelligence, shuttle from the logic of an ant to the wisdom of a people of ants, leaving behind the world of words, the social securities, the quarrels between pity and hate, between virtues and vice, the thick, yellow cloud of slogans. Each may use his personal boosters, his potent brews of words, sounds, chemicals, exercises, explosives and songs. And how awkward in these takeoffs one can be! Or are those enchanting viewpoints the privilege of times when religion is less a welfare nurse and more the great art of getting high and sitting on those lookout posts?

Now that Edison has taken away from us our most simple soul-catcher, the cool and healing solitude that settles on us with the darkness at night; now that one is bogged down with worshipping the economic wheel, high-flying thoughts, friendship-drugs, kites for the eyes and sciences for levitating our minds are needed. Wretched soberness has been so long my pride. Wretched celebrations where we applaud an even sharper plow, toast to each further mind touching down to help level the ground and where we cheer each other for every inch we add to the waist of our GNP. And tell me, is there a healthier high than to simply look danger steadily in the eye?

A peephole, please, for us who endlessly circulate in the guts of our businesses with our minds safely tucked into a condom of rationality and barely a window in our subway tunnels shooting by. I realize now that from kelp fields to beyond our skies I am surrounded by my living memory where the rational gray of my brain is just one colony of cells and mainly the mental powertool of my ego. Is it not for this reason that in sacred ceremonies or in desperate quickies, one lures one's attention away from constantly staring at that familiar spot that is the personal or mankind's bag of memories and so finds relief of being so terribly conscious of the ego? There are so many great ghosts calling long distance on which our inspirations could draw yet they are held at bay by local busy tones.

When a people evolves into a worker's society, the Sundays, the Sabbaths and many kinds of carnivals become their wild mind's refuge. In these times, all practicalities are banned. In these feasts, our spirits can vibrate with unabashed dialogues with faraway friends, perhaps even directly with the gods and purge themselves. Would it be for this old die-hard need that a busy man banging, sickling, hammering, data-crunching seven days a week may still need to sneak out sometimes and buy some kind of crack that stops for a treat his working mind and gives him a quick, instant Sunday respite?

It will be my mind's Mt. Everest to make for me of science, religion and art, a trinity in which none wants to boot the other down to bag a first. The good outcome becomes more difficult when a talent is present in me that charms me to make of it a child prodigy demanding fame.

91

Only halfheartedly I can cuss and snort, now that I
have gotten a hunch that all acts may be children of
God.

When I think of criminals, rare and fascinating critters, ugly ducklings,
fairy-tale toads, thorny shrubs, the poisonous Pacific yew trees, wild-fires
and meteors start to become synonymous with such unusual women and
men. Bare of any obvious values that seem profitable to geometric
thought, I cannot yet figure out how such outsiders fit into the puzzle of
life's ebbs and floods. No doubt life uses some of us for ventures we simply do not know. "Down with them!" we nonetheless may impatiently
say. "Give no title to a sunny place for such useless loafers to grow their
sour fruits." Our persecution and our orchestrated hate can fast make a
ruin out of such tramps. Is it not such psychological pesticides we use
against them? How we can needle such extraordinary people. Any tenderness that could make them breathe and smile should be stifled. How the
sun is blackened for them. Their minds may panic. Such ill-cursers may
corner these visitors from other worlds into loneliness so cruelly cold, it
shutters their soul. Yet slowly we start to wonder about the side effects of
our psychological herbicides we use to control the weeds flowering in our
collective soul. Slowly we start to worry that in our soul gardens the swallows and the insect-folks are disappearing. Alarmed, we also note that
organisms persecuted for their undesirable traits tend to gradually
harden. After the revenge effect bacteria add to their immune system more
guns and build up their own defensive toxins. Look how our glorious
antibiotics now fare—and look how strong the early Christians got from
persecution.

However such unpractical women and men seem of quite ordinary
origin and akin to the wild cereals that grow and hide between the rows of
our sorghum fields, akin to voracious caterpillars, the butterflies and all of
God's highly paid clowns to cheer up our monocultures in which we produce our boredom and exclusively our food. They might be sisters to that
arch-rascal the mosquito, the bat, the merry chickadee, the rays of an
evening sun that countless years have been dancing together here in the

Arctic's glorious rites of spring. They are from a vanishing tribe that has often astonished us with their rare ideas, qualities, their headlines in the news, their unexpected symbiosis and unappreciated experiments.

Yet these ordinary "weeds" have little to do with the rare mystical people who are lightning bolts and supernovas in our sky; the prophetic saints gifted with the power to wake up in a dreaming desert of ashes green fireworks of lust, joys, and tears; or the mighty undertakers, blessed with an equally formidable plow to bury these fireworks under and ready them again for another season—daimonic men and women of cataclysmic strength who are born as far apart as eclipses in our firmament and who become nearly extinct in our time.

Nonetheless, might we not help create the criminal's horror story ourselves? How readily we capitulate in our intellectual search and go for elegance and comfort in thought in order to quickly rest in a conclusion. How readily we give up any puzzling act to the horrors of crimes, pests, garbage and hells and put those presumed wrongdoers out of sight. The poet in us suffocates in the enormous waste we produce in our minds and we are running out of prisons and of other disposal sites for such hazardous wastes. How convenient to call all those powers which do not submit to our personality cult or our five year plans the evil powers. Yet look how depressive for our psychic growth such convenient mental DDTs have become.

As one may now see, the western religions have turned out to be quite wasteful religions not only for our fellow life but also for our merry souls. There is much refuse created in our courage, in our longings, acts, thoughts, diversity, options and our means of transportation into higher spheres. How many options to forgive we have lost. Billions of turbulent souls—explorers beyond our credos—have for our peace of mind simply been damned. Many treasures can be found in the dump sites that are the hells, sins, demons, vices, witches and crimes. With a long-range economy in mind, many gems of wisdom can also be mined there. Some of my guilt feelings are land mines cautiously buried into my mind when very young. They are triggered to automatically explode into a curse, shouting endlessly: You are damned!, as soon as I sidestep the patriarch's rules. And look at a zombie for what a curse can do. To not feel guilty I need the courage to grow up so to stand mentally on my own.

145

I look at this wonderful land behind the fence and it fills me with optimism for the future. Didn't it handle problems that tame our doomsday wailing to mere bites of fleas? It survived a hundred doomsdays, ice ages, enormous pollutions of oxygen, great floods, shifts of the magnetic field and continents, population explosions, the mutagenic powers of radiation and plagues, the impact of meteors. More encouragingly, it's on such cataclysmic helpers the evolution of this wonderful Earth seems to thrive. Thanks, over and over, to that ladle that stirred and stirred the "Nothing"—till that "Nothing" exploded into a firework of stars. Thanks, one more time, to that ladle, that stirred some more till that premordial soup started a dream to become more than a soup. Why wail and beg the creator to stop his story, to stop his ladle from stirring what is cooking?

I look at this wonderful land—this stupendous success story so much of it seemingly "useless," even "brutal," so many of nature's stories are "crime" stories yet are wonderful tales to me and I have to remind myself over and over: "Theo, never give up, walk twenty times around a crime or garbage-act, around any waste, cast away, perversion or sin if needed to find in it its hidden use and rhyme." Have faith that there is something worthwhile about it, even though all the evidence of the senses is to the contrary. Maybe all things that have happened to me are qualities of God. Name anything nasty or sweet, murky or clear—my hunch: each is the right answer to a riddle—and some are riddles only for grownups to solve. More of us now ruminate in a more organic way of thought, so that our lawbooks may not become as deadly to our mental fauna as DDT has been to our countryside, so that our safety measures may not become a clue so sticky it immobilizes us.

It seems not so much our comfortably holding hands, or our agreement not to offend but to be logical and act polite, that created our keen sight, but rather our dear hunger, our dear opponents the mosquitoes, the dangers and the meteors, our jealousy and envy, our monkey-businesses, and our enormous capacity to survive as unequals that created our sight. There was no known logic for the mud to start wriggling and to form eyes. Creative openings of disorder and free time in an omnipresent order, a chance to be a saint or sinner and mixtures of stability and chaos are dispensed by our dear devils among our souls' routines. This free time in an universal non-linear harmony seems life's most creative achievement to

146

me. And so, for a special treat, life whirls my ego round and round and drives it to the edge of madness with its logic shattered to pieces. On this hot edge, new information is continuously cooked for life's feast. It might well be our prodigious capacity to dare, blunder, move out of step, clown, lose our pants and sin that cobblestones the road to our profusion of inventions and to our platforms in space.

Yet it is perhaps not from the above capacities to be spectacularly strong and bold that our most heart-filling moments arise, but from our being strong enough to be soft and able to be the greatest givers and losers, without going bankrupt. The holy spirit might well be disinterested in my aspirations to be personally strong, perfect and whole. She, the mother of evolution, seems fond of sending corruption to break perfection's deadly marriage; to break a strong-box stuffed with a stuffy goodness and integrity. Her evolutionary mischief seems to thrive better in the soft, unstable ooze of imperfection, amorality, leaks and corruption than in a state of individual equilibrium. She seems fond of her temptress—the goddess of the blunders, mutagens, doubters and sinners, of the inventors, perverts, tunnelers and astronauts, the diva of aberrations. And thanks to evolution, that blessed healings process of all these little crazinesses, mess-ups and mutations life daily forks into its harmonies, nobody needs to wake up in the morning yawning: "Do we have to do this again?"

This world becomes to me a musical instrument with more strings than I thought; many sounding too loud, too aggressive, too dark and base when played near my ear. Yet when I climbed a distant tree yesterday, I heard some fall in step with Theo and with you.

92
More from my fascination with garbage dumps.

When your mentality was so far off mine that it confused me beyond tolerating, I probably did as does a frightened skunk; I drove you off with hate. I found this formidable mental repellent can protect me from chaos and unbearable provocations and mental pain. My refined mind could not digest what it heard from you and I vomited it as I do food that is too rich or crude. Is this uncontrollable and messy outburst of mental indigestion what we call hate? Is it for such helplessness that a highbred mind, erring into the overwhelming plenty of the wild, gets indigestion or starves— dreaming about thoughts that are killed, cleaned, selected, whitewashed, boiled and ABCed?

These thousand "I-hate-this-I-hate-thats," are they the symptoms of partial blindness we seem all to some degree afflicted by? The task: to put lamps in those blind spots of which only the most serene seem to have escaped.

What do I know? Maybe also hate is turned behind my back into just another shovel that is put to good use, a blind shovel with an overdrive, a shovel with enough furious obsessions and sweat to build in defense of the frightened shoveler the deepest ditches and the highest mountain walls. There may be no faster shovel among God's tools that can take as much pain and strain. Up on top of hate's wall, others might be freed of the blindfold and invited to look around and down into a land they have never seen and to rub their hands, pleased. Up there one wonders whether one should not thank that blind hardworking man with his shovel whirling furiously up and down.

Up there one might also let go of all handrails of prejudgments and for an instant recklessly wonder if the State of Israel would now exist if there hadn't been that terribly hateful madman of magic Germany? Think of the worldwide change of tide in feelings about this people that madman finally caused, after many Europeans, who have feared this people for whatever reason, decided finally "enough is enough" and sided with it. Such subtle connections seem altogether invisible from the flatland's scenic views. I fear while I prudently stay on my island of local goodness and do not break out from the spell of such a sheltered mentality, I will never find out.

Would it shock you if your friend could compose a song so puz-zlingly profound, that it could even light up the estranged love that drives a rapist's heart, after our frost and dispassion for that desperate man in flames may have given his act its horrible sting? I suspect we are here to compose this song. Yet it could well be that the mischievous answer can-not be taught. Each might have to find out by himself where that desperate malice, seemingly beyond ever being socially acceptable, is coming from.

The anguish of discovering could be so great that it might only be bearable to those who, in a rite of passage to a reality of larger scale had stripped their mind of all its ornaments and looked for this hissing firestone with all their passionate strength. Yet who knows? In this other Pandora's box, dedicated to faith in goodness for all, an unsuspected key to forgiveness might be found.

93

Some amaze me with their compassionate strength. They generously advertise their vices with bells as some lepers did in medieval times.

You can trust that when you hear my defensive outbursts proving to you how good or right I am, you have hit my sore spot. I have learned from advertising laureates. They recommend selling tobacco and tar-in-the-lungs with the smile of a beaming youth wandering in the limpid air of a pine grove basking in a summer noon. When I am depressed and vulnerable milling in the pits, I am counseled to puff up as blowfishes do and shout bliss.

He told me of the great faraway places I am invited to; he showed me an upsetting new answer that my intimate mind for a long, long time has urged me to accept, yet my prudence was so terrorized, it scared the hell out of me to change my course. It is for this I had to snort at him twice as hard. I had to out shout him; I had also to out shout my disappointed soul who still urges me to leave the warmth of old credos to go for that further goal! That attack from the front and the rear made Miss Prudence in me fume.

In my business of making a living, I am barely removed from the world of the spiders. I mostly sit in my web. I am glittering with motivated goodness. I am glittering with attractively baited hooks. There, my communications with you are strictly dazzling advertisements and cover-ups. In this trade one learns to steal freedom and how to sneak a lifelike dummy into a deceived mind. One learns from the cuckoo how to plant one's eggs.

After all, what innocent generosity is there that would need advertising? What compassionate man would need to shout his noble soul into a TV crowd? What benevolent moral is there to be hammered into the wise old soul?

When I shut Theo up and allow that wise old soul a spell of solitude, she quietly starts to cook and bubble up into my mind medicine for all my imagined and not imagined kinds of colds.

94

Our shy mental capacity to fly into a high, to look down on the forests, the oceans, on our families and towns, on their pattern and currents and on the ripple Theo produces in them, is to me a gift that is infinitely kinder to life and never to be confounded with our ever offensive inventiveness. That gift can transmute me into an ecstatic spectator. I hold my breath for fear of missing a trick, circling higher, lifted by my admiration, by my joy of all I can see, and I warm with confidence.

When I am down with wings or legs broken and heaven is closed, a crisis-alert fires up that corner of my mind that can invent for me a pair of stilts. When my corn is miserably thirsty, the logician in me wants to become a little Hitler and does not let me rest to sleep and defecate in calm anymore. All in me is mobilized to invent that deeper well that can secretly drain the water under my neighbor's fields.

Often, a crisis that rains iron, hate, fear and adrenaline is needed to switch on a people's inventiveness. This overload of stimulation can erase all inhibitions and shame. Our patent-system also reassures us: we will protect your inventions for your greed—go for it!

When a nation that lost its trust in life asks for my admiration for their Great Commercial Hunt to swiftly round up the Earth, they ask much. Then I know, this Earth can serve me better than to become simply a giant udder to fatten us. To be a spectator and fill the belly of my soul is the better half of my joys.

Also my dark inner states of war with you or her are amazing spells of inventiveness. In this blackout, I synthesize an arsenal of high-tech thoughts often as impenetrable and deadly as tanks, often exclusively built for getting you out of my way.

Ultimately it seems not to be the happy, the seer, the wise, the serene who are the inventors and technologists. Who on a blue transparent day, when one sees the mountain of unclaimed gifts begging to be opened and seen, would want to hammer, scheme, compute, dig irrigation ditches through paradise by the sweat of his brow and rebel? So when life goes on a warpath of inventiveness, it ties a scarf over my eyes and cuts my vision in half. With egotism, its Creator fractures my vision. Soon I see only one generation far. Soon I see only a world full with broken off and bleeding ends that is an imperfect and messy sight. I goof. I start to cause friction and to make enemies. I wander into mosquito swarms and twisted thoughts that only open up generations away. I stumble into dark underground cities with my vision too short to turn on the lights. That darn blindness infuriates me into trying any new trick to come quickly out of this mess. Miserable, I bite into anything showing the slightest hope for a fast ticket home. I roll up my sleeves to give the Creator a lesson. I start to revolt, to experiment, to invent, to mutate, and to make that broken world a better place for the blind. How much I dream in that blackout to stand in the spotlight of fame. Is it with this illusion the Creator blindfolds me so I become a willing helper to make his dream come true?

It seems it is the prisoners, those buried in wealth or a slide, or those who have lost their courage, or a leg, maybe their North star or their faith, who are best predisposed to figure out models and gismos to create that "better world" that is custom-made for a short vision just one generation tall. In the absence of the spiritual, technology can unhindered step on the gas. So, if you wish me bad luck, wish me to live in an inventive time.

How well our species fits now these chores. Our prodigious capacity to get entangled in curled thoughts, make grimaces, get mad, sin, step in gopher holes, forget our children at home, be clowns who never know how much is enough or never fit into their pants may well turn out to be our gusher of inventions, surprises, mutations, new tidings. And who, after all, does not dream to run away from Miss Perfection, that good old maid?

Yet the progress that purrs in me best seems completely unfamous, uninventive and laissez-faire. It tiptoes the opposite way of the inventors, the fireworks of the celebrities, the twenty-four-hour news and fatter ears of corn. It simply transmutes my anger with God into applause while missionaries, world improvers, engineers, Theo "the hero," and other angry people, all seriously at work, are passing me, hurrying the opposite way. To let myself be turned on, to let myself be filled with metaphors and thoughts which draw no blood but simply make me dance, may bring out the only acts in me so inactive that the whole creation can throw its hats and tails up in applause. To remain an apprentice in the architecture of beautiful and lasting relationships is a career I like.

Through my blindfold I feel a faith warming me that ultimately all the pursuit of knowledge will maybe mischievously but irreversibly lead toward a deeper esteem for the community of all life; sciences inspired by war or by the wonderment of Mother Peace, the sciences that are baited with the sweet joys of revenge, fame, or hefty bank accounts; science for pay that might come close to being a spy, the big, corporate science that mutilates the intellect of its researchers with monocultures to fit its collaborative research will all lead to this end.

The pursuit of knowledge cannot be held back. It is the critter who knows more and loves better who will survive. The highest prize may go to those sciences that never lift a finger but simply explore and acquaint us with how well we are taken care of. Here, we, the actors, are off for a Sunday and invited to get high on the beauty we see and scoot a little closer to that legendary ecstasy.

Ah! With just a glimpse on how incredibly good this world already is, which of us apprentices would get up and meddle with it?

95
I wonder why I hesitate when the advantages are so obvious and bright.

I am nagged by a gut feeling of doubt that mingles with my enthusiasm when I proudly board our miracle, the 747 plane, and hand over all my controls. I am an old-fashioned, all-purpose man, unfit to break a record of any kind. I am an unspectacular centipede who never tried hard to develop one of his legs much bigger than the rest of his legs. I still jerk a little when a nail is driven through our families to make that fantastic 747 bird go up and fly. I realize that our profuse and loose world of emotions—discreetly compassionate with every living thing, is the biggest hindrance to fast technological success. To make and fly that fantastic bird needs from us the discipline of a Prussian army. Yet the guidelines from my intuition prefer the flight course of butterflies. I doubt that a people made of warm, strong families could ever hatch a 747 bird and make it fly.

The success of a country's economy seems to depend on how fast its society can break down its members into their components and how shamelessly these women and men can let their talents and commodities be strip-mined. And the more naked people are on the beach, the more pressing it also becomes for those who remain shameful to strip and overcome their shame. However life seems to ultimately favor inter-species cooperation; it watches our local success like it watches a lost son.

Did you ever wonder why the birds didn't invent airplanes but went for wings? Technological inventions are seldom self-improvements. They are invented, fabricated and operated by cutting us in two or three, many to end up as a caste of eternal mirrors to labor obediently in some dark bowels. Our minds are felled like we fell trees—and they are cut off from serving an individual's autonomy. Exquisite parts are tricked into working on life's scientific projects that may have ultimately nothing to do with man's survival or well-being. It is in a favorable impact statement on the autonomy of the individual that many of our inventions fail.

When I am tyrannized by some talent and I start to tilt that way and to limp, I become a sweet, oozing mango attracting every employment agent who offers to buy me out for exploiting that talent. "Come in, become an actor, act out with us the new society our master composed!" I am offered reinforcement from billions, generous welfare, even fame. I am guaranteed a comfortable niche in the society of technologists if I join and allow that talented part of my mind to be mined and the product sold.

I wonder whether a new caste of high priests may be forming—a team close to the dream of magic Germany's "Herren-caste"—where heads were cultivated separately from the bowels, and the "saints" were cut loose from "crimes" and relieved of pulling nails; an elite with a superbly cultured rationality that presides and lordly strides through our

inner gardens to freely choose and pick their tools. They may choose themselves as a caste of holy master bakers to knead and thump that dough of
human minds, blood and loves strictly according to the credo of their
Church of Reason.

When I muse this far, I get a little cautious with my hurrahs, when I
step aboard those miraculous 747 flights.

96

After Faust feasted on the extraordinary powers
derived from loans which he charmed from generations after him, did these debts turn into a millstone
dangling on his neck?

I am confused. On one side: The promising invitation to join the powerful brotherhood of all my contemporary Fausts—with its price: my vow
to chastity for my intellect. Unprecedented success, exemption from nature's space-time traffic laws, hair-raising speed, a conveniently simple
geometry of the circle and the straight line, miracle-rice fields, the magic of plant breeding and raping, impossible progress, ambulances everywhere—all this becomes possible in that pure and seedless plot we
cultivate in our "dirty" minds. By its deeper nature, that unclean and
fertile mind tends to be endlessly motherly, endlessly pregnant, endlessly foresighted and hindsighted, ever so fond of seeds and weeds and always late and worried about some child to come or left behind. Ah, to
take leave of God's all-forgiving, all-patient, unnervingly permissive
unison and to make a slick separate pact on a fast track, a kind of Teamster's Union for a couple of generations of man, and to transcribe one's
soul to the magic of its chaste science, what fantastic power over all the
creation can, for that nick of time, be had with this trick! All life will
tremble with respect when we contract into this cataclysmic melt-down
of our fusing intellects.

On the other side: that rather shady and seedy community scattered through the endless generations peopling Eden's gardens whose
untold members are mostly invisible, and rarely listed in telephone

books. Here the initiates often seem to live ten miles, ten thoughts, ten generations or sets of genes from their kin. Here symbiosis is seldom seen in pairs but comes in triangles, octagons, and heaven knows with how many runners crisscrossing in life's relay run. Here are legions of good neighbors across the fences of species and of times, who all delight to love, chisel on each other, make gifts and build new bridges and rhymes. It needs more than an understanding mind; it needs a soul to compose an impact statement when so many different neighbors like to be questioned for their needs and how a new need can be fitted in. Here are unusual flowers with their twelve petals made of twelve blue springs that we mostly see only in dreams. Here in Mysteryland, we are unnervingly patient. We might be asked to clap only with one hand; yet your hand and a hand clapping ten generations ahead might meet and make in our souls a sweeter, fuller clapping sound. Deer grow very long—sometimes fifty generations long. Trees are engineered to last a billion years—and make my impatient logic often despair.

Between hauling line and landing fish and depending on a thousand experts to keep me afloat, I look from my boat sometimes up the foaming coastal cliffs—and I congratulate a soaring bald eagle for being such a great and self-made flyer. I hail him for his independent sight when he spots one of my throw-away fish from a mile away. All this that great bird has over generations patiently invented without signing over his soul to some sorcerer's society that draws a magic circle around a generation or a species to declare: Let us work and care inside this circle. Let us forget our elusive side-effects on the outsiders. And we will be free to become for an instant the fastest miracle machine the Earth has seen. Much of our progress makes wonderful sense while confined to such a circle.

Instinctively I am skeptical of fast miracles that seem made possible by a pact to throw down that mysterious dimension in our souls which keeps us from shortcuts and from growing fat and flat or from thinking in straight lines and circles. Shame spoils my appetite to bite into Eve's apple; to enslave one another and just together with my contemporaries to ram shortcuts through this forbidden door with the six billion minds and shoulders welded together into one single sledge hammer; to storm the heavens, and to trample down the eagle, the fishes and the daisy who, helping each other, are also on the way to that legendary upper room.

155

97

Only a huge emotional rearrangement can pull me out
of my addiction to think conveniently in sweet
humanistic rhymes.

I am still a refugee loaded with much baggage trying to hold out with others in the uppermost floor of the humanistic edifice made of man-centered thoughts. I am still one of those fabled camels too big and rich with convenient assumptions to squeeze through the needle's eye, yet I see our whole space needle up in flames and under siege from our own mental success. To intellectually mature, I realize, I have to pull myself out of this feathernest and make friends with many unaccustomed thoughts that seem now hostile to us. I am to beach-head on a larger reality with the mythology of Man-the-chosen-people left behind. That chick-in-the-egg mentality has to give and my mind to be stripped of many protective ideas in which we have cautiously wrapped and decorated it. Swift in its new "string-outfit" it may yet slip into an enormously infectious and fecund mental world. After all, even the beetles and the jellyfishes have experienced winter frosts, ice ages, shifts in continents and in commandments, the addition of visions shattering their event horizon, and they learned to thrive on such provocative gifts.

Ours looks like a time when our spiritual evolution makes another beach-head, deeper into the new savage element of awareness. Surprise, surprise, studying the psyche of the living earth as a whole proves so much more rewarding than singling out the ego of a species or of a woman or a man.

See, I lay a comforting arm around the shoulder of Theo. He seems always so afraid of what he may be asked next.

98

More thoughts about a limit for flat
socialization.

When the many wisps and puffs of wind chase each other through the woods, clearing out and clearing in, making the cedars, the aspen, the blueberry bushes sway and hum and rest and again sing, it makes me wonder: do we do well to channel all our own wisps, lulls and puffs into one single terrible blow, uniting and focusing six billion freewheeling minds to march, chant and storm behind one single flag that leads us into the Great United Hunt to round up the Earth?

When we pierce that membrane between you, her and me, when each of us pulls down the pants of his mind and exposes his secrets without the slightest shame, when we snowball our strength into a six-billion-legged dinosaur, a shameless Internet looming from here to Japan, what hummingbird, what lily pond, what outsider could escape our control? We could become one giant corporation of technologists, so fat, sassy and flat, that it squelches the biome of the Earth, wherever it eats, chants, rests or breaks wind. Who dreams of a time when all women and men, the winds, our arts, the laughing waters, the nightingales will all sing our kind of International Hymn in one united awesome refrain? Prayers for this kind of unity often sound to me like swearing, "God damn me." The lasting success story of the ants may well lie in their maintaining diversity in some 20,000 different species and so remaining small, agile and versatile. Who knows, that unfashionable god who dispersed the mighty labor union on that glorious tower of Babel by differentiating their tongues might have been a wise God after all.

No, it is not our individual egotism not yet unionized that still stand stubbornly between a man and united mankind on Earth. It seems rather our inborn, stubborn tenderness toward all life beyond our neighbors and fellowmen—our unseen need for it and our unconscious devotion to it— that is engraved way down in our archetypes. Yet our hyperrationality might have no eye for such far-reaching love, calls it naively brute and puts it down. It seems to be our sexy multi-generational mind from which barefooted thought has not yet been swept out and steadily obeys morals that are of a society greater than man, that still revolts against any conspiracy to band together just by ourselves and inbreed our minds. The notion that a man deep below the graft of civilization is an egoist is one of the most enduring superstitions. Compassion is a law of nature as is crystallization.

The ticket needed to enter our anthropocentrists' club seems ultimately always to be a form of intellectual chastity. And so, in a civilization of love-your-neighbor, I wish you the luck to be a close neighbor. For if you live ten generations deep in the belly of a woman and man, you might very well be out of favors.

How ignorant and high-nosed one can become about our deeper and humanistically speaking, rather "asocial" character traits that have guaranteed us for so long an orderly relationship with all the world's life. I suspect that Freud entered only into the antechamber of our hidden memory vaults. Our deepest psychology that often is defamed, can only be understood with gusto when a mineral, a tree, a pond, a mosquito, a tsetse fly have remained members in the society we have for three billions years been building in our minds. They are the spirit of all my ancestors combined. Our visionary scientists now make us realize that our deeper psyche is rather green and that this shady, loose and witty wilderness is our wife. I wish the Western mind this breakthrough in relationships.

What a sweet surprise it is that advanced physics also show us now so well how we are ultimately closer to a higher truth when we are not thinkers but part of a thought, when we are not perfect solo players but instruments on which life plays its music for our souls. This idea seems related to the "Stop the thinking!" of the impeccable warrior.

We seem invited to an even more poetic life than the one I assumed.

99

Just teach me to think one compassionate thought a day and you will put all my other friends in the shade.

When I can remain uncertain and curious long enough, holding my verdict back, I often find a hidden good in the sting which the thistle drives in. I can also keep on reading a diary full of stupendous thoughts which that adventurous weed has been writing down for me. I can see and respect in a dung beetle an international enterprise that for the last two billion years has been paying its debts avoiding bankruptcy. Could you help me decipher the happy message in the roar of a flood? I am a man who has been blinded into docility. Could you be my strong friend and revive my clairvoyant eyes that can run so fast, they outrun any bad man and see him from ten generations ahead catching a glimpse of a spicy affection in him?

Would you see me on the fast track of progress if I cold polish his dark meanness and make it bright, like scientists lately have polished the image of the viruses, showing us how behind their malicious face they are mainly good-natured ferrymen ferrying genes between the different species, helping them to evolve? Will you remind me at the tree festival to also celebrate the trees' roots that suck and loot?

I like to become kinder with my own malice and to keep it as my muse and not to impatiently throw this devil's advocate out. Maybe its outbursts simply remind me to do my share of pulling nails. Maybe by making peace with one's own shady bursts of temper one comes to accept also the others' rugged beauty, smiles, rages, pimples, avarice, peacock-feathers and all. Taking it kindly in, a meanness might thaw. Its sting might even turn into a spice later on.

Making peace, to me, has little to do with stopping the yelling or the gunshots. It is rather the lifelong, personal undertaking to slowly silence my anger, my hate, my criticism—to make peace with the crimes, pests, forest fires, sicknesses, stranglers, parasites, sins, sundry Hitlers and with death. Name anything else you cannot stand. I have a hunch that all the rascals, children drowned in ponds, gays, gamblers, horseflies, tyrants, executioners, saints, weirdoes, the master and the seduced maid—name any critter docile or wild—are all dear to the Mother-of-All and provided for well. And the implications: Christianity and its competitors become part of that beautiful wilderness—the jungle out there and the jungle within our economy, our towns, our hearts, those who abort and those who fight this new need—all seem to abide by the same law and its hierarchy. It is for this hunch that I like to make peace also with the wildness that still survives within me.

And for a catalyst: Goodwill to all that seems good. Goodwill to all that seems bad.

100

I suspect that only a course in generosity, which makes many of you chuckle with amusement, can restore in me that shameless sight of a child.

One should never abolish the reform schools for those of us who have become retarded in our intuitive minds. Places are needed where I can take off my mask and learn from an ecology with telescopic eyes, places where I can think without shame, look with a fearless eye and dispel the acquired mistrust in all life not yet missionized; places where I can enter the spirit of the countless species, all thinking, all experimenting, all in one great colloquium conversing. These experimenters all beg to be seen, to populate my imagination, give advice, make me sweat, laugh and be wise. To emerge from the intestines of mankind, to lazily sit on a windowsill just for a lookabout is a luxury I like.

The free, instructive lands, festivals open to every living thing, are much more than places of recreation and romantic sports to me. They are my brain. They are the lands that cook the long-range thoughts my emotions thrive on. They let me think in likenesses and free me from the leash of words. It is where all deep symbols and my space-time ideas are stored. The language that can best be visualized is born from these forms. Everything there fills in my sense of orientation. Everything there becomes oxygen for my soul. When I erase a weed, I erase part of my brain. The first resource of any creature is its memory.

I suspect that out there is a creature for every subject in my mind who has experimented and thought longer and better about it than I have. Have not the bats put to use the Doppler effect millions of years before us? And it's all written down, waiting for me to find the ability to be a medium and to plug in.

I like to think here that every creature is unique because life needs it for a unique research assignment, perhaps on the project of locomotion that is not flying, wheeling or walking, on chemical language, or better economics in photosynthesis; on digestion of cellulose, on copulation without a male, on mutating lead into gold, on refining any of the unlimited kinds of existing elixirs that we do not know, on kibbutz-living for cells, on infrared vision, on an architecture based on hexagons; on lubricants that outsmear those of snails, on projects that put bees to work on a royal baby food which, translated into our biochemistry, can give a thousand years of life to a chosen individual—and they did it too! Projects in air-conditioning where termites figured out to regulate their buildings to within one degree Celsius of thirty-one degrees Celsius with outside temperatures between three degrees Celsius and forty-three degrees Celsius; all this without warring for the oil of Kuwait. All to enlarge the gnome of life that is our memory bank. And so it seems not to be the common in us but the eccentric and the freakish that count.

This free land is the keeper of balance for the mass media in which the church of Reason makes my mind pragmatic. When just breathing in man-made thoughts, my mind is living on candy bars. Watch out for boils, the scurvy of the mind in an intellect that works only with "yes" and "no." It might be the TV death of a soul. The voice of the free land broadcasts a basic system of ethics that works ten times longer than the appetizing types offered by the various chains selling fast food for the soul which, it seems, have to replace their recipes for inadequacy every few hundred years.

Did you notice this shy, curly idea clinging to that soaring bluff? Even that lichen might be a thought more beautifully and powerfully recorded in our communal brain than the theorem Niels Bohr could create for our fame. To make this shy little symbiosis homesteading on this bluff last and fit, the Holy spirit has perhaps fingered and molded it for a billion years.

I belong to a tribe of creatures that became beasts of prey to such an excess that I do not need more of this carnivorous knowledge that gives even more such power to me. Why think out an even better mouse trap? The knowledge I have gained which encourages me to become weaker, softer, less fearing and more giving now serves me best.

Ah—when I remain an undecided apprentice, what could God be teaching me! Things could start to happen to me.

101

While among people I keep on falling onto our highway system of thoughts that bustles with the exchange of our mental commodities. Soon my world view is biased in what I see and do not see. Soon I become a puppet of the media obediently cruising only along the highways of our practicalities.

Every creature has many different forms—some are just part of larger forms or are days in forms fifty generations tall.

When I was trained to see of all these shapes but the one directed by usefulness my world began to shrink. The speech of the silent things has gone. The ghosts that are the Theos of the future and the Theos of the past have gone. By and by my world held only what I was trained to see and hear. I started to bang into many things that became invisible to me. I became that spell-bound wasp that erred today into my pilot house. Slave to her sight she banged and banged herself against the front windows trying to get out. Ah! If for just a minute she could have pulled out her eyes and stopped her way of seeing and thinking! Blind she could have found the open back door and the way out. She would now happily sip from the brew of rotting plums and buzz around.

When nature produces a solitary woman or a man in hermitage, does she not make a gift of some unique binoculars to the whole world and more so to her tribe of man? Some are delegated to become loners and beat the bushes away from our information freeways and motivated love affairs. Later they perhaps come back from their errands into the unexpected, and thrill us with news.

Some are driven to be solitary fanatics and to dive to a depth few minds dare explore. They walk away from a comfortable routine. They are Marco Polos, Saint Francis, self-made astronauts, Johnny Appleseeds. They are the happy fools who endanger their lives when living safely is cheap. They stubbornly continue to think by themselves, refusing to buy the latest fast-model the public mind produces on its assembly line. They do not depend on cooks who butcher and prepare knowledge to nicely serve it in books, but like to pick and decipher by themselves the language of the natural sights and sounds. Courted by the warm crowd of five giggling girls, they nonetheless prefer the sober company of a hen with her ducklings, of mountains and of other long-distance calls. They may invite disasters in themselves—floods, mindquakes, obstructions, the battles between the seasons and between the uncertainties. Filled with an ardor equal to a shaman praying for rain after many years of clear skies, of dust bowls, and of thirsty souls, they may invoke flash floods in themselves to wash the piles of garbage away that formal schooling and its efforts to make us storm the heavens alone have piled up in the backyards and basements of our minds. They

162

may trigger slides in the sediments of their minds, bringing to light memories that have been fossilized. They fast while others bask in the supermarkets' plenty. They drug the cash crops of docile thoughts that have been cultivated in neat monocultures all over their minds. This for the simple delight of watching what might grow in a free and asymmetric mind. To us they might seem to be in hell; and they are having fun. I see women and men who can become oracles, maybe guides into other worlds. And they seem so modest—just asking not to be reformed. Yet they can cook better refreshments for us than the Brothers Coke. They can be yeast that raises a people's collective soul.

102

Maybe there is no other species that is losing so fast its hold on the dimension of time and is becoming instantly so smart and so powerful.

You may be puzzled that some among us take off now in a different, more vertical, direction to socialize and leave our neighbors in space for neighbors in time. No, you need not overly worry to missionize these "asocial" minds. They do spy on the news of technocratic progress with some quiet admiration—from a safe distance. You might even develop a liking for them. In their motherly preoccupation, you might rediscover your own anima, devoted to fertility, to diversity, to the curls in our love, to the dream of the Earth. Unfit for hair-raising braveries which seem to be the privilege of a prodigious shortsightedness, these minds are nonetheless fascinated by the new visions with which martyrs for knowledge excite our daily news. You might want some of these mental drifters to survive, intact and on proven ground, regardless of what happens to world improvers. These "savage" thinkers might spin a good yarn for our kids with what crystallizes from the enormous sacrifice, when others furiously hoe and burn themselves up in that spiritual magma that wells up in our minds. They seem the mamas, always late, always dragging behind, always worried about some whining child, full of compassionate thoughts that do not sell.

103

It seems obvious that we should freely share knowledge—yet is it? Stand on your head and look again!

Is it good for me to drive over to the neighbors with the slightest trick life confides to me, to find its value on the knowledge-mart? Should I freely spell out my mind, pawn or sell out my inventory of secrets, until there is no personality and no Theo in me anymore? Each of us seems to be born with his own set of patents. Her own mixture of the known and unknown makes a unique subspecies of her. What a colorful flower field! Yet I notice that the minds of students and their answers the world over rapidly become uniform showing signs of the Burger and Cola syndrome.

Mephistopheles, God's minister of mutations, perversions and evolution is recruiting, whispering into my ear: if each of the six billions of you link up on man's side of the tag of war against all barefooted nature—here is my promise: You will turn upside down every tree, every mountain, every gene and every turtle in Turtle-Land. What riches could be piled up on our side with such a united prostitution of our minds, what storms not flattened out? We could pluck the whole living world of its feathers and make of them that fantastic communal featherbed for us called better world. Our individual leisures, dreams and curls, the robins' evening songs, the creative disorder of youth and the fireworks of the setting sun, the wonderful follies of our feelings in love, the dances of mosquitoes and those of whirling snow, the endless braid of generations arguing in each soul—could all be nicely stuffed into a uniform and sent off with the troops of rationality to their front to wage war against the one hundred and forty-four irrational worlds where for these troops the light has already gone out. In the power binge of such a union, we could push most plants and animals into prostitution for an alm of fertilizer, water and grain. We could render them stupidly tame. All this power will be ours if we become informers and trade the secrets of our souls.

But I also note that when I become a collector in some special field of knowledge, other sections of my world view get dull and obscure. Might it

164

be for this reason that some of us intuitively resist becoming the best at anything?

I wonder if when the mangroves along the lagoons, the hoppers, crawlies and chirpers, the mice in the fields, the centipedes, and Theo's follies, when all the forget-me-nots are forgotten and there is no wasting time on ghosts and critters not mentioned in our golden resource book of the 144,000 friends anymore, when all these arbiters mediating between you, me and a future child are left out and do not cool our intellectual greed anymore, then might not a meltdown in the core of our mental powerhouse occur?

A few of us stand back and miss the chance for a golden job while in others their feelings are systematically dried out and they are bred to a useful indifference for the sake of more power, expertise and speed. Then many mental eunuchs who are clean of emotions are needed as functionaries in the courts of our economy's empires. We suspect it is those obscured roots that now are rapidly cut off in us which can channel our love to and fro among the flora and fauna, up into the future and down into the unrecorded past and can keep our hillside to heaven's ecstasy land well-rooted and safe from erosion. We mistrust our own uprooted consolidated strength. We think that also in the pursuit of knowledge cancer can occur. With awe we witness how a billion minds detach from individual souls and contract into a cyclone of raw physical knowledge and blow out one by one the subtle lights in the meadows, in the woods and in the spirits deep down in our own jungle minds. Yet, the soldiers of precise and unified knowledge seem well-started in the direction of mental socialization and are looking for more hands. After a long period of refinement, diversification and decoration, a season of motivated science seems now in a hurry to melt down that profusion of fanciful knowledge to one gigantic economy and hammer, one currency and trap to subdue all of nature's tribes. For myself, I like to pinch myself awake. I want out of our parents' addiction to bossing ever more energy around, out of that crude materialistic cyclone we seem to become. You may study how to recycle an ax or how to get more mileage and more axing power out of it. I wonder now how I can bury one of my axes; how I can become more curious and accommodating, and a little less powerful, feared and cunning.

Let me be carried away and add this:

165

When a loosely social species is pressed against the wall by a cataclysm like the over-competition in a population explosion and cannot afford all the yellows, the greens and blues of individuality for each of its members anymore, a merger may form. Each is then asked to remember and to regurgitate into the open his most practical mental treasures and become an informer. Information will be weeded, sifted, classified, usefullized and the essence consolidated in the expertise of the expert. Mountains of life's luxuries, including the peacock's wildest feathers, are buried and left behind in this forced exodus into that new utilitarian lifestyle. Biologically consciousness may have something to do with the transfer of knowledge from the individual to a society—culture forms a society's "genes." (Think of the bee language where individuals publish information with symbolic dances.) Maybe becoming temporarily conscious has happened in the prelude of all highly socialized organisms. Might at the same time this extraordinary mental trophallaxis or explosion of information regurgitation become the new social reinforcement and mutual grooming—a social cement—the great hive's comforting, inner identification-hum and music?

104
Ah, the importance of ignorance!

Cut the communication of a sparrow with the mass media of the flock. Let that sparrow fly into isolation somewhere in the Galapagos. Soon a new subspecies of sparrows may develop.

Take a seed idea away from the hall of mirrors we may call the mass information freeway or Internet. Offer it a hermitage. After filling in its ignorance on its own, might that thought nicely lost in endless option not finally develop into a whole new species of thought? On the other hand, does an information explosion create new information? Look what such an explosion did to the million local ethnic drinks after it united us behind Coke.

I wonder whether belonging to the generation of six billion side glances should make me proud. In life, that glorious rebellion against unity and practicality for three billion years, didn't more and more creatures go to "Washington" their very own way?

105

Why has it become so highly respected among us to whisper the answers to a man who is failing his fitness test?

When from long city arrest my peripheral vision gets blurred, I may shrug off as stupid the geometry of the fish who builds his pyramid deep into time and spawns in his fertility rites new generations, each in incredibly generous numbers again and again. With each of his generations, the fish also generously sends an invitation to every neighbor in the sea to swim by, be an artist and nibble and chisel on him and his brood, have a feast and to drive him up, purified, once more thinned out into a single point or fish. By and by he has been metamorphosing this way into a higher quality of life.

Obsessed with the practicality of the moment and with a terror of running out of personal time, we seem to rapidly be leveling out our own organic pyramids. No selective hearings are held. No such costly invitations to nibble and to chisel on us are sent to the zillion artists with which the Garden of Eden is filled. No berries for the birds, honeydew for the bees and yummy leaves for the caterpillars are cooked in our camp. None of us is allowed anymore to fail the fitness test that wants to patiently, thoroughly sift for our future generations' best. Do we not encourage whispering and cheating in these tests and make it a great virtue to do so? Every newborn seems to be hurriedly cultivated to maturity, no questions asked, and put to work. We do not worry about long-range defects. We have the clinical health-care industry to cover them up.

To raise a child and to allow it to take a fitness test, risking its rejection and its death, is an unusually generous gift a people could make now to its next seven generations. This quality control has become an unpopular, even prohibited, generosity. Are we anxious to produce inexpensive throwaway labor that suits our economy?

Still, with this stupendous organic geometry of the wild in mind, I might have seen that maimed snapper and also felt a confident joy, even after a big wave has stranded this fish. I could have excitedly watched his metamorphosis into a feast for maggots and how a swarm of steel blue flies soon flew from that merry maggots' nest into the sky. High above the dancing sea, the sun coloring its wings, I might have seen this metamorphosed snapper looking down on me with a thousand eyes. From tragedy and birth I could have rhymed a new creature, even more fascinating than a fish. What should I call that wonderful creature that flaps, swims, wiggles, crawls, flies and thinks, that drums and hums many songs? But why frame it again in a name?

An inspired act, an individual creature, or one lively single lifetime seen by itself does not make sense. An intuitive man, a people dedicated to all life, even a species, seen by itself does not make sense. They seem each but one of the endless expressions of Mother Nature who laughs, sneezes, digests, undresses to dress more fancy again. Shiva, mother of all the ornery and beautiful things, is surrounded from midwives to undertakers by her tools.

There are countless moons in the cosmos of our minds waiting to be explored. When peeking into Symphony-land with impeccable faith, one might see beyond the wolf and the caribou, the snapper and the fly, beyond Theo, my ego, who may only see a lawyer as a horsefly biting him. The wolf—caribou symbiosis—might come into sight—link by link. One starts to see creatures and acts with their complimentary actors and acts firmly attached to them and rhymed.

And so when I watch again the sculptor ecstatically chisel and nibble all over the slab, I will take his show as a simplified lesson on how, over the generations, sickness, malice, parasites, dangers and death have also chiseled on Theo.

106

Nature has decreed that for many the call to have a romance with a child and start a family needs not to be sent.

I note that in many the old spicy desire to start a family has turned into a rusty yellow leaf that is gliding from them, maybe to be replaced by a new creativity in a new spring. I see young professionals anxiously wait and experiment with new relationships. They seem to listen for inner guidance and to ask for a new script for their souls. They seem eager to usher in a new community complete with laws that can be good to them in their new careers. This change of the social order is still confusing me. I wish I could adapt better and feel more at home in this new company of singles and couples wholly dedicated to careers.

I am a man whose family has remained in sap and my body enjoys swaying to this old season's predictable winds. Yet more and more I live on the negligence of that new society of professionals, on its loopholes, on the garbage piles of its junked thoughts, feelings, music, joys and on its thrift stores. A monogamous life with five rather homemade children in which I do not march to the tick of a clock is good to me. I am not disappointed enough to join the prayers for a better world. I feel no blinding hunger that holds with savage hope onto any promise to get out of an old broken home. My twosome togetherness for thirty-some years turned out better than I was told to expect. If paradise is on earth, it is *this*! I saw it twice when heaven was open. Thank you, dear God, thank you, Clara, for this luck—in this lottery in which we see now fewer winners.

For this I am handicapped to join with the many who work hard toward a new commune where one seems soon to produce our children with even more efficiency and boredom than one produces our cars. To be a loose fisherman, a dreamer, a handyman, to see Clara in old-fashioned love awaiting me on the beach, her purple skirt fluttering in the wind, are the best treats I know. Clara, it feels like walking around in one slipper when you are not here.

Am I living the late days of an old summer doomed, it seems, to be replaced?

107

I like it when Theo is not just a good, severe shepherd to his thoughts, strictly rounding them up so they may munch like mad to produce only meat.

In a world of so many wonderful things to welcome in, what is the point to rebel, trying to become useful to only man?

That slick soul-catcher song, "For a Better World," gives me bellyaches. Why this cultivated anger with the state of affairs that has plunged us into this uncontrolled activity to reform this mostly undiscovered world? When I make a headstand for a change and look again I see that it is our endless whining in front of God, our "pork barreling," and the many of our glorious little betterments we slyly sneak in just for ourselves that now give the Ark a bad list. *If you can't beat God—join His Way*, I tell myself. *Stop to be a pioneer, conjure up thoughts that do not produce new gismos for now, but simply evaporate my anxiety, learn to love the Earth, stormy as she is right now; it may beat Odysseus' fabulous trip.*

I only now realize how exhausting for the Earth an eager achiever or world improver can be: to bend all the rains, the sunflowers, sunrises, and vines our way, to comb and straighten all of Gods curly creeks and wriggly laws; to become master of the legions of caring thoughts my soul wants to friendly send into the woods, the ocean, the fields, and put them day and night to work controlling the rodents, the riverbanks, the moods, destinies and meteors, to write a new lawbook for all of God's 144 worlds so that all may slave for us, and to grit my teeth while I so comb the earth—how exhausting can such a "better" world become. I might end up an orphan in a luxurious dormitory playing solitary games.

When humanism broke out on the face of the earth, much land and trees, the curly minds and hairs soon distorted into symmetric forms. This new environment, so strange to my soul and so charged with crisis-alert, affects the fertility of my thoughts as "The strange object or strange situation reaction" from an IUD can trigger infertility in a womb. I like to wean my mind of the naive forms of this adolescent geometry. They are crude, ungiving, as egoistic as a wheel and life seems not fond of them. Why should one generation be proud to have its own Darwinian fitness improved at the expense of our species?

That lonely goal of caring for man's United Nations alone and legislating the whole Earth in our favor is also provoking an ever-inching tide of angry miserables in nature that each morning make us hurry-hurry more to think out even smarter and more brutal techniques to raise The Wall around our world economy. As for the wicked so for the victor there is no rest. He remains haunted by the revenge effect. Damned be that bold moment in which it was decided to stop the march of the seasons. How much longer will I be cursed with a mental crudeness so shallow that I want to know every living creature just by the single immediately most useful quality it owns?

My thinking that has to compete just for mankind's applause becomes hindered. It has one eye glued on that pretentious crowd. How, with only one eye left, can I catch thoughts from afar, from left and right and from behind and become finally able to forgive and understand? When I am sunk into brooding about my own business of living and sharpening my thoughts as others sharpen arrows, how can I see her dreams, listen to my children—or not bump into a tree? And I soon need a white stick for the blind.

Thanks, Theo, for letting me also mount a peppy thought that did not go to school and lets me fly on it through unknown land as we do on an eager horse not tied to a plow; thanks for letting my mind at times go free and not fixing it with a chastity belt of slogans and the condom of a credo, free to let it get pregnant with poetic ideas that do not sell.

I am intrigued by her secret; how does she remain a song so well composed that it rivals the smooth flow of a swell licking swiftly through the jagged rocks of the shores? If I could learn to listen better to her dreams; if I could get so tiny and in my thought-mill so still that I could slip into her world and look around, I might then want to be less of a boss. I might then be happy to just be with her and the exotic garden she grows in her and let her be my catalyst.

Theo, make yourself a boat; escape from the island of Theo's point of view!

108

Although we like to trumpet how freedom-loving we are, are we not all a little handicapped in some domains for that scary height? Do we not hide behind our backs all kinds of suspenders crutchers, helps, partnerships and loans that we need to stand erect?

No doubt a disabled man must hold on to his stretcher and its crew. While the crew laughs, sweats, makes love or plays ball, he gets time to brood and somewhere grind himself to the sharpest edge. He may well succeed in making of his broken feelings or legs a solid million dollar throne. No, I do not expect him to fight for dignity and freedom of movement for the jolly men of burden who shoulder him around. To make good his defect, to be welcomed in, to command respect, to pay for his "sofa on wheels," he does well to train hard at becoming brilliant at one thing. He can high-breed his capacity to give orders, juggle numbers, heal others or bully them around or to spit from ten yards into a pot and become the best at it. He can cultivate a clairvoyant shaman's mind. He may just domesticate himself into an irresistible high-yield sugarcane so it will be all sweet plea-sure to have him and to carry him around. And while his friends shoulder him on his journey high and gently over the rugged land, kill the fish, man the guns or tend the potato fields for him—he can select, sit on, breed and hatch some unknown idea. Sometimes a woman or man may so become the celebrated flower and poet on top of the stem. Here no desire will hatch to fight such life-giving dependence; no Independence Day will be pro-claimed; no bill will be signed to ban the use of strong, sightless men as roots or beasts of burden decreeing equal treatment for every woman and man.

In a technological society, a partial handicap, a humpback mind, a lean-to man, a myopic sight, a memory with a convenient tumor or hole, a head obsessed with pity or hate, take any obsession you can think of, is it not precisely these "failures" that turn into treasures in this new order of man? How would a freestanding, freedom-loving general practitioner fit in here? Is it not these obsessions and shortcomings that bring out the com-pensatory excesses which are the stuff such societies thrive on? A person with such treasures is the favored aspirant for such a society. Without options, second thoughts, regrets and doubts, he can plunge into that door which nature opens to him. There will be a seller's market for him. Is it not the man with the longest shortcoming most eager to build better stilts? Money or fame becomes for such a one-sided person important; what else would keep up his missing sides and corners?

It seems the more a person is forced to cultivate a cash crop in herself, tilting her whole personality this or that way, the more this person becomes a promoter of technology; she chants the credo for united man loudest among the crowd. She prays her God to make man progress that way.

172

I wonder here whether socialized medicine has not become the guardian of personal unhealth and dependence, the breeder of incompleteness, deformities, congenital defects and of castes, the promoter of expertise and talents, toolmaker for technology, the creator of a society whose members will plug into a thousand social connections to function well.

When you watch me again when I weep, preach, argue, jubilate, cheat, command or throw my anger around and trumpet freedom for all, you might want to know something about my blind spots, my health, the holes in my courage or broken strings on my musical instruments, about my need for cash, about my talents that are overdone. You might want to wonder what kind of dependencies, help, crutches, credo and suspenders I need for support. You might want to find out in what orbit I am caught, what friendships I need to protect for plugging my leaks, for fueling my chair on wheels, for tickling my humor, for giving me loans. You may want to check what shade trees I need to shade my delicate ego from thoughts too hot or bright. I might be less free to think, gesticulate and trumpet for freedom than you guessed.

Maybe to become fledged, versatile, to invent a lifestyle that is featherlight and have the option to fly to a higher society than the sect of man is what our love of freedom is all about. Then who would want to become free to do as he pleases, to wrestle himself from the leash of Grace, to become a heavy maple leaf tumbling in a freefall from its tree. I was told that independence is a lonely, barren place—a campfire left behind to burn itself out.

109

How warm it felt when you had your old mended sweater on and did not come to visit with a mission in mind.

I am slowly discovering that beyond a businesslike approach that politely rapes another mind, there awaits an exotic vacation land; I found that communication can be a love affair. A conversation I share with you can become an ascent we make roped together. Yet when I trip and slip into self defense, you need double strength to keep your foothold and not to let us slide into simply quarreling about who is right.

In a kind moment, when I dare the luxury of opening all windows, locks, credos, assumptions, cover-ups and doors, my sanctuary begins to vibrate and sing to the ripples of your heartbeat, to the chirps of the birds, to the surf of every heartbeat of the world. Freed from my commands, my intuitive mind loses no time. It leaps, yelps with joy, and falls in step with that great song that also sways the grasses to the winds and in the East is called The Way. The world then shows itself to me more as one wonderful brain in which every pebble, every colony of moss, even computers all have their input and their say. I have heard of gifted women and men who can tune in to the voice of the free world so finely that they can hear and visualize the outburst of joy and the downpour of tears of every chirper, buzzer, whiner, drummer, and lover performing on Earth.

Yet when hordes of people sweep my thoughts into emergency thinking and barest ego-defense, every shortcut seems then allowed. My mind is swept into a frenzy and I become quite deaf to your intimate boos and smiles. When I sink into the thick yellow communication cloud of all our attention snatchers which orbit the planet now, your timid signs from deep down take hopelessly long to seep into me. Your deeper messages wilt before they catch my eyes. And so in our meanness-breeding crowdedness language has remained less and less an exchange of gifts but had to be reoriented to become one more arm of self-defense—some times as misleading and deadly as my deer call I use to hunt. Did you see the nymphs on the bottom of the pond hiding in coats of mud and sticks? We more and more need to hide underneath words. Why was I trained to meet you with my spirit of a pioneer, ax and hoe shouldered, advertising and cover-ups in mind, calculator in hand? In our communication wars I wish at times I were a clam. Yet conversations are also among the most exciting gifts I have received.

It is good a town has its tea gardens, its sanctuaries for the intuitive mind which is such a curious and delicately sensitive child. It needs a shelter from the rudeness of the dull rapists of the mind who are desperate hawks, diving into that innocent child, throwing it with slogans up in the air and then again on the ground until, its feathers strewn around, it breaks down and falls in line.

174

It seems to be for their unnervingly patient long-range science, for their inborn shame of quick practical cunning, that less formally educated people, who are still crowded with voices and live closer to the land of children, are such misfits in the flat and rude high-tech land. Highly cultivated and refined people, like refined sugar, seem easier to manage and organize. They are brought down into one world alone and into the realm of short distance calls. When dealing with them one deals with one ghost, not with a thousand ghosts.

Early in the morning, when still a little drunk from dreams and my thoughts are not yet combed with a credo, I am shamelessly all ears. I do not like to squander this high of the dawn to read, to argue, to plan. In this soaring time of a breaking day I like to fool and walkabout just listening to what my guardian spirits may say.

110

Hesitantly, we now find that it is to our advantage not only to have biodegradable plastics but to remain perishable ourselves.

It does not feel right that I should let myself be initiated deeper and deeper into the grandiose conspiracy to keep each other alive at any cost—not so much in the fight against the beasts of the woods, but against our future children whose hearts tick in your soul and in mine. Are we trying to rid ourselves of our fall seasons that can so nicely and completely rejuvenate a woman and a man in another spring? A society obsessed with body-veneration, with hospitals, longevity, personal rights and liberty, a society that holds the right of the individual to uncontrollable healthcare more sacred than the health of mankind, seems to me not very much in love with its children anymore. This mentality does not make good moms and dads. Is this not also the message in the songs of our young? We seem stuck in a soft ethic—in an ethic that tends to make fat, ugly, old, too numerous and stale, and constipates our love affairs.

Was not sickness for a long time seen as one's personal test, a bullfight, a way to new strength, or as arguments with death to put a man's doubt to rest? Yet it takes so much courage to see it this way. It seems now preferable to kill part of the new generation just quantitatively before they are allowed in. No chance for that vigorous new shoot to lengthily, expensively prove itself—with no questions asked—simply a whack with a deadly solution of salt. Still, this little woman or man seemed just a few apples and carrot juices away from us all.

Should one lightly, contemptibly call them diseases—these discreet, little chisels that have for eons tirelessly fingered all over the human edifice, hardening under their hammers our quality and probing for soft spots? Should one heroically fight life's contempt for safety, its gusto to get high on experimenting and danger—and to storm beyond? These microbiological chisels seem ultimately also a creative and farsighted population control. They seem to me as compassionate and inspired as a parent's or a doctor's thumb pointed up or down when a child asks to be let in. And has not the partnership of the elephant with its "diseases" been doing well for millions of years?

In this brighter light maybe these discreet little inspectors that the god of dangers and sicknesses sends us should be listened to closer and personally argued with and not simply be rounded up by some health police and shot on sight. Who wants to shoot all bulls because some bullfighter got horned? We might soften into helpless pieces of blubber plugged into a health machine if allowed to skip those personality tests. In life's population control, who will test and question us now? Who should have a short life cycle that is all delightful follies of youth? And who should in a lengthy cycle mature—and become loaded with seeds? We might naively exterminate the little quality controllers and wonder-medicines nature keeps in its medical chest to keep us trim and slim, to keep us few, so the animals and plants may remain plentiful. The obsession to prevent death among us becomes soul-sickening to more and more of us.

Yet I also see life is endlessly inventive to give us and to preserve for us these precious gifts of birth, of pathogens, of death. Obviously our naive eradication of these intriguing "medicines" will make life breed smarter "medicines" to help us contain our malignant population success. Cancer, that deadly ego trip of confused cells, may be one of life's answers to our own ego obsession. The whole body, every cell, every deeper thought in me, seems to defend this incredibly fruitful cycle of birth and death. No, it is not strong, brave death, but it is grim, man-made death I

176

am dubious about; for it produces enormous waste of youth and vitality and tears and many slowpokes that cause in life the traffic jams.

That loss of our multi-generational vision sickens us with an obsession to prevent death among each other; slowly we lose our capacity for apoptosis, slowly we get blind in success management. Consider, *e.g.*, how our arsenal of antibiotics, so victorious on the level of the individual, ultimately dilutes our species and helps make it huge and ugly—and with exploding our population may damage our vitality more than would a nuclear war. Obsessed with body armament and protection—so much so that we are now the animals that have become ninety percent horns—our intellect neglects the brave science that keeps our species healthy; our economists have declared war on our own five generations ahead—and we are winning this war, and starting to limp in circles.

That we remain free to bring our children into this world to our hearts' content and without limited entry has turned into a blind feast with a sad ending, as we can now see. Addicted not to take full responsibility, but to hook up to a technological society's welfare, one will have to grant, against all our hearts and tears, that new mother a control over the coming of our children whom we now abandon so freely into her lap.

May the business of clinical medicine with its body veneration pass on for now its Nobel prize to a new science that renders mankind youthful, slim and in its relations with the earth beautiful. The best work researchers in clinical medicine can now do is doing nothing (disarmament). The Earth grieves under their success as the oceans grieve under the advancement of our fishing technology.

Musing so on a more generous scale one might come to a more forgiving attitude toward pathogens. One might see how in disease, microbes confront each other and can ultimately learn to live together in colonies of bacteria. Evidence now hints that our bodies might just be such colonies.

One might then also wonder who will help the herds of wildebeests and the fleet of vultures to defend their savanna from our frenzied urge to confiscate their grassland, and to castrate and farm the world after we have destroyed God's ingenious gift to the savanna of the blow and tsetse fly. Are not these little freedom fighters better than all the good Greenpeace people at keeping these no-man's lands humming, breeding, con-

177

cocting, cricking, blooming and diversifying among us?

It is a relief to know that we are not alone in having to deal with population control. All species do so when an extraordinary spell of inventiveness carries them away, so the neighborly life may catch up with them in their forced march to success. Did you ever wonder at how carefully a species of trees figures out how many seeds per tree it grows, how far the seeds should be allowed to fly, how sour or sweet they should be, how hard to be nibbled on, so its kind will, after a thousand years, still just dot with many other kinds of trees a harmoniously diversified forest that can walk on many legs and not one kind of trees will multiply into a great flood?

In our time, in which life seems to be so fond of acrobats, perverts and clowns, I learn also to applaud a man who walks now on his head and prefers a thicket of mangroves alive with crawlers, flamingos, paddle ducks, tunnelers, creepers and pinchers to a dozen human lives which could be saved by macheteing those Jacks-in-the-muds down—a man, who amid a human tragedy, setting some of us back, discreetly comes up with a smile. He seems to join forces with that mosquito-paradise and the flamingos, which tremble day and night with fear of the "first-world" countries and their Development Banks. He shares a little of their happiness about the new lease they get when a human tragedy occurs and we lose a "tooth." "Thanks, Lord, for a few less people who are after us," this endangered stand of mangroves behind the shrimp farm might sigh. Do you also see a needed ring of growth on our world view forming in such an intriguing mind seemingly walking on its head?

And so, blessed be also the weeds, the chickweed, the water hyacinth, the cleavers spreading between the corn; blessed be the weirdos, the gays, poets, hitchhikers and surfers, the bashful and loafers among the great utilitarian crowd. Together they keep our ambitious population or production down. Why yelp at leaves that rustle in the wind?

When I crack the paradigm of humanism and excitedly hatch from that golden egg, surprise!—the color of our brother death is not at all a somber black. His color can be a friendly flaming yellow and a pulsing amber red. I discover that hailed longevity may be a stagnant lagoon hiding behind dunes from a lively indigo sea who loves to recompose herself. In this openness, a tragedy might turn into help, a brake might accelerate, a wound inflicted might be a healing salve, my periodic migraines a help not to stagnate in routine. Mean aggression may take on a smile and turn into all kinds of fingers plucking at zillion musical cords.

I note that other species, when engulfed by their own prosperity and strength, also make use of their cannibalistic traits. They bleed and thin themselves. Why is it that the blueberry bush brings forth each year a thousand leaves and lets them die, to shower fellow lives with the manna of its biomass? Why does that bush not hold onto one set of leaves and become a giant evergreen? Over years a blade of grass could grow a mile into the sky, yet prefers to have a yearly "give-away." So fond are all creatures of death that this art has now been cultivated for three and a half billion years.

I have always felt hesitant in front of a religion motivated less by adoration and more by intervention, attributing to itself the mission to domesticate our spirit with soul splicing rather than to turn on a lamp in the menacing shadow of man. From deep down I am advised that the more a man tiptoes, trying to be "good" close by, the longer a shadow he casts further away. The punishment for so doing good and for favoritism seems fame. I feel that a philosophy which remains in a humanistic shell and does not hatch into a wide open ecology is a Napoleon on Sainte Helene. Surprise! The leap beyond humanism is even better than a gloomy Europe discovering America.

Don't run away. I am stammering here a thought that is too big for one man alone to say.

111

My life seems to function as one huge penis maybe eighty years long. The harder I think, plan, try and boss my life around, the more it says "No." Yet when I let myself go and I surrender to faith, it miraculously starts to grow and grow.

If I could catch again that trust of a child; if I could dare to just let myself be pulled by my nose by Mother Grace down into her grandest canyons and up to her hairiest peaks without being chicken and buying an insurance policy against her tricks and treats—I could become again a merry Curious George riding her roller-coaster to all the dreamed-of places, yelling with awe and with joy and just holding onto faith. I feel spellbound to just a few man-serving thoughts that are huge miracle-potatoes cultivated in my brain and said to give tubs full of food and safety for all the gluttons and cowards hiding under my skin. With the goals consumer animators whispered into me, I became a fat man in a tunnel. I became dead concrete anchored in dancing gravel skipping merrily down the river's way.

Would you teach me how to sniff out my favorable winds and sail more swiftly the zig-zag tacks of my moods, hunches and dreams? I barely remember how to ride those hidden forces the vulture uses when surfing for hours the updrafts without flapping his wings. No, our intuitive guidelines are not base. Climbing a scenic viewpoint, I find them bewilderingly generous, bewilderingly all-loving and caring for a thousand generations before my willpower ropes my zest and reorients it toward labor in the sweat of my brows simply for our contemporary egos.

When I finally laughed at my little schemes and let my thoughts escape from labor camp I got a sweet surprise. I was dumbfounded by how well I can be served by all those physical powers released when I let a dream become true. When I give in to faith and do not yell at the Mama when she changes my goals, all magnetic fields seem to start falling in step and to favor me—and I become a "natural." When I give her my hand and my mind and do not endlessly pester her with my advice, I seem to be let on unexpected hanging bridges and curves to unexpected friends. I fall in step with streamlines that only my nonsense thoughts seem able to make out. All I do seems to become then of better quality and boredom is dispelled.

I was addicted to the straight line—to bulldozing mercilessly at my goals as we hack mercilessly our freeways through the land, presuming this land became our enemy and is our neighbor no more. I was trained to march to the tick of the watch and I have lost track of my biological clock. When shame or an exotic idea tugged unhappily on my sleeve and pleaded to be also heard, I was instructed to simply step on the gas. Yet when I look back, I am appalled at how much shamble, waste and angry fists, flippers, and tails such heroic stubbornness leaves behind. Great opportunities, sweet relationships I never tasted may have gone to waste while I grit my teeth bullying toward my target. Lately I allow myself a mischievous smile when Theo doesn't get his way.

Although cheered for being a compulsive thinker, a loud or silent talker, I have a hunch that wisdom comes rather from tuning into the muffled grouches and joys behind one's well-dressed speech that mostly is advertisement and cover-up. It comes from listening to the rustling of leaves, from watching the snowflakes whirling through the naked trees. It comes from walkabouts in unplowed land that remained a billionaire in catalysts for my mental chemistry and is out to enlarge and refine my local kindness, compassion and generosity so they may root and ramify swiftly into the unknown. Wisdom seems to me this kind of unglamorous knowledge that makes a sexy high heel out of something with claws that can climb, leap, tiptoe through high grass and trees, heal and repair itself, and defuses a sex attractant too—a gadget we simply call paw. Wisdom is a slowpoke. Smartness is an expert and goes for speed. Wisdom comes from considering and learning from all things. When you tune out of my chatter and charm and for once simply look at me, you may learn something about my needs. And so to listen to your story I look at your face, your hands, your breathing, your pose and at what you don't tell. Or do you want me to strictly listen to your speech and risk that I bring you snowshoes for the dance? I am still dizzy from surprise at how amazingly well I do when I dare to set fewer targets and rather trust and drift with all my antennas out.

It might well turn out that for my deeper nonsense mind the straight line of always or never, yes or no, virtue or vice and taking sides has always been the longest, deadliest line running blindly over the homes of great jugglers, daredevils, teachers and clowns. What a relief not having to succeed. I can get into the only competition that feels to me absolutely right—I can compete with my older self.

Tomorrow I may be a little less of a grouch when I do my exercises in flexibility which life is daily sending me.

112

Yes, laziness may also be a gift, perhaps now even a more welcome gift than the love of seriously fumbling with sickles, keyboards, pesticides, fishhooks or hammers. Ask any snail, fish or tree whether this is not so.

"Stop the action, Theo. Remember, idleness was the primer of your lucky strikes. Stuff cotton in your ears when a crowd whips the doer in you on with applause." I wouldn't have done a good part of my fishing were it not for my overdone training to work hard and compete to pay for a band of applauders.

As a fisherman it itches me to realize that when I slip into a frenzy to kill just to impress you with my bigger catch and how deadly I can be, nature mindfully plants a parasite at my side. She always seems to provide finally a mad overproducer with a complementary woman or man that mops up the mess of his excesses. Imagine a nation entirely made up of outstanding providers—no dancing, walk-abouting, tripping-out and singing—what a horror story in ecology such a nation would act out. Imagine the tremor of anguish such an accident would run through the oceans, the tundras, the jungles, and through all the merry lands that do not strictly produce calories from their soil but cook the delicatessen for our souls. Think, what a catastrophe for our poetic minds! We, the greatest generation of GNP generators, may also want to remain fatherly and watch over our awesome capacity to catch, to produce, to pack the beautiful Earth away. Otherwise, we might provoke the Holy Spirit to trigger a rain of gentle loafers, brakemen, dreamers, quitters, free-loaders, suckers, sniffers, eco-fanatics and welfarers on us and to invite the fools to rule and fool the fools to blow away the stench of such a one-sided battlefield.

I will have to watch myself for that overkill that seems to impress the fool in me and in others so much. What comes of it, if one doesn't live one's own share of daydreaming and lazy-time, but loads down on some other man or generation all that tricky, fragile and explosive burden? Here is a thought that makes good graffiti to be spray-painted into my mind when others flatter me with compliments for being one of the best fishermen.

To be overaggressive and become wealthy involves so much doing wrong to others, spreading misery in nature, and one becomes less loved and more feared. No land, no mind, no watercress likes to be owned and put to work and paid. A wealthy people is a lonely people, feared for leaving much shambled freedom behind. Just as a wealthy person, so a wealthy people seems also endlessly followed by a swarm of flies pestering it for crumbs.

Mother Nature may like those equally well who surf, dance, live in huts of mud or are simply addicted spectators of her show, who giggle and yell, smear their bodies with paint and have pie-throwing competitions in thanksgiving joy, as she likes those among us who seriously shovel, drill, hook, brood and compute, thinking she needs a face-lift from us. Gifted with the aversion to swing an ax and the lack of ambition to outsmart or to kill, our loafers, poets, freeloaders and all the other gliders and surfers are specialists in leisure time, helpful parasites, that nibble the tumors of our excesses away. They even might be saints in the shrines of all nature which we have not yet erased or hired on. They are saved from living the trauma of the practical life to its shallow end. Blessed be unemployment and strikes; let creativity jubilate!

I can replace raw physical solutions with mental solutions. I can find good reasons to admire you for the smaller car you drive, for the fewer miles-per-hour, kilowatts and work hours you need to cruise your soul around, for your greener technology and the narrower trail you leave behind, for building your better home not with bricks but with comfy relationships, for your lightweight lifestyle that is so streamlined you can wriggle swift as any eel through life. I think that the rise in our energy consumption corresponds to the fall in our spirituality. How to become butchers who drive knives through the joints so swiftly their edge last for years? How to rediscover the green connection in our psychology and give my domesticated psyche back its eyes as Greenpeace cares for the great wild in our countryside? I dream of a lifestyle so elegantly lean, there is barely any bulge for the ego-promoters to hold onto and to lead me into the underworld of forced production and consumption.

May I linger a little on the idea of complementary chores and add that your character traits and mine might better fall into place when each of us is seen as one shade in humanity's psyche now in crisis alert where a million women and men are her hasty outbursts of overdone pity and another million of us are the fits of overdone destruction in that stressed lady's soul; where a woman's depression may well be the mere symptom of a man in distress although these partners may have never personally met, where her love turned into pity or fertilizer here and into hate or pesticide there.

On an even loftier level of thought, one can muse that we are primarily cells and only secondarily men. One can think that in the body of the living spirit we are, in the first place, just cells and building blocks, rich with millions of primal ideas; that each is triggered without being asked, to become in one lifetime a molar, perhaps an egg, and in another lifetime a brain, an unknown lymphocyte, a sky lark, a lull or storm, a fingernail. There, each organism may become one of the zillion keyboards on which Mother Kali improvises her songs. One may then also start to wonder whether it is the fittest this or that or whether it is simply the fittest ecosystem that survives.

Daring on the knowledge-ladder still one small step higher up, one can thus guess that our unhumanitarian character traits are also beautiful and needed.

And here's an informal essay on living with faith. To test my soul's IQ, God forged a fish hook so big, it takes an hour to walk from its eye to its tip. He baited it with five bank accounts, ten roasted pigs and ten thousand fools applauding that hook. He baited it with whatever the Sears catalogue is offering us. Name any goody that can be hung on the neck of a man—he hung it on that gorgeous hook, and he glittered it with fame, tempting me, testing me if I am still of quality. Did I remain wise or did I become clever and go for that hook loaded with handy shortcuts and tricks? Did I become fit to shamelessly think, wonder, listen and look, or did I remain a giggly minor fit only to be sent off to a labor camp to safely work in the sweat of his brows?

113
Of great unknown women and men blessed with weedy, seedy minds ten generations long, who remain unfit to become the darlings of one generation or of mankind alone.

Yesterday, this grove was lush with wonders. Its pond was filled with many hues of greens and blues, with the epic of algae, with aquatic beetles, with the honks of Canadian geese, the mirror pictures of clouds and reeds, surrounded by wise old trees. It was there you could listen to the frogs' evening serenade in the month of May. It was a cheerfully chirping puzzle teasing my mind to catch its rhymes. That cosmopolitan meeting place is now bulldozed flat to a docile construction site, all ten acres, by Jimmy Cracker: a man to respect, with an impressive string of scalps to show from his bank account.

Earlier I introduced a new fishery for sting-rays here on this tropical coast. Most of the rays have been hooked and cooked by now. "Please, a cheer from the crowd for this laudable man," one might say. Yet this praise does not make me happy now. Deep down I now realize that to wring out of nature still more food to sustain even more of us has turned into a negative success. Take any of nature's trillion eyes and look through it; you will probably see little quality in what I did.

In the fight between the agronomists and the surviving free savanna land, a new dry land rice has been engineered so another million acres can be made into our slaves. For ten thousand years this has been good news. Now, while the Earth staggers more under the impact of agriculture as it would in a nuclear war, is this still good news? Such thoughts have tears in their eyes and are not easily lived with.

In spite of a cultivated taste for heroes who pull down more than their own daily bread, or tame the rice or work hard to exile our brother death, I feel now closer to those among us who do not burden the land with tombstones of any kind. Asking an elder among the trees about such curious stones, he might make us understand that he does not know of any monuments that do not smack of humanistic arrogance. Deep down I have always been fond of women and men who least polluted their spirit with personal or humanistic acts and are not fond of private favors. They seem to me the best-mannered guest at the festival for all the living things—the legions of great women and men who manage to stay rather unknown; women and men with just enough healthy malice to drag them down from the pedestal of the anthropocentric elite to which they were lifted. Take a fingerful of fame and lick on it. To be so intensely liked by just some individuals of just one species in just one speck of time most likely has an aftertaste of favoritism to it.

That slandered corner of malice beyond reasoning in each of us might well be rooted in our inborn yet battered pledge of alliance to all forms of life, morsels of our defamed love reserved for that devil's advocate in us who reminds us that we are not meant to fry hamburgers only for ourselves. There are vital chores in the journey of life that only stout, unmotivated and unperturbed wickedness can do with a calm hand and a gleam of joy. This troublesome character trait, which we thought we could conveniently delegate as an appendix of the soul, might still prove more vital to our long-range well-being than we thought. That naughty brat might even turn out to be a courageous, bright child when better understood.

Our terrible and indestructible capacity of self attack and to be whispered into sinning against our fellow man may well be life's tool to prevent a species from clotting and becoming a wart on global life. When suffering an epidemic of virtuous zealots, our own version of the parasites or drones which a beehive holds dear as dead ballast, might well protect our own species from swelling into a huge balloon and taking off into the pure and lonely sky.

114

She preferred to be God's idiot and not to take sides rather than go for elegance and surrender her intellect to pity and to hate.

She told me, "When your feelings toward others become harsh, imagine how every single man must spend every single day and night urging his imagination to construct for him a purring happiness." She reminded me that right now all women and men on Earth sit in the middle of their personal tolls with all the lights available to them turned on, searching for better answers among the pictures that their fate lights up in their memoryscape; billions of us, each busily fingering his own jigsaw puzzle of composing another happy day. At the side of each of us are his poisonous thoughts and stingers. There are also his instruments of music and charm, maybe his advertising agent, to attract the goodies for which his imagination or appetite longs the most. There are the "scalps" that menacingly decorate his belt to impress—and the trophies and bank accounts. There are her inborn stars to help her navigate safely. There are also personal clouds—all the tenderness she missed—that blot some of the stars out. There are fog banks of slogans that slyly can turn his course around. There are broken loves, shoes and promises with holes, and parasites, extra inches of waist loading her down. There is his personal set of potions, rituals, ladders to heaven with which he may be helped to reach for magic highs and impregnate his mind with sights of other worlds from which he may also choose advice.

He often seems a troubled man, quite inexperienced in translating his longings brought from a lost sweet home into that soul-testing battlefield of a career to which he was lured. Yet when the tempest lulls, she may listen with all her ears to the surf of all her many worlds that's rolling in on her. She may see the ripples sent out by heroes and weeds through the sea of time nicely woven together and rhymed. What a thrill to step so close, to step between all those waves, splash, yell, tumble, go down and shoot triumphantly again up into the open air. Yet, what if her eyes are hopelessly blurred or her cracked eardrums don't hear? What if some blinded man stepped on her power line and in her soul the lights went out? What if she could remain connected to long distance calls and he, a local man, could not fall in step with her anymore? And then while he fumes she might seem to him radiant with bliss and strangely unconcerned.

She also reminded me that each man is biased differently and that he may see his neighbor as a darling or a badman, depending on whether he is inclined to see his neighbor's good relations into space or into time—street neighbors may love what gives our neighbors in time a bellyache—and she was very insistent about this.

Snowed in or basking in a thawing sun of May, are we not firmly in the grip of the incorruptible law that drives the sapling to its apparent source of light twinkling through the canopy of all the other greens that also wriggle, tunnel, elbow for the sun? Do we not all itch to make "straight" for that speck of opening and for the brightest happiness we are able to figure out?

She made me realize that to ask for forgiveness and to learn how to forgive has a fabulous prize. There is no other teacher quite like forgiveness to make me ask far-reaching questions and discover more Americas.

Ultimately, I feel asked for something more exciting than to endlessly haggle about advantages or to better the world. One by one, I am to handle and inquire into the personality of every "dirty" act, of every inconvenient man, bugger, weirdo, and flower of evil that most of us wouldn't stop to inspect with a long stick. I am invited to explore how to forgive and light lamps in my shadow. Maybe that is what becoming serene is all about. Maybe that's how one charms a ticket from God to enter His legendary gardens of fun and games.

115

When a woman feels hurt for being left out of many rights, I wish these thoughts could rest her anger a little while and make her smile.

Could it ease your anger to consider that when I hesitated to introduce you to our bookkeeper's justice, I feared I would lose your balcony with that far and breath-taking view you loaned and kept up for me? I feared your leisure time might die. I felt I was your roots. I split. I war. I provide. I lie. I am your worm digging for clever ideas and getting my mind dirty doing so. My eyes are rather glued to the ground. I saw you as my flower, my look-out high on my shoulder, my devil's advocate and animator, my cruise ship to exotic places, my lover and catalyst, the daycare center for my guardian angels. And you are the pond toward which my sperms run when they catch fire.

Buried underneath my grotesque terror of sharing with you equal rights to prostitution and its pay, there was also my doubt that I want to succeed in that rude overachieving world. I was hesitant to invite you in as partner in the mills of the macho progress that failed me.

Yes, you can surpass me in cleverness; yet could it be that you envy me? Now that my masculine traits of a subtle killer have so overgrown my anima's tender joys that they brutalize my whole intellect into becoming one square brick of practical thought—all cock and no hen, now as never before, I wake up each morning to the fear of seeing our meadows faded, the songbirds gone, another sun shot from the sky. And I look at you with the same worried look, for fear that you also, one sad, sad morning may be straightened out. I think of how much your soul would have to give up to join that splendid parade of the many proud experts in careers in egotism.

It might come from a silent fear of failure that I wanted so badly to see you as an Ark of Noah or a wilderness to be spared who could float me out of my debris again. To me you remain my deep unemployed pond, with its endless stream of unpredictable happenings and wonderful uncertainties welling up in me, a sacred power spot I am drawn to, to be inspired and judged by a goodness beyond the tinkerings of my common sense. I count on your unharnessed courage to help my stale repetitions erupt into a new spring. I count on your unspoiled anger to tear my sterile philosophies to shreds and plow them under again into fertile soil. I may now shiver in cold reasoning were it not for you getting me lost over again in the mysteries of your jungleland. I count on your strange ideas to attack and plunge me into a creative sickness again and again.

It seems I am not so much reproached for the cocky show of my manhood but because of our exclusive brotherhood of all the Fausts. This is our order of crusaders for a chaste, self-satisfying mankind. Our hierarchy rewards the selfish and seedless. We kill the fertile. We fatten our rationality by castrating our mind in removing our emotions as we fatten a pig by spading it. We court the ego so our businesses among us hum well. I see this pride is now turned loose to also nibble on you. I fear an elegant misunderstanding between a woman and a man is being cultivated. The harsh feeling it discreetly seeds makes all of us losers, but the stock market will smile.

I cannot forget that it is your unschooled generosity, generous enough to wait a patient hundred seasons, which, in spite of my offensive awkwardness, picked up again and again the broken pieces of my daring projects and stuck them back with my roots. Your clear, barefooted sight that gently boos my ridiculous shows of strength when my mind is hit by a kind of rabies and runs amok, does me good. Standing apart, you rather applaud the successes of my heart, ignoring the shouts of applauding fools when I tower, dumb as any gladiator, over the victim's pain.

You have kept that ecstatic high of falling in love alive in me. It was this psychoanalysis in the wild that shook me with the power that made my dreams come true. And often it is only through you that I can hear the magic flute in myself.

You might say, "Look how brightly that drake painted himself; how proudly, how loudly he waggles around; what a macho man is Mr. Drake.

Remember that cursed show might be to attract the hawk so that "devil" goes after him for the kill and overlooks the ducklings and the hen." When you see me with all my deeper anatomy killed just bragging and begging for fame, remember that drake. So we the machos are expected to live six years less than the females.

When you also have to swim across to the technological age, I wish you the luck that you do not need to surrender to hate. Our political psychology, our whole science and its technology, seem rather a lone Adam looking for an Eve.

116

About television at home, I am a little like the prudish fellow who joins Alcoholics Anonymous although he is no drunk. Television seems to me such a huge open barn door to a home and I do not trust myself yet to be strict enough about who may be my guest.

How well the puppet masters behind the screen make me sit in front of an all man-made landscape composed of dots and to forget the stormy uncontrollable world I am standing on, to gently make me hallucinate. They boil my envies and make me one of the crowd. Too often they court the coward in me. Sometimes they lobby for one of my capital sins. They daily can sneak a hundred super-salesmen into my home to kindle commodity dependency in me. Television can spread a convenient epidemic of rumors faster than any other tom-tom drum. It has become the chemist and manipulator that can turn the heat up on the screen and synthesize at will a people's mind and mood. You need a dosage of hate, of pity, of applause, of thirst, of fear? Television's attention snatchers have the prescription and can administer it! Often they turn my mind into a confused bull who goes for the cape which is a fictitious happy land thirty inches wide. I wish they would more often court my private courage and make me think of faraway things.

Television is such a huge barn door to the mind. Many super-thieves, elegant hoodlums, parasites—even Trojan horses mingle with spirited guests that march in through that door. How fashionable this culture of voyeurs has become. The hands are neatly resting in the lap. The mind is led away from the fury of a man's own boiling love and sap. Uninvolved, one can experience through the peephole of the screen a completely man-made mental atmosphere. Here is sport and an exercise machine for the mind, the new Coliseum for the crowds. Here is a meeting place where most have nothing to say and a very few have all the saying. With seventy percent of the television programs in the hands of a hundred international corporations, this tool has also become the bulldozers and the slash-and-burners roaring through the awesome jungleland of our minds, preparing our minds for Western thought and to become farmland and commodity-dependent. I see a billion gray-haired pupils who daily go to school with Rupert Murdoch and his fellow media kings. No doubt here is public school Number One.

In the explosive inversion of our communications from a loose dia-logue between flora, fauna, and man to a quasi-organic mental hook-up strictly from man to man, television has become the effective censor and mind-conditioner. Under its dome no mind seriously at work will be dis-tracted with disturbing question marks and unwanted comments, applause or boos. No swallow, no mosquito, no lindentree may directly comment on what we say or do. A man under this dome might well have freely walked into the most secure, most protective confinement ever devised for him. And so television seems to be the ideal "fly catcher" with a billion minds glued to it at any time to be soon mentally lost when on their own and so in need of a permanent hookup to consume only the man-made information and indoctrination the media sells. This business has also become the convenient leech we put on our kids to get rid of their exuberant vitality. And there is no Red Cross to intervene.

This imitation-life might well fill a vital need. Here billions of frus-trated workers are made to passively and contentedly sit holding onto candy or cool beer. They need not swarm, when freed from work, through the prairies, through the souls of their spouses, through the woods, to revengefully shoot, loiter, kick and nag their frustration at anything that still remains free. The screen can inexpensively imitate our adventures which would become far too consuming for nature, should the six billion of us roll up our sleeves and go out to do the real thing. Imagine, six billion adventurers all out there, what a holocaust to nature could such activity bring. Television becomes a scape-goat that can make a forgetter of an angry man and cool him down. If the lemmings had television perhaps they wouldn't need periodically to wander over cliffs, inviting the raptors to a feast.

There are so many newly created occupations for which we have, so far, no inborn pleasure-centers. There is so much Friday night fever for the pleasure-dealers to cool. The screen seems to turn into the most gentle and widespread hallucinogen. Billions of moths, also, are whirling with us in the spell of the brightest screens. In the hand of advocates for the endangered worlds, this fantastic invention can also become a mighty spoon to stir up what has fallen asleep and settled on the bottom of our souls.

117
Should it come as a shock that to overindulge in the sweetness of being "good" has also its price?

We—the species of supreme lawbreakers—claiming unlimited goodness and wealth for ourselves, we seem now endlessly on the run and breathless from out scheming the latest retribution of life with which it tries to bring us back to the center of its *Way*.

In spite of our presumed master minds, life seems to remain our good unimpressed mother and watches over us when we dare too much. When drunk with success we seem often to rush hypered far out of sight. But she has her ways to call back our tribe and does not let us get lost. She may load us down with all kinds of freeloaders and ballast, so in a delusion of grandeur we do not balloon into a grandiose loneliness. I notice that she keeps every martyr and pervert and every crime ever committed remembered in our genes and, to the horror of my moralistic mind, deals out those self-attacks and killer genes well-meaningly to correct our overbearing number and our splendid blunders. In moments when we brutally enforce our own success, I notice she sneaks all kinds of delinquencies into our society or swiftly turns the light off in many of us to bring us back into harmony with her thirty million other tribes. A whole cheerfully inviting world sparkling with sex goes dark. In that blackout new emergency scripts might be lit up in many of us. Gone are the old healthy fears; gone too maybe the sweet familiar folly of having a romance with a child or investing in a glorious future five generations tall or being a good boy and working hard tilling the earth. To slow us down, a desire for a modest comfortable house-arrest in a fine career of egotism somewhere in our society's bowels and an inordinate love for safety and an indifference for all that is not local news or sports might be triggered instead. One is baited with pleasures which come from undoing a past that has been nailed together too grandiosely and too fast.

Such auto-immune "diseases" and self-inflicted wounds seem to be latent talents in us that are called into action to brake a success in power we cannot contain—to break the spell of that legendary apprentice that goofed and called out the non-stoppable broom. These wounds may become the cracks for creativity in a few.

Take a species' long-range health care system and try to fit in our worthy Red Cross. Strange questions will arise. Take our great clinical medicine catering to the personality cult. Why is it that in the wake of its mesmerizing success mental misery often spreads through nations we newly disinfected, enlightened and vaccinated and we are cash-cropping now? Why do these people often stop to dance and sing? I smell here a forgotten science that begs for a seminar.

With a heavy heart one may notice that for having prohibited death among us for too long, not only a man-made epidemic of abortion is now triggered but the dark urge in some to slowly sedate themselves. Giggling, they pleasure themselves aborting their own being with any of the ego trips, Nintendo and other solitary games. How tempting it is for a society that invested so much in being "good" to now cover up the side-effects of such favoritism and its unsuspected involvement in the mishaps of degeneration, to burden some dark power with it, and to postpone one more time the payment of its debt. Ask yourself, should such painful connections remain invisible for good? Will the connection between antibiotics, overpopulation and rain forest burnings never be understood?

Maybe the fashionable urge in some to remain a cute little chick, who refuses to hatch and to rather enjoy a cozy self-absorbed egg-life, is a high-level cure.

That uncomfortable old Chinese saying, "No good deed goes unmended" annoys the Christian in me.

118

When our forebears built the Great Wall between good and bad, they started to produce more waste in their minds and homes.

No invention has created as many jobs as the notion of good and bad. Billions are now busy elbowing around God's grab bag of gifts, mistrustingly sorting what to keep and what to burn. Others keep huge fires burning where all the undesired is going to hell.

For a short and hurried mind one generation tall, it was a great relief to be able to throw anything that is too long-range or without an immediate answer, use or reward over that Wall. Would you lend me your thoughts to now kick a hole in that Wall that shames my intellect and plugs my well of ideas. I suffocate from the stench of the "do-no-touch" and "do-not-think," from our twenty thousand pages of laws, from the overflowing prisons and dumpsters, from all that our safety measures kill, from the billion pounds of DDT soaked into the ground, and from the ever-growing corner in my elegant mind that was made into a dump site for its throwaways. Now that we need another million lawyers to sort and dispose of the garbage our puritanical legal systems produce, could you help me to explore the notion that the powers of "saintliness" may correspond to the powers of "crime," like brother and sister who hold hands and like speed and mass are one. Each dependent on the other, they have been kept separate by that Wall for so long; they now first sit in my mind timidly together on the opposite ends of a bench, arguing, feeling each other out and when encouraged, they may scoot closer and win the other's confidence again.

In a world of an all-justifying Creator, a world that promises never to become stale, it needs but the ordinary mind to see the light in a common good deed and to feel good about it. Yet does it not take a complete blindness, or a terrifying far-sighted extension of the mind rarely used, for a man to commit an apparent "crime" without flinching and still remain serene?

My mind also seems to have complementary parts. On one side, I have the rational thoughts and body guards. Here I am eager to create ease and make rocking chairs, to chop off mountain tops, to spread dear comfort, unity and peace, to fill the dumpsters and pave over blue blossom-land to go for speed. Here I am always busy with some kind of bulldozer to plug mischievous volcanoes, heretics, geysers that gush difficulties, multigenerational question marks, creative fevers and dangers bubbling from deep down in my soul. I am also probing every living thing as to whether it should not be plowed under to make compost for our vegetable fields. Here I seem to dream always of a rest, of a bench, of some soothing new law.

Perching on a viewpoint a few generations tall is my intuitive mind. That lively mistress creates the fires and wars, the curls in the hair, the voltage in my powerlines and love affairs. She thinks out chores for me whose paychecks arrive maybe in a hundred years. This Diva of all creativeness tirelessly adds new knots to the imponderables in the living work of art. She teases my intellect with endless question marks. She scatters boulders, gophers, grasshoppers, unknown seeds, nettles and other "flowers of good and evil" in my manicured golf course lawn. Much of her time she wastes for children who haven't even been born.

I suspect that above this hierarchy in the mind there is a lamp waiting to be turned on. In its light nothing might need changing and our wastes and our sins may ultimately also provide somewhere good music and good cakes.

To be allotted a mind that likes to fly and to land on many scenic points or view to ask around, "How do your people and critters view this improvement or that act?" Surely this is an impractical gift. When making a moral judgment, I'm handicapped. I can never quite forget my suspicion that any argument may have, stretched out along its road, as many pros as cons, as many boos as hurrahs. American natives had a saying: One should walk for twenty days in his moccasins before one judges a man.

Yet I have to decide. And I take sides according to how well my mind can fly and on what viewpoints it can land. My reason, Darwinian and practical, tells me to side with the successful, the winner, the strong. My deeper mind, where I'm more than a man and rather motherly and brave, prefers to side with the minority, the endangered or far out, the feminine, the child. Fitness in engendering diversity might be life's dearest fitness of all—to become the fittest potter on the potter's wheel!

When I respect a Sabbath for the mind; when I stop my inner jabbering and there is no ripple of thought on the pond, the mind may become part of that magic mirror-mirror-on-the-wall, mirroring the ups and downs of every sand grain; it might catch the tremor of every heart. And lo; I may succeed in seeing a little through your eyes and stepping into the first stage of a trance. My mind a fabulous seismograph!

And as the tree shoulders the fruits, so my reason is Saint Christopher, patron saint of travelers, shouldering my soul across one more season: one, an eternal child; the other its brave chauffeur, who knows all about the latest mobile home in which that soul seems speeding to some home along hair-raising curves.

119

Mozart created a perfect refuge for my intellect, so perfect, it leaves no window, no crack for an outside wind, a paradox or even for a late friend to come in. He also hooked me on a harmony that makes me less forgiving and more strict.

My faith tells me: goodness is all around. My reason complains: that goodness is altogether too overwhelming. Give it to me simplified in a garden fenced off within Eden's jungleland. In Japan they like that beauty spoon-fed in their tea gardens.

When you compose for my reason a mini-paradise, perhaps of thoughts, of colors, of a beat or sounds, you give it a place to safely stretch out and relax. With that tightly woven nest of sounds, thoughts or colors, you surround my mind with a model of the world, in which a thousand awfully great seasons are so shortened and simplified, they make sweet obvious sense to the section of my mind that is reserved to serve my ego and thrives on gossip, local news and neighborly love. Here, the grandiose dance of the foxes with the hares is simplified into a simple carousel. Here, justice performed in one hour replaces justice made in a million years, and I may get a little dizzy and heavenly drunk on the repetitions of its beat stroking me, swaying me back and forth as others get entranced by rosaries, rock, massages, mantras or litanies.

This is a simple, comprehensible re-creation of life's awesome goodness—the ocean storm served in a tea cup. This is indoor justice—with a happy end within my event horizon guaranteed. This is idealism in sound. On this man-made island of logic my ego can calm its panic after it has faced the higher justice of life at large and has become terrified. Here is a perfectly balanced book to my personal bookkeeper's delight. Here a God is modeled to whom the overwhelmed logician in me can take refuge— and worship it without rendering himself up to faith. He can go back to the daily work in the hospital, in the bank, on the boat, even in the concentration camps it is said, without being followed by nagging question marks and doubt. Music knows a custom-made beat for swaying any of our levels in the sense of justice.

In that hush when my guard is in the spell of such obvious harmony never to be found so obviously in the wild, a golden chance for a fine leisure may also visit my soul. That spell on Theo, the hardworking man, may let my deeper spirits slip free to roam the tabooed worlds, unless I just lay down on that nest of sounds and sleep blissfully away.

Mozart created a wonderful fetish for my rational mind which, confused and overwhelmed by barefooted nature, needs also some kind of orgasm to stay well. Here is musical architecture. Here is a snug blanket that feels warm when tightly wrapped around my thoughts after they have roamed inconclusively in the cold out of doors. Music, our beautiful gardens of sounds; here everything is under our control; here our anxiety finds a refuge. Yet if I overindulge, may not my mind become a spoiled brat; may not wisdom in such safety and comfort fall asleep? I may never again want out to where the warrior-winds whistle and thoughts grow seven generations tall and as strong as weeds. How easily one's expectations are misled by such simplified and man-made harmonies and music. Still, when heaven is closed, these intellectual feasts are usually as close as I dare to come to God.

Beautiful music taught our parents to be good girls and good boys. Raw mathematics has now replaced ceremonial music to influence and tighten our morals, our limitations and sense of justice.

A repetitive lifestyle soothed with routine provokes in us different neurochemicals than a life at large; hence our tendency to seek refuge in dance, prayerwheels, litanies, the psychodelic rhythms of music, when we want to invoke our endorphin system to flood us with peace.

When I tiptoe out of the man-made world ornated with docile harmonies of thoughts or sounds and step into pagan land, I turn a mind-boggling "poem" loose on myself. It makes fun of my tidy beliefs. It pops my cultivated system of justice as easily as I pop bubbles of soap. It frolics with the wildland and paradoxes in my life. It boils my explosive sap. Bewildered, I face a Creator who doesn't order his daimons into hell, but makes good use of them. I like to try myself out making love with naked nature, outside the refuge, for a spell; to roll with it, yell, tremble, shout, my unleashed mind steaming with enthusiasm and with awe. I slip into a life that is a cubic light year big. This steambath unclogs my mind.

In this light, the Greeks have not enlarged my sense of harmony much but have rather given my confused intellect a superb fetish of humanistic aesthetics. They often court my ego's haughty intellect which crowned itself Napoleon, emperor of the world. Aristotle already cultivated this schism in my mind. Homer tells of brave Rambos rather than of men who learned on their voyage the art of being tolerant and forgiving. Even Socrates was a mutineer and put what serves his Republic before what serves life. Hence his low esteem for the wisdom in feelings and intuition and his obsession for a justice spread and fulfilled not among all life but among his clan.

Idealism is a charming painting and is still unchallenged hanging in many a broken mind and home ready to comfort, mislead and break us again.

I think also a man and a woman are musical instruments, flutists, drummers, sometimes whiners of God, among trillions, where forms squeak and rattle when they try to play well by themselves. And so a Beethoven symphony starts also to squeak, makes the birds fly off and the worms to tunnel deeper, when that beauty in a box is exposed to the storm of life, as does an idealist who tries to flute with mankind alone. Music!— and I can't stop my fingers from tapping, my toes from wiggling—dancing! The stars, the molecules, all play their signals. They ARE the cosmic music. Every cell, every gene in me gets itchy to dance to that universal Twitter. Every molecule is responsive to the others; a man dances with mosquitoes; the ax and the oak dance with the moon. The oceans play long deep sounds in this music. Neurochemicals sprout, or do not sprout according to that mental weather. All act in an intelligent way.

Ah, when her love mingles with that thawing wind, breathing out and breathing in, humming through the forests, bringing fall and bringing spring, breathing a poetic life into her man, playing on her way every bud, every talent, every branch, and fluttering around the fiddle heads of the fern and around every twig. Is it not in this taller harmony where a tree, a kingfisher, the murmur of melt-waters, an angler, and a boulder become a riverbank in love that plays its modest tra-la-la in the one great symphony?

May I add here that a religion needs not become a welfare institution and a refuge for confused and helpless minds wrapping up their open ends in some harmonious credo. It can be the sacred art of getting high; a modest shaman's initiation for the ordinary women and men, creating hardship, intoxication, obstructions, hunger, danger, dizziness, the gold of mind-quakes and routine breakups, soul-catchers, sky-ladders, an opening of eyes.

120

Here comes our law. Watch: one set of laws; one size of pants for every woman and man, old or young.

When we harness ourselves with one more set of laws and pat each other's shoulders rather self-contentedly, my body tightens a little. Are not good laws and bad laws a ring in our nose? No heart, no bull, no mind, no dog likes to be told what to do. To me laws written to iron out the depressions, highs, curls and bumps in our relations seem as well-meaning as refined sugar. They make me lamer and purer and easier to handle and to store. They sure make me more of a bore. I become a lot of useful calories and not much more. They breed sameness in our minds, make us less forgiving and shrink our idea pool day and night.

Life does not seem to thrive colorfully without those shady trace qualities sparkling in the vices and virtues alike. It seems to be the busy little outlaws, mutants and explorers in each of us, the dreamers, the lusty and lazy, the eccentric and crazy, the greedy, miserly and saintly, the weirdos, the acrobats, gays and jugglers of virtues and vices who ceaselessly mold the human clay of flesh and mind, metamorphosing what of the most complex is most ingeniously simple into splendid butterflies who ultimately fly. A vital people can be proud of each little craziness gladdening some heart that it can afford to let go free to err, to fly, to risk, to explore and does not have to leash it with a law. Consider: do we not with each new ordinance amputate one of our personal wings and responsibilities?

To be safely caged in twenty thousand pages of laws does not stir my pride. It seems to become a needed addiction, a curfew slowing our huge masses, reducing the risk of all kinds of traffic-jams when we are milling around on our worldwide market square. It feels like shackles on the Gypsy in me. Here is lubrication for our automated iron brains yet feels like arthritis for the soul. Did kindness become a luxury in our crowdedness? Did our inborn kindness become so lame that we need so much dictatorship? When a leg is lost, surgeons give us a wooden leg. When compassion is lost, moralists give us duty to limp on. Should every nettle and thistle, the marshes and the towns of ants, every lover's lane and paradise for thieves, the creative distractions and self-inflicted wounds, the fancy of exotic souls, all be plowed under with an iron law and the souls planted with potato fields? The itchy little insect that has been working perhaps for a million years on nature's project of infrared vision and carbon dioxide deduction, should we, because of its table manners, simply write it off as a pest? Should orders be given to cut all the long fingers off because some impatient fellow used his to dig out our seed potatoes? I see millions of minds stalled in front of millions of non-entry signs.

No, I don't yet feel so tired that we should outlaw the cuckoo eggs, the creatures with stingers and thorns, the night birds, the uncertainties, the lovers, the roller-coasters, the unsprayed fruits and souls, the lesbians, skateboarders and vagabonds. By declaring war on all the weeds, the daisies in the meadows and the poppies in our souls, on all that cannot be profitably sold, do we not outlaw the deepest source of wisdom? Wisdom seems to grow best where there is no furrows, no watchman, no lawyers, no shoes.

In a heroic battle for a simplistic and obvious justice that should neatly settle in one lifetime of every man, do we not often compose new laws to protect the coward from the courageous, the present from the future, the elders from the incoming tide of the young, the neighbor from the stranger, the leaves from the tree, the mediocre from the bright, the efficient from the wisdom of the wild and the greedy spring from the rotting fall? Should every blade of grass that shoots swifter against the light be chopped off, and distributed to those that drag behind? The notion that a new law is born from compassion is one of the oldest convenient superstitions. Imposing a new ordinance seems to me the opposite of compassion. It comes mostly from some personal grouch that gets its revenge.

My courage, my inborn decency, my wise spontaneity have been caught in the web of protective laws so many times, I barely recognize beauty in their disfigured faces. I feel it important that my courage gets its daily bread and has its dangers to wrestle with, so it is never forced into one of the many kinds of vandalism for its last way out.

Thank God, the flowers of permissiveness and weeds and the outlaw in each of us also tend to form an immunity against their old enemies like the mosquitoes do. A heavier dose of law, a deadlier pesticide seems needed, so strong finally that even the legislator's own inner songbirds are silenced. Thank God, humanistic haughtiness builds in also its own remedy. It drowns itself ultimately in the flood of agencies it has to create to control the wonderfully uncontrollable world.

It rejoices the heart when lawmakers before all kindle our fever of creativity, and watch so that no meek bills are signed which protect a majority of docile voting adults from youthful, courageous and rowdy minds, who still dare to risk getting burned and burned again by a thousand different suns. They are lawmakers who are first city fathers teaching in a Socratic spirit the one kind of knowledge which is of supreme moment: knowledge of how to make one's own soul and those of others so permissible and wealthy in options that only in rare cases does a problem have to be given up to a written law. Why curse ourselves to become personally so unimaginative and irresponsible that we have to be herded through life with ever sweeter carrots and meaner sticks? To create awareness is so much kinder than to hurriedly persuade with the stick of a new law.

Does not every new law strap a man's mind a little more? Are not these "do's" and "do not's" straitjackets that keep us from jumping far? Laws can make a man wear a pair of pants for life that are intentionally made too tight just to wear him down and tame him, just to keep him from jumping a fence. They seem to be a sort of help that also makes us a little more stiff, a little less responsible and kind. They can make a mind lose its trust in its ability to support itself. Only now do I realize that giving orders to a man and helping him may be disguised synonyms.

When I yodel "halodidoo" into the mountains, isn't it "halodidoo" that's echoing back? When I trust you to be kind and thoughtful, it will help you to be kind and thoughtful; when I expect you to be mean, meanness probably will echo from you. When legislation expects us to be uncaring, dumb and to remain minors, it helps us to become dishonest, unkind and unempowered—and makes of us also great rabbits tunneling loopholes out from under the fence of the million "you musts" posted around our souls. Does not legislation often amount to rubber inflating the roads so that there are no flat tires anymore?

I also note that mass-producing, selling and applying laws have become industries bigger and more profitable than baking bread and that the cartel fosters the demand to sell more. For a safe job go into the lawmaking business. It creates its own demand to sell more. You behead the magic dragon and behold, she grows back two heads. It will be the miraculous multiplication of your daily work and bread.

Consider this before taking the grave step to tie one more string to yourself so you become a puppet with the government agencies for your soul. Did you ever make a promise to a deer, to a stand of trees, to a client, an opponent, to yourself or a skunk with no lawmaker other than your own mind to check and flog you when you have failed?

121

It is amazing how long we did not need to huddle together into a super-society exclusively for man but could stay young, invite danger, associate with ravens, mountains, trees and fan out into our incredibly profuse diversity from which our imagination can now draw.

I was wrong when I thought I could get rid of my native courage, my loose generosity, my unfocused thinking, my angry October storms, my dreams of being a vagabond, by whacking these troubling character traits on the head hoping they would simply drop dead. To be tamed, I realize, is to be taught how to artfully "masturbate." I exercise daily in making love. I exercise daily to live healthy. I exercise my generosity with giving alms. I walk my fitness-miles to nowhere. My emotions that have to remain undelivered are stillborn on some high-tech wailing wall, boxing pad or in a meditation hall. I neatly spill my sap that was born as a river of fire heading for cold dormant land. Also my sports are such acts that are not allowed anymore to go out and mix vigorously with life at large, my inconveniently lively passions in house-arrest, so to speak, my fire-birds defused. Sports are dead ballast. They might be our first rather uncreative attempt to reorient zest. Hence the aftertaste of boredom the sports leave behind in me. We pay the price for becoming more social.

Now each day thousands of hectares of hemlock, cedar, spruce have to come down, not to keep us warm or to keep the rain from running down our necks, but to feed a huge industry that should tickle our boredom or distract our homesick thoughts, when, with tears in their eyes, they wander off to the gentle "brute" in us which we still love but society had to paralyze. Are not a billion women and men each morning sent out to fell, to till, to compose, paint, film, striptease, clown and televise simply to feed the wild in us, which we keep jailed for life? Do you realize what staggering chunk of our GNP has to go into keeping that zoo in our minds, to keep the wild in each of us behind bars and pacified? Think of the entertainment value of the Gulf War. No, that loose spirit which I thought to kill in me with one good whack is not dead. That lively muse, which is no meek angel with a lute, is under arrest yet alive, still pestering me to be heard, dressed and taken for a hike.

Look now at the apparent "beast" who the pious made me behead. I see it turn into a monster who grows multiple heads. A head, for instance, spitting out bundles of money for getting drugs—another head sending helicopters and troops to round up the gauchos who cultivate the stuff, a head who preaches cowardice and the needed safety of an insurance company, another head who takes me to the movies to dream of braveries. Many such quarreling twins still sit at my table with mighty appetites. I will have to double my fishing and providing to keep these kicking bedfellows quiet and full. A man with such multiple heads has little time to peek out of his routine and be an ecstatic spectator for a while. So we now work longer hours and dance, sing, celebrate and storytell less than tribes that are tied looser together than us.

Yet slowly, the enormous altruism that so elusively animates the wild shows itself to us and starts to court our trust. We get inquisitive again about those troublemakers in our own personalities which we simply threw into dungeons or buried in our unconscious misusing it as garbage dumps. We start to reorient our love more creatively. Our minds become a guest house in a new way—welcome in!

122

When a man in his late golden days wants to lighten his load so that he may not crash when shaken from the tree, he might want to make an early gift to the young and vote for them and not for himself. Why wait and remain a sour plum to the end?

When in democratic justice the adult commune outvotes its children and decides to become master chargers and to charm from Mother Nature an extra ration of her air, of her botanical gardens not yet plowed, of her trees still living free, when we quite legally gobble up her most expensive riches on credit so that any motherly soul would get all red with shame—and we expect our kids to pay, we ask much of them. I think I can learn a thing from the saga of the salmon who, when mature, seems content to fight the river upstream to spawn and to slowly, purposefully, decompose its body to feed its brood. I think: as in a salmon so in a man, for each of their seasons there is a different sense of justice triggered. To proclaim equal rights and justice naively for all, whether a person splashes with her lusts wide open through her spring or ripens to an inviting juicy-oozy mango in her fall, only misleads. It might well wrap us in a seedless justice that is as convenient and as impotent as seedless grapes. A man who wants to be more than one man tall breaks that circle of justice and refuses to remain *just*.

In an us-generation where only adults vote and where the just man and woman are the heroes, democracy soon becomes a sad story for the young. Nature shows me a model of justice that she stretches a hundred generations long and she gently pooh-hoos a just man. She builds in a merry give-away for the mature on behalf of the young. Student loans become wings freely given to the young fliers and she would consider it cruel to have those wings clipped and later on returned. She models a democratic living among the generations that seems to make a cheerful place for young and old. It is for such reasons that, to me, a wise decision is different from the majority voice of a million selfish votes. Glorious democracy with all its inhibiting rites may try to suppress an enormously fruitful but unnervingly long-range system of differentiation between strong and weak, experienced and inexperienced, mature and immature— briefly, a natural system of castes. Yet this equalizing proves as difficult as to level duty and rights among mother and child. Glorious democracy, so dedicated to individual rights has also imprinted me with devastating legal self-interest. It might so well turn out to be the quiet breeder of ego- ists when its side-effects are better understood. Doesn't democracy show itself now as the ideal cradle for corporate socialism? Nature shows me that, unless we are all clones, democracy is a biological impossibility.

Much of our progress comes from feasting on the "seed potatoes" of our kids—and they will pay for our nasty trick. Oh no, not so much with money. Their minds will become banal and square in a cash-crop land that we made banal and square and is not allowed the luxury anymore to also produce inspirations in them. As in the adversity of arid land plants tend to grow spines, so our kids will also grow more meanness to elbow through hordes of fellow men and endless traffic jams we cause with our soft ethic and our overloads of possessions in our homes and our minds. Maybe they will pay with having to wear oxygen masks, with many kinds of abortions, diseases from stress and degeneration and memory holes, or with spending half their energy to mislead each other and be liars. More children will be born physically and genetically deformed, mentally retarded, in need of a permanent hook-up to a health care machine; and when grown up, fear will prove for them a stronger bond than love. Many will have their curiosity so often plowed, sprayed, weeded and boiled, their minds may end up in wheelchairs or in videoland. And our comfort- able featherbed will ultimately cause them great stress. Add any idea on side effects of your own.

And so I watch the children pay a high price for our civilization that often loves its technology's ego boosters more than them. When home from our careers, is our love not often that mighty Rio Grande that, after

205

watering all our cotton fields, our self-pleasures and careers, is, for our kids downstream, no great river anymore but a tired trickle? That's how after we emptied ourselves in a career in egotism we may leave our children in a drought of love and many will be our luminous flowers no more.

Still, are we not invited to feel tenderness between the generations and hug with a fleeting thank you smile all moms and dads for the gift of a habitat which they loved and tended for us and did not leave soiled with their industries' feces. In spite of the applause a high yield career can rake in, a few of us have broken that spell—and we promised ourselves not to rush with a cash crop mind into our children's inner world, exploiting it as land developers might, disregarding sound inner ecology.

Organic thoughts are shy plants that prefer to feed and to grow in the great open of the wild or in the dreamland of the night. There they feed on land that is a billionaire in ideas. The land of emotions is also tropical forest, oceans with sharks, lily ponds and spotted owls. These are fragile and endangered plots. Yet are they not our children's sacred power spots? One wants to watch out that a high-yield education does not recklessly log those rain forests and drain the lily ponds in a child's mind to cultivate strictly cash crop knowledge in their place. In our legal system we could build in a refuge for the wildlife of their minds. It is important that in their memories our children never run out of good virgin ground lush with endless options and ideas.

When one gets older and matures into that oozy juicy mango, one is also nicely helped to forget the names, the reading glasses, the business tricks, the numbers on the dollar bills, the lies, the details and cleverness that made us firm providers and sour fruits. The thoughts, the penis, the will power, the heart and hands get softer. Our personal memory weakens and becomes second in command. The greater outlines of the heart and our universal memories get the upper hand again. One might get a little more generous, nibbled on and better loved.

For the mature and strong, there may be nothing that purrs better in them than lobbying for the young. I note that mature women and men who can cast their vote against themselves and for the young do not play solitary games.

123

Tell me, who among the modest and the generous could ever fill our space rockets' enormous fuel tanks? Might it not rather be from professional profiteers that the huge loans for such fantastic happenings will come?

Some of us are born with shallow roots and are not meant to dig into the dirt for food. No vigorous health, no fingernails, no leathery skin, no deep fluffy lungs, no mind to kill. Instead they are made to rely on their wits and on our industries' regurgitated food.

This might be the man who specializes in terror, composing pictures that should shake and frighten me. He spreads addictions and makes them pay. He lives on strikes, on breakdowns, on the desperation of my heart. He may hook me on credit cards. He may polish his nearsightedness to a microscope so perfectly focused on our today, he simply "out observes" in details his more poetic friend whose left eye likes to wonder off to the clouds and whales, to the future and past. He may live from dubious laws, from pebbles he sneaks into my soup. This wizard may juggle my figures and zig-zags his thoughts so heavenly fast, that he leaves my pockets empty and me dumbfounded in the dark. He mumbo-jumbos my drowsy mind into some invented shame and carries a sweet, cheerful absolution in his pocket for sale. He is the father of psychology who learned from the gypsy matron the skill of how to probe for my weaknesses, my secret cracks, bents, vices and hang-ups, the holes in my integrity, my penchants and cowardice. If I let him, he discreetly fills my heart with thorns and offers to pull them out again taking a chicken for pay. At night he might very dimly hold up at lawyer's point my children's piggybanks. Graciously, he dearly loans us back a bundle when the sun is up. He might do the same with a country's potato crop. He maintains himself from his cuckoo's eggs. Maybe in good housedog fashion he just gives me cheerful companionship to be fed. It is sound goodness in his moonlit mind, to have the advertising agent talk sickness, envy, fear into my mind. He might discreetly plant a hungry flea under my pants. Later he will have his salesman with the remedy drop by. He ridicules my inborn shame and soon after sells me a condom. He is the fox that charms the crow to sing and drop its prey. In our sullen routine of a working day he is the cheerleading storyteller, swinger, attention snatcher, pocketing discreetly the best morsels for pay while I gape in awe or joy. He might be just a patient friend who hears me out to earn his day. Such seem the unobstructed freeways life has allotted to his joys.

There is no doubt, this magician has also been sent to me just as another adventurer to test me, to tease out and mobilize what great spirits I have never guessed are dormant in me. Should I be mad at this fine teacher from whom there is so much to be learned?

A hardy parasite for every great provider to mop up his surplus, is that not what nature's wisdom recommends? A well-mannered profiteer for the deadly efficient fisher who buries himself in dead fish. A surf bum poet for every overachiever under whose whip the earth is grieving now. Here seems another elusive symbiosis not yet mentioned in *The Wonders of Nature* book.

There are many such suckling mistletoes that the great spirit wisely plants in our tree to grow. These experimenters in survival probe after every possible bug and fault in us. They drive their roots into my weak spots, into my cowardice, my thoughts that fell asleep, into my warts, fears, cracks and nooks. And they make good use of all these faults. There are those predisposed to simply become filthy rich and to be colleagues to those ants chosen to serve as huge living storage tanks for the ant people's honeydew. What clowns, what imaginative inspectors for our wits, what wonderful fund-raisers for our dear and daring projects, what sharpening stones we have here!

Should the creator have put me in charge of the project to send a species to explore space, I could think of no better suited scenario than this perverted, over populated, hyperrational, gadget- and grandeur-loving, adolescent-minded human society, with all its hilarious and abominable trimmings—orgasms by phone and all—which is replacing now my old idyllic home.

The more I find out about how you are made: your health, your pimples and crutches and suspenders, your memories and the holes in them, what you have been told and who are the secret crybabies in your soul, the more I find that the way you live is the best way for you to survive. I wonder whether we are not a little like the raindrops that trickle in puzzling zig-zags through all kinds of winds, turbulence and clouds never quite sure they will end up by a dormant nut, in the sea, on a rock, or maybe on my cap.

124
Of three-dimensional and of multiple socialization.

Why in two and a half billion years of creative tinkering did life not also contrive a pill of socializing hormones for us? Why did it not provide us with a "love-your-neighbor" drug akin to the witch magic that drums a "people" of the slime mold into a love march, each fall uniting these microscopic creatures of the woods into one body and brilliantly yellow flower to do together what an individual cannot yet do. To the contrary, it granted us a formidable system of rejection, borders and fences that animates each of us to be a self-replicating subspecies of man and to diversify bringing out each his own model, keeping up her own studio and world.

This immune system in our love is a horizontal barrier, wedged loosely between the creatures—a repellent discouraging them to unionize just flat and between peers and snowball into an avalanche. It keeps the daughter from falling back into her mother's arms. It seems life's master stroke for diversity. In Gaia's quest to dot, stripe and color herself and lace more exotic cultures and blossoms into her hair, I see ourselves blessed with such a system of chemical lies, of anti-neighborliness, of keep-off signs, and all kinds of taboos, codes, and mental skins to keep our many races and truths from mixing to a sullen gray. No life form without a membrane of some kind is known. This now hotly disputed barrier for short-cuts among us has, up to now, elevated us above a flatlander's paradise and is the hindrance to practicalities. May voracious investors in the international assembly line reflect on this. Then it seems that each time a commercial colossus doubles its stake in the big board game with a new break-in, it also doubles its contribution to boredom in the world. One may wonder here, what worthy, lasting joys the giant Mac Cola may derive from gulping down our world's million ethnic foods and drinks which our forbearers have patiently embroidered into our routine for so many years. One might further wonder why some giant religions insist on missionizing local religions and breaking them with their soul-food chains.

The task given to our economists: to level our ethnic diversity and cash in on this simplification, to modify a hundred generations' economy to fit a five years plan. In this process our bursting lawbooks become our bursting garbage dumps where we bury our mental refuse. Billions of options, of long-range ideas, many subspecies of our cultures are "incinerated" to get productivity on a faster and faster track so to avoid its own footprints. Do puritan economists and legislator do the same with our options as we, the puritan eaters, do with the fish? We head, gut, skin, bone, fillet and finally nibble on what's left, wasting ultimately 77% of the blackcod.

Yet do we not also catch ourselves time and again applauding mother earth for talking in as many different languages as there are in the tundra kinds of grasses, mosses, lichens, bugs, and flowers and for having such a profusion of flutists, hooters, howlers, whiners, whistlers, and drummers performing her Pastorale? I think that a born thief or parasite who puts all his "colors" into becoming good at what he is meant to be, becomes a happy colorful thief, and that a born helper doing the same becomes a happy helper. To outgrow all role models, to become a brighter poppy all by its own with no obsession to missionize among the daisies, the buttercups and the goldenrods—is that not how one becomes a natural and one of nature's saints? A life seems to me not necessarily a great life because it is "world-improving," Noble Prize-winning, heroic, or greatly entertaining. It might be a great life because it does great in becoming in all its beauty what it is meant to be; be it called to be a messiah, a cheesemaker, an expert forger or fermenter. Maybe it needn't be a guru, an Aristotle; perhaps it is a handyman, maybe she who can dance on deep snow without leaving tracks, who gets from life the highest prize.

Still, my growing rationality might ultimately turn out to be that new social hormone that in an emergency can break open the immune system of my love. It can slowly make the personal secrets public which each individual has pledged to guard for its offspring. It can salvage a limping man in a joint venture and put him to work as an informer. It might be my being subconscious of my most vital functions that protects me from leaking and becoming unscrupulously such an informer.

In spells of glorious strength I am also lured into a positive routine-breaking crisis leaving me full of leaky conclusions and cracks of promising doubt. In such ego-shattering bangs, a woman's or a man's credo in which the ego has egged up may burst. Windows fling open. My mentality gets invited to seductive new views, perhaps showing me a whole new string of forgotten relatives to welcome in who live far in the future, under the bark of a spruce, maybe in my obscured heritage deep in the past. Unnoticed little thingies on the other side of the humanists' fence turn out to be my dear neighbors and partners—welcome in!

Neither one loaf of bread nor a whole pile of loaves are a happy field peopled with wheat, with starlings, chamomiles, farmers and butterflies swaying to a soft blue September song. Yet I thought I could lick my egoism by simply exchanging in my thinking the "I" for the "we." I forgot that even humanism is a monoculture.

125

Wilderness is explosive company that whispers dangerous ideas into Christian ears. Yet tell me, is there a gentler drug to break my stare than wilderness?

When I hear preaching for more and more holding of hands and minds in a circle, claustrophobia starts itching me. When so many side all their psychic powers with just rationality, the accident might well happen that these "circle-men" will generate a mental cyclone that whirls a society of egoists around itself so fast that it will uproot and draw into its center everything: beasts, plants, genes, our love and our thoughts. And where the eye of this uninspired knowledge-storm has passed, the lush land out there and the lush land in our instinctive world are left in shambles and tears. The potency of our nuclear warheads will seem but a trifle in such a shattering fusion of ego-minds. Can you think of any critter on earth that would not shiver with fear should all the troops of mankind withdraw from life's society into a sect on the fast track and among themselves make a separate pact? Such cleverness should soon know how to audio-harvest and process all the fish of an entire bay in one single haul and make us forget how to live neighborly with the fish. It could empower one desk of the commodity exchange to suck up the entire world crop of sugar cane in one particular way, leaving the stumps and the stench of a million dead hopes and joys all over the world thrown into the skies to fall out as a black and silent spring in our children's minds. I note a rapid shift away from pursuing and passing on knowledge that strengthens the autonomous individual and its relation to the cosmos toward producing and disseminating knowledge that strengthens the dominance a society has over the individual. Think, for example, of the power over the autonomous individual that is given to such a society after the Human Genome Project is done.

A "forbidden" knowledge seems to tumor from such a separate pact which asks each to bring in the secrets he guards that make him unique. Informers are promised in return regurgitated food, more information, self-pleasures and security produced on a common assembly line. Yet the pursuit of this kind of knowledge may forget our young, for it still aims to engender a robot, Miss Technology, as our maid rather than to wake up and nourish the poet in a child.

And so one may awake in the morning to the sour surprise that over night the crowd has driven one more stake into one's inner land, to claim another of one's rivers, another secret, to clear another plot where a person tended his own little crazinesses and joys, his brain children, his poetry, his unique kind of clover and grass.

The whole world seems to me a dialogue between natural expressions that talk, that hiss, grimace, explode, smile, communicate in perfumes, signal or simply shine yet might ultimately rhyme. Names are pieces of a jigsaw puzzle that slowly defuse when their underlying form is revealed. Patterns become visible; things made of things become visible. To withdraw from this great society into a sect we call humanity could become tragic to our minds when one considers that our deeper forms of thought are so intimately rooted in a picture language of the whole flora and fauna that give us the wonderful capacity to see in likenesses and rhymes. Might the fable of the Tower of Babel be prophetically speaking about the United Nations and the Common Market and their ambitions for us? Might it be the divine old tempter again who takes us for a test on top of Capitol Hill, showing us all the temporary riches we can gain if we subscribe to him and his projects our souls and we join in one common market, one huge club of shameless informers, one Internet, one hammer, one common economy cooking food only for man?

Have there ever before been so many missionaries at work? Many who seem to have not succeeded well in their personal world are trying to make good by preaching some kind of united nations, a gentler, meeker world agreeable to handicapped souls, a gospel of socialized health care, better safety, comfort and pest control, an ocean with no wind and waves, sanitized ponds and minds, a kind of Teamster's Union of our souls.

What a treat for my gloomy mood that I can also think about the first few among us who plunge into a daring change in the way they socialize. They break out of that hoop; men and women who prove stronger than their old taming and wriggle themselves out of that colossal all-providing lap. They cut their cord to humanism, and escape from that egg to love out in the sun, the rain, the hail, the winds, to socialize less selectively again. We hope to disperse more freely our compassion which our dear neighbors, dear potatoes, dear sheep, and cows have monopolized for so long. We plunge into this enormous undertaking to rearrange each his own personal mythology and to harmonize it not only with the needs of man but with the needs of life. We train to become general practitioners—to become fit and eligible to join that cosmopolitan meeting place that is one step beyond man in the hierarchy of societies. We wire together clusters of ideas that have been ferociously kept separate by laureates of mental domains with their compartment logic and we make one thought picture of them as we start to wire symbiotic ideas into the ecosystem of the Amazon. We are after a break through in our science of relationships that implicates all our applied sciences.

Maybe it is this kind of scooting closer to God that the age old love to be free to see is all about? And so we follow the raven and leap from the Ark.

Would you have imagined that at times I become so homesick, I can barely breathe? I need to be out in this land we spared from our success, to be loved by it, hurt, and made fun of or impotent, thrown down and teased, to bathe in its infinite chemical languages that modify behavior so to keep that great society in tune, to freely breathe in and breathe out all those wildly exaggerated thought-pictures that flood me with an intoxicating beauty beyond the reach of a humanistic vision. I can wonder about all the wonders that litter it. Wilderness is the kind of soil I can seed with my wildest questions and watch their answers grow. To my mind wilderness has sex appeal. This is a love enslaving me that seems not different from the love for a woman. Who should not gladly give a hundred comfortable hours for a morsel of its gifts?

Einstein's theorem that light behaves as both particles and waves remains unexplained, yet that faith has worked well. The simple faith that all life is one organism is for me also such a fruitful unexplained theorem.

126

> I am fascinated by the koans lived by nature's great sinners and saints and the bewilderingly grand logic that seems to hide behind them.

A hunch tells me that the awareness shyly budding in us can slowly catch up with wilderness. In this joyride over the edge of my common sense world, I dive into my psyche beyond what has been domesticated and herded behind Sir Humanism's garden fence, beyond my own reproductive zest, beyond my allegiance to man. To qualify for this fabulous ride I have to lose my old innocence. I think we all have to. That newly discovered wilderness will not be peopled by the innocent and the primitive of yesterday's health nor by the simply virtuous, the good boys and those that kept their minds all spic and span, but by those who got sick with anger, have overfished, blundered, sinned, goofed, drifted, been bored in seminars and waded through mud, got kicked out, split in two, yet ultimately became lucky and got beached as pioneers on a new reality that is larger than man's welfare. If there will be vagabonds there, they have wriggled free of many myths, slogans, refuges and traps before. There, a woodsman will have excelled in creative thinking and in biology. A future pedestrian will have driven a million miles. If there will be innocence, it will be an earned serenity that survived a cataclysmic world in which our five year plans collided with nature's million year plans. In this mutagenic happening, tougher thoughts may synthesize that can give me mental immunity against banal slogans like: "work for a better world for man," that have echoed through my mind too long, and played havoc with all life that could not readily explain to me its use.

Every act has to finally cross the fire line and recombine with the associates of this new multiple mind: my fishing, the phone calls, my relationships and preferences, my mythology, my pest controls and heroes. In this new light everything I know needs on a higher level of knowledge to be born again. There will be new "do's" and "do-not-do's," new tears, new celebrities, saints and other Nobel Prizes; poisons may turn into medicines, garbage into a resource, vandalism into surgery in this change of scale. The fisher who needs to kill and brings in the smallest load to survive may then become the hero. Every action, every feeling, every savage beauty existing begs to be seen, reconsidered and also loved on that eighth day in the epic of our growing awareness. Old forms will disintegrate while being integrated into their underlying form according to a new multi-species view of the mind. Creatures will not only reveal their form into space but also their form into time.

What could an innocent man know of how sadly a graveyard of stumps looks at us after a forest has lost a battle with our saws? We of the generation of exterminators and feelers, we have seen; we should better know how depressing such a relationship finally becomes; we learned the hard way how a forest looks after we degraded it into a tree farm, dragged it into slavery and it lost its soul. We know how eloquent a storyteller a forest can be that we respect and allow it to keep its underbrush and elders and to remain free. And now when we cold-blooded clear-cut a forest we are with a friend that dies. Did you see that "apartment house" out there with its hundred different little tenants cheerfully chirping, munching, experimenting, chopping and singing away? The blind see in it just as old dead and no-good tree.

Also we highliners of the fishing fleet out there who fished our minds bloody and sick, after we got drunk on the success of our fishing machines and lost track of how much is enough, we can daily hear the sea pleading us to become a friend. We can be the first to become pensive about what we do to our blue mistress, the sea. We can start to wonder whether creatures in their undomesticated state of intelligence might not be a little closer to the way of the gods than we are when we step elegantly out of line to put on that golden captain's hat, to become virtuous men, to shout orders to paradise. You may say: lion and fish are crude, a weed greedy. Don't laugh at these acts! They have been refined for three billion years—our virtues and our super corn a mere two thousand years.

I try to rid myself now of my weird sense of value as old as the legendary Job ending "flooded" with his numerous cattle that still infests my veins. Why should God have buried him in such wealth for recompense?

No, our newest probes and instruments for better vision need not always be used for strategic information and for locating enemies or prey but can again be religious instruments and magic carpets simply meant to give us a high. Gradually their capacity may approach that of our soul's binary vision in which one eye is placed into the now and another inner eye seven generations and species away. Slowly our conscious is initiated into The Way and also allowed to know. Like ants we may have to build these bridges and ladders to better viewpoints, bridges made of our pains, goofs, losses, sins, and of throw-away people so others can safely walk over and upon them and finally land on that promised mind. We may still astonish the old economist in us and discover that to seed the wheat together again with some poppies, chamomile, caterpillars, moles and butterflies can be closer to The Way's baking good bread for all.

It will be our cocky adolescent science growing mature, humble and wise that will lead us there, our macho-science that has found an Eve; the science of the daredevils who bite into any weedy, seedy idea to feel it out, and then the green, motherly science of the mamas who seem always late, who slowly, intuitively ruminate the crude chunks of all our hair-raising thoughts. Quietly the science of social laws and appropriate rights, after incorporating the neighbors, the women, children, the blacks, greens and gays, will also bring into our social circle the marshes that harbor our songbirds and the foaming shores that house our neighbors the barnacles and the crabs. With each farther penetrating lens or thought which helps us to follow farther the ripples of our in and out-going acts, we may find new unexpected members in the circle of our relatives and friends. This, I feel, is how our intellect may compose that Great Society. Did you realize that when you act, the destiny of every thing big and small in the cosmos changes? So, when we make decisions, whether we like it or not, we each act as a president of the world.

And as a treat, are we not all blessed with the joy of bragging about our finds? This sweet self-reenforcement is surely one of nature's catchiest baits. Is it not the father of great insights since our history began? Did it not find recruits for its deadliest discovery raids? What has not been done for these peacock feathers of the mind?

You may wait for some fellow to write the new laws all rhymed and polished with a rocket launched into the sky. Watch out! Can it really happen this way? We probably must each add just bits and crumbs. We might never know the full scheme until we go.

127
Is it good to go for a safe mental environment and whitewash the world?

Later, our time might well be remembered as the revolution for orderly, docile light—a revolution that should fill our retinas with only man-made and inoffensive forms and information which make sense and are harmonious to hyperrational minds. To help us to forget a nostalgia for the bewildering sense of beauty of our animal soul, every visible surface seems to be landscaped, painted over, weeded, simplified, its ghosts busted, and domesticated. Under this sight-conditioned dome for simpleton souls, the face of Mother Earth is lamed, freed of questions and sanitized. All moles and weed flowers are kept from surfacing in her lawns. The volcanoes are sewn closed so that a mind seriously at work might not be infected by strange, upsetting ideas. No uncensored messages, no weed thoughts, mental germs, no creative chaos, and mosquito dances; no paradoxes, no rotting apple or daddy-long-legs; no fierce passion or long-distance calls from generations away should disturb this orderly working scene. When a symphony so simple is played, we needn't be poets; soldiers, fishers, data crunchers can fall in step with the thrill to know it by heart.

Is it good that nature's chorus of messages is whitewashed and replaced with a few easy assumptions, slogans and credos? Is it good that we culture the children "in vitro" in a greenhouse for rationality, keep them safely within an egg, shelter them from the natural sounds, sights and signs so they may never have to learn living with anxiety but may remain eternal embryos in a society's bowels? Should one plug the children into controlled running water and information as soon as their eyes burst from the placenta into light and spring? Should we nicely surround ourselves with a beauty wholly adapted to our logic and mathematical skill?

Break two eggs into a pan—one, a ranch egg from a rooster and hen that knew nettles, dunghills and worms; another from a hen in a battery cage and compare the quality of their yokes. Take two men: a utilitarian man, freshly baked from the mass education's assembly line; and a home-made man, raised and educated on the periphery of our society's dome, and compare the liveliness of their souls.

What is the haste to rub out nature's awesome picture language which we cannot reduce into words and control, but which keeps seeding yeasty question marks, triggers neurochemicals and talks to us in awe-some rhymes and metaphors? Should fading flowers quickly be carted to the dump so an unwanted wisdom that defies our personality cult may never again be stirred? Do we do right to surround ourselves with just our own few memories, our own great deeds and heroes, with our dear cattle and fields and cut off our dialogue with the free animals and plants that are all great professionals begging us to be heard and seen, so that we may undisturbedly keep on living in our dear mania of superiority? Do we for-get how little in man's nature is manmade? When withdrawing into such a golden egg, who is going to lead the merry army of amnesiacs?

A person with an organically grown mind can handle and enjoy bewil-dering scenes, all seedy, all pregnant with questions searching far and soar-ing higher than the tribe of man, full of turbulent beauty, unsellable values and dangerous advice. She can dive into deeper thoughts than those of our paradigms, concepts and credos specially modeled for our own peace of mind. She can visit outdoor schools for mental courage that lure us into a world even more fantastic than the one of Public and Bible schools. She can watch an outdoor play about justice so forgiving that her learned sense of fairness gapes in awe of all the options for forgiveness she sees acted out. Here a poetic, stunningly beautiful mind may form that can arouse another mind so to spurt forth its fecund, hidden ideas as pollen and sperm.

No, I am not an E.T. from another world whose mind needs to be sealed in a globe to walk this nifty Earth full of infectious sights. My thoughts need not yet tiptoe on wall-to-wall carpet, so to speak—for fear of breaking a bone.

There are other forms than the forms disclosed by common light that cannot be whitewashed so easily. When the poet in me falls in love with the land I am standing on, with a woman, a dream, a mighty tree, a roaring sea, with a splendid idea, then magic light floods the stage: Everything lights up; the pimples, the eyes, shady ladies, thunderheads, sicknesses and snores, thistles, forest fires and sins; even a visit to a lawyer full of foul play may then turn into a humorous play.

I nearly went blind in those greater forms, in which everything is so superlative, it seldom fits into our context, alphabet, generation or fence. I see now better how blindness to this audacious harmony was well-meaningly bred in me for fear that a fine-tuned sensitivity could disperse me dangerously beyond the immediate grim needs of our numerous herds of men who now avidly elbow about. Instead a bent for more raw energy, better defense techniques and ever bigger mousetraps is triggered. It seems to be this crisis of wicked crowdedness that has blotted out my luxurious vision beyond the useful and makes my generation the most practical, the best exterminator of ghost, soul and wilderness yet.

Still, in this dangerous light, faster than light, I get a chance to see a tree with its blossoms of a thousand springs hanging in it. I can see winged carrots. I can see landscapes of many full moons spread up and out into one single scene. It makes me carefully step and sidestep as if other generations and species were just other neighbors like you and myself. Maybe that magic light gives a creature clairvoyance so it can mend now what later others will break. Maybe in this light a fisherman wants to hover over himself to ask his ego for an impact statement and find out whether he lately has performed to his heart's content or not. Perhaps a woman can see the hoop around what all she cares about and find out how tall or how small she is.

And for a souvenir: are we not all invited to be playmates of the fabulous Odysseus sent away from a cozy home on a voyage to the demi-gods to be instructed, thrown into the churning sea, to Yama and Hades, into the tangle of nuclear power and the international businesses, lured to Pandora's "Grand Opening" of the human genome, led to hear the sweet song of the windwaved grasses and the saga of an old thorny acacia tree?

Maybe we can even outdo Odysseus and learn a little better how to pardon. You know, I remember nothing that I wish hadn't happened to me. Sometimes I wish more tumult had happened to me. When I failed, some expected me to repent and moan. I like to simply say: "I learned."

If we make it through this latest purgatory, imagine the goodly pile of new experiences we can claim.

128

I nearly forgot that in luminous times "to become wholly practical" is a damnation referring to a mind that is to be exiled into the world of simpletons.

The rivers, the woods and our children seem to become in many adult minds the same. They become resources that are to be well-prepared, fertilized and used. They are to be pruned, straightened out, the wings of their minds clipped and shaped into good shovels, good workmen, nurses, horsepower, memory banks and telephone poles. The advice given to our children then becomes useful advice, always practical as well as useful advice. What terrible advice is this! Why this unbridled effort to lure our children into the trauma of a practical life? Why this terror that our children might choose a more poetic lifestyle than we did? No wonder that years ago Gila, one of our daughters, begged me, "Please, Dad, don't ever use that terrible reminder—be practical!—on me again!"

I hear the whole planet quivering with hope that we may overcome being its practical freaks, and become its poets and improvisers instead.

129

I have bent and tried to smooth this kinky thought in many ways and still it leaves blisters in my mind.

To fall in love—one man and one woman—to chisel on an individualistic world with few outside commands, a world many generations tall, to plunge into its dangers, to be romantic about it all, to be a subspecies all on its own, was that not our own wild life and one of nature's seven wonders for a long, long time? The oceans so deep and sparkling blue, the steppes covered with their flower quilts, the taiga, the rain forests, the Himalayas that get us high, so many continents can people that homemade mind. And it seems such a privilege to be the king or queen of it all—and to have no middle-man to one's own soul.

And now this awesome happening of a six billion and still mushrooming crowd that may turn us into each other's enemies soon. This tremendous friction, this emergency combustion of each man's psychic power to raw physical knowledge of how to more aggressively elbow around seems an emergency self-defense that comes close to the sea cucumber's eviscerating finally its inner anatomy to distract an enemy and save its life. We fatigue and bleed each other in our traffic jams. We evolve ever meaner immune systems in our minds to deter the onslaught of the many hordes of fellowmen that replace our old predators: the lions, tigers, the smallpox and sundry suckers. The overload of stimulation erases our inhibitions and our shame. We react biologically as any plant does that's too much nibbled on. We brandish better dressed meanness, mental toxins, hyperrationality, killer thoughts and tougher lies. We become such tight egoists that we become even immune against the creative fevers of our own souls. Some end up a ball of lice on a dead cat and became each other's prey. No wonder there is a frenzy to horde and to speed as time, love, food, friends, homesteads and elbow room seem to be running out.

Will we become ten billion wicked foxes milling ever smarter on this little physical world, endlessly outdoing, out scheming, out advertising each other to charm the ten thousand ravens to sing and drop their morsel of cheese? Or will we call back brother death from exile and allow him to be again our dear allotter of ample elbow room, the good habitat for kindness, the habitat that retires meanness, thorns and gloom? Think of the staggering amount of our energy, GNP and time we now spend to mislead and impress each other and to puff ourselves up. Will we spend more hours on display bowers than the bower birds do?

There is now a discreet hope lingering in myself and others too. I wish our children the good luck that they can be mentally braver than we are and overcome the terror to change their personal mythology in order to give preference to save the endangered no-man's land from us instead of dutifully hacking it down, infusing its raw energy and its dead meat and wood into failing human lives which otherwise come to the end of their term. I secretly hope our children will rebel should we try to shackle them to our sickbeds and make nurses of them. I hope they will be less pre-occupied with saving human lives than us and will learn to better enjoy the nostalgic soul song of the floods and ebbs, of birth and death. I hope they need not overly flinch when our huge masses need to be thinned out.

No, you need not feel obliged to go out to feverishly drill, log, inject, cultivate, transplant and ship more grain around and lobby with Mother Nature for one more loan to extend my years when heaven lets down the ladder for me to ascend. When we can't bear watching a person suffer and die, our kids will inherit extra troubles from us.

I wish you could prove me wrong and show me a remedy that has become socially acceptable by now.

130

A field of cabbage is an unhappy dog pulling on a leash. I turn it loose and zoom—it dashes to a more stable level of unity.

Unstable unions might come from my dependence on the corn in your field. They might be a merger of ITT and IBM, a natural gas pipeline from Moscow to Paris, or Roger and Bill deciding to shut up and join in a polite and profitable friendship team. They might come from uniting the Hps of a dozen happily chattering creeks into a hell of a power dam. These are explosive liaisons that walk tipsily on high heels. They are soap bubbles always anxious to burst. Often they thrive on hiding tears and fears, on sweat, on holding back, on love in a rush, on walking the tight rope of being polite, on lawyers' whips, on cowardice, self-denial and cover-ups. Continuously they want to be weeded, courted, painted, patrolled, lied to, reinforced, bribed and greased; if not, they squeak. For in these unions there seems so much shut out and ordered to play dead. Much of what I cannot spread on my daily bread or take to the bank or to bed or does not pay me for my love is left out. Even my dear soul might be left out in such a pact. In such company you soon get goose bumps from all the smiles that squeak.

For others not so gifted with that heavy-handed practical sense and happy to be skipping pebbles in the creek and not bricks, for those who are still staying unpretentiously out of town and have not yet melted down, our need for unity might have become instead an exercise to see better; to drift with grace from sight to sight, learning to enjoy a meadow without a fence hugging itself, to find the links from you to me or from an anger to the mental image relieving it. We love to discover likenesses and metaphors. We may take into our circle of neighbors a fireweed, a weirdo, a banyan tree, an exile, a thought that's kicked out of town, an evening sky full of fireclouds. We listen to the tricksters in our souls that reward us well for considering them. We like to fish in God's bag of tricks and play at fitting whatever we fish into his puzzling work. Name anything; it seems an eager candidate to show off its rhymes. Here seems a science at work that enjoys to simply turn on the light in what I do not like. And is there anything purring as well as to be wealthy in unabashed relationships?

This seems to me a time of many diggers and not so many seers. Still, some of us who have a bent for a more poetic life, we like to toss all kinds of mockingbirds and forget-me-nots between our formal unities. Name anything that comes to mind; we find if kindly invited in, it stops to squeak and horrify and starts to lubricate our relationships.

131

Looking down from a 747 do we not seem a kind of smallpox? We leave so many scars on the face of the earth.

When I go through an agricultural fair, it is a grain of sand in my eyes to remember that in some early cultures agriculture was a sacrilege. In that ecstatic time our planet's flora was a goodly pile of flourishing weeds free to give and go as they pleased. Mother Earth was fond of being awfully diverse. Man, beasts and plants grew part of their stems, leaves, fruits, part of their ideas, seeds, biomass and genes to set the table so each species may be the other's guest. The trails were woven in all imaginable directions then. It was an enchanted loom that was free to weave day after day every rhyme etched into the genes of every living fiber deeper into space and deeper into time into a more exotic tapestry.

Nonetheless, we got bold and introduced agriculture—our effort to monopolize an ecosystem that loves to cook food and send invitations not only for us but for all. We chased everybody else away from the table. A heartbreaking tremor went through the forests, the plains, the marshes, the buffaloes, the fleet of dragonflies. Even the flora of our minds shivered with fear from the harshness of which we become possessed. From now on, it was proclaimed, there will be only one direction for the trails—the one that leads to man.

We picked from each appetizing species the most perverted for keeps—the lazy, the cowards, the too fat, those that docilely walked into our traps, the too sweet, too sour, too big or tender-skinned for their own good. We picked those that broke the law of moderation. We inbred their stupidities and excesses. We made them kings of a feedlot paradise. We spent our time to enlarge their "sins." Every leaf, every stem and branch, even the sunflowers, were ordered to bend over our way and prostrate themselves. The plants were prevented from humming their own songs but commanded to blast, each species, one single note in the international hymn of man; a working hum, a number in our commodity exchange. Much like a man would be spared just for the extraordinary size of his balls, each animal and plant had to report a deformity that made it especially useful to us to be legalized and invited in. A wart, a bulging talent, a mind with a horn, an organ that is a giant or dwarf, a fruit that's all sugar and no seeds, a neck of a giraffe might be the ticket for getting in. And so the holocaust in our sour companionship with the family of life began.

"Eureka! Food for another billion men!" echoed shouts of pride. And, judged by the endless supermarket shelves, it infected many of us with quite an eating binge. True to the Bible story, " . . . to toil in the sweat of his brow . . . " we also wake now each morning to the lamentable bellowing of all nature we mutilated into such helplessness, it can only feed and drink but from our hands.

My forebears were pioneers. They were the missionaries who baptized the forests, the brooks, the pristine land. They must have slept with their axes in hand, they were so much in love with that mighty tool. That pioneer spirit still haunts my mind. Yet I realize that this heroic slave hunting crusade through Graceland is now out of time and has turned into a negative heroism. How welcome now is a science that is fascinated with

224

more exciting things than to fulfill that prophecy and make of the landscape just a simple extension of our bowels. How welcome a feminine science, finally, that is not exclusively out to lick more of Mother Nature's land. How welcome scientists that are not chickens endlessly scratching for our advantages but lift their eyes from the ground. Has not a bird in the bush now become worth two birds in our hands?

Who in town would have thought that it is not the malaria, not the Russians, the Gypsies, the tsetse flies or a stock market crash, but that it might well be our gently munching cow that turns out to be the deadliest pest of all attacking the quality of our lives. With every pair of tire sandals I wear through loafing up in the Sierras and down in the countryside it strikes me more: It is this dull animal that hooves and munches the very soil from underneath our feet while slaving for our exaggerated hunger for meat—and it is our excessive lust to eat that deadly muncher that needs now our pesticides.

Genetic engineering may consider that its effort to force the corn to bulge its ears one extra inch has become the unneeded effort to bulge our world population another inch. Agronomes can remind themselves that for each further insect, blackbird, iguana, tumbleweed and sundry creeper they can evict from the fields, they invite one additional man to squeeze in. Are our morals and our science not still geared so that there is every hour a thousand more men and a thousand less birds? When on Sunday the mind has the privilege to glide high on a kite, it might well decide from up there that our obsession to save human lives might have for now become an unwanted effort in the epic of our planet's life.

Let me expand: you may be a scientist who found, hiding deep in a still free semi-desert, a sapote tree, happily sunning its sour fruits. Heroically you might be out there in that baking sun trying to whip that no-good tree into a lush orchard giving us commercial fruits, big and yummy-sweet. Deep down, where I am more than a man, I hope you fail. I wish you would find out why I am so mean. At times, maybe you also now wish I would come home empty-handed from a trip and I would not get that last happy fish.

And so the woods, the deer I hunt, the uncensored thoughts that bubble up from my sediments, my mistress the sea, everything alive that offers me help—I do not want to see them anymore simply as my resources, good only to be used, traded, kicked around. They are not my underlings. There is a head for the flora and fauna in my divine trinity.

Do you know of anything since the last ice age that, in spite of its miraculous instant success, has brought a nastier bellyache to the earth than our agriculture, our inbreeding of the abnormalities in her animals and plants? We plow under what is healthy and keep alive the freaks. And one might here stop and wonder: in spite of its glittering prospects might not the Common Market, with its tendency toward monocultures, go down in the geology of Europa's soils and minds, short of a nuclear war, as the most cataclysmic happening since the last ice-age left this continent? Will this pact be remembered as the dark triumph for the international corporations?

When a people gives up its shame; when it goes topless and joins a Common Market, a common bed, one kind of pants fitting all, simply for materialistic gains, when it skins itself alive and invites in every Turk, every German, every salesman, the fruit flies, the Coke Empire and the bees from Africa, every Theo, every spy, it might be in business and soon rake in dazzling profits. Yet I wonder, will this latest form of communism not soon give Gaia a bellyache?

Many of us have lost our pride to be Napoleon riding on a white stallion through the wonderful lands and command the break up of the symbiosis of all life and make each useful kind of plants to march separately in lonely fenced off furrows—prostrating themselves in front of us and our Reich. We do not want to compete anymore among ourselves to cultivate the fattest warts on the face of this earth. We do not need to bathe in mare's milk while the paddleducks don't even have water to drink. Meanwhile, wilderness so successful in imagination still tries to subsidize the failing mentality of practicality in our towns and fields.

Thank God, a new breed of women and men are again on a high and they clearly hear their intuition teaching them that bending every creature our way heaps contempt on a wisdom that has served us well. Imagine if we would dutifully pull down every man on earth to the purely materialistic standard of the soft, cushioned living the superpowers brag about. Might such a tragedy not drag down the whole familiar world?

Who knows, all might yet turn out well. In the grand opening of the Pandora box the wonderful double helix of DNA is showing itself to us.

What a fantastic and timely chance is given to us. Biotechnology can become our stomach growing food for us. Land now on our leash could be turned free to dash for wilderness and grow again inspiration for our kids, should we succeed in not squandering this latest gift simply for piling up even more human biomass.

132

Theo, do not forget that when you act tame you only survive because somebody else does the wildness for you.

No, the animal qualities of our nature that we have defamed in the individual and supposedly left behind, in order to behave humanely among our neighbors—they are not at all dead, not left behind. But society's immune system has decreed, "No more self attacks!" And now we have dutifully jailed our personal wildness and entrusted the key so to have it orchestrated by the nation. In this new setting our wildness can express its brave animal instincts under new respectable names with greater grandiosity.

As mitosis also differentiates and tames "wild" autonomous cells, pressing them into specific functions in my body, making each forget 99% of its genetic memory and capacities, so a step further in socialization, Theo, the autonomous individual, is tamed by pressing him into specialization. Society, with artfully induced forgetfulness, sports, and other masturbations helps me to suppress my native capacities which it finds unsuitable for its mental engineering.

Most of the wild traits of individuals are now discouraged. Freewheeling, yelling, unashamed thinking, judging, reforming, child care and schooling, spying, punishing, fighting, vengeance, lying, educating, slaughtering, bearing arms, baring teeth in menace, and healing have been consolidated in a nation's PR schemes, radar and missile belts, the department of agriculture and that of population management, the CIA, Social Security, its corps of diplomats, the Seventh Fleet.

In order for you and me and our country to survive in the jungle of nations, the political princes may need to act wilder than Machiavelli's lion kings. A nation is as a wolf or a tree: it would soon perish without robust "beastly" qualities. Theo, remember this for sweetener when you are shocked, that out front statesmen do your animal chores so under the umbrella of these "mean" amoral men you may enjoy a "wall to wall carpeted" indoor ethic and your clan can nicely huddle together in good manners. Out front the shepherds and their dogs dance to the ethics of the winds and wolves. Remember this when the ethics expected from you and those of the political realities become for you painfully at odds.

And so, after I acted out my specialty in our natural functions: killing boatloads of fish, I can then indulge in being a good boy playing at being tame, while the other wild chores are performed by different players. A leader, though, is he not the conductor? We expect that person to tell us when and where to act wild. This is how we behave tamely.

And now, one step further in socialization. I see a new experiment that consolidates all of the national ventures in which we socialized our animal qualities into a United Nations. In this superanimal, made of tame and specialized nations, we join our aggression to a grandeur beyond precedent. Here the bulk of our onslaught is reoriented through technology and agriculture toward our wars with the fauna, the flora, the minerals, the other planets. And here we allow ourselves to proceed with the wildest morals. The whole biota of the earth may soon quiver in terror should that "Great Animal" not soon create its soul.

The "Great Animal" brandishes omnipotent horns, the swiftest invisible wings and deadliest stingers: superlative pest- and herbicides, international arsenals of antibiotics, global resource management, GPS, Red Cross, gene raiders, the corps of engineers, the Internet on which we inbreed our cunning. It employs all these to exterminate, to enslave or to cook our neighbors, the flora, fauna and landscape. We hope to relieve ourselves of our sufferings by burdening the other animals and the plants with our pains.

And for a treat: note that lately also our most wonderful wild capacity: to wish others well—(a biological law that decrees that the cannibal discreetly cares for the neighboring village and the fox for the hares if their future litters are to be well fed and prosperous)—is also uniting forces. Maybe the green movements: the tree spikers, the Earth Firsts! and other corps of protectors, the whole global "Conspiracy of the Mamas," are our collective psyche's first tentative biological response—a joint mental undertaking in natural healing. Look, that Great Animal is not just inventing a deadlier stinger—it is starting to create its soul.

133

It amazes me to think that even a stink bug that does not pull a plow can be the success story of a struggling walk to a hundred different North Poles and back, and that the details of this saga are all written in that creature's genome.

I am struck by the idea that the wild land might be the deepest spiritual resource I have. Maybe this is the reason of all my fuss to keep that wild with us. There is lively land whose countless professionals tirelessly reflect, create, exchange genes, make outdoor tests and stubbornly refuse to specialize in making hamburgers and bread for just us. Think how much every minute the spirit of life is inventing in her oozy, yeasty test sites along the Amazon. Imagine, the ants sifted for 20,000 different kinds of social structures and as many kinds of procreation, greetings, and architecture; they came up with 20,000 backup systems of most of their vital functions. This place hums with thinking. This is an arena of unlimited knowledge and is littered with inventions more fantastic than we could have guessed. Here are a billion baseball games in progress. Here I can be cheerfully lost in the belly of God. This land is my parents whom I respect. This is wilderness.

I like these kinds of thoughts. They are the sort of help I need in a time when the more courageous of us start to give the thrift stores some of their too much. We become more careful of what we buy. We consider how the making of a product influences lifestyles. We consider how each time we buy, we compromise a little more of our autonomy. We consider how a dollar spent often turns into a whack of a machete, another hole drilled into the Ark, a bullet spent. We consider that with every thing we now produce we also produce a pile of waste. We dig again ponds for the homeless toads. We breed trees with thorns for the spiders to anchor their cobwebs. We allow some of the Grandmother trees to die and rot by themselves, after we realize how great a housing shortage there is for most critters peopling the woods. We prefer to dive into all that's wildly green and wash the graffiti and slogans off our minds instead of buying Jacuzzi baths for our homes. We are after more mental solutions to needs like safety and trust so that we can wrap a thousand unneeded RPM's in a box and make it a Christmas gift for that lively Lady in Green. Instead of adding their own child to our troops some feel better to adopt a piece of that beautiful land, a laughing river perhaps or a community of a lily pond who needs help, and to live for making it happy again. We can slowly redo our habitat and let it be a garden of food, of companions, of ideas.

Now that we get more signs that life might be one great symphony, no lively mind will want to touch the slogan, "For the betterment of mankind," without being aware that this seductive saying has lured us into an ever more luxurious quarantine.

No, I will never sell my Sunday time. It is the stem of the apple. It is then when I tease my mind to come out of its niche or its mine or from talking fish. It is then when I can get a gentle high and let my thoughts get a little wild, so they may jump a discipline, a career, a fence, may seed and be seeded by wild oats. It is then when I may become a child again who excitedly tiptoes on top of our fence to that legendary enchanted place to get a glimpse. A woman or a man exposed to untamed nature in and around their minds will not see themselves exposed to dirty company anymore but will blush with joy and jubilate in surprise: "What a spinnaker for our minds we have found!"

Wilderness is the show that still gets me away from the immediacy that infests every nook of every day. There, I'm a fish trapped in a well that finds the ocean again. I plunge into a mind so wide, so permissive, so deep, I need not be shocked by whatever you do. And I see reasons for being a little less shocked by what happens to me. That land does to my mind what water does to a fish. Everything there is thought in a grander scale. Members of that association do not love only their neighbors yet do well. My mind loves to sit under this waterfall of ideas—and get a message. If there is a place where wisdom is cooked and served, this is the place.

When someone participates in Holy Communion with this in mind, this person projects a therapeutic picture into my mind.

134

To make things come and go, to make them grow in curls, in lines, in red, in blue—do not the pleasures need as many shades as soils are in the woods; some pleased to rot, others all smiles to make the sapling grow?

It seems that nature programs each of us with his particular pleasure center, a custom made bait for each, designed to lure him swiftly to his personal niche of work—maybe to pull a nail, maybe to add a nail to this world. When unpopular tasks are distributed, of which nice people would hear nothing, an unusual and compelling bait is hung into a mind that can handle the contempt of a crowd.

Are we not all blindfolded differently—each so he hurries straight to his studio—no side glances needed, with no distraction of the mind, no vertigo. In each of us different clearings are opened into what all can be known, a little like cells are triggered to express different genes of their genome according to their environment. Without the blinders no hammer and no chisel would fill the morning air, no hooter's mating call would join the evening serenade out there. Who would still argue with God and compose new thought combinations to even better decorate the world? We might just sit and indulge in applauding the same old merry-go-round, with no one getting up to add a new kind of banana to those already out there. When we take from the river its boulders, its rapids, its falls, do we not take away its murmuring song? Who is Theo defused in comfort? What music comes from a guitar whose strings are relaxed and do not dream all night long of being touched?

I suspect that our minds have a controlled access to all the memories ever amassed in our evolutionary ascent and that we start out as primal cells faintly capable of being triggered by our environment's universal twitter to bring out the character of a "saint" or to favor the traits for the dirty work of some outcast. Inhibitors are activated to blur this or that spot in our memory pool according to Mother Earth's needs for building stones or wrecking crews. Why shouldn't any function of life be allowed to be done with serenity? To momentarily neutralize for a treat the fog-forming chemicals in our memoryscape that focus us on this or that project and to

231

refurbish our faith, the great spirit makes us also gifts of flares, spirited liquors, drugs, mind quakes, holy days, power spots, peepholes, and mountain tops. No, I do not see that we are free to choose the clearings in our minds which make us each walk a path with different curls and curves. It seems that my mind has seldom the mask with the right size of eye openings to appreciate what others do. What a presumptuous belief that life can be beautiful without hate, without betrayal, perversions, lies, teeth, flowers and farts. I am glad I don't have to sit in judgment to earn the ticket for my stay.

135

I like to better learn how diseases fit into my life, how to personally argue with and get the best out of them—and to enjoy what these little rascals in God's menagerie quietly contribute, maybe to me, maybe to the world.

In our obsession to keep and mature every troubled human life, be it faulty in the body or have a knot in the mind, be it a mutant, a freak, a mind in a wheelchair or fallen in a well, do we not also produce the most extraordinary people, criminals, saints, artists, neuters, monks, suckers, missionaries, clowns, all the useful and not so useful neurotics and geniuses, are we not coaxed to produce those experts with a grotesquely one-sided brilliance on which the phenomena of technology thrives?

When the health industry asks me to come to their counters or when it exports health to countries more accepting of death than ours, I am told that health can be given or acquired like a better pair of pants. I wonder now whether this is so. Is health not ultimately the wisdom an organism acquires over its generations as it fights its way out of every new tangle, slogan, pest, virus attack, pit or trap it falls into during its journey of living by its own body and soul? And so a woman and man, as an insect and a tree, we each seem to be given sickness as a biological learning process and a periodic purgatory test that nobody else can pass for us. The glorious state of health seems the prize for a successful effort from within.

For long I naively followed the pretentious slogan that to help others will allow others to afterwards help themselves. Yet might that assumption not be a fashionable coat dressing up one of our less glamorous psychological wants? "Help" and "take over" may be close to synonymous.

No, my good deeds are not bad, but they do limp until I see their complementary side effects. Below my politeness, I suspect that this enormous joint venture in medical research and clinical health care becomes over generations the enemy of personal health and strength and the mother superior of fast socialization and the unofficial foundation of eugenics for a new order of man. It can be the golden chance for unemotional brains to become commanders that may knead and mold this softened human mass according to their idealistic views. With nostalgia I note that robust, autonomous women and bold men of many capacities become unwanted pebbles in their dough. I know of no other science that storms us so irreversibly and quickly toward that brave new hive of men. Many, many arms are now stretched out for help without the least of shame. Many people are ready to gladly step down as their own kings, ready to melt and transcribe their souls to this unison so to be spared a personality test, all thankful to become servants and saved. All this on the assumption that sickness is not a friend. Yet is that ultimately so?

This latest generation that is partly produced, jerry-quilted and kept going by the health industry's clever shortcuts is now also submitted to quality control. Experts find this generation duller, slower and more obese than previous generations, and more diseases of degeneration are showing up. Experts find that our health got to be a spoiled brat hooked on convenient service and repair.

Pathogenic organisms also seem nature's busiest gardeners and ferrymen. Ceaselessly they ferry the genes around. Ceaselessly they cross breed and plant genes on new ground. They help us not to be wholly prisoners of our own immunity. A woman might say, "This sickness is my mountain to climb; this is my walk to the North Pole; this is my sharpening stone." Sickness seems nature's favorite routine-breaking drug. It can produce invigorating mind-quakes. It can produce cracks in the egg of our mentality and make it hatch. There is much that this shock treatment can awaken in a man which—while in good health—he knows little about. He might be coaxed into strong shameless thinking again. Sickness may also be the grandmother of all mind-altering trips and of mental diversity.

Are we going to be freeloaders and shoot every sickness on the spot? Are we not each allotted a little extra strength, planted with a seed of mutagens or craziness so we may contribute to life's ever more fantastic spectacle not only with our self-replication and manure, but accept the diseases with their mutagenic powers to do their research, their experiments, their magic? It might after all be those disease-forming little buggers that invented the raven's wings. Remember: wings also grew from deformities.

Do you know other hints at Mother Nature's riddle: why she is more fond of sickness than most of us are fond of gold? And consider: would it not be a mediocre god that whispers into my ear to heal and green again the golden birch leaves in fall just to please some obscured souls?

Only now do I realize what a long-avoided hornet's nest it is to find out more about what help means and stands for. It is the least understood word. For some special persons who wish me a break-out from my comfortable merry-go-round, compassion may have little to do with healing and comforting. They hesitate to swiftly extinguish my fevers and fires and stop my whining when I am aglow and being forged under the hammer. They realize that dangerous and great things may be about to come to light in me.

God willing, I will heal of all my sicknesses in one lucky strike. I will realize that in these uninvited happenings, I am made to break camp to become a pathfinder again.

136

After a bold rebellion and tasting the fruits from the science of shortcuts, we shamefully looked at each other and realized that our unfaithful minds were naked.

The magpies, the lupines, the creeks, all the other members of the great rowdy family were up in arms and protesting. How they scolded when we did not wait for our turn; even our souls snorted at our foul play.

On this sultry noon of protest and enraged tears, it was decided to cover up that naked mind. Since then this disloyal corner in our mind has been vesting itself in endless philosophies to our glory and other intellectual fig leaves and rhymes competing for titles in parades of the best-dressed minds.

What a relief to get out from under that disguised intellect, out into the breeze and learn from direct observation, out to the Great Spirit that answers without shame, to gorge on its spectacle without a fig leaf on the mind. What a joy to plunge with the mind all naked into this beautiful land of the koans, so puzzling, so forbidding to a brilliantly dressed mind that is busy applauding itself while it tiptoes in high heels.

I have opened doors in my cultural-imposed limitations and—yes—I caught a cold. But come, see what all there is to be seen!

137
To purge the mind, to become entirely medium for a while, to become from head to toe one giant ear.

Life on earth staggers under the cyclone of our united cunning and endless moaning for a cure of hunger. Breathless there is no rest for applause, for thanks, for giving. Round and round we scheme and struggle for dominance in life's coop, where I have never seen permission to remain a winner. I sense that the whole planet pleads that I become of age and cease to remain a teenager that naively takes our species as the center and attractor. Our humanistic mentality is meant to be temporary—a kind of placenta for an embryonic mind.

Think as a man who is more than a man. Let yourself be touched by the untouchable, I tell myself. *See the unseen, walk bridges mined with the fury of local minds defending their domains; look also through the eyes of an owl, undo the western, rather Marxist and Freudian knot of thoughts that prudently limited psychology to a humanistic drama and nailed it nearly into a box for man alone. As if the history of our loves, of our relationships, of our joy and guilt would have never reached beyond man, woman, work and bread. Risk that dizzying freedom even if it makes you a stuttering fool unable to conclude.* Self-assurance makes great, but ignorant doers.

For this I like to walk about in land we did not simplify and lame. It teaches me brave thinking and not to simply suckle on knowledge that has been killed before, regurgitated and served in books. I can unlearn to simply talk, write, teach, argue in neat furrows and chapters, meekly think in dissected chunks of thoughts one has cut out from the living world and, for a convenient clarity, butchered, sorted and cooked. So many new explanations are opening now that it becomes suspected that sicknesses like overpopulation or cancer may be caused by a retarded intellect which has remained a lifelong fetus and keeps talking in rhymes of the unborn; now that in our notion of good and bad fantastic new bridges are spanned so goodness or badness even misfortune are not certainties anymore, bridges also that reach from our prayers for rain to a downpour the skies boil in response. In such openness the sciences are surprised bumping into each other in front of what seems to be one living system for all. Mathematicians are becoming the artists who paint in our minds the most revolutionary works of art. With our breakthroughs in our science of relationships, how can one remain a complacent humanist nicely curled up in his egg? After the quest for a cooking fire—now the quest for light!

Humanism has for our minds been a seaworthy boat. "Ladies and gentlemen, all globetrotters, we have arrived!" And who would want to stay aboard and not dare to step on an exotic land?

I am booed by my own arbiters when I abuse my thoughts and have them, like oxen, work, day after day, in front of a plow. I am booed when I am chicken and just settle down in a nest of assumptions, when I swiftly capitulate to conclusions. What a treat to sneak out from talking man, from under the cloud of RPM's and all the momentariness that overcasts most of my days. Instead of remaining a clam I can become a curious lad, never quite sure; so many things can then happen to me.

And so as a man so a town should have its sacred places, its tea gardens, its telescopes and boosters for our intuitive mind where executives can take off their mask, be surrounded by life's awesome wealth of memories and be gaping apprentices for a while. I think about places bubbling with life and the phenomena of the elements where one can wash one's mind that suffocates in banalities, places where one also can simply be one's own spectator and wonder how well Theo's drumming, fishing, fluting and whining fit in.

An organically nourished mind can itself become a powerful reservoir of landscapes. It can bring back to life thought pictures that are remedies equaling those of the drug industry. Thought combinations can physically light me up as much as vitamins can do. With all the "bloodlines" from the seen to the seer, from the felt to the feeler, the stinger of a mind can also bleed another man to death. And have you noticed that some know how to dream up their inspirations so well that when in such dreams they walk in the sun, they wake up with a tan? In my dreams my spirits often act out the advice I need.

You look, dream or think your way and I am quite changed. You look at an atom's core or at a dozen arguing crows and they are not the same anymore. I am constantly surrounded by the wake of my thoughts: battering, licking, caressing and always remodeling every of my named and unnamed shore, every information, every word, every form—constantly recreating and rearranging what I see. Your thoughts are powerful songs. Their resonance in me quietly spellbinds my world into other rhymes.

Yet I found an even better remedy for me than courting my own thoughts: when I stop for a treat to stubbornly hope, to set goals, to argue and to whip my own battery of thoughts into battle, when I simply open wide my arms, my mind, my solar plexus, my beliefs and conclusions, my home, my goals and my reputation, when I become one giant ear and vibrate to the zillion hymns with which the earth is serenading me, I find that the spirit of life can do exciting things with me. "Theo, stop your thinking and you stop being the center!" Why should I only listen to Theo—does one not become all that which one becomes aware of, smells, loves, hears or sees? And so tell me what you have seen—and I will tell you who you are.

It seems ultimately not to be my victories but my mischievous little cracks and when I missed my goals, or when I found myself to be wrong, that make me amount to something; I am such a tight unhospitable fortress, yet, in spite of the blindfolds keeping me on target, I slowly become instructed through these cracks in my determination and filled.

138

Christianity seems to have done to the mind what agriculture has done to the land. That soul revolution has brought our minds the miracle love; that green

237

revolution has brought the land the miracle rice. Both successes appear to have comparable long-range side effects.

Although admirably successful on the level of the individuals, the Christian paradigm seems to now be entering a crisis of its unpredicted long-range side effects on global life—our environment—for taming our undiscriminating love and making it with all kinds of fertilizers and pesticides exclusively useful to man, for being preoccupied with the individual's fate before all letting mankind become obese and so endangering life's wealth of diversity.

I wish we could stop proselytizing and fertilizing, sparing some native minds and lands from becoming simply humane. I wish we could overcome the psychological need to spread our gospel of practical love.

Like a lion, a man needs a large territory so he may freely swing his arms to the tick of a vigorous soul. Yet do not a million failing lives saved from setting and in good time rising again ask for ten new laws to restrict our movements and to keep that constipated crowd from bumping into each other in a traffic jam? Here I see a dubious pity at work that can breed the viciousness of a cornered animal in our heirs seven generations away. Here I see lighthearted lifesaving teams devotedly seeding Mother Earth with our overpopulation. I see the World Bank in naive philanthropy spreading that same deadly virus with its thousand charming masks.

In this light, a versatile mind might want to scrutinize with an ecologically-minded eye the greatness of our great white jungle doctors. A truly modern mind that thinks also with a third eye placed generations away might then note that this humanitarian greatness nicely exploding our population there can ultimately cast a great shadow over the flora and fauna of the jungle and stop its people from singing and dancing.

How could I so misunderstand nature's gifts of birth and death for which our ethics are becoming blind? I sense a time when many a surgeon might rather be seen as a brilliant acrobat or magician, who hands the hat around after his dazzling show. In an advanced birth and death control for a world with numbered seats, a surgeon may soon, before he saves a failing life, first have to find a child he is allowed to abort.

Most founders of our practical western religion were unfamiliar with the wonders of birth, pathogens and death. They loved to awe the crowd with feasts of resurrection and healings. The soft and embellished intellect that their ethic produced led us to become excessively numerous. This triggers our children into helping the opposite and becoming more competitive and selfish. Are the wealth, the obsession for practical knowledge and the prestige that people cornered in towns now frantically seek not a bid for better chain saws, faster wheels, sharper knowledge and stingers, tougher locks and hides, impressive bank accounts, more kilowatts, horns and power? Is being competitive not just a more elegant word for being mean, hard, a bigger tooth, deadly and sour? Did we have to reorient the poet in us to help us becoming better calculators and hammers?

Maybe behaviorists also give us a hint when showing that crowdedness triggers meanness among rats. Maybe to retreat into hyperrationality simply means to become superbly mean when seen impartially. That a wildly permissive wisdom becomes finally neutered and becomes rational may have to do with a more general law: crowdedness or captivity triggers loss of reproductive zest and the loss of multigenerational vision—our soul—that goes with it. That reorientation brings a storm of inventions, of armament, of venomous thoughts, of practical minds complete with condoms and better lies and tanks. It engenders aggression so superbly refined it passes for compassion to all but the most attentive minds. It creates new kinds of porcupines pocking quills of missile silos into each other's face. When minds ceaselessly rub against minds, do they not develop a thicker callus of rationality to protect themselves, a little like a wind-ridden tree ducks and adapts his pattern of growth? Who would have thought that whining pacified by impatient charity ultimately fathers meanness? Yet I find that this revengeful child lives only a few mental steps from its parents' elegant home.

The phenomenon of non conscious interaction seems to have little respect for our moralists' advice. Ignoring our soft ethics it triggers into play among a society corrective character traits needed for cleansing and long range health.

The more we become sick with crowdedness, the longer we seem to go to school. We need to unlearn being patient, trusting, curious, generous, wise, kind and universal. Frantically we learn how to outwit each other and Mother Nature, our allotter. Logic becomes as cruel as the logic of the wheel. Many become sorcerer's apprentices. Let me expand: every year every fisher now thinks he needs to add to his boat another ton of gadgets, another tub of hooks, another hundred horsepower to outfox the others while we run faster and faster after less and less fish. This is the legendary miracle broom which leaves ultimately more litter than it sweeps.

Some of us parents want less of that purely rational education for our children which slowly breaks their "undisciplined" souls. We encourage our gifted Curious Georges to leave the formal schools with their credos after eight basic years and turn to enlightenment, learning from all cultures and things. Do children really need to formally learn to be courageous and to shamelessly listen and look? Do they need to be taught to touch things, to directly observe, to relate? Do they have to learn how to copulate? Do they have to learn being good? Much wonderful knowledge we get as a birthday gift.

So the universal denial of the heartache born from suppressing a deeply known friendliness toward our brother death seems to have become a mental sickness that is so afraid of its diagnosis.

I am intrigued by that native's mind which seems to have been able to hitch a ride with a raven high up on a wind, to confidently conclude: "Today is a good day to die."

139
A father probably loves his son more than the son loves in return.

Justice as I learned it at school, and over which I quarrel with you across a business desk, does not make me purr deep down. The use of money has put my sense of justice under house arrest. Below the disputes in my confused mind of what is justice between us, I feel I am rather made for another justice which makes a cheerful rhyme of the enthusiastic abuse by the young and the carefree give away of an older person when she ripens into her golden days. My life is just a wonderful berry. No justice, no conclusion is meant for it. It is meant to happily sweeten and ripen and to be merrily eaten up. I note that the milk between the mother and the baby and the sap in the grasses and trees also run mostly one way and do well. I note that the root, the trunk, and branches and the fruits stolen by some nifty little thief, all affirm this puzzling justice and they seem happy about it. That organic justice that takes God knows how many species and generations to catch again its tail seems endlessly pregnant and pays the dividends to the young. It hardly looks back and it turns the commandment of respect for the parents on its head.

I try now to wriggle free from the assumption that justice should be strictly satisfied within our own species, within one generation, or within one lifespan of a man.

An underlying law is surfacing which says that it is ultimately the strongest kind that does not survive. The Chinese say it's the nail that sticks out that's hammered down first. When a species transgresses the law of moderation and cannot balance anymore close to the middle of the Way but becomes a Hitler, all the menaced tribes in Graceland, even our own souls—band together and defeat that injustice. So I dimly begin to see awesome sense when out of this same puzzling long-range justice, which seldom acts linear, life trespasses my parents' ethics and triggers in some of our young people longings for failure, for mutilation, for being quitters gently nibbling on our excesses while living off welfare checks. They become brakes for our runaway success. A dormant urge to be wrathful and to pervert the excessive fertility of the farmer and his farm, the excessive soft-heartedness of the good Samaritans who nicely doubles the tribe of man every fifty years might be switched on. Such complimentary character traits seem fast becoming needed and popular and are heavily advertised by more and more of the top songs of the week.

A pest we provoke, be it of a runaway bug or a delinquent breed of men, seems to be a message from the holy spirit whose ethics we betrayed. Pests, as delinquency, are nature's ways of creating justice. They are not overcome by police or chemicals; pests are provoked when we leave the Way and they are persuaded to retreat when we make peace with the land and our deeper selves and find the trail to the center of the Way again. When we break diplomatic relations with the great forests, the oceans, the animal kingdoms and go to war for a world empire of man, we also provoke the whole menagerie on the other side to pit their enormous inventiveness against our chaotic excess. When we get obsessed with herbicides, insecticides, federal predator hunters, with sanitizing our minds and arming ourselves for such an ego trip, life helps us with pesticides like epidemics of competition, viciousness and mental confusion, with bad dreams, lame erections and perversions, with cold, money-oriented, misleading educators, with "fuck you" campaigns of our young, with the interception of our vision and with perpetually mutating pathogens. Synthetic chemicals in our pesticides start to mimic the effects of our own hormones and start confusing us. Evidence suggests that our toxic agents in the environment have reduced the average of our own sperm count by forty-two percent over the past fifty years. The whole life on earth might finally be called on to sneeze out our menacing excesses.

In this emergency time when we are now so indebted to our fellow life, this taller justice may also make some of us walk straight past every man and go to work in benefit of the fourth world that might be the world of whales, of elephants, dragonfly ponds and owls. A woman might be asked to go over to the other side of the scale and to serve the oceans, a coral reef, the battered woods. She may open an orphanage for eaglets or baby bats and dispense her love on their behalf rather than add another child to our side of the scale. Yet do such "ungrateful" people not start a greener revolution than the one chemical agriculture has in mind? They do not do what is natural for man but what is natural for Life.

No, the holy spirit does not always send us manna, candies, Mother Theresas and rain. It also sends us plagues, Attilas, druggies, tree-spikers, forest fires, worriers for the Mother Earth, not so much as a whip of wrath but rather as benefactors and cures.

140

Should a man try to settle comfortably in a labor camp? Should he exercise to better fit in, to better work and become relaxed—or should he remain angry and dig a tunnel out?

To make good with exercises; to do aerobics with practical thoughts and to assemble them into a more impressive muscle which better defends my little world; to vacate my mildewed, workaholic mind out in the wild with the car stuffed with goodies I bought in town with the fees I got from renting myself out: these medicines I am recommended to use.

I am told: relax the mind when torn by rebellious thoughts, swallow shame and shyness inhibitors, serotonin enhancers, so I can better work and take abuse. Suppressers of long-distance calls, soulblockers, anti-wisdom drugs are to "cure" rushes and stress and give me peace of mind when the Internet between species and generations, my soul, rings the alarms scolding me for enforcing our success too brutally and too fast. Do your push-ups in your mental fitness course, cover up stress in a health spa; meditate, sternly concentrate on a goal you dictated yourself while aborting all undisciplined thoughts that love to stroll, hand in hand with Grace, into the fantastic world not taught at school. Breathe deep, deep, deep and drown troubling memories in oxygen. Be like a hawk after the thoughts in heat, quickly neuter and focus them on useful work, then reunite each morning your mind with the minds of like-minded believers in a ritual circle of dance and prayer and reinforce your credo so all may disperse thereafter invigorated for daily abuse. All this is recommended so I can lead the ox in me refreshed to his job, so I remain that goldfish in a bowl who tries to become an ocean goldfish by simply exercising vigorously and beating his tail. I now wonder whether this is the way I can seduce grace to walk with me.

No, it will not do. I found that it gives a misleading satisfaction "to have done something"; it gives me a complacent feeling of strength. Is the want to exercise not often a want that clenches its teeth to make a wrong feel healthy and seem right? Is this not the madness of the fool who day after day falls into the same pit, yet is wholly proud to know the trick of how to climb out of it day after day?

I have been on the ocean successfully hooking fish for thirty years. Mostly alone I have probably caught fish equal to the food needed by a hundred people during thirty years. In a time of six billion machetes, hooks and chain saws, what good results from exercising my mind and my body so that I become truly a superman of prey, enmeshing even more salmon, halibut, skates, sharks, snappers and snooks? Should I feel satisfied that in some kind of daily workout or sport I can again and again wash all this blood off my mind so I become an even sharper tooth in that terrible mouth we have become?

> "I vigorously walked on the spot.
> I relieved myself of my tears with some psychiatrist,
> confessor or wailing wall that did not react.
> I warmed an unresponsive rock with my love.
> and mannerly spilled my unwanted strength and sap.
>
> Hugging myself I relaxed.
> I exhausted my stress on an exercise machine
> and I declared peace.
> I was terribly alone."

Do you know this song? I am replacing now some of these imitation acts with natural acts. I am not going to be that prisoner who very seriously installs himself quite well instead of furiously starting a tunnel to get out.

"Theo, your writing is your tunnel out!"

141
The stepladder game.

An act never ends. Often it starts with one big splash—that discreetly radiates out into a swarm of ripples. I follow this act for a few mental steps. I soon tire. I stop. I freeze what I see and frame it. I give it a name and may call it good or bad according to whether my awareness horizon stopped on a crest or a trough of the ripples.

A name or a word never ends. It is the top of an iceberg each sees differently—especially the fishes. The whole world may cling to it out of sight or underneath. And how different each person's depth perception can be! Could you describe the earth without knowing the sun, or a sand grain here without including the sand on the beach of Hawaii? Could you know Paul without the raspberries he tends behind his fence? Blake saw behind one sand-grain the entire world. Some can make out so many symbiotic thoughts clinging to a word and bring to light so many roots of a science that their network of ideas may ultimately enmesh all sciences and the world. And so for some a mountain is not a mountain, a hero is not a hero. For you a bridge might be a fulfillment, others might see a leak.

From a glimpse high up through a giraffe's eyes I got the idea that a man's whole life may flow opposing mine yet can be well spent and full of divine fun. It flowed "upstream" when I first saw it from my basement window looking south, backwashing a fat boulder that rested happily in the middle of a stream in space-time. Seen by himself alone this man in reverse cruised directly into my favored course. Yet his turbulent life that seemed contrary to my way of doing things became exciting news once I saw him from high up on that giraffe's neck drumming his part of The Fugue on his yellow drum, mingling nicely three generations ahead into the cheerful march of all the troops many offspring long.

Remember, Theo, you go one step further up and your blue may turn red; your anger may even turn into a "Wow, I would have never guessed!"

To compete on the stepladder leading to our deeper minds, who dares a step, and another one, up without vertigo making him plunge down; do you know of a more exciting game?

142

When you criticized me, you also quietly put your arm around my sagging shoulder and you didn't let me sink.

When I think of how few of my thoughts are more than sarcastic, defensive or better than P.R. schemes, and of how seldom I spend a minute of my thinking for a listener, Theo the Great becomes so embarrassed he wants to pull a shopping bag over his head.

When I break into your world and hurl smart piercing thoughts around, I feel deep down no better than a squirting skunk. Even a splendid idea remains a sour plum when not cooked in compassion but simply hurled at you in raw arrogance. It brings down a man by wounding is pride giving his mind the runs.

When you harshly broke my pride, I was that nut that patiently waits for a rain in May whose husk you suddenly hammered and cracked it out of season. You stripped my mind and I got all confused and out of breath when you forced this new idea into me. Is it not the kernel in each of us that knows best when it is time to crack its husk and push feelers out? When I cold-bloodedly proved you wrong and slashed your pride, I slashed one of your vital skins and I made you bleed with my splendid idea. Criticism takes so much softness to become more than a bullet hole. Maybe such explosive word-gifts are better left on your doorstep for you to decide when it's time to take off the pride, come out, softly unwrap that gift, dare for your mind a bikini, ask questions, open to foes, bugs, options and strangers and get a tan.

For a long time I wondered why pride is such a cherished old coat and so vital to us all. I think I have gotten a hint. Pride might well be the guardian of our deeper logic of doing our own unique chores for which we often have no rational defense. Its the bran of the oats. Wisdom is childlike and on a different scale and eludes the language of rationality, hence it is speechless when drawn into a rational argument.

To make each of us play his part of the script, are we not all blindfolded differently? Pride might be nature's ingenious blinder, so I may see here and be blind there; so each may love a different niche of work without being sunk by too many options or zig-zagged around by doubt. There is no better truck driver than a near-blind truck driver, proud to see all of what's on the road, nothing more.

When my faint capacity to wish others well bubbles up, even the criticism I risk seems to become a gift—a gift no credit card can buy.

143

The economy has become that elegant multilingual prostitute who wears a tie and does business with every race, with every color, with anything that promises to add another point to the score. Her offspring has become a man-made locust swarm. It gnaws on every living thing. Why should that great hooker remain exempt from birth control?

When a businessman can make a new customer, this seems a happy day to him. Now that we can export rainbows, garbage, birth dates, birdshit, the skin of worms; now that women also seem to win their right to a career in egotism and to freely produce and consume, to drain their own golden pond in fall and have it quarried and sold—there is little left without an owner and fortunate enough to be worthless and unsellable among us. "Bringing the stuff—any stuff—we create the need for it," the advertisers say. And they stand in my sun to sell me a winter coat in the smiling month of hay. Yet the science of spotlighting and cover-ups is now beseeched to become the big brother to all things alive and not to turn into a Roman vomitorium that helps us to consume, and to throw up, and to consume again. The new generation of public relations people is beseeched to become more than the elegant charlatans who spirit the bad conscience of the business world away.

Where does this obsession to ever increase the GNP lead? What happens to a pig that tries to eat ever more? This mania seems to me as sickening as now encouraging women to have more children. Will it become a competition of meanness—each man showing off how many scalps he can hang on his belt, how many bathrooms he can hook up in his home, how much waste and luxuries he can afford, how many more antennas he can show off on top of his fishing boat, how many zeros he can add to his accounts? Is it going to be a live chess game where, just for kicks, on their big board, entrepreneurs shift up and down whole peoples, whole forests, entire world crops simply in competitive games? Is it to be a race among the data merchants who can prey best on our privacy and put our secrets up for sale? How could we run ourselves so trustingly into this blind alley? There must be a more imaginative way to advertise one's creativity than to outdo the bower birds and trip through life with a ridiculously wasteful display of wealth. Are our possessions not our backpacks and the earth a very crowded bus?

Yet consumer animators still spin my head and dizzy my thoughts so I will stumble, so I will produce waste, buy more and produce jobs. Men are paid to confuse my braveness, to blacken my faith in my own resourcefulness. They batter my self respect so I need a flashier coat of luxuries to prop up my shaky little self. Have you noticed that, now that we've traded our love for enlightenment for an obsession to produce incessantly, we physically change the world so fast, only the hardiest critters like the cockroaches can adapt fast enough?

And so to reverse the GNP spill that still unhindered belches its sweetly intoxicating offspring into our minds, into our homes, bellies and the land, and its feces into the oceans and the air, every advertisement will soon carry the warning: "Do it with tenderness for a child—consuming has become harmful to global health." Then our international economy may well have become the child abuser Number One. From every niche of the earth, from every generation still to be born we are beseeched to reduce the birthrate of our economy, become poets and consume more inspiration from this inspired Earth.

When I buy, no blood is staining my hands. I also can nicely forget that when I make a purchase I ask another caste to do the killing, burning, felling, drilling for me that inevitably occurs when my purchase is produced. Money can be a deadly bullet when targeted at a prey. Feel how the ponds, the murmur-creeks with their pussy willows and lupines, how the skins of terns winging yearly from pole to pole, the trees and the bloom of the Arctic sea, how all tenants not sanctified by our commodity market tremble with fear where this heartless child of our prostitution is homing in. Listen to their scolding and their prayers that a Pauline enlightenment from above might strike the International Monetary Fund with the question: "Soldier of the empire of man, why do you persecute my children who you cannot cook and eat and whose nature and chores you do not understand?"

Money gives me the right to have somebody slave for me. When I have this option it has become common sense to go for it. Yet should I? I want to become more careful about how I use those vouchers for selling myself. I got so used to naively sending my money as a war party on a raid without much questioning from where it will bring the prey. It is in this sense that a dollar spent can become a silent bullet that shoots another hole into the Ark without bothering the financier's mind with its BANG and with what it sinks. To spend money involves more responsibility than I guessed. Why spread our hungry standard of soft living to every tribe?

Lingering a little longer among these strange thoughts, I notice that the more my acts are free of charge the more they become natural and light me up. I try to be logical about them and fair—and the light goes out in me and I fail. Capitalism seems to turn me into a seedless bachelor, always ready to crawl back into the safety of some kind of womb. Its economy discreetly becomes the opium of the folks. We seem to be the only species so devilishly just that we need to use money to get somebody to do something for us. The acts that give me a more natural high are those I do not do or receive for pay but for their simple sensuous joy. They are my only bridges to you, him and her, that now still stand and which I did not build to be pulled down with some payment immediately after a raid.

144

Unhappily I find that some of the pity cultivated in me comes from my educator's lack of mental courage to think in more dimensions than in "yes" and "no." I cannot be deeply proud about this mentality anymore.

I look around and I am not alone. Others also don't hear clearly anymore the call to keep fighting in our revolution to flatten our lively planet for more safety, for accommodating more of us, and for letting our vehicles eat up more miles. We experiment with lifestyles that allow more risks and allow the land to grow more health food for our souls. And I promise not to whine when I pay the price.

I feel overeducated in our neighborly pattern in space and underdeveloped in our neighborly pattern in time. I am now rudely awakened by the costly outcome of our grand one-generation vision that has the whole of God's menagerie up in arms for allowing our technology to take those crafty shortcuts that gave us spectacular instantaneous advantages and our population explosion. That vision centered on the individual is so out of focus to show me the wonders of life, it has turned me into one of the inconsolable whiners, unquenchable inventors in the Garden of Grace.

I need a break from studying ad infinitum how to make even better Humpty Dumpties for us that should function ever more efficiently as our devoted secretaries, bulldozers, farm machines, and maids with their love looking out for us. I need a break to explore those divine animal laws written down by the Creator in me, in every creature and in every grain of sand. These grandiose laws closer to the roots of my mind were silenced for being less humanitarian, more oriented toward relations between species and more tolerant than the ten commandments written down in a scroll by some lonely and very humane man. They were silenced for standing in the way of our short-cut economy that could only become miraculously successful when allowed to harshly trespass the other species' private properties.

I see our present mania for cleanliness, whitewashing and castrating our world and souls, as an emergency measure of a population in explosion preoccupied for now with hard logistics and physical power. In a crisis, there is no time for a poetic vision. Each needs to become a steamroller; wonderland is nicely flattened and planted; the laughing crows are silenced, the lush jungleland awakening in our children's souls is simplified and put under the plow for some mental monoculture. The sciences are rushed and are to play puritans. They must isolate their experiments, hypotheses and models. They must cut a phenomenon's roots and its zillion uncontrollable connections; they are to deal with cut flowers and streams that flow only one way and to come, with such simplifications, swiftly to clear conclusions.

Still a kid at heart, I gladly keep my discontentment open and am in no hurry to sit back as a mastermind. I think that those itches in my soul are a well gushing adventures for me. I do not want for naive pity to plug that well. I prefer to toughen my thinking. I like the joyride of an unsafe world that sparkles with birth and death and I am glad that not all the opponents, curves and uncertainties are straightened out; I secretly still pray for my daily dangers along with my daily tortillas or bread and try not to pity myself or others too much when suddenly we enter a hairy bend. I see good economics in replacing a thousand rpms of power with a slick mental solution in order to let more land produce wild ideas—the health food for our minds.

Trembling a little with the terror of the unknown, I like nonetheless to remain all ears. Listening to nature's hottest adventure stories, listening to its animators and troublemakers, figuring out how everybody in God's zoo has managed to be good neighbors for so long without a Bible at hand and without driving on the right side of the road—these I think are ways to become a well-behaved spectator, stamping with the feet in awe and joy while watching the game when it's not my turn to perform.

Advanced physics with quantum logic is again breathing life into our old respect for the brave nonsense intelligence and its creative disorder in us. Thinking of our grand idealistic ambitions for all the personal: the dear personal freedom, the clinical medicine, personal justice, personal psychology and health and personal Nobel Prizes, a personal seat in heaven or hell, I note also that life never had much use of any kind of personality cult. I hesitate to steer all my pity toward the whining leaves when they are shaken from the trees. I am a pupa ready to hatch and to become wonderfully confused. I am a shy legislator out to enlarge in me the ten commandments beyond the old anthropocentric chest-beating. I welcome now other saints, other heroes than those who made us into the master chargers of the world. I wonder whether our parent's charity did not often simply postpone a problem and what their charity had to do with wisdom.

I see humanitarian help and good deeds discreetly increasing the terrible fever we have become on earth. And then I think of the meanness and the extra ice asked of those after us to cool down that fever. It seems to me that only a people that is preceded by generations of headhunters, warriors, cannibals, may for a while overindulge in good deeds without their children being born indebted and the plants and animals remain many but the people remain few.

I find that by taking my imagination into free land for sightseeing, comforting thoughts can be found that are more cozy than woolly slippers, more reassuring and softer music than a pension fund, more protective than security guards. I find that by kindly inquiring into nature, by asking all these shy, experienced helpers for advice, by picking thankfully their berries and their ideas instead of shouting criticism and commands at them, I am shown how to synthesize therapeutic metaphors which cure gloom, delusions of grandeur, doomsday fever, mistrust, injustice and make peace between my pity and my hate. They protect me better than savings accounts.

I like to compete more in the art of dispossession. I am one of the happy fools who are unfit to remain underground or in the safety of careers. We are chicks eager to wriggle out of our eggs. We are homesick ocean ducklings raised on a ranch. We are the good boys and girls itchy to hatch our minds from the safety of humanism. Instead of endlessly hanging on the phone we like to discover the use of the power lines from you to me to our children seven generations away, even the sidelines to acacia trees and bumblebees; all these lines have been spun ages before Bell intro-duced the telephone. All these sidelines we may also lose should we get too much hooked on and isolated by our own electronic World Wide Web. What wonderful "nonsense" is awaiting us.

I wish myself the good luck that for four festive days a week I stop most strategies of self-defense, maybe even the telephone, step boldly out on the balcony and truly listen to somebody or something else, to listen more through the navel and less through the ears to be completely without fishing or career, to read a woman or man and ignore our twittering.

145
This world is more nourishing when I discover it than when I just eat it up.

Truths are shy organisms I found. These lively creatures start to run or dive when I enter the scene thinking hard how to capture them. How well they also recognize when my mind is not a loaded gun.

When I am simply a curious lad nosing about amongst what other creatures have found out and am happy with the crumbs of wisdom I can pick from them, when I leave the fish knife, the motives, the briefcase and the best pair of pants at home, everyone seems to invite me right in. Every creature likes to show me around and brag about how it is worth more than Edison. When I imagine what after evolving for two and a half billion years these little tufts of grass have seen and how many tests they passed to still parade in that glorious workers union to build the earth, I am impressed.

I sense it is a step down and a lack of intellectual zest to erase a thistle, to exterminate a weed, to wipe out a crime, to missionize a gay, to "heal" and make a mute man talk, to put a stove on the North Pole and make of it a cozy nest. Ask any elder among the trees whether that hunch is not a lit-tle right. I also see it as a hell of a step into an ardent sun to boldly ask such puzzling phenomena: "Where are your good deeds?" Maybe every crea-ture has a name like Columbus, Buddha, Edison. Maybe every act is a love child of God; I have sometimes an irksome ghost of an idea that this just may be so. When in such a bright noon I meet a freak, a pervert, a "loose" woman, an acacia full of thorns, a mute, a one-legged man, a clown, a gay, a filthy rich man, a faker or chameleon, they might proudly say: I am an explorer of the world of freaks, of fakers, of the loose, the world of clowns or of altruistic love; I am king of the unipedes; I am fundraiser for a trip to the moon; I am grand master in camouflage or pantomime. And so life without the option of homosexuality, e.g., seems to me a poorer world. Why this pious urge to halt and reform every man, to pull the explorer back from the periphery of society to the center and standard again? Why this rage to breed sameness, to fit everyone into a black and white uniform? Why not let her be a meteor? We can take the heat and the "loss." We are many; we are strong. We don't need to endlessly censure God's variety show. Suppose we are in some way outstanding in God's menagerie. Might this fancy gift not come from our prodigious capacity to wander off, to fall over cliffs, to break our legs or minds, to forget, to dress up our motives, to cut a new grimace, to peek through the eyes of a giraffe or to become perverted, off balance, sick and so unpractical that we can crack loose from common sense and become Amundsens or meteors?

We could invoke a time of Odysseuses and of psychic adventures, of inner refinement and better mileage, and of Olympic games for the souls. I wish us the luck of an infectious fever to get high and complete to see whose soul will shine with the most kilowatts.

146

To know my standing in ecology, I first count my possessions; I count my slaves. I get then a good idea how well I am liked by this planet's freedom-loving crowd.

When I go on a "wealth hunting trip" I want to remember that I depart on a discreet slave hunting trip and go as gently as possible about it. Are not my possessions my slaves? Is not my money the certificate of how many heads I can command?

When I show you my property, I show you my slaves. You might see a woman, once jubilant and free, now meekly serving me. You might see trophies, once mad with joy to be alive, now hanging dead over my fireplace to impress you with how deadly dangerous I can be. I show you my bank account and you will know how many mornings and afternoons of my fellowmen I can command to labor for me, and watch out for the lawyer's whip!

The hay-grass, the bees. MY woman, a patented idea, a field, a parrot, an assumption, the air I force into my lungs, all that I want to possess: they are my trophies. They are my enemies that suffer me. They are my only enemies. But why remain a shackled barnacle trying to possess the rock by not letting it go?

When thoughts are owned and put to work as beliefs and they are not free anymore to curiously come and go and to grow ultimately to abracadabras that can turn an enemy into a friend, they become ballast and make the mind sedentary and obese. A mind that has so lost its wings and soul and is not able anymore to take off will have to mill around in one lifetime alone. To tempt my slender hand to squeeze through the legendary needle's eye, to grab loot and ball it into my fist without enough leeway to pull that heaped hand back, is this not nature's ingenious "monkey-trap" for those who want to possess too much?

How often my search for freedom collides with my search for property. Ah, to dare to become generous, and to let go, to remain lean, to be dangerously free, to become that daring barnacle that gives up its rock and learns to fly—is there a better gift for which one could wish? See—Theo gives himself a lesson and yelps at his own pack sack full of dead meat.

147

There must be better cures for our ills than to send out an ever bigger fleet of concrete trucks to pour around barefooted nature an even tighter chastity belt.

Why brag that each morning we can start up a more powerful army of big Cats, of earth movers and pavers and engineers just to hack more freeways through the flesh of wonderland that begs us to be seen and loved? Why this unquenchable anger with the asymmetric land full of wonders and our urge to slash it with ever more and straighter speedways? Why this weird desire to be superbly boxed, superbly bored and to be effortlessly and with no side glances freighted at a hundred miles per hour through adventureland so to be swifter put to work?

I look around, asking myself, how does a community of a river, a raccoon, an elderbush, an angler, a thundercloud, a farmer and sundry associates get to know each other and share their concerns? Deep inside my mind I find less offensive trails laid out than the maze of highways we roll out pushing every living thing aside. I find trails that zigzag more peacefully from you to me to our children three generations up the hill and back to a stand of maples that settled in between; trails that make me walk the puzzling longcuts of the soul which turn out to be less frictional and do not need even cobblestones.

The great adventure to tour and travel has become banal and rude. Packaged, we are wheeled around. I imagine that a person needs to learn a deep dispassion for nature so that he can be jubilant and proud when cruising Interstate No. 5. Did you notice that we never move with more friction in our minds and our habitat than when we move in freeway lanes? Listen to the music when people meet and "relax" in a nice little traffic jam. We never seem to move so savagely through our land in green and pink and blue as when we are dead meat with a foot on the gas.

An obsession for speed seems to come from highly specialized and patchy interests that create in our vision vast tracks of blank disinterest or enemy land which have to be hurriedly traversed and left behind. Imagine what we pass up for the sake of our venerated speed. And then one might be dreamer enough to consider here that it is also our fine road systems that drill holes into the diverse cultures and make them leak as a sieve, draining their wealth of diversity into a kind of universal manure.

Ah, the beauty of walking! When one thinks that our walks are our truest ballets and dances. What a privilege to walk! To walk the slender walk of a free body and an unemployed mind holding Miss Grace by her hand; a walk that is allowed to follow the music of inner rhythms and rhymes, to be a Curious George and investigate at every stop and step— and shake hands—to become physical and walk inside this fantastic picture book, to greet a passing chestnut tree, to ask a mountain what he thinks about our mania of leveling what's low and high, to ask mama nature why she invented hibernation instead of a refrigerator, to follow a dashing thought without ending up in a ditch—what a treat! Thanks, good legs. Thanks for a life that needs barely a car. I can rub elbows with many people and things and be cheerfully puzzled by them. Walking is such a good experience to me. Three times thank you, legs, for that treat.

In a deeper sense one can measure a people's friendliness and its trust in each other and in all life at large by the fewer miles of freeway it needs to force onto the land. One can often tell the warmth of a people's affections and its children's kindness by the gentleness with which it weaves its roads into its habitat and by how well it tiptoes doing so.

148

When I snoop around in life, I notice that its Creator must have an extraordinary fondness for lies.

I wonder what is the great idea behind this profusion in games of hide and seek. I am surrounded by amazing high tech systems of immunity and chemical lies that prevent disturbing truths from seeping in. What a wealth of membranes and skins that keep vital truths from leaking out. No organism can do without them. Here are thought-contests in progress older than the Olympic Games. We attack and repel—penetrate and deflect, testing the armor of each other's system of thoughts. Here seems a benevolent power on the individual's side at work that can swiftly turn an incoming bullet or a spy around.

Our lies—some hate, others love, may be simple no-entry signs to give good dreaming to seeds softly curled up in their husks and still learning to sprout. These tricks could be just brothers to the chemical lie the cabbage invented for its leaves to repel a soaking rain so its leaves would not decay. My lies might simply be sturdy barriers that keep you and me from mixing into a sullen gray. Your lie could be your intuitive "No" when you run with your message through "enemy-land" and I sneak into your way flashing a fat tip so you may sell your message to a spy. A lie may be the husk of an unripe truth reserved for a future spring, the wrapper of a gift perhaps meant for our children's joy, the "go away!" to a mental beast of prey.

A man who has no hair, no bulging muscles, no coat, how would he protect himself? God might have given him a bag of splendid lies, in case he has to drive some sucker flies away.

I have been living here in the tropics among a lovable, individualistic people among whom a swift smooth lie is a sign of health and strength and more respected than karate for self defense. Here my fellow fishermen ridicule and bark at my honesty when I brag and freely tell the places where I catch a lot of fish. Here friends scold me for being as truthful as a bucket full of holes.

When at noon the sun pours down its heat, how cool it feels to have a shade-tree to stretch out under; to happily watch from the shade the sky boil in the thunderheads a refreshment for a blistering day. Also the mind may need a shade and can have a form of sun stroke when no truth is withheld. As an episode to this point: Chuy had a hen nesting under his beached and overturned canoe. Ten curious chicks had hatched. Another one was patient and still hiding in his egg when the big wave flushed everyone out from under the boat, drowning all but the one egg holding tight that rolled to high ground, hatched nicely in the dry later on, to be adopted by Chuy, my friend.

Are we not all messengers, each with a different destination in the edifice of life? Are we not all, in a way, sequences of information in Mother Nature's DNA—not always allowed to conveniently shortcut to a neighbor but often commanded to hold tight maybe all the way down to a blistered toe, maybe to the following generation, maybe to a child far away in time?

Good for me if I can learn to also love that old-fashioned heart which seems not yet ready to conveniently spill its inner truth as easily as I wish, and cannot give up the dimension of time to grow as freely sideways and flat as good Christians encourage each other to do. Why should a person who cannot quite give up her privacy not merit my respect? Why then should I insist and ask questions that should not be asked? Are there not sacred places meant just for one single soul or for a very special form of leaf to fill? You would have to fool me with any good distraction or mimicry to keep me from bursting into there. I have seen people crumble when panicked into a truthfulness or other giveaways they could not afford. How easily truthfulness turns into an open wound! And so we respect the apple tree that holds its apples well and will not let them go prematurely but waits until they are ripe to be picked and nibbled on.

There are many things too explosive to be told. Many thoughts are unique snowflake crystals. If spoken, these crystals would melt and metamorphose into a flash flood of melt waters tearing up the beauty of the billion individualities that make of the land such a colorful quilt.

I am being infected with a banal truthfulness, an epidemic of informers that seem to be praised. I am encouraged to disarm, to skin myself, to become tame and told to do it with pride. Might it be for the individual's wildness being tamed and that wildness passed on to the state, that the state becomes even more a wild, aggressive animal? Might it be from these billion personal meltdowns, from these prairie fires, the great raw power of feared nations comes? I am one informer in the information explosion. Here the wisdom acted out by millions of individuals erupts and disintegrates into a kind of megaton mushroom, releasing enormous raw knowledge and energy for physical solutions. Its fallout may wipe out the personal zoo each keeps in his deeper mind. Thus I may also understand why an individualistic people, proud of its own patents and colors, may see tourism as an invasion of spies.

One wants to think about this when crusading for that convenient horizontal truthfulness which can nicely supply a childless comradeship billions of man-hours, billions of barrels of raw mental energy. Then organic truths are no power dam but a thousand wriggly trickling creeks that may well first have to water many other trees before they are allowed to join and reach for our orchards and fields.

Yet when the mind hitches a ride on a high cloud, from up there the view again might change. One might then wonder: are we meant to remain worms and eternally true to our nature of being worms—with absolutely no leaking out or seeping in, with no mutations at all allowed to trespass our immunity defenses both ways: Or are we meant to move on from being true to our rest stop and routine? Are we to be thrown into the fire of life's experiments and be consumed? Is it not natural not to be natural? How otherwise some of these worms could mess-up so much what came natural to them that they ended up with eyes and ears and left the tunneling to other worms? Up there I feel cheered to become an acrobat and to balance along the edge of being giving, leaky and vulnerable without becoming exhausted and slipping down into dependency. I am cheered to dress up and be pacified by the least of rites without being worn out by the friction of aggression and opposition. I am cheered to become as generous and giving as I possibly can without being swallowed by the crowd, while I evolve into a self sufficient subspecies. Why transgress the law of moderation and play it excessively strong, safe and armed with too many lies? Why become excessively sour and feared? So if you look for an honest person—look for a thin-skinned person with an explosive temper.

When next time you make a cut into your skin, and become truthful to me, giving me of your "blood," I will remember that you are making me an extraordinary gift. I will remember that your bleeding for me is permissible only when you have a surplus of love.

149

When my mind is wild with joy to be alive, I can sometimes perceive dangers, aches, doubts and itches as favors. Even the stingray stinger that traversed my leg and that has been lifting me out of my dear routine for the last two months while I have been fighting for my leg, starts to turn into a masked gift.

I have heard of men who drove bone hooks through their skin, hung themselves on poles and swung as in a carousel. Thus they exercised the art of bravery. They wanted to be ready when the heavens opened their purse of gifts.

In my meek moments I prefer to hide behind a tree when volunteers are asked for risky gifts. I have never really learned how to welcome such rocks aglow that are laid on my heart, challenging me to be taken in to be forged and carved. On the contrary, I am trained to cut such demanding gifts in two and four and conveniently share them with our high-security society that has become our greatest insurance company, spreading pain, dangers, mountain tops, and joy equally among all, spreading deep and high, black and white to a smooth and level gray. I am trained to swiftly shoot down danger and pain and to avoid the chance to ecstasy.

Still, to see and single-handedly welcome such challenging favors, making them a stepladder for my soul, remains for me pure, naked art that is not dressed up for a nifty fashion show. I suspect that also an anger or doubt or a ghost of an idea are hidden seeds that are paining to crack their husk. So many things I know remain bottled up in me. Just a little extra courage and the cork could pop. So many aspects of life I dare not tease out into the light are waiting to win my respect. Hence all that wasted activity squelching cigarettes into my soul where there never was a viper's bite. Hence all my useless yelping up the tree where leaves are rustling in the wind.

I suspect that with every discomfort mingles a little of the sweet prospect of a hurting woman soon to give birth. When I sweat and cuss in pain, the thought of this exciting prospect may work better for me than Aspirin. My few feats of mind have come from such kernels that hounded, itched, and ached me, asking my "Yes" to become my brainchild and challenge the old clowns and acrobats in God's show.

When you march alone behind inner voices and blow happily your own trumpet, when you dare adventuring into that oozy, yeasty world sparkling with dangers, caprices and rewards, you are good medicine for me. Your one-man show, in which you march to your inner science of no shortcuts, no castration, no straight lines, makes an old silenced fever in me again acute. Your courage does to my mind what yeast does to a loaf of dough.

150
Is it wise to engineer the whole flora and fauna into one giant udder so even more billions of us can be squeezed in?

When the crowd cheers what seems to become negative technology that increases the excessive, I doubtfully scratch my head. Take the love for our dear cattle: from life's point of view, our cattle have become the primary pest. Yet don't we invent more vaccines that help this deadly muncher to spread and spread?

Our success story in plant breeding and cash cropping also rapidly replaces God's permissive flower fields with tissue-cultured clones forcing its native populations to hit the road or to set the table for man and man alone. Monocultures look and sound like desert land to me. Are we going to be the bedeviled technologists who can chase away every little beggar who also serves himself to a nice morsel at that great feast where each species is the other's guest? It would become the meanest, longest high-tech war if every undomesticated creature were declared illegal and were so provoked into becoming a guerrilla or terrorist. They were expertly examined and fingered: some were selected for labor camps, others to be exterminated, according to their serviceableness. We too have gloriously committed such a genocide with much of the flora and fauna and do it now with genes. International corporations do it with the diversity of lifestyles, languages and food habits. Western education does it with human mind pools so that the ideas of global youth may soon to be stan-dardized and neatly dressed in black and white uniforms. And so in a few months it might be that historic day, when for the first time we will have succeeded to willfully and completely (even in cold storage) extinguish a species (smallpox) whose only known benefit to us was to help control the growth of our population.

Yet is not the gene pool of any savanna grass in itself a tropical forest whose unattractive strains should not be pushed over the cliff for purely practical reasons? After all, the "weed genes" are also inventors who have been laboring, spying and recombining their genomes for a billion years and are with their memories standing by in a healthy diversity of options and recipes that should not be simplified in a holocaust. I feel that, as now the fishing technology, so all our other superbly anthropocentric sciences which give a pragmatic label to more and more organisms and eradicate others for our security and ease, should themselves become subjects to arms control.

We have truly become the generation with Faust's magic spirit that could turn the whole living crust of this planet into a fabulous supermarket, for a limited time, before we will be burnt out in our own hell. I know of no other generation that, instead of singing and dancing, had to put 95% of its energy into eliminating one by one its dear opponents, microscopic or gigantic, and to press nature for its own safety, its physical comfort and hilarious amusement. Did we become such demented crybabies that we cannot live without some kind of pacifier? What if tomorrow there were no murmuring creek left that I could simply lean against its bank and have it soothe my sour mood and wash my dirty trust in Mother Earth? What would become of me had I no place left to go where there is no other man and where I can take off my mask? Imagine a man whose mind could remember nothing more exciting than to superbly play his calculators, to sharpen his fishhooks, to arm himself with ever more pesticides and vaccines?

Have not idle hedges bristling with thistles, caprices and nettles, with nifty little thieves, with marigolds, elder bushes and banks of flowering weeds twinkling with flitting, fluttering butterflies and droning with hunches, bumblebees and advice, produced for us a solitude which can tell a whining mind, "get up and walk"? Does such entrancing solitude not come from simply respecting and listening also to the gulls and fiddler crabs promenading the same beach with you and me? In this free living memory a hungry mind that's undernourished by learning from multiple answer quizzes can gorge itself on a wholesome seminar.

Is it not our wild capacity to reproduce and refine ourselves a thousand times over and our shy inborn tenderness for all those thousand cycles sleeping in us that is the wise spoiler of our neat logic for just personal success? To function smoothly on an ego trip that psychic masterwork needs to be jammed.

As our bodies are guided by melatonin through their seasonal rhythms, so also our spirits seem to cycle through seasons. An epoch of analytical thinking, of mental autumn and decay, engrossed in the sciences of herbicides, composting, bulldozers, of docile love, of hoarding, of pacifying our outer and inner world and hibernating in peace, seems to be followed by a season when warm organic thoughts again flood our minds. Emerging from our winter dens we again become animated by our sweet little crazinesses and highs. The dream of the Earth is whispering to us. Cheerfully we start turning again back and forth with all the fires that are breaking out in us. A science of spring, of heightened daring and of ecstasies then prevails akin to our religions of youthful times when technology is, before all, the tool of our creativity and getting high. In these peak times we synthesize again formulas from our primal ideas that build impossible bridges, thaw assumptions, permafrost and credos, sweeten sour relationships, pierce horizons and husks, laugh at unionitis and cowardice, shake off gloom, hangovers, cocoons, fling open windows, light lamps in evil and night, sing the sweet song of the symbioses and create consolations, delights and happiness. And we become again merry pupils who skip school to visit wilderness for seminars.

In such a blue expectant spring, I follow the beaver emerge from hibernation and I expand my local psychology to include again the psychic network of all life. I can weave in between you and me many of those minds, seasons, actors and believers that in darker times seem personas non grata to me. I can pull concepts like health, justice, being social or helpful out of humanism's timid common sense into the wide open again. I can transfer and adopt these ideas to a larger mentality with its life forms many species and generations long. I do not even mind the contradictions that occur when I commute between these different levels of knowledge.

Why continue stepping on the gas and going for ever more power— and friction. It's those with less power—and more vision that are in demand. So many doers still, so few seers! With my surplus of strength and time I can do better than performing some good work to improve the world, even better than building pyramids; in such a luxurious blue spring, I can dive into the science of serenity with an uncommitted mind that is all ears, and for a treat simply intoxicate myself with the goodness of life; and who knows, I might get my first taste of an unsinkable high.

151
There has always been a distant voice in me that absolutely refuses to take sides for you, myself or for mankind. It is the intellectual troublemaker in me.

I am trained to hold onto a mind-rail of prejudgements and not to let it go. Yet a voice still whispers to me: "Wriggle out from that protective cocoon of manmade imagination which overcautious educators have spun around you. Girdle your mind in the loosest credo that still can hold you together in the confusion. Take courage; think of what an emerging butterfly can do." Convenient assumptions that endlessly fuss in me to be groomed, worshipped and reinforced have kept me in protective house arrest too long.

When I can lure my eyes away from prudishly staring into my personal memories which I have mostly turned into my defense department;

when I tease my curiosity to come outside the camp of man, here is my golden opportunity to fish for and explore other living memories, not as a fisherman does but as a man does who simply enjoys becoming less feared and more loved. I can learn from memories that fly, root, glide, crawl, hop and remember how to turn compost into corn and pebbles into philosopher's stones. I find catalystic ideas and seminal thoughts that are so hot, only daredevils may want to plant them into their minds. I can invite the fantastic to put on its show and be ice cream for my soul.

I can take a deep breath of faith and step into the abyss outside the knowable circle in which I have nicely installed myself as dictator of a miniature world where in a sterile environment I inbreed and cultivate humanistic thoughts. I can be a little witchy and taste a wheensy bit of that divine madness beyond the garden fence of our collective convictions. I can taste our privilege to see boldly through the eyes of Moslems, ducks, Bedouins, of mildew and crocuses, pygmies. Buddhists, street neighbors, faraway cities of stars. I can marvel through these trillion eyes life invented for its associates so we may all circulate among its tribes causing less traffic jams and more rhymes.

I can wrap the bark of a spruce around myself, wriggle into the pants of an enemy or walk in his moccasins twenty days; I can act out to be a river, a spotted owl, a banker, a pulp mill worker and exchange identity— others call it group therapy. And then I can pose my questions more impartially. It might be the only way to understand.

To do so I may have to get Theo's watchdogs in my mind a little drunk and gently push them out of the way, while I tiptoe out of their sight and risk getting seasick from what all I see.

Dangerously free, I can breathe in the communications of the whole twittering cosmos on the move, not to possess the messages but to breathe them in and breathe them out again to get my script in tune. I can tune into this surf where each ripple is the soul beat of another creature. To drop for a festive moment all written morals, all guards, all tattoos, so that the whole body may become one luminous eye linking my mind to the thoughts centered in every creature of the world; to let my mind become that medium for me, here is a Sunday's employment I enjoy. And for that moment I may fall in step with God's breakers, pipers, hooters, whiners and flutists with my own battery of drums.

264

When I get lost in this way, Lady Prudence becomes all nervous and pesters me, but my curiosity has one big happy smile sensing new Americas that beg to be landed on. I become vulnerable to the goodly pile of friendships the world is pouring down on me. Here, hardship mingles with reckless joy that pulls down doubts, sins, shadows, garden fences, boulders and preferences in its way. Here I stand at the scenic window of the second floor of understanding and look into a wondrous world more fantastic than fairy tales.

May I add a thought on how that cheerful troublemaker in a mind may be preserved? It seems to me a child is lucky not to be drafted by educators when very young for society and for the school to be tattooed and have a speck of its useful intelligence farmed in a monoculture. Allowed ample time in an organic environment, it can explore the smells after a rain, the picture language of a new morning bathing in the sun, the mysteries of the impractical world, the high level songs of night and day. It's imagination can breathe in thought pictures, that are more nourishing than those made of numbers and words and later can pull a confused mind together again. It can learn to chatter with its million guardian spirits that are the trees, the clouds peopling the sky, the happy fools in love, the eagle, the mosquitoes and the wolf. Every creature remains a lawyer to her dispensing free advice and happy to give a seminar about how to keep the earth a cheerful home. In brief: a child's emotions can mature. One should give that little inquiring George this chance.

When a child learns to read and write, becoming literate, his communication soon shifts from his loose dialogue with all things alive to the intercom in the bowels of man. Let educators wait to get a hold of a child, to turn her into a worshiper of man and sacrifice her to the world economy as an expert worker. It takes hours to break in a colt. It takes twelve years to break in a youth so that our economy can ride on him. It makes me wonder to what degree our schools serve now as protective confinement. After twelve years of sitting on the hind, drawing trees with lots of fruits and no roots and reciting credos, there are thoughts and things only those can think and do whose souls had a chance to root well before they were broken in for work.

The psyche of a child becomes a good seaboat when drawing deep, keeping her center of gravity low. When all becomes smartness and gadgets up on the bridge, and there is only a shallow draft below, that smart top-heavy ship capsizes in the first big blow.

152

When he takes off his mask, his pride, his hat, to pray, does it matter which name he chooses for the address of his petition?

May she be allowed to call it Vishnu, the sun, the psychiatrist, the Mother of All, God the Father, Gaia, Holy Mary, name any name that makes your mind fly, does the address or the name of the mediator to this healing state really matter?

Does it matter that some people do not like to give their mediator or catalyst a human face but prefer geometric forms, or a golden ox, or a wailing wall, or no symbol at all?

Does it matter from what place I prefer to dream up and send off my wish list and my thanks, as long as my heart can freely stutter its speech without stage fright that for many comes when facing a crowd? Does the language matter? Should we go to war with our neighbors because their minds prefer to flower their red instead of our blue? Yet it does matter to me that the knot can open to which the ego has tangled so I may become vulnerable, humble and nimble, an apple with a stem. It matters that I can step out of the center and for help I can turn my mind away from Theo when he is sick with too much ego and toward The Way, and crawl back into the warm belly of God. The teeth stop gritting when trust replaces Aspirin. In this simple trance I may get tuned into the twitter of all of the universe's creatures that for their Darwinian fitness may all be to each other prescription drugs, advisers and doctors.

I can stop drinking from empty hands and lead my ego to the well. A corporate director can leave his straightjacket, his willpower, his push-ups, his tower of solitude, his mask, desk and name and be for awhile a naked emperor without a telephone simply soaking his fears in the sun. Thus, he may not end up with a constipated soul.

The assumption of a God as the creative force has proven to me a helpful catalyst to the humility needed when exploring the Way of Life.

This universal biological need of the roots of the mind to take advice from a deeper source of wisdom than man amazes me. What wealth of languages, what diversity, what a colorful flower field!

153
Are not my acts also my children?

My acts are not only cheered or booed by the few imposing motives our society has up its sleeves. They are also watched, remembered and commented on by the assembly of all life's zillion of more discrete members for whom my intuitive mind seems to reserve ample forum seats. According to that assembly's impact statement, it is voted how many pleasure strings or drums of pain should be played in my soul for my recompense.

When I am a good parent to my acts and find out where they go, what mischief they may do, how healthy and how well-behaved they are and when I curiously follow the ripples they cause well beyond man's garden fence, I think I become more adroit. I may then step less on others' toes or trample on their joys. A happier tape may then be chosen to play in my soul.

When I follow the tracks of my acts, I'm surprised to find how often I was not that parent to them but simply a businessman who orders them to come right back with a fat profit, and I gave a hoot about their impacts. I find that my faint capacity to wish others well is even fainter than I thought. I find that to become better in that faint capacity, I am a completely blind and helpless worm. I know no trick of how to steal, catch or buy these divine meteors. It seems they just strike me and light me up or strike me not.

When I am very still in the middle of my activities to curiously follow these visitors I send out and wonder how they benefit the world and how warmly they are greeted on their trips, I add more road signs to my luck.

154
My daimons seem to be the Gods who did not yield to you and me and to my simplistic way of reasoning. They still rebel when I snobbishly socialize just among men.

My daimons are the undomesticated Gods in me that I locked out to shut them up—the Gods who may not reward me in my seventy years but are in charge of truly long-range chores and seeds that are packed in husks so hard, it may take them a hundred rainy seasons to bloom. These voices seem to be divine messengers that my personal guards never learned to identify at church or school. They have been left out in the cold. They knock on my door. They pound on it. They hound me in my dreams, pleading, sick, desperate from being left out and unloved. Yet when I take the cotton out of my ears I discover some as formidable saints always out to compensate. In a way that eludes my personal little logic, they seem out to make good the blunders of my short-sighted campaigns in which I zealously fend just for myself, my toys and vegetables and for my contemporary friends.

My deeper mind seems to come with senators for every organism peopling this world. Often those daimons counsel now in favor of interests other than those of our cows and roads, of our economy or humanistic goals. With a mind breaking love they may negligently dance on my neat, profitable garden where I cultivate chosen and refined fruits and thoughts for myself and my chosen friends.

These spirits form my dear background and seem guardian angels of my deeper self. Often they are overruled by the loud-mouthed, naive goodwill of the logician in me which, panicked by the overcrowd, has become an all too zealous watchdog for my ego. Yet it has become obvious that these tricksters can nonetheless quickly crumble the ethics of the day when a generation ventures into excessive success.

With their impartial fervor these spirits raise hell when, drunk with self-esteem, I dance round and round myself clapping my hands for my own applause. They plant healthy harshness in a generation whose parents could not take the whining when life heated and forged a woman or a man and so remained minors gorging themselves sick on faintheartedness and pie. Caringly, these spirits are busy trimming mankind down to a healthy stand. In a time polluted with our overkill and the feces of our frenzied work, they whisper laziness, welfaring and tripping out into our youngsters' ears. When drunk by a thousand men to the left and the right I stand in blind obedience in front of the Reich of Man, they turn into bugs itching me awake. These voices sneak up to me at night, surround me with

268

placards, with storytellers, symbols and traffic signs, and often awe my common sense, and they ask questions I have not learned to ask.

These spirits are the ant-eaters, good old family friends—when you ask a people of ants. These spirits are the ant-eaters, terrible rascals when you ask an individual ant. If you listen to the contraceptive ideas mixed and rhymed into the love songs the youngsters are now avidly taking in, you may get hints of how these tricksters are working on our long-range health.

These spirits are also the busy chemists in my dreams. Tirelessly they recombine my archetypical verbs; tirelessly they fish for new ideas and rhymes without getting Theo too much hurt. In their savage activity, I hear opinions of other people, of jungle trees, of other worlds, times, realities, of cockatoos and spotted owls. In my dreams they try every possible hat on me—some I have never seen—and they flash remedial pictures on my screen.

My daimons seem to be the left side of my inner voice that is a pea I was told to split. They argue the cases for the storms, the mosquitoes, for all the unfamiliar critters, for the clams that would not readily open up, for my own firmness, for all acts that are hard to rhyme and seem to me non-sense or crimes or meant to benefit generations I do not know. They are voices in my DNA that can teach good and lasting rain for all. They might even be my messengers who are closest to God. The Christian Trinity-God-head is rather the humanistic psychiatrist I chose as speaker for the right side of that paired pea which has strongly committed itself to our person-ality cult.

To get my relationship with the Earth in tune, I like to telescope my feelers into land that is clear of our little schemes; soak in its universal lan-guage as others soak in the sun, get my mind and my blood waving to its song. The signals of the universal twitter effect the distribution pattern of species of which each writes out with its dances one letter of the holy script. Each species, each individual is continuously updated in a way which reflects the whole world. It seems to be such a high-level description that switches on and off neurochemicals, inhibitors and dreams and realities producing in us whatever passions, actions and prohibitions needed.

Why then the campaign to bleach and iron out a soul and bust its ghosts? Why simplify goodness so to become obvious even to a mind that's only in black and white? Are there to be no more orgies to gratify

269

these spirits we figure we do not need for a seedless and symmetric life yet that keep on sowing weeds, winding roads, curls, unnerving patience, paradoxes and forget-me-nots into our minds? Why should we already abolish the sacred intoxications that give those wild guardians in us at least the chance to a workout? A pitcher of wine, please, for my mind on a leash! And off she races into the bushes, to come out with unsalable treasures.

One wants to watch that one does not suffocate in the stench of one's own psychic waste, now that we just throw out front any inconvenient spirit, arbiter, or longing we think we have outgrown. There is barely any carnival anymore to gently, compassionately strangle these outdated ghosts. We should perhaps openly give social standing to the shady brotherhoods who can sneak drugs to us that yield wild dreams, safaris, trips, quickies in ecstasies that give us rest in our forced march to reorientation. We could elevate that vital need to gently wean and launder the mind of unneeded ghosts and nostalgias to a respected science that disposes compassionately of those lobbyists in us which we consider too yeasty for our dignity or with too long a memory for a presidential term or a five-year plan or for a personality cult.

When my intellect scrutinizes a common good deed, we seem always to be the winner in the first round. Then my investigation mostly ends by triumphantly shaking hands. Nonetheless, in the third round I start to run into nasty side effects. I also begin suspecting that the hells we created have surprises for us. I begin to realize that in these dumping grounds for inconvenient ghosts, unsuspected medicines and benefactors can be found that serve all of life and not only individuals or species, medicines so great they eclipse the Nobel Prize.

On a clear, lucky day you might better see that many of the apparently dirty, vicious and abominable traits in yourself and me are really the grotesque forms of old, deeply beautiful and bewilderingly far-sighted longings that were misunderstood and left behind when one descended to work in the dark of a society's bowels. Now that we focus all our vision on our advantages, those voices of a more universal ethic are not loved. They become orphans, revengeful feelings and terrorists.

I begin to realize how wastefully I hoed, hacked and strip-mined into my spiritual heritage to make fast profit and to become an instant "good man." The miracle love of Western culture shows me more and more its disturbing side effects, a little like its miraculous green revolution does.

You and I and the atoms all seem to be ultimately just communities of little specks of the rays from all the suns—the big suns and the subatomic suns, the faraway suns and the sun on your porch. In graceful times one may step out of the cocoon of man-made thoughts and get a taste of one single, unobstructed sight. Just consider the thrill when in the mind more and more such specks unite.

155

I listened pensively to this simple song of the street: "Did you find something more exciting to do, Jessica, than to follow the string of appointments our dads have booked for you and me?"

True to the tablet's law: "You shall honor your father and mother," our children ought to be duly chained as servants to their elders' egos and nurse their comfort. The more I think about this commandment, the more I suspect that its author had little love and fun with his children, filled with their forward pressing sap, and with springtime coming up. Watching the pumpkins ripen in their wilting foliage, or looking at the wrinkled seed potatoes after they did their job; I wonder whether life has not also dictated this commandment into us not in reverse but in forward drive to honor our children first.

What are your thoughts when mistrust finally eats up our teenagers, after we treated them to our stony confidence in our tablets of right and wrong which we cloned in them, an ethic that has brought us to such disharmony with the earth? What should we the parents confess to our children when they feel so helplessly caught in a web of tight and sterile thoughts that some want to roll themselves in glowing coal, in acid or dope to burn from their minds those slogans that we crafted into it and lock them up in boredom. Can you visualize a pissed-offness so black it pours raw acid all over a young mind to burn the cuckoo eggs planted in it by a society that fell more in love with its economy than with its kids?

Tell me: when one delegates a young woman, pregnant with adventurous dreams, to solder every day a thousand chips or wire a hundred telephone poles, how should she soothe her aching body and mind? How to appease her neglected dreams again? Think of a noble savage silently crying every night because he feels downed and degraded in the work he does. Would you castigate his appetite for a sip of a drug that for awhile spirits away the blinders of his mind or that lets him sneak out on a trip or climb on a high and feel as if he were again a king? Drugs have become for some the poor man's space ship, the poor woman's safari into jungleland.

In a hypersensitive response or anger beyond hope, some seem pushed to starve or strangle themselves, slowly, deliberately, in a suicide rite, as I have seen animals in captivity do, as plant cells do to isolate an invading virus, as I have heard some tube worms do when they literally throw themselves to pieces under attack, depriving an enemy of a meal. This for the sheer humble satisfaction that at least they no longer support an adult society they cannot see as a good parent but rather as a child's world abuser. They might be martyrs of a kind, strange to our common sense, defying the public agent sent to confiscate the "sword" they are driving into the marketable part of their brain. The officer might say, "They could escape. We might not be able to ever use them again." After all, don't many of us bank on our young to warm our feet later on?

It is a tragedy that those decent people among us that create the need for drugs frequently do not know that they do so. So they fight in a rather godlike wrath with their accomplices whom they refuse to acknowledge, but who nonetheless fill the void that the worshipers of practicality leave so painfully amiss. Isn't it from the womb of a society trying too hard to be practical and "good" that this naughty child is born? Isn't it our animal spirits ordered rudely into exile by which many of us secretly long to be animated with for a festive little while?

That forced march into flat socialization catering to an adult commune has opened the crack in the trust the young have for their elders. They trusted in vain that their seniors will be as generous to them as the seed potatoes are to their young. Any crime, any powerful plant, any trick that gives the slightest promise of a ticket to escape now seems good to those most desperate.

In the present ecological confrontation, the bravest of the young people charm, spike trees, walk on their head to beseech their honorable elders not to abuse the children's world for simply fattening our darling—the GNP.

Our old habits and rituals have been a ship that has brought us from far. Yet in me the fear to jump overboard is now surpassed by the fear to remain on that ship while breaking up. How do I overcome now my terror of leaving our dear habits and of changing course? "Give up the wish for better shepherds farming meeker sheep," I tell myself. "Stop wailing for another law, another savior, a wonder drug." Stop shouting, "God give me a better world!" Wriggle swiftly with less megawatts and RPMs and more spirit toward your joys; beware of slave hunters hunting souls to make them customers of their "soul-food" chains. Have faith in the wisdom Mother Nature dispenses in her seminars; snoop around in her land and catch her ideas that fly as clean as a kite. This, I tell myself, is how I may dance more in harmony with my magic flute.

I have a mischievous notion: there is a cheerful place waiting for us where there is no war, no sickness or pathogens, no pests, no crime, no undesirable holes in shoes, no need for dope, missionaries or death. And you know what? Nothing will need changing to make it happen—absolutely nothing but our minds and eyes.

156
I live for the few moments I can explore another mind not as a fisherman, not as a missionary, but as a friend.

It can become a long depressed work day evenly overcast with all the little "you must" when my thoughts are not allowed to return to the curious child I still am under the uniform. When on duty, I drive my thinking as we do our cars, oxen or jets. I cruise my thoughts in lanes, to endless traffic commands; no trespassing, no loitering, no drifting, no ears for the humming of the bees in the pussy willows celebrating spring. My thoughts are laserized and magnetized to yellow traffic lines leading to success that often obliges me to unite with others into a mad army of driver ants ravaging in their unstoppable success through our children's flower fields. My thinking is fodder for the GNP and hired out for the crudest labors, ego trips, fun or wars.

It seems not to be a higher wisdom, but a prodigious and incredibly fruitful shortsightedness triggering a feverish inventiveness in us, that sets us apart in Eden's Park. A brand new happiness for those who lost their souls and became tame and myopic has to be invented. It is this highly personal vision, so rare in nature, where the I and the others become extremes, that helped us to become geniuses in self-pleasures, ego-defense, superb technologies; to become the plunderers of the world. My higher intelligence however left school underdeveloped and darker than before. Yet I find it is this poetic vision which is not learned but, in spite of Theo, seeps into me through every opening of my skin and holes in my will, that can unveil the whole of God's menagerie as my deepest self, as my extended brain, as my most patient friend. That permissive vision makes me less offensive, less inventive, less humanitarian. It makes me also more curious, more lazy, tolerant, trusting and adoring, maybe sometimes even a little serene.

I live for the few moments when I do not need to put my thoughts to work and I am not locked behind a credo. Ah, to be able to sometimes ignore my butcher knives, my practical thoughts and cunning, thoughts that are just stingers, shoes, cover-ups, fishhooks, raw power. I can dive into a mind deeper than the sea and amicably play chess games simultaneously against every creature in the world. Ah, after the season, to take my 33-foot fishing boat—a Norwegian built double-ender, 120 HP Chrysler-Nissan diesel—up through Neva Straits into Nakwasina Bay; to take her at high tide through the Narrows into the inner bay, dodging the kelp and the rocks, and drop the anchor. It's incredibly quiet here alone, beauty everywhere, to the left, the right, above, below, the closest man twenty miles away. Later I push the skiff overboard and paddle to shore, to walk about, sit against a beached log, to look, to listen to the Way and to smell it; and with all the feelers out to look yet again; to simply be a satellite dish, without counting the hours—what a treat! And for a moment I may be the fisheater, the fisher and the fish.

After all, am I not also offered the chance to stand for a treat behind every single eye on this planet and on any spot to wonder about the cosmos, visualize its many worlds, the waterfalls that fall up into the sky, September storms, thrills in May? And some of the impractical things I then do and think may become my spaceships to other worlds.

There was the whole assembly of good, educated reasons voting against me when along my life I did the few strangely impractical things that still are purring in me. Inaudible to that elegant crowd there were also a few illiterate voices cheering me.

When my mind is not employed, I can look around, get acquainted, stroll into the poetic world, shake paws and hands. Every man becomes a new continent then. To let me land on it and explore do you know a better gift for a visitor from another world?

The whole scientific community, perhaps all nature, is in labor to give birth to its poets. They are its eyes. They are the charm and amulet, the joy, the pride of all those who sweat, suck, lie, fish, compute and hammer for this child. The poets are the seed crystals on which the latent capacities of a people can precipitate. These unemployed scientists, experts in the art of enchantment, are society's radar eye that sees many species wide, many ages deep, many generations high. They weave our confidence to a cozy quilt. They compose the stanzas of our thanks. They paint, teach, sing, story-tell, dance and televise morsels of the law that makes God's merry-go-round the most wonderful twenty-four hour show. These tricksters make us a little drunk with awe, wonder, confidence and reckless joy.

157

Only with a pity that will earn me but boos from those that lifelong stick to the same notions of good and bad, can I integrate myself into that great society of mutual help between you and me, the shade trees, the gorgeous butterflies, the rolling tundra, the storm-petrels, my dear enemies, and a roaring sea.

I rediscover that I was born with a pity that is a compassion so generous and so wide, it bewilders my educated mind. In its world there are winged people, green people, insect people and the people of man. That brave mind of many minds may ask me now to become spikes or thorns for endangered trees; it respects you and it respects equally our compatriots far away in space and time. It is so outrageously generous that my educators have said it is wild, and shook their finger menacingly in its face. Yet its feelings still purr within me. In long, boring sessions these outrageously patient long-range compassions were to be put under house arrest and monopolized for us, for our house dogs, pear trees and cows perhaps, and occasionally even for the generation next door. By pouring all our dear love down on this one single time, spot, and kind, look what a deluge in our planet's history we have become.

Much of the pity I learned could have remained an innocent child—a child in a circus and full of delightful laughter while we, the serious people, bemoan our balloons and our mad successes popping; while we bemoan the cows for refusing to go to their slaughter, while we pity those the Creator thumps and squeezes through Her fingers to even more fantastic bubbles and curls.

Now my feelings are confused. I blush when I have been good to a forest instead of to our army of loggers. When I feel good in the company of life at sea, when I simply snoop and wonder about it rather than pester it with my longline gear loaded with nasty hooks, my cultured mind may mistake this friendly time for laziness.

Our children are now left with the unpopular task to make our impatient pity patient again. They are asked to stand back and let the butterflies by themselves slowly, slowly unfold their wings and not to blow at them warm wind. I wish our children the luck to be strong enough to say "no" when asked for their tears so a soft, seedless science may buy even more credit extensions from our fellow life to stop the whining when we take a test. The winged people, the insect and tree people, the 15,000 different grasses need a Gandhi and a nurse now more than ever—more, certainly, than ourselves.

Underneath the feet of our glorious economy still confidently advertising itself, I feel the whole earth quivering with hope for a generation that will have less desire for even more material riches and will become fascinated with cultivating beautiful relationships and get high on dancing to these relationships. Or do you think our economy should simply keep on stepping on the gas until it runs out of victims and comes to a halt?

My soul is sore from claustrophobia. Too long my psychic energy has focused on a merry-go-round for man alone. This neurosis without a name has now quietly become my rebel leader who gives me new ideas where and when to be sad or to cheer.

In my mind other forms of life have now become as precious to be preserved as a failing human life. And so let me take the boos, if booing it must be.

158

Deep down it appears a perverted desire to me that the grainships loaded with public relations grain and with the plight of overpopulation should be sent to soul countries and to stop also in them the journey of the seasons.

The above is an agonizing statement and I knelt to share this thought hoping it might come out more than just offensively. Do I do good to cast this idea adrift so a finder might talk it over with me? I discovered that people who are poor of gadgets but rich in spirit have a colorful string of joys and smiles of which a man in a high-yield society knows little about. Although it would comfort many highbred minds to shoot down with consumerism the remaining soul countries and bring them into our reality, I wonder whether we should try so hard to plug this source of nostalgia? There is a rare fragile beauty in these other worlds and I have a hunch that we should not lightly intervene. After all, they might be the new Arks of Noah for the life at large and for what in us is deep.

A desert people is among the paloverde and the ocotillo one other desert plant. In the drought the ocotillo sheds a thousand leaves rapidly and a desert people may quickly shed its share of women, children and men. These plants then withdraw, turn inside and so contribute together to a sacrifice to preserve the many special desert joys. And then the rain comes—and they all celebrate colors Mr. Safeway will never produce. What do I know of those joys in a desert soul that would allow me to send grainships, DDT, credit, earth movers, better pumps, and create a tyrant in the desert life? Would I do right to add these special people also to the herds of men milling between hamburger and soft drink joints?

Savage love may also become beautiful when one considers that the dearest neighbors of a fecund man may, after all, live in his testes and of a woman in her womb. It may thus be the spoiler of a generation that conspires in a one-generation plan, invests in it all, settles in this one world alone, huddles together for love, protection and warmth.

Below the graft made on my soul that lets me produce seedless love, thoughts and grapes highly convenient for my generation's selfish goals, I am still that lively pollen sack that learned to independently walk yet still loves to court its blossom of a thousand successive blooms. To me this courtship has remained wonderful. And the woman who God settled close to me thirty-eight years ago has become a magic box of gifts. As soon as I pull one goody out and look away, that box is again filled. No other favor from God has come close to this gift.

159

Every hero and thief, every fern and moss, every mind and leaf, even buggers and braggarts, all abide to the Law; all fight and wriggle ahead to meet the source of light which becomes visible to them after that light is mirrored through the garden of time in who knows how many zig-zags and curls.

It is said that beyond our attraction to light we also possess an extraordinary capacity that's itching in us to sprout. With this fabulous gift we might even out spring the light. Think of the thrill when with an organic cyclotron in us we could accelerate all memories into one single scene.

For now this is to me barely more than words; it's a tease; a crack with a fantastic view which I do not want to heal. But consider, what a thrill for a daredevil mind to be invited to trip out to where there is no time to separate the victim from the crime, entering a world woven so tightly, it leaves no crack to drive a fence pole so to keep the good grazing separate from the mean.

Yesterday, I looked in puzzlement at a book page full of pinholes. I saw no sense; just random holes. I would have never guessed that marvelous happening which pinholed my old dictionary's page one hundred seventy-eight. Only when I read a hundred pages earlier and a hundred pages later in that book and noted other random holes did I realize that in that book there was a well-planned termite's nest. In the book of time, one is also for a treat sometimes allowed to read from back to front and see that it makes sense. In that book a life may start a thousand years from now and lead to Napoleon's tent.

I suspect that beyond the wonderful gray of our brain, there is also the history of our future in reverse time joining our memories of the past as the guardian angel or a supreme I Ching counseling us, perhaps even allowing glimpses of an ecstatic vision.

160
Are not the moral trails the rather down-trodden trails on which it would be hard to find anything for the evening news and worthy to brag about or reward?

What could be the fabulous project on which we are being assigned work, now, that nature allows us to be its most sinful, wasteful and daredevil tribe in its procession from the sea to the land to the gift to understand? Many of our old noble talents are being laid off. Farsighted species preservation that would meddle with a man seriously, self-sacrificially involved in a test is blindfolded at our test site. We seem to be sifted for some strange usefulness that gives a hoot about personal happiness. In this project a jellyman, a neurotic, a pervert, a braggart, anybody hyper in some way seems higher paid than the stable, the happy and the robust. A gift of prodigious shortsightedness seems to be sent to make us blind to the danger the side effects of our work is earning us. I surely feel driven from a cozy old home.

Yet I have a hunch that for the spirit of life there is no waste. Every act is written down. A motherly lie, the shift of a pebble in the surf, a hug for a maddened friend, her step into a perversion or a sewer hole, a life spent sharpening nails, a species ending in extinction, everything seems memorized in the unused forms to be used as a roadsign later on. The blank space and the building's openings are full of meaning. In the steep climb of life to an ever more fantastic world, does not every step after being made become a precious misstep that is thankfully marked off and its result filed? There my goof-ups and failed experiments never fail. They simply seem the road signs to luckier strikes. Why should I give my failures hell? Are they not also my teachers? Later my spirit uses these roadsigns to better reassemble itself. Brighter stars may light a darker night.

Our prodigal capacity to blunder, to act in paradoxes, to excitedly yell at each other or try any imaginable perversion on us seems to come from the abundance of adventurous oddities clowning among our docile, good-boy genes. For her experiments, Mother Nature needs to lure many innocent organisms to step forward as candidates and to risk their innocence. And for her suicidal tryouts, we seem her perfect and eager applicants.

Yesterday, when pulling fishing gear, I impatiently knocked many thieving starfish from my baited hooks. Today science tells me of the wonder: these poor starfish Theo broke in two will each soon turn into two healthy starfish instead. And Theo fished himself no fish but a lesson: life can even turn his failures into successes.

The Creator needs us to be a little angry with him. Why otherwise would he blur and scramble our vision of his scheme with all kinds of fog-forming chemicals, inhibitors and blinders, making us disgusted jump off his merry-go-round and perhaps err into a new way of making wings for his horses and swans? Why then repent? Is this not how we do his work?

Some are lassoed with gentle dissatisfaction into trying out what a good citizen should no try out. The Creator shifts others into overdrive with anger, even hate—to make them eagerly pull his meanest plow. If I think of how many mutations it takes till an innovation falls again in step with the Way and is welcomed to stay I become more forgiving about our "sins." How come Theo never learned at school that it was the bad boys who pointed out the poisonous mushrooms?

161

It could become sound business on Wall Street to invest in bogs that make good breeding grounds for frogs, for wisdom and all kinds of great undomesticated thoughts. Do you realize that soon a flower in the wild, an untamed thought, an innocent hunk of soil will not be sold for even its weight in gold?

No doubt our generation has lived truest to the Bible's story that declared us the masters of all creatures and told us to brand every organism on earth in our name. How seriously we took that command! This part of that sacred book is offensive to those of us who feel a kinship with all the other actors that perform together with us in God's circus show. Above all, we feel it has long misled the thoughts in our minds and the axes in our hands.

Nonetheless, the whole population of this planet has been thrown up in the air for grabs. That turmoil is over by now. Every leaf and creek, every boulder, even the manganese nodules hiding in the night of the ocean floor not yet explored and the guano on the cliffs of its shores seem now to be branded by an owner. Our need for ever more possessions is furious to find each blade of grass already labeled. I want to watch out. That frenzy for wealth might now turn us against each other, luring us into out-studying each other how to twist the other's arm and mind so he may have to drop his share; each pondering on how to slyly undo what the other has patiently done, and to patrol one's border—each forced to out think others in the art of changing the fence poles without being caught.

How easily we could hurt each other, businesslike, smiling, and keeping our harsh relations under an elegant hat, each humming the music of politeness to cheerfully keep up this drama.

Yesterday when I left my cocoon of slogan thoughts for a walk, I overheard a family of alder bushes worriedly lamenting to the Iris Meadow spread out underneath, "Do you remember when the God's Son proclaimed a love-in for man? Yet we know of no dragon that attacks us now with as many bulldozers and chain saws, of no spider paralyzing us with as many venoms as those men do who went to school with that wise man of Bethlehem. How come it became the children of these very people who spread now so much fear among the woods, meadows, the fauna, the sea?"

One should watch our children's education so that under that dignified biblical license to tyrannize our planet's life, we do not produce a billion little Hitlers terrorizing and cleansing the Garden of Grace.

Some, though, decided against this advise and we see it as the challenge of our lives to physically make do with rather less than more. We polish and streamline our lifestyles and go for quality. We like to zoom and wriggle through our fellow life with a minimum of possessions and friction. It's our idea of how to provoke less enemies, to progress in our leisure time and collect more friends. We see ourselves as modest colleagues of Scott. We explore life styles and do our own kind of little South Pole tours. We are merry fools who think about giving some of our IBM stocks not to you, not to charity, but maybe to the few herons still wading between the beer cans, shrimp farms and mangrove roots. We are fascinated by a justice in exile that reaches even beyond that mentioned in Bible stories and comes close to a wise old oak tree's generosity, when at the end of his legendary way this quiet companion finally lies down to give himself to whatever creature is in need. We have realized that a prickly pear unceremoniously braving the scorching desert sun is quietly also earning his nobility prize doing his fieldwork out there, his daily tests, his recombinations of DNA.

When a people dedicates a day in its calendar not to its heroes, not to itself but to the life outside its fence, does it not invent a festival that helps its public relations better than any professional campaign? Imagine a kind of sacred carnival in which each man, woman and child plants a "weed" tree, or together they buy out a piece of enslaved land and turn it free—a little like Potlatch festivals where some Indians released slaves. In such an Earth Day we could be good with our thoughts that sow wild oats. We could become a new breed of pilgrims not known in Jerusalem and honor in a tree festival the trees we have to fell. At such feats no chain saws, no fishhooks, no practical thoughts, absolutely no profitable effort will break that festive truce. Maybe the Jewish community could teach us what such a Sabbath means. What impossible bridges our minds could not build in such a drunken day!

162

What an assumption it is that people do not want to die.

The soul song that loves to march us into battle—does it not also want to lead us cheerfully home? Yet to make our economy hum, promoters spin me around myself. They seed me with preoccupation and with fear of death while I am dizzy. They smear my telescopic vision with mud. They make people die sour and hold onto the tablecloth with the porcelain while going down. Windshield wipers, trust, windows in our horizon, serenity, and chimney sweepers for our minds are not promoted for fear they make the GNP lean.

Yet imagine: we break out of this dark attitude; mad with joy to see we start to build even more powerful seeing instruments and we dedicate them to exploring the mysterious goodness of being alive with all its beauty of being born and dying; we promise not to profane these sacred tools with the vulgar sciences of panic which know little about how to give and how to leisurely thank, but have only in mind: fast—fast!—we will give life the psyche of an ox—we will market it. We would not be the first to build such "Sunday instruments."

In a time when dying has become so precious and needed, plentiful death among us becomes the rain many of us seem to be discreetly praying for to heal us from a scorching, meanness-breeding crowdedness.

I feel it is the tragedy of my time that in our perception of death the light went out. I can think of no blackout that brought more confusion in front of the legendary gate than the loss of our vision through this gate. We have become this huge somber crowd loaded down with clinical medicine and with provisions, everyone piling up and encamped in front of that gate of death and rebirth. Some are terrified, trampling and pushing each other, others are terrified, helping each other; all are out to postpone their own passage.

This cloud in my vision has shrunk my curiosity. It has exchanged many opportunities for limitations. It has reoriented our fundamental science of serenity to a science and technology that is preoccupied with personal eternity and with rocking chairs and is selling our children's world cheaply. Its personality cult litters this planet with grotesque tombstones with which many of us now try to perpetuate themselves. It makes me a stranger to people from other cultures of other times whose apparent friendliness toward death is beyond me and puts me out of tune with them.

Am I alone, or do Faust and his colleagues also hear our fellow life in tears pleading their case, "We were kind with your terror of death. We granted the tribes of man to hold onto one billion, two billion, six billion more men. This required an enormous sacrifice from all the other populations on earth. Please set your zealously applied sciences down for a while, your scalpels and lifespan stretchers, your earth movers, your microscopic endeavors. Make Sunday a day of inquiry, a day of science for just the heck of discovery and let your amazement at how well you are being taken care of be your thanksgiving. Please allow more of your people to die. Please make us this gift." The delegation of trees were desperately insistent for this when they called long distance.

Yet slowly we learn from the forest and its fires, which we have fiercely extinguished for so long. We let some fires take their course and see their benevolence. Even more slowly, nearly every old golden rhyme in my heart snorting, I have started to translate this wisdom behind such fires into the great thicket of man. I run into implications my tamed mind is barely vigorous enough to pay for and accept.

Climbing a ladder in a lull of the battle, I am also getting a little high. I marvel; I breathe in the sight of this enchanted planet and my confidence in the future soars before I am pushed down again into faith and the blinding steam of the battle.

When I brood over nature's plans, I am amazed how well we are being taken care of by nature's nifty inventions of birth and death—and I get a little drunk with confidence.

163
I know of no intellectual troublemaker as stimulating as the stupendous wilderness.

How could a man fertilize his intuitive mind, were he not able to also become a hummingbird darting through free land, sipping wisdom directly from builders, wreckers, renovators, crawlers, concocters and fermenters—all creatures who are also great philosophers, freedom fighters and explorers, all helpers to restore his rotten faith in the mother of all? Might he not slowly become deficient in tall, seedy ideas and become a pale eunuch in his mind after he has been lassoed, corralled and harshly ordered into a niche to just reason and to work? Soon, his docile mentality might sicken him with fright when he peeks over the fence and faces that rowdy crowd at large. Life in this no-man's world can look terribly courageous and "misbehaved" for a tamed mind. It enjoys spontaneously shaking itself to pieces to better reassemble the pieces in another try. To not trip in such wild waters, a man's eyes must remain sharp and his mind ready to jump for a foothold up into his imaginary future or down into his mineral and animal past, pricking up his ears to the hints of everything slow or fast. Out there, where he listens to the zillions of waves that nature creates, licking, pounding his inner shores, flooding him with so many messages at one time, he must have ten ears of a hare.

It is not just my penis, it's my whole life that gets an erection or goes lame according to what it experiences and sees. Watch my behavior closely, watch my growth—and you read my biography. I am the reflection of what I experienced. I am mostly echoes. I am the cook of my neurochemicals and proteins—my environment is the client who puts the order in.

When children are incubated in controlled isolation, fed sterile, regurgitated thoughts spooned in by the hour; and for every question allowed to choose just from the three most simplistic answers, when the voices in them from wonderland are so cut out, they may become good robots and office equipment. They become apprentices of good work. Yet I wonder: will they not lose sight of a fantastic world where a mountain is not a mountain and a sin is not a sin? Their intuitive intelligence with its advisory board of guardian angels may die.

When our children spend their play time in that once bewildering wilderness that we simplified into an "adventure place" for simpletons with a swing, a metal slide nicely fenced in by flora that's geometric and trimmed, may then these youngsters not soon become siblings to the psychotic zoo bears intellectually locked in endless, meaningless pacing and swaying movements when not performing their acts? We may, of course, invite them later to docilely get their kicks in videoland.

Yet for someone who can keep company with the pitiless and the hateless no-man's land, with its whispers of amoral ideas from all its seedy weedy greens, with its shady ladies and its shady woods, with its chewy thoughts and mighty songs of thunderheads, these barefooted companions will never turn into monsters for them. Wilderness becomes a teacher, benefactor and ally. How could one ever become a widowed mind in such a playful crowd? I have heard of women and men who were driven so much by that unfashionable lust to taste nature's prize for danger and pain that they left a neat profitable desk for good, just to become involved actors in that great outdoor show of love. Out in that unhygienic world every possible sight is a potent seed crystal for those wholesome thoughts that are tantalizing foods for our wholesome souls. Wilderness is land in love. Its refuges are our meditation gardens.

In town my mind learns mostly from other men. There we have shifted from a general awareness to a highly selective species-oriented communication—hence our wonderful verbal language capacity. There my mind eats mostly dead and regurgitated thoughts. It eats white bread and candy bars, so to speak. When my mind is arrested too long in town, it becomes a fat farm fish that dreams of the vistas and of the dangers in an open sea. When I dare and leave the egg shell of classic logic, I step into that awesome openness. I become apprentice of a trillion different masters; each the expert in his field—the poppy—expert in drugs, the skies—expert in shades of blue. Some plants study electrostatic ballistic to shoot seeds, and the dear mosquito might be experimenting on vertical take-offs or an infrared vision for you; each works on his unique project in life's edifice in which they have been tinkering and thinking perhaps for a billion years; each is a magnificent living experiment in the art of living that absolutely no one can duplicate. There, my mind can enjoy a wholesome meal.

While in town the million fires of the Friday night fever are noisily burning, but few of us are still allowed to be out on an island of no man's land. In this delightful isolation where no man watches out for me, information comes from awareness and the need for verbal language is drastically reduced. There we hope that our sixth sense is switched on and tunes us into the nonsense wisdom of grace with its language of super luminary speed. On that different network of news, we can submit our problems and our finds to a larger crowd. Then the mind has different levels in its language. All is not twitter, words or written in TV dots, but is analphabetic communication best perceived away from the rude neon lights in town. In that upper room the goose bumps, the pleasures and the stings we give and take may sometimes be read in the timebook a hundred pages away from my ego. There, a bellyache may come from different things that from unripe plums. Yet to jam the revolutionary voice of that freer world, which is meant only for those able to stand mentally on their own, still needs to be the first commandment when the great spirit programs a fine and undistractive welder who can perfectly weld a pipeline's thousand pipes. So, I trust the advice of my solitude more than the applause of a crowd.

But behind all those romantic fantasies I have hidden a more closely disturbing question. Tell me how I could ever love you below your surface after I'm hooked on cleanliness, on obvious justice and on aesthetics, and I cannot stand you in pants that are not pressed but simply mended, after I cultivated in me an aversion to all that's yeasty and seedy, to the asymmetric and the daddy longlegs and to whatever is wild in you? Is not your mind behind its mask also wonderfully alive with bats, with nettles, lilies of the pond, spiders and beneficial worms, with peaks and depressions, with horseflies and fifteen thousand kinds of grasses!

At times I think how a young mind that is loved and not hurried, is the most amazing butterfly unfolding gently, very gently, a hundred wings; each wing meant to fly that mind to a different world. I then also think how a society catering to the adults might push this tender mind into school onto a bench and impatiently rape it without feeling shame. Could it be for this that many among us end up with the defiant, revengeful psyche of a violated child out to sell itself at the highest price for the rest of its life?

I heard of an educator eager to show off his butterfly's success. He took this future flyer in the warmth of his palms, breathed on it and the butterfly rapidly unfolded its splendid wings, fluttered excitedly and fell back in his hand, dead.

164

You may think it is our nice gifts that make our friendships grow. I learned differently.

It seems to be our shortcomings, our indigestions, fits and sins: when we lie, steal, disappoint, explode or drive testingly a strange idea into a friend, even when we are angry and vicious, and when we can forgive each other and make such difficult acts wonderful and good with our tears afterwards; all this, I learned, makes good friendship grow. From these compassionate tears, I discovered that your daimons and my daimons, missing elegance to have them publicly exposed, may nonetheless belong to the most enduring and vital parts of our personalities.

When I do not simply clam up in accusations when her mind has indigestion, burps or breaks wind, I can enjoy our most wonderful capacity: I can explore how to make of that ugly duckling in her jungleland a blue and red cockatoo to add it to my territory of love. The deeper I probe into my own inner wilderness the less egotistic and the more bewilderingly generous I find myself. That merciless psychoanalysis confronts me way down with my and your inborn disinterest for all that is merely humanistic and in its narrow sense good. At that level of my psyche, I seem steered by a morality that ultimately does not favor us. It seems to be at the edge of this mental abyss where we made that legendary change of course, proudly stepped out of the Way and headed for our master-of-all-life complex.

In such ideology-wrecking inner disputes in which we become vulnerable to our terrible inner strength, we knock down fences, the deadlines of our egos, no-entry signs, and the virtues favoring man. In that brainstorm, we may discover that it is for our imperfections that we are all brothers and sisters after all. There, in our untamed depths we are more brutally beautiful than exploding stars.

To hang on my dear imperfections, to celebrate them and not to quickly shortcut to some personal mini-perfection, to remain vulnerable, to hang even a lantern over my openings, notches and hang-overs, my needs, doubts and "sinful" depressions, holes, exaggerations and missing corners so that others can grab me, get a foothold and hang on, is this not how I invite you to step right in? It might be for this that a mountain climber is not angry at the mountain for its pinnacles, cracks, warts and holes but talks to it as one talks to a formidable friend. It seems to be the precious imperfection of the flower bleeding honey that becomes the opening that begs the bee to come in and do its magic. With so many highs and depressions, how can a good wheel be round? And so personal imperfection works smoother and with less friction than personal perfection.

To offend somebody and to make up for the offense afterwards may prove more revealing and rewarding than not to offend. Are not our most intimate and lasting bridges built with such difficult "gifts"? Are not offenses also invitations to get to know the mysterious wildness underneath the dressing gown of a friend's mind which may be as beautiful, challenging and profuse as any jungleland?

May I ride that uncomfortable thought to its next stop with you? On the level of global psychology, "sins" may ultimately fulfill chores similar to viruses when they trespass boundaries and ferry genes between the organisms. To sin might be our mysterious and feared capacity to take here and to give to unexplored destinations, transferring love from the empire of man to kingdoms of other species, to unknown worlds, to times ahead or past. And are there not many vital interdependencies we do not yet know?

And so I am suspicious of clearness that is clear, of knowledge that is obvious, of goodness that is good, of a talker that talks swift, of roads that are straight. With so many unfamiliar tenants living up and down, yesterday and tomorrow, to the left, in the middle, to the right, how could a good road be straight?

An act that is obviously good or obviously bad may ultimately complete itself in the fallout of its many shady side effects that it showers somewhere else. Then also an act has a personality that is larger than its obvious ego.

Yesterday, puzzled, I listened to the song of a passing wind: "Hold back! Don't shoot your opponent; you might never find a better friend." Today I begin to like this song.

Don't think for a minute that this beautiful Earth is made by meditation. Look, summer is hunted down by fall. Yet is this awesome hunter not also the manna that feeds the soul? And so, from these zillion nasty little pinches, bites, quakes and thingies there is this beautifully chiseled world that has become ever more alive for 3 billion years.

165

Are we ushering in the time when a computerized bureaucracy becomes a digitized Louis XIV to royally declare: "L' état, mon cher, c'est moi."

When I am tired and feel beaten, when my refined mind whines and is fed up roaming out of doors, I am reminded not to be a fool but to swiftly take refuge in one of our many brands of "huddle-together-isms." There my shortcomings can become the notches and holes in the key that lets me in. There a man's failing virility can free him for a devotion not open to others whose seeds in heat endlessly are itching them. Here a love story that failed on its own can be socialized, turned into a success and insured. The gardens are socialized; cowardice can be, reproduction, compassion, even the sex organs might soon be. A radical simplification seems realized to raise a penthouse built by a million hands, isolating us from the menacing jungle of life.

A man who gives up wandering alone but joins such a commune, how much can he not give up, leave behind, be blind to, care less about and forget! How many holes in his courage, wallet or soul can he leave unmended and still get by.

When I trip, lose my self-assurance, blunder or sweat in the heat of a creative crisis and I tremble in awe, is it courageous I give up at the slightest inconvenience, to put personal missteps out of sight by joining for help some crowd, to ask shamelessly for relief, a lifeline, food stamps, a cooler and support? Should I readily abolish my kingdom and unite with other disposed kings into a royal commune of hardworking nobles? When our wonderfully impractical love for our toddlers gets temporarily sick with a mania of grandeur, practicalities and luxochic, should we without a fight with this sickness rapidly institutionalize the semi-orphaned children in daycare centers and pat each others' backs with pride for having so elegantly got rid of our kids? It seems to me such a grave decision to amputate a swollen leg of my soul and ask society to step for me.

I am beseeched to dilute my grief, my itches, my ecstasies by lowering myself with others to the level of a human hive. Why should passionate love become mediocre, shared and cooled?

Deep down I feel it's not yet my place where twelve failed captains run together a boat. And so I keep holding my own course.

166

Life advertises jobs for a new breed of business leaders. They are to invent ways to operate with stocks we grant to our children, to the oceans, to the rivers and the forests, to all of nature's wonders and, of course, to ourselves, all sharing good relations, profit and vote, all having board members when decisions are made.

Will Harvard and Oxford leap forth to the revolutionary challenge from the Earth and give us a breed of visionary businessmen?

In our businesses we have remained quite cannibalistic. Under the disguise of our corporations we can now legally cultivate egotism to its perfection and do it anonymously, fooling our shame. We are slow to enjoy the most simple kindness when we produce, buy and sell. The PR people of our businesses seem to be still great ink fishes and clowns paid to distract a worried crowd. They sure are experts at public diversion and beginners in creating good relations between business, our children and the Earth.

It would be a benediction when we could finally also give our businesses souls. Without them they will become a horror story to our children and not because of the rift between the rich and the would-be rich who do not mind cold feet standing in waiting lines for their turn. Our success story could become the story of how we marketed the Earth, pushed this glorious planet into misery and left all but the closest of our kin in a poverty of desperate meanness and tears.

This change of mentality seems to me a subject that cannot be conventionally taught. Answers how to escape that blind alley start to trickle in from strange sounding seminars. Here the apprentice is probably more knowledgeable and less hung up than the master economist. This leap to interspecific, intergenerational vision will quietly prepare itself with the help of many, many who think and dream about it and do not mind making the old patriarchs chuckle over our own hang-ups and beginner's clumsiness. Yet I wish us the good luck that a supercritical stage in me and many others will soon be reached. And then the avalanche or the hundredth monkey effect—a group of monkeys learned to wash the sweet potato before eating. Instantly other groups, completely isolated, started to wash their potatoes. The rush is on, not for gold, but for a new and dazzling vision. We become the revolutionary generations that truly defy gravity, and think, feel and commute freely between different levels of knowledge and different worlds.

We are shy apprentices of a new economy. We do not enjoy serving stockholders who got stuck in just playing banal points on the rusty, old board game. We think about how to deal with our fellow life more on equal terms and try to live the proof that it can be quite agreeable to be biofriendly and to give for what we take. We are children of a proud technological society, caught in its own quicksand of temporary solutions and we are full of doubts. The more we enforce our old humanistic ethic for solutions, the more we seem to sink. We encourage each other to become humble again so we can hold onto the help and wisdom barefooted nature is offering us. This business revolution rumbling in our minds will dwarf the enormously anguished and bloody conflict out of which slavery became a crime.

Slowly we do not take anymore only the low dollar sign as price for what we buy but add the repetitive stress injuries the land and the minds of the workers suffer when forced into monocultures to produce and sell cheap. We help each other to outthink the naive assumption of economists: one needs to own much to live well; this notion is really incompatible with good relationships. We turn to nature for therapeutic thoughts to fight this sickening belief that turns us into chic monsters with ten maddened heads: one head to give jobs to thousands advertising cigarettes, another to pay thousands to advertise against cigarettes. One head that in an obsessive hatred of germs makes us whitewash the world; another head that injects us with the germs to educate again our immune system that became dumb and information poor.

We are weaning ourselves of our parent's mistrust that made them endlessly whine and charm our good Mother Earth to reveal more of her great sciences to us; not for getting us high by her goodness but to unceremoniously snatch the insights granted and run to hide them, to make another hammer with such gifts, another killer in our chemical warfare against much of her flora and fauna, another whip to coax her for more favors. Can we ever again voluntarily give and scatter some of our energy, of our crops, of our thinking, time, vision and biomass for the raven and skunks, for the rodents, the muskrat ponds and all the laughing creeks that also love to celebrate spring, for simply giving our thanks, as did some Indian tribes?

Our almighty remedy has become to produce, always to produce more physical solutions. When a mental tool is mislaid we replace it with a tool of steel. The gospel of the better chain saw, of better fishfinders and mousetraps, another injection of money, add another head to the monster, another tooth, another policeman, another kilowatt, another inch to the waist of our output. When our warmth for our spouses catches a cold, we quickly build a fallout shelter for our battered wives and keep the men out with three locks. How physical we have become to offset our vision that is getting dull. Wasn't it mostly such aggressiveness we gave as a motto to our scientists?

Yet in a lucky morning alight with all the suns of a sparkling dew, I may for a tiny spell become all eyes. And I stare at our bulging speedway system and in disbelief I see a slowly mushrooming bomb spewing a huge poisonous cloud into the stratosphere at a trillion RPMs. It is in this sense that our businesses may have quietly become a sad story to our children.

After our great success in vaccines, pest controls and vagabond traps, I hear now a cool question asked: who will protect the savannas from being overgrazed, now that all the female blow flies have been fooled with sterilized sperm, although these little rascals were the savanna's guardian angels since unrecorded times? One by one the misbehaved organisms we exterminated for being freeloaders to our businesses, they turn out to have also been qualities of God.

It is for these present circumstances that the nifty people from institutions like Harvard and Oxford are asked to deliver us now a new breed of heroes.

When one becomes more social with the whole rowdy community of comedians life settled on earth, one can also listen to much delightful and encouraging news on the business of exchanging gifts. Yet beware, would not the love of a woman or man, who have acquired such divine goggles they can see far into unborn generations and well beyond man's garden fence when searching for side-effects, look rather shady and not at all economical or heroic to a domesticated mind? Would persons with such a tall moral not be far removed from the business ethics of our dear old heroes, our beautiful people, and celebrities, our bygone saints whom we picked with a farmer's eye rather for their usefulness and whom we applaud for being the brave bankers, soldiers, clowns, missionaries and sundry chauvinists, who better imposed man's Reich on the planet's life? I look at the results and I get an irksome hunch that the highest ethical standard is lived by wilderness which our patriarchs systematically advertised as our archenemy. Theo, don't deceive yourself. No humanistic, no high-bred mind may ever enter that legendary garden of serenity and survive. To thrive in God's heavens and hells needs the mind of a weed, impartial, pitiless, tough and versatile. If I ever get a glimpse on wisdom I expect it to be such that many will only have the harshest words for it.

167

In defense of the profiteers, may I bring up a less arrogant point of view?

Although I do not know of a creature that is not in some way a beast of prey, is it not the physically or emotionally disadvantaged and rather unpopular man destined to prey on his fellowmen to survive who needs the sharpest rational mind? He has to know all about my blind spots, my carelessness and doubts. He has to use the holes in my memory and shoes and has to be expert in Achilles' heels. He lives on what he can get out of my cowardice. To feel comfy and secure, this man without much muscles or skin needs to wrap a sturdy blanket of wealth around himself. He might only survive on premasticated food and physical work that others do for him. And so he has to become more knowledgeable than the stout anteater, the fisherman and good-natured farmer who can conveniently prey on the dull corn, ants, pigs, wheat, fish and clams. Is there a niftier inspector probing in me for soft spots than the profiteer, a more pressing animator, a better psychologist, a more arousing whip that God sends to drive me on and sharpen my wit?

In the saga of life there seems to have always been a great need for profiteers, outsmarters, mistletoes, freeloaders and parasites. These visitors seem to know more about their hosts than the hosts know about themselves. I might fear them for this. Maybe I should also take off my hat to honor their wits.

168

Love is the wisest magician and She might again have a surprise up Her sleeves for us. She might once more bewitch some of us and this time make us care for any needy creature in God's menagerie and do it with the same sweet old feeling of hugging a child.

In the past we were blessed to fall in love with our children. This was for most of us our high, our most ecstatic dream blossoming so powerfully that we put all our songs, perfumes and colors into it. To fall so in love gave us a taste of having magic eyes. This was also the time when even a hardened warrior like Crazy Horse, when his infant daughter died of cholera, lay beside her body three days, such was his pain.

Now I notice that whole nations are eventually losing their ability to fall in to that old-fashioned love anymore. They are losing their most natural and gentle drug. I notice that the eyes of many people slowly, slowly shift, a little like the ancient adaptation of the flounders did when those flatfish settled on the bottom to live and their eyes drifted to one side of the head. We adapt to the cataclysm of a crowded world. Many have come to see children from another angle: as a punitive burden. They feel a sacred urge to march and to fight for the right to be left alone and free for a career. Others feel they should demand help in the "burden" of having a child and be rewarded for it. Deep down, and still obstructed by many old, golden rhymes, I reluctantly discover my respect for that difficult sacrifice.

I am from a generation that is torn apart. The fragments of its native soul take off in blazing meteors on their solitary flights. We became handicapped to share a law, a lovesong, a public bench. We are now so much scattered through the chores and seasons, we cannot swarm together anymore like we used to. While some are still born into the sweet jubilant hopes of a romance in May and having a child, others are born for a solemn sacrifice that asks them to happily make good our excessive multitude and to bury the colossus we became.

In a large sense we seem also polyphonic. We produce different psyches in response to seasonal cycles. Traits well suited for conditions encountered in overpopulation seem now triggered in many. Yet I am confused when others who are apparently so similar to me bump into my heart and rush righteously in the opposite way.

For a long time we could till our lives to the same seasons under the same sun humming one love song fitting practically all. We were born and again pulled down for similar reasons, all orderly and predicted by that same constellation in our genes and in our sky, to supersede ourselves in another round. We were born to be rivers that flowed into the ocean and at the same time to be the ocean that transpires puffing up the rivers of clouds that rise again into the skies—no holding out on one single career— raising only up and up, or pouring only down as if we were an irrigation ditch.

Caught in this terribly interesting time between the self-sufficient people we were and the experts we are going to be on the run to specialization, we are whirled around in a mighty confusion of our needs and feelings.

Many suffer now the trauma of one of the many kinds of abortion which seem not only to come from the need to poison an ovum or keep the semen from spurting but from a terrible need to poison the whole so tremendously vitalizing love story that kneels like the three humble kings around the child. Many are suddenly asked to invent a completely new way to bear flowers, to give themselves, to fill their need to be joyfully consumed.

What's natural to us is after all not as boring as a beautiful tape played over and over again. Thank God it's also natural that we are born with a seed of craziness in our souls.

169

There was this intriguing man from Assisi whom our economy's PR people may want to choose as their patron saint.

The art of public relations is invited to a change of heart and to stop walking on its hands. It is invited not to be a handicap but to be an advocate for better ecology. This science of better relations can become the science of public enlightenment and of cultivating among us a fascination with better relationships with the sea and the land after it has rid itself of all the little Goebbels that the industrial Reich now thinks it needs. A collection of good relationships may be the only wealth worth striving for. This art of beautiful public relations should never fall so low that it corrupts my mind by bribing it with slick slogans with which I can conveniently blur feelings of guilt toward the earth. It should not get me drunk with a psychedelic language that dispels my question marks. It should not be an ink fish leaving me in clouds. And I say, "damn it," if it should breed the slick lawyers who defend ecological crimes.

There is a shy public relations team in my deeper mind at work that does not take sides but teases me to join it in sniffing out, exploring and simply advertising the good will between you, the maple tree, the sand dollar, the wolf, the eelgrass and me.

Note that in the epic of evolution it seems not to be the strong, the rich and stout, not the gloomy whom fear converted to become a saint that finally survive, but those delightful organisms that have been most fascinated and productive in bettering their relations with all the populations on earth.

There are a few Nobel Prize winners, a new breed of highly educated yet career-disoriented tinkers and thinkers; there are Earth First! people, Green people and other ark-builders, there was this intriguing Francis, saint or flower-child from Assisi, all had or have fun devoting their lives to promote our good relations with our fellow life.

170

There are no vices which I haven't seen transformed by nature into good shears, explorers, shovels, composters and renovators helping to better her show and to amaze spectators even more.

It seems that a crime, any crime you pick, has its turn in the journey of life to be precious and to become blessed. To make a change of season less offensive to minds easily terrorized by change; tricksters are asked to sow sand into old-fashioned eyes while blinders with a new matrix are tied around our minds. They give new attractive names to prohibitions and crimes that finally are triggered to orbit on the Medicine Wheel into duties to be done and to join the troops. Plotters help to erase obsolete love songs in our souls. Neurochemicals switch on different clouds changing our vision. Clearings appear in our sky with messages from the contraries where before it was gray. Shadows forbiddingly stand in some of our sweet old ways. It is the promise of nature never to become locked up in one game.

Isn't it our capacity to cultivate selective forgetfulness in us that gives us the obsessed daredevils who can push alone and blind to mind shattering risk to the most hair-raising peaks or extremes; daredevils who forget all about our sweetest old romances in order to mind walk the edge of schizophrenia, risking a meltdown in a full blistering sun? Thanks to our prodigious capacity to forget whole sequences of memories while spotlighting others instead, we can also conveniently create new heroes and saints adapting these role models to our ever changing needs. Our sins may, on so large a scale, do to the ethical code of a society what mutations do to the genome of the individual. Both these mischievous transgressions save the world from boredom and from locking into repetition.

Life, after all, may not have been foolish when it blessed us so lavishly with vices and when it hung all these glittering lures on the mischievous trails that branch off from our fine system of safe ways. Our notorious capacity for perversion might prove to be one of her masterstrokes on adaptation. To make our morals self-regulation might turn out to be one of her great ideas. Who of us moms and dads would have guessed that some of our "sins," like abortion, would in many of our children turn into benedictions while we are still around?

We may still want to keep some hopelessly incompatible rascals on the other side of a fence. But what a wonderful shock absorber and painkiller we have found once we start wondering whether these fermenters, sinners, and decomposers might not also do a job for God—and sin is never certain anymore. My task: to reprogram my biblical world view, choosing a fitter recombination from my archetypical options so that I can live in this evolving world with less anxiety, guilt, doomsday fever, with less anger with the Creator, with less need to be a grumpy world improver. It is not the object, not the world that creates information. It is the seer who creates all information including the one that renders serene.

Who knows, if the whole inner topography of a man would spread out in front of me to be clearly seen—his eroded peaks, his lowest lows, his depressions and hyper highs, his rifts, faults, permafrosts, his abysses, deserts, love-forsaken masses of ice, his mutagenic happenings and his Grand Canyons, his uncharted jungles and forbidding swamps and his Blue-blossom-lands—maybe the way he lives might then turn out to be his only way out—and all might be forgiven.

171

Slowly this amazing flower we walk with, protectively nested between our legs, is in many ways losing its petals and undergoing a metamorphosis, maybe into a new love tool still unknown to me. Slowly we may be elevated to a tenderness beyond the sexes. We shall see.

The above is an old harmful splinter in my mind I try to pull out. I wonder whether in the process of socialization, homosexuality is not a prelude to a wider asexual sharing, a stopping point to a love scent that can cement a new society together with affections freed from the pollination game, with collective procreations, and custom-made pleasures that hold together the neuters such a society will need. What an amazingly foresighted gesture of life to discreetly cultivate for million of years in advance an assortment of oddities in our genes to be ready just in case. Here, out of the old love hormones a new altruistic love lure might be invented. Here nature may give our overcrowded world a tenderness with a built-in birth control. Strange new aphrodisiacs seem triggered into action modulating our sexuality. May nature not reward those whom she had to drive away from their old familiar homes with new pleasures lubricating their new relationships?

I see many are now invited to shed in neutered love games with each other's help a bewildering dimension that has become an unneeded burden to them when they enter their new careers. The confusion of the sexes now seems to come from a retreat of many to a basic asexual love with equal rights for all which might well be more deeply rooted in us and older than sex. In a deeper sense does not such earthy, "non-procreating" love more and more also flourish between women and men? In the many careers that the rational world is now distributing among us, no distinction of the sexes, no women and men as such are needed; neither female lines and circles, nor male management are needed. Now also she may come in from mystery land and have equal rights to think in comprehensible forms and obvious rhymes that please the rational mind.

Paul, as a good Christian, had reason to ponder on how nature in us would finally physically and mentally react to the neighborly socialization he taught. I wonder what he really thought. Be prepared, Theo, you will become what you act out. You reorient your love so to act as a Christian; you will physically become one. Shake hands long enough according to culture. Slowly an arm will prevail for just such a function.

And there is news more encouraging than a baby shower card. More of our children are pledging now their lives not to multiply the troops of man, not to build our success five stories higher into thin air. They dedicate their lives to the success of that shy and discreetly wonderful creation, which our troops, when storming to their triumphs, have left behind as unworthy. And so one morning one finds among the family pictures the picture of a most lovely seaslug pinned to the wall.

How much I need forgiving thoughts to keep up with our love life that races ahead. I want to feel good again with these gentle fellow women and men who are gays, or whose sex is more loosely defined than mine, after my civilization has invoked a terrible curse on them. They may, after all, be genetically best predisposed for an advanced social life among us. Great things in nature seem to start 500,000 years in advance. But how would one fit such long things into our short morals of the day without getting complaints?

172
More on the beneficence of paradoxes and lies.

When an unschooled person from somewhere in the uneducated land talks and lives stronger than me from her soul, she often puzzles me with unnerving paradoxes, non-logic, a taste for apparent injustice and lies. After I made a few unaccustomed thoughts I also realize that this person might well be engaged in a career many lifetimes tall and so lives higher up in the hierarchy of mentalities than I. There seems to be plenty of time in the multiple world of her unfocused mind to comfortably accommodate double-talk and let it become truthful in one of the many layers of her world. From her scattered perspectives, her paradoxes might make more sense than my "two and two is four" or your tennis match with me. People who are seven lifetimes tall follow a higher moral than I. Often they seem whispered into protecting some unknown friend who is too removed for my ego to be considered a neighbor and to care about. They have not yet fully tasted the trick to use shortcuts in love and time and to take refuge in a one-generation philosophy that's easily rhymed. They happily, and with the trust of a child, seem to walk the soul's winding roads curling through its many worlds to reach me maybe another day, in a separate reality, perhaps in another of my lives, perhaps as a benefactor to a child of mine. And what's wrong with a person who is loyal not to me not to mankind, but to life? Who said such "wrong doings" become not right in a mental step further up? What's wrong with a millstone having faith in the river's flow?

Gradually these ingenious systems of lies, membranes, hard-hats, repellents, immunities, antibodies, pride and paradoxes in the body and the spirit, that guard the many individual worlds from clumping together in a flat one-generation plot and stand so forbidding between the clover and the grass seem to start dissolving in us. Do we not now freely trade away our most vital personal truths as no one could have once dared to do? Every truth seems to have a for sale sign on. Do we not fast become informers without the slightest shame ready to breed a generation of mental clones that adores its media-fabricated heroes? These defenses give way to aggressive psychological enzymes, which break down secrets, spirit, shame and souls. The science of mind-altering breaks down the pillars that keep us horizontally separate, diverse and erect. Its experts nibble on our individuality and drill holes into it. They make us excessively neighborly in space, practical and flat and leave underdeveloped our communication system, the soul, that gives us seven lives. They deflate our dimension of time which gives our reasoning a soul stringing our thoughts evenly through seven generations of life. How useful and predictable we become when we shrink ourselves to become truthful slaves to one generation and its goals. How untrained we become in mental self-defense. But do you believe that somebody can be mentally "skinned" and in such openness still remain alive?

And here is this idea seen from another point of view:

A galaxy seems to turn just around itself yet it also remains firmly in the arms of the paradoxical pull that makes it waltz to the beat of some attractor common to every galaxy waltzing through the universe. The flat merry-go-round of a reasoning man becomes a helicopter freeing him to spiral swiftly, purposefully, visiting the other generations of life above and below when so following the paradoxical forces on his soul.

A woman clinging prudishly to one step of logic on the knowledge ladder might well remain a grounded feminist until she takes heart and lets go.

Missing such creative paradoxes, wouldn't a man remain simply a macho and a prisoner of one world alone?

I notice that it is the woman whose will remains weak and is not imposing on her soul who can be fearlessly strong. She rides a horse that's broken in. Hasn't the porcupine that contradicted itself by promoting its slowness instead of its speed become the fittest and the evolutionary survivor of its tribe? Such self contradictions might well have something to do with the great art of moderation and with how much horizontal truthfulness or armament is enough for an ego. The question: How much of my mind has to be tied up to Theo?

Why then grumble about the antagonism between flesh and soul? Do these contradictions not give the ego a helix and make it into a helicopter that can soar and land and soar again? What contradictions do you see in air filling a balloon which holds onto the wind or in a man who breathes out and breathes in?

173

What if, after all, no species, no man, no star can ever outfox the others, as Darwin's theorem seems to suggest that they can, and we are all in a way apples which cannot outfox for long the apple tree?

I suspect that on the journey of life, any invention of one organism is in a yet unknown way ultimately ferried and occasionally made available to all other creatures to be shared if needed. I suspect that every organism dips into the gene pool and that infectious disease, even "sin," may have something vital to do with the transfer of genetic knowledge and that for eons gene and mind-splicing has been practiced in a more mysterious and profound way than in our biotechnology and our world wars. We might not only be colonies of completely integrated microbes, as biology now suggests; we may also be seen as colonies of thoughts and genes. A species does not only develop. It seems to develop in a way that is needed for life's general well-being.

With so much sharing of knowledge and ferrying of genes between all species, should one lightly speak of survival of the fittest as if all this creativity were a boxing match? It seems rather that life changes, once in a while here and there, its coats and socks. On one clear morning we might wake up confused by the suspicion that it is after all not just the "horse-ness" that invented the horse but that this work of art, the horse, has been composed by life's innumerable composers all together: beetles, clovers, amoebae, horses, Indians, ammonoids, viruses, minerals and all. One might then be less offended when the Holy Spirit asks a horse to do some-thing "against" the species of the horse and makes it plow under some of the horse's grass. One could then even forgive a bit this spirit when it asks some of us to work against humanity and to pull some of us out as if we were a runaway weed.

That an organism is triggered to become a killer cell among its own kind and may be asked to clear elbowroom for other species than its own, is still a shady goodness to me. The science that will unveil this puzzle of interspecies communication and of their mutual help will have opened more doors to forgiveness than the apostles could have hoped for.

To grant us its ultimate prize and make us serene, I suspect, life asks us to simply discover the good intentions it has.

174

Slowly the mamas among us who protect the marsh-land, the magpies, the innocent air that gives every-thing its breath, will also want to add our impractical moods, our "illegal" character traits, our oozy juicy tenderness, our soul-made storms, our laziness and grains of craziness to their list of wonders needing protection.

When I dared go beyond man-made education and news clippings and let all my ancestors, the Johnny Appleseeds, the grasses, the algae, the minerals and trees also teach me, I got a surprise. I learned to respect that grandiose native selfishness in you, in a meadow and in a cherry tree—my deepest self, what an orchestra. Those who have the privilege to be trusting fools and still curiously stroll out from under our thought-conditioned dome to get directly involved in the Holy Spirit's outdoor seminar, we pick up morsels of the beauty in that "brute." Slowly unexpected wisdom begins to trickle from it and we are excitedly sipping it. When out there I mount on the back of a great wind and look down, our elegant goodness in which we like to dress up seems still little more than a politeness greasing our relationships—a refined lubricant of snails.

When a woman becomes pregnant, is she not starting to live more from her roots? Do then not the rules of our civilization game become declipsed in her by her analphabetic, radiant soul? Her egotism becomes twelve generations tall and makes her bewilderingly beautiful. When a man can become pregnant with what he daydreams about he also becomes awesomely beautiful.

I also have discovered something disturbing. I found that it is from this untempered and endangered world below our civilization's graft, teaming with nettles, mosquitoes, thieving orchids and buttercups that the most moving and spirited pictures bubble up. There dwells Miss Muse, saint and courtesan. There more spirited danger and fun await me than at the mental square dancing to which orderly thinkers are inviting me. I find that my inner sun raises, my dearest obsessions, the stuff of which ecstasies come to be—they well up from below where preachers and teachers have passed with their tattooing and their plow. I have found that the men and women who have shined a vision to me have fished it up from below where the "noble" graft was made. Then, how could a mind hazy with tears of pity see far and understand? Daring one's imagination in all its native clairvoyance without the safety net of rites, one might even see that beautiful sunset when a man goes under.

Yet rationally I have always been deeply afraid to stand up for my naked desires. They are mysterious to me, intangible, overwhelming giants that do not nicely court the ego of Theo. Might it be for this reason that in our rhetoric we endlessly dress our desires up with pity, with hate, with help, with all the soothing virtues and goodness humanism has created to please our whimpering reason and our eyes—a little like we the Christian and Hebrew people dressed up our history so that we can see ourselves as God's darling people on earth. I wish these hints can be better understood by some than just as an offense. Think how sensitive to other believers and critters we could become if we can free ourselves of such complexes of superiority in which we protectively wrap our fragile intellect; how many impossible bridges we could build!

In our unspoken depth, we may well be so terribly great, so mysteriously beautiful, so incomprehensibly lovable and loving that our reason has to dress up these fountains gushing mysteries in neatly comprehensible poems and rhymes. Is it for our terror to look that terribly overwhelming and puzzling beauty in the eye that we have to cover up our bare animal desires in political rhetoric, in humanizing attributes, in poetic philosophies before we go to the parade? We might all be naked emperors who desperately want to see each other with clothes on. How inventive that willful misunderstanding and the garment business for our mind and motives has become. Deep underneath those jewels and gowns we might be, though socially still unacceptable, much more than just humane. It might be a trick that nature has played on us. The need to cover up, as old as the feather business of the birds, has it not made of us the most productive inventors and decorators in the zoo of life. Yet good thoughts, as fine flowers, come also with their own attractive perfumes, and that's where the charm of our aesthetic arts comes in. It takes so much resolve to accept that in my deeper desire I am a happy emperor without clothes on, that a naked mind is stunningly beautiful. In my beginner's mind, where I am not yet tattooed by common sense and confined to its bubble of perception, I am still quite a promiscuous "bridegroom," eagerly wondering how the lively "bride" looks and loves without her gown.

175

Our shy capacity to give one's mind more free time to loaf, to wonder and to understand may become our greatest happening yet and turn into the eighth day of Genesis. Here is progress I like.

We must stop simply being vandals and create new jobs when free time is at hand!

To those of us who have children cheerfully nibbling on our fat and our love, it should come naturally to be considerate and sensitive to our future. Is not an archaic lesson in ecology also nicely curled up and sleeping in our chromosomes ready to wake up and transform a woman when she gives life to a child? Are our children not guardian angels posing in their untempered clairvoyance creative questions for us? Are there not things only children can see?

There is now a siblinghood of neuters rapidly filling the ranks, becoming so strong, its vote can soon become the law. This may be a new powerful guild of adults dedicated to seriousness and careers. They have few children nibbling on their paychecks and luring them away from work; yet they still have the aggressive strength to support ten but need to provide for none but themselves. Many are well into Genesis's eighth day, yet are still hounded by an old need to frantically provide and to come home every day with a full load, as if they still were moms and dads—and they may end up with constipated souls. How to spend that surplus of love and time more inspired than to work it out on a full time job and to simply empty it in binges for luxovaganzas, soft living and banal fun which all seems to give our planet a bellyache. Never before were so many of us challenged to create a completely new generosity for themselves, to give themselves and be needed in a creative way, now that for the many childless people the old obvious reason to care for more than one generation and to be joyfully suckled is gone.

I like to learn taking more gently from the oceans and from the land, now that my children are grown up. It's my chance to become a little bit of a poet, a scientist, to finally wonder and understand. My old provider mind can learn to be less productive and more creative. It becomes now obvious that an inorganic justice in which we justly divide up all the riches

306

of the Earth can be a deadly justice for our kids. Imaginative justice can do better than impose equal rights for a tree that labors under a load of apples and for a tree that is asked to produce shade, flowers, firewood, good-will or poetry.

Now that I have the capacity to kill ten times over what I need, I can learn from the lion's population and consumption control—and be mostly playful, curious, gentle, even poetic and on Tuesdays and Fridays only a serious fisherman. I can distill my surplus, quickly readjust and turn my free time into all kinds of original pregnancies.

176
What an assumption that to sink more and more into horizontal unity is a universal remedy.

The argument for unity—a picnic for the crowd. The argument for diversity—a solitary sailing around the world.

When a man is invited to come down from the wind blown tower of his native solitude into the warm lap of a maternal society, when he is offered a niche to specialize and to become good at his allotted job, is he not also invited to leave a fantastic view point behind? No balcony on the dust and elbow-ridden market place is quite as scenic as his. Yet safely taken into that new organism's bowels, even a troubled man can become brilliant at knowing the structure of the one ant mound to which he chained his mind to investigate and he may even parade a Nobel Prize. His brilliance in his domain is the gift for sacrificing an unfocused view. It is his reward for accepting mental house arrest. Yet slowly, in perfecting one talent or one virtue in himself, his capacity to make a general statement leaves him. Slowly he will become one man more to be asked precise information and one man less to be asked advice. He is gradually relieved of being directly responsible to God or his soul. Without worrying, he may follow that society's agencies' ethic codes.

The gathering place is crammed with people and more are protesting to be let in. What an epidemic to socialize! So many are begging for careers to be just handed to them. What if there is no one left to sort out all what is brought in with broken off beginnings and ends and can weave of it a lasting smile? What if the positions for wisdom and its poets that knead the clay of all the raw sciences alive, remain unfilled? It is for this reason I wish that in a triumph of insight, the elders decide to let the Jacks of all thoughts alone.

When I shrink myself to be rented out for work do I not also shrink my responsibility? I become a barge in tow of a tugboat. My towline no longer reaches to heaven. This is how among us much accountability is lost.

In the history of our intellect the shift from indiscriminately mingling with all species and all times to focusing on a temporary merry-go-round for man seems to me the most dramatic happening. Maybe it has to do with the new symbiotic rearrangement some now call the Great Society. Life sometimes gives failing individuals a second chance to do together what neither could anymore do alone. In this simplifying reorganization, the tools of self-sufficiency, capacities such as to think, to gather food, to procreate, to decide, to digest, to cure oneself—are gradually eliminated one by one until only the one outstanding and highly cultivated function or commodity valuable to that brave new society remains.

With so many specialized minds, the democratic system soon is hijacked by the professional tricksters of the mind. With everyone dispersed down somewhere in the shafts of our knowledge mine, who after all wants to be asked, where and for how long should the sun shine. Should those working underground be asked, the fireflies, or the sailors of submarines? Should all be asked in good democratic fashion to vote regardless of their blind spots, their expertise or what they care about?

In spite of all the historic cover-ups, democracy has to live with the biological fact that there is among us a system of castes. In the process of further socialization the leadership will retain finally but its name. Sun and firefly will never have equal right and equal time to light up a summer day.

The nostalgia of a soul that is taken in by the kingdom of rationality, subdued, usefullized and socialized, seems to me one of the most helpless sadnesses yet. It is evolution's old soul ache without a name. It surpasses the neurosis of the layed-off sex appeal. This trauma is not meant to be healed by society but amputated. To heal it needs a single-handed revolt to shake it off.

This time seems to have a foul climate for vast unfenced minds that know how the seasons of evolution, how penguins, trees and men, how opponents, generations and friends can together socialize. It makes me wonder how wisdom grows. It cannot be cultivated nor taught nor bought. You touch it, transplant it, fertilize it, protect it, and it spoils. Scholarships and grants often make it wither and rot. It does not do well in comfort, in safety or on the freeways of our laws. How wrong was I when I thought I could pursue wisdom by clenching my teeth. Rodin's *Le Penseur* has misled me to believe that wisdom can be found concentrating and just staring in one's own little bag of memories. I found that the best of my mind is not its storehouse but its mirror dish.

I suspect now that wisdom has to grow somewhat like a weed, needing only our permission and nothing more. When a man wants to brood and learn the terms of his soul, does he not rather look for a weedy, seedy neighborhood? When he stops a while his mind from willfully focusing and staring and he allows the world to look at him, unaccustomed questions arise in him. In this separate reality, his mind can ask guidance from uncommitted spirits which may be trees or grasses. They are the most tolerant prophets I know.

177

I note that many of our common accusations as I hold them back and send them to my backland to think some more and ask around for a possible pardon, they may soon come forward converted by one of nature's tricks on how to forgive.

When his mischief pushed me beyond all my resources and my best imagination was failing me to fathom the good of his provocation, all got black in front of me. I turned into a curled up hedgehog panicked into hurting, to give hell, to be left alone. When my intellect gets tired of looking for a sign of God in a shady act and capitulates, I may well settle for hate and killer thoughts, or to become a reformer.

Where I learned to see a wrong, I also learned to rush into that handy conclusion of "sock it to him." I am of a civilization that follows a simplistic moral. What we call good or bad seems to have little to do with trying to read the mind of God. These notions simply seem to point out what appears convenient to a contemporary majority or not and we prefer to trustingly parrot these judgments. We seldom bother to personally wriggle, backloop and patiently tunnel after a possible pardon. Yet by entering a confrontation with the goal in mind to prove somebody right or wrong, haven't I stopped being a lively apprentice with the free ears of a hare?

I was not encouraged to hold out on the hairy and scenic edge of impartially hearing somebody out to the end without soon sliding down to take sides and become a man with one eye. My mind still limps from wishing some well and giving others hell and thus is missing the beauty of the dance.

It takes so much more courage and eclectic thinking to forgive than to simply take sides and accuse. When somebody becomes this whiz lawyer of multiple eyes who can swiftly juggle his thoughts between the different levels of knowledge to outfox any accuser and gets for the "misbehaved" instead of lashes, cheers, does he not put all the other lawyers in the shade?

In ecstatic moments, a man may fly so high, he gets a glimpse of an uninterrupted goodness. With that eye-opener an inflammation may begin in him that never again quite heals. From there on a faith in an all-forgiving goodness that creates no waste cruises quietly along with Theo and takes in his fits and hates and fictional "better worlds" with humorous disbelief.

I wish myself the luck of becoming more patient when I think disturbing acts out and track these vagabonds through heaven and hell, to find where their gifts finally turn up again on familiar ground. This takes more patience than I can learn from al the sea stars promenading the tide flats here in Sitka Sound.

How to make good use again of all I learned to condemn, waste or hurriedly dump into some kind of hate, garbage can, or hell. So many options, so many purring feelings and relationships are left to rot for some trivial temporary gain.

I am going to salvage some of what Saint Paul, a much stricter dualist than Christ, took from me and threw into the fire of hell and call back the damned, the exiled, find their meaning, integrate them again. This, I imagine, is how I may become whole.

Maybe an organism, including man, becomes more of a saint, a contributor to life, a creator, the more separations he can take by going it alone. When this way he surfaces as a new subspecies into the Zoo of life, to entertain with his own show of tricks, the heavens serve music and beer.

To live with the fewest assumptions and beliefs without going under in confusion; to remain surrounded by the most options and a barn door open to my soul, is an intellectual freedom I can understand.

A few, I don't know why, seem gifted with imaginations so vast, that they become new suns to us, with such serenity radiating from them, that in their presence I become tanned. A man or woman who comes close to serenity is a saintly person to me. Here is finally an organic high, with nothing knocked out with some dose or some hammer.

Maybe serenity is the best protection against the punishment of celebrity or fame.

178

A man who can chatter with himself, laugh at himself, even take sometimes his ego to court, stays a cleaner person. Shampooing so his mind, he can rid himself of fleas, fears and incantations that infest his thoughts.

In our obsession to make our children's generation the most rational, sober and productive ever, it seems necessary to abolish the personal, home-made prayers with which we daily healed and cheered up our bleeding psyches. It has been realized that this simple tool for discovering oneself, with all the beauty, dangers and resources of one's wonderful jungle land, works against the growth of our GNP. It obstructs the easy recruitment of new accomplices for our miraculous economy and it makes bad soldiers. It makes us reflective, visionary, dangerous and trusting children. It can make fun of many acquired ambitions, preoccupations and possessions. It can render unnecessary some of our learned hate and of our work. It does not create jobs. Since we left the garden of innocence, has not this stammering, homemade form of psychoanalysis retrieved some of our lost memories and trust, bringing us back for a peek daily to the fence of that legendary enchanted place?

It has long been known that only a deeply unsatisfied and neurotic people—a people angry with the Creator—can be plunged into a productive binge. Also these pyramids are made of fear and boredom, not serenity. One needs to break a horse and fit it with blinders to make it pull a plow. And so our seven capital sins have hired an impressive cadre of lobbyists to cultivate their causes. These job-producing sins have now become the very heart blood of our economic growth. The fear of discomfort, of danger, of grace turning on the lights, of learning from direct observation and risking death, of not being as hardworking and docile as an ox, of being different, the fear of being God's fool seems to become a modern feeblemindedness so appreciated and cultivated by a consumer society whose high priests breed their working force. That cultivated mistrust can make of us superb consumers and gluttons in everything we do. Here the best chicken is the one that never hatches from the egg to ask an opinion from God. Yet think how could in our wrung out homeland the fattening of our GNP still be the measure stick for betterment? Such imagination seems now rather fit for cows.

We can stop each day a weenie while to hoe, fish, invent, compute, fumble, outsmart and so halt stress and adrenaline from furiously spin the ego-generator in our brain. The whole assembly of advocates from every niche of the earth can then call in to boo or maybe jubilate; We can crawl with our dirty minds every spring into the steam of some stone lodge and sing, pray and sweat our minds all spic and span; we may become true poets for this festive little while. Imagine what we might heal. What excitement such a bear running loose could bring to Wall Street. Might it be for this reason that the professional producers of more consumption must spend public relation's billions to jam the conflict creating voices of the free world and throw mud into my vision so that I will not rebel against my learned helplessness and tinker with autonomy, so I will not start to have faith in my own resources and guardian voices again? What feisty old economist would be that hearty fool who would not smile should also women and men put each other under siege? Think what a windfall for the Dow Jones average a civil war amongst the sexes could bring.

When you come home from work, you wash your hands before you eat. When you come home from work do you wash your mind before you speak? I passed a family of Huychol Indians going home up into their Sierra leaving many wildflowers strewn along their trail. They returned from work on the coast threading tobacco leaves. It is their way of cleaning their mind before they come home.

When a man is able to remain open to the scolders, teasers, balms and question marks of his deeper self and his thoughts remain not simply defensive quills of porcupines, his spirit is less likely to become constipated and to break wind. No, our deepest prayers do not defuse into the empty sky, but seem to be powerful mental RNAs whose messages go directly to the corn and triggers it to grow. They seed clouds and can make them come down. They produce echoes. They connect our telephone lines to all the memories of the world. They make us face and hear ourselves so we may come out of the closet. They make fire breathers of us who can defrost shivering souls.

The baby cries; the mother's milk flows. We pray for rain; why would the sky not respond?

When two persons fall in love, do they not pray together and jubilate, do they not daily save each other from stepping into the pit of a routine? In a heated mating dance their souls then seem to come out naked to mate. I barely dare to breathe in their presence so open and vulnerable do they become. I suspect that for many of us to fall in lust and love is as close as we will come to ecstasy and to God.

When you held so humbly still that no thought, no reproach, no wind would come up, you became my mirror-mirror on the wall with no ripples on it. I could finally see myself and what my virtues and vices do in the shadow behind my back—surprise, what a gift!

For every day that we cannot mumble with ourselves and listen to life's lobbyists meeting in our souls, we produce another cemetery of stumps in the woods, another cleansing, another million tons of carbon dioxide mushrooming into the stratosphere, endure another Hitler and we have to harness another billion freedom-loving Kilowatts to our meanness and our plows. And for all this mess-up our enchanted planet has to pay.

179

Do you know a better medicine for our race that grows out of control than the gift that a man is also a sun; that he can in all his splendor rise and set and in good times rise again?

When I consider how with so little shame I became addicted to a greedy science of bending every living gene and fiber our way, to make our summer noon last and last, so we can squeeze in row after row of additional fellowmen, I feel ashamed. From that meek commercialized pity nicely boosting our GNP, I feel a bellyache with no name. The whole biota seems sick with fear, that I play foul, now that I have been thoroughly programmed to yell at God and revolt, when God tests one of us personally and makes him go back for a new start when he fails.

I feel I should whisper less to you when you take your tests. I asked a friend who lives seven generations further up what he thinks about our honorable mania to ever more help each other to save our lives from setting at whatever the price. Seen from the level of our species or from my friend's balcony seven generations up, healing others is often plainly not this wonderful virtue but a rather egoistic practice—a whole generation in love with itself. Excessive mutual helping to hold onto one's life may turn into a nasty trick not to pay the price of autonomous health. Few seem willing to find out where this compassionate cheating will lead. I also note that nature seldom seems to go for this ruse. And this is probably why in the free, generous, most beautiful world unaided by us, I have barely seen anything that looks like a hospital or looks like a shipload of wings sailing for those birds that lost their own, yet all seems balanced and in good health.

When a science unashamedly studies how to bulldoze the remaining free lands and to grow a super crop of rape seeds or sugarcane as fuel for the tractors which might well till the rape seed fields, this to me has become an obscene science on an ego trip that eats for the pleasure of defecating. It is better I die five weeks earlier than to get a life-extension out of such a land abuse.

Did we forget the law of moderation to come into such disharmony with all other species? Did we become excessively armed—with ever more vaccines and immune defenses, with antibiotics, erection pills and aging retardants and God knows what other wonderful arms in defense of the ego and to bolster our generation? It will benefit us when medical research enters with life an arms agreement. Then even the cannibal needs to watch this law and live in harmony with his neighbors if he wants his grandchildren to enjoy a meal.

For those many who took the words of the Bible too seriously: be fruitful and multiply, fill the Earth and subdue it, have dominance over the birds, the fleas in the hair and the fishes in the sea and over every living thing, genetic engineering can be the supergun in their biological warfare to modify and make all critters on earth submit to us. Will we becoming an eerie ten billion Rambos who invest all our mental powers into fighting for supremacy over all the other creatures? I see so many celebrated scientists competing to feed and keep more of us alive longer. They cater to the cult of mankind's egotism and increase our excesses and risk making warts of us. In the arena of medical research I see gladiators showing off their competitors' heads. It is in this sense that the orientation of the present science and its ethics puzzle me. I see science with a pot belly and a meager soul.

How welcome becomes an insight granted when we excitedly light another lamp in our shadow with it. How rapidly that insight turns into a rabid dog when one monopolizes that gift of insight behind the barbed wire of a patent's fence.

Now that so many of us have narrowed their faith into a man-god, listen; there must be a trillion voices to be heard from out there which desperately pray from every niche in this world, asking the Great Spirit that more of us be taken home, that also we learn to die with compassion and with strength. They fear that Humanism's Ark soon has no room for them all and might turn into a floating clubhouse for man alone. Among us, however, the generosity of death seems stubbornly to remain the ultimate pest.

This beautiful autumn gift of death, though, has for long come well-meaningly down on us as a purifying rain. It gives us birthday parties, honeymoons, orgasms. It makes us young. It gives us the least exploited joy, the simple joy of giving. So many times it lets us wake up into a new sparkling morning sun. Is it not the best washing powder of all? To accept this gift is also the most faithful "yeah" I am being asked, and my mind is submitted to a loyalty test. Caringly life has watched over us from deep in our souls and has helped that enough of us may die. When the accident happens that we get in a jam and become too many, I note that God is no miser but soon sends us a good stout broom that sweeps away our excess. I leave it to you to choose of what that broom should be made. But try to choose. That mental process is beneficial for all of us.

I fear, my robust native feelings in this respect have been whirled around, dizzied, misled and abused. They have become pale, virginal and are not well-meaning toward life anymore. Seducing people to stay on and become customers of a hang-on industry should slowly be phased-out as, for opposite reasons, we now outphase catching whales. I try now to heal in myself this drunken attitude.

180

No, one does not survive on the full belly of a green revolution alone.

The last free lands where the Creator displays still most of her works of art—should they also be entered with a calculator, a Red Cross, a plow?

Our latest chemical rebellion against the economics of Mother Earth kills much food for our souls. We spray the USA yearly with a billion pounds of herb and insect killers, mainly alachlor and atrazine. Hidden in the shade of our agricultural success, we also threaten many species with genocide for simply standing in our way. Aside from the yummy for the tummy, a person needs room to walk about, to radiate her inner heat, to give her soul ice cream and some solitude. Her legs can only be tied so much, so that in this flood of foraging fellowmen she may not constantly tangle "horns" with other foragers.

Why is it that we became such virgins and misers and do not do our daily best but save our selves for some prolonged old age, as if there were no children waiting for nicely renewing us? Isn't this obsession to hold on fast becoming a somber curfew for us all? To forestall traffic jams, soon no one may go out; there will be no side and high steps, no vagrancy, no nomads, no wanderlust allowed; each will be allotted a niche in a feed lot paradise and cushioned in a cocoon of laws. Each in his niche will seriously do his one thing, cooling his other fires with a thousand channels of substitute adventures on the screen, with voyeurism, solitary games, do-not-do's and fetishes. Because of this man-made flood we have now come to this painful question: should a few more of us or the last of the pandas instead be heaved on the Ark? I side with the Noah's Principle and do not opt for a more numerous mankind. I opt for a richer world.

316

In those of us who are rethinking our lives, we are sad when the few Noah's Arks still floating safely from the flood of man-made goodness are also boarded and usefullized. My soul will break should I keep on fishing as heroically as before. I also note that materialistic nations still love to be sharks, cruising the Third World, circling them patiently, politely, completely self-assured to paralyze their future customers with loans. Do you know of a better hidden and paralyzing sting than the sting of a loan?

Why try so hard to lure the few remaining soul people and their lands out of their own separate realities? We might hatch from dark prejudice and arrogance and, fascinated, listen to their daily news as we once spellbound listened to the *Thousand and One Arabian Nights*. Instead of further injecting the "amaterialistic" countries with envy and complexes of inferiority, why not give them for their strangely gentle lifestyles a Nobel Prize? Our cultivated whining and pity for them might shake to pieces and reassemble into curiosity—even a nearly sacred esteem—as we have lately rediscovered to gape with awe and joy at the other seven wonders of the world. No other tool could better protect this world so fabulously rich in ideas from our consume-consume syndrome which lands together with us, a little like smallpox did, each time we, the business people, the tourists, missionaries and humanitarian soldiers with our gospel step onto its shores.

When I am a missionary and weed out an impractical religion, is this extinction of one whole subspecies of our mythology not as tragic a loss to our heritage as when our economy pushes one more weedy wildflower over the cliff? Missionaries and viruses seem to have a common trait. They cannot enjoy that others are different from them. When invading a host, they both command: adopt my DNA, my doctrine, copy me!

We could call off our conquest, bring Peace Corps armies and advisers in our chauvinistic economy home and replace them with apprentices who go empty-handed and empty-minded to these power spots for seminars. They still may observe a system at work where the principals of conduct in a very long range economy are acted out. To unriddle the beauty behind that economic riddle, to become guests in this feast of imagination may make us wealthier than higher sales of Coke, one more crop of Christians and workmen or ten more shiploads of pulp.

Free land of which some of its critters' sacredness is the only usefulness to us may be sacred a thousand times—turn it into a potato field and it will be sacred but one time.

181

We might still astonish ourselves with our own goodwill and eclipse the lizard's power to restore its lost tail.

The whole seedy world of emotion is hurriedly to be given up to make room for the huge six billions of us. Will we turn the whole world into one symmetric quilt of fields?

No wonder that we are now so suddenly pulled into such a sharp turn on the roller coaster of our love—and we are shaking in terror and thrill of that change. Who of our moms and dads would have guessed that a love which cares for a menaced stand of willows with its song birds cradling in their nests can become as dear and as precious to a daughter or son as to whisper one more answer to a fellowman who is failing his test in his autonomous health. Our oldest daughter, Lexa, while working on her doctorate in marine biology also nurses orphaned baby bats.

For 2000 years we have proudly cultivated the arts of whispering the answers when life testingly pointed its finger at a fellowman and asked questions. Have not these compassionate cheatings discreetly become the most sacred deeds to most of us?

I hear now a new shy dedication sound, less from the beautiful old song of man, woman and child than from the many childless women and men who could outgrow their fetishes of the playboy and playgirl paradise. She told me that she longs to spend herself more gratifyingly and more imaginatively than to simply join in the Thank-God-it's-Friday fun. Here something great is happening. Here young people want to make good when an epidemic of self-gratification among their love-sick parents has made this wonderful earth into one great killing field. They might procreate by cradling a mind-full of that wildly permissive weed-life that their parents have driven from their own elegant minds. They seed again my whitewashed mind with nettles, cockatoos, paradoxes, yeasty question marks, gentians and crocodiles. They can be the beneficent mutants,

318

who became immune against carcinogenic slogans that trigger us to multiply our excesses in physical power and self-defenses and give our killer thoughts ever more guns. They have thought themselves free from those myths that hoaxed us into believing that we are the world's master minds. Their sciences will for now forget miracle trees, better life preservers for us, more immunizations and kilowatts. Their sciences put mankind on a diet. They are not interested in piling up more advantages that fatten our excesses. They feel that the curative instinct of life would only have to counter with another surgical bombing, pest or pathogen to save us from loneliness should we put even more distance between the fellow life and ourselves.

These gentle rebels remind their parents that with every further kilowatt of energy we use to elbow ourselves through life, we also create one further kilowatt of enmity, that for every energy we enlist for us—clean or not so clean, renewable or not—we provoke a counter energy. They think that a blazing ten-kilowatt man leaves a ten-kilowatt wake of friction behind. To them nature is a hedgehog that grows sharper spines into our faces when in a frenzy we fell, butcher, and cook more than our share of her.

In a time that pleads us to be less energetic and more giving, this new kind of lover loses interest in distributing arrogant human rights or plowing the Antarctic to grow supercrops of snowberries. They are the weird lovers who seem asked from a supreme court for ecological debates, seated deep down in our mind of minds, to go out there and make good where their dear parents failed. They retired in them the myth of St. George blasting the great and shady wild in defense of elegant Lady Humanity balancing on high heels.

Among these exciting people are a new breed of lawyers who study biology and life's social science and initiate us into an all-comforting world of one amicable togetherness. They realize that a tree is sustained by roots that spread much deeper than its roots. They show us that out there each critter is the home of a spirit who quietly does its scientific work and gladly gives us advice. And so they like to provide all of life's scientists, even the squirting clam, with a defender. They also notice that the more social we become among ourselves, the more antisocial we become outside the fence. Maybe they will become our psychiatrists curing the trauma from the incest in our minds. They will hold hands between all disciplines and listen together to that neurotic soul that witnessed the holocaust brought upon all other life when we, the parents, worked so hard to exterminate the unsellable part of Mother Earth and made the rest into our slaves. They tell us that serenity is the result of mental progress and has nothing to do with how much our economy improves the world.

Here are adventurers who prefer to remain all ears instead of diving into the safety of a profitable career. They encourage each other to live materialistically leaner than us and do so for the same reasons others like to live in a bikini, to flex and think freer, to be closer to the sun, to be bio-friendlier and more alive, to have more free time, to get a tan. And is it not a wonderful new way they have found to have a child?

Biology with its advanced sociology will be studied by our children's children with the ardor of a blistering desert people praying for rain. In this confused time we are starting a systematic examination of the interaction between our morals, our learned feelings and our environment. We are starting to ask our acts for their impacts, not only on our dear bank accounts but also on our children who live seven generations up the hill. When asked permission to pass, these acts and ideas will also have to prove their goodwill toward the oceans, the mumble-bumblebees and the grasses.

Some of our young learned from the lizards and regrow our lost "tail"!

182

If you can teach me for every day to make just one compassionate vote, you will put every politician I know in the shade—And do we not vote every hour, day after day?

I suspect that in my larger, more discreet ego, which is quite a zoo, I am also a democratic state. There I am a "United Nations"—birds, daisies, fleas, Theo my dear ego and all. I like to call this "United Species" my soul. Who knows perhaps I even house a lobbyist for every creature promenad-

320

ing this world. When I cast my vote from that mind of multiple minds, I might surprise you—and vote against Theo. I found that deep down we vote bewilderingly generous and we might even be programmed to be benefactors to the whole menagerie of life.

Yet democracy in a generation stampeded by its sheer number can turn into a looting mob that swarms through every soul leaving the next generation shivering and bankrupt out in the cold. It becomes a democratic "everybody-for-himself" crowd. When I panic with this maddened crowd, I cannot stop that herd of would-be dictators from looting my own home and soul. A million strong, we could then lordly stand over any man hesitant to join and shout: Hand it to us! We could nicely win a majority vote and ceremoniously grant ourselves the right to loot our eighteen-year-olds of their dances, their great ancient trees, their drinks, their heritage, their skateboarding, their rainbows. We could strap our toddlers to their chairs if we are promised two cents less on our insurance bills. To make a law for others is an act of mistrust—and I get mistrust in return. It started with my intolerance, with my little inconvenience that somebody's joys came from a different tap than mine. It started with this tiny droplet of poison. When I got bold and asked for a new law to force that outsider to my side, I went for the big cup of poison. It is in this way that a new law and its makers encourage meanness, hostility and crimes.

And so when the ethics of egotism consolidate in the ethics of some "ism," I simply see a quantitative change. I see a million selfish hammers join and synchronize their banging. Yet I add to these ethics the dimension of time and my pronoun "we" explodes in an incredibly creative Big Gang.

Only now I realize how much greatness it takes to handle well such a difficult vote in which a woman or man often needs to risk nothing yet is given the chance to put his thumb up or down and support or oppose a minority such as our children and the owls have become. Did you realize that a democratic vote trusts every woman and man to act as a good wise queen for all? Still, it's quite a mouthful to say: "I have a heart a thousand people big—let me govern you!!" A majority who is not tolerant to other ideals and worlds could legally cart everything that you and I love to the city dump.

To illustrate the idea, think of a great, cheerful apartment house whose tenants, to reduce their common utility bill, voted each month in good democratic fashion whether for any given floor the power switch should be turned off. And this is how in this cheerful place of minorities slowly, one by one, the lights went out.

When seeking restrictive laws, how easily one oversees that we are trying to demolish each other's personal joys. In this destructive game in which we can immobilize each other with walls of "Yes" and "No," I will be given a turn to be after you and you will get your turn to be after me, to put one of my dear fancies in jail. In this game finally nobody but Lady Boredom wins. Whether we love a cow or a cat, a beer, a joint, skateboarding or collecting stamps, whether we are thistles or buttercups, our personal little crazinesses that gladden the heart are mostly vulnerable minorities that can easily be voted down by the sheer number of all those who are indifferent to those rare little joys. Slowly, revengefully, we could pick each other's meadows clean of all the flowers from all our dear weedy seedy greens. We could transform that rowdy assembly of ten thousand joys to one giant golf game on one common immaculate course that is rolled flatter and made uniform with better rules. But I can also become adventurous and boo at this chance to meekly put my thumb down for life at large.

Here I also think of the many "crimes" that anger me in absolutely no other way than for mocking my learned narrow sense of justice that harmonizes our juridical symphonies of which I trained so hard to play my part. The howling of wolves, a nesting sparrow in the symphony hall, a broken love or string, a man loving a man, the whistle of a train, a latecomer that upset the symphony played by my judicial orchestra may commit such crimes.

When seeking for more laws, remember it was four our privilege to be the most tolerant, the most sinful, trespassing and adventurous species on earth, that we discovered how to flower all of our twelve primary joys in nine hundred ninety-nine different hues. That prodigious looseness is now caged in twenty thousand pages of laws. Remember also that the selection pressure on criminals imposed by our juridical system breeds super cons who can keep one step ahead of our enforcement. Note what fast learners microbes became under the pressure of our antibiotics. Our juridical system is more important than we thought in shaping the way crime evolves. It should be sparsely used for similar reasons that we sparsely use antibiotics. Luckily there are also daredevils out there who gladly take the heat so that our dear daredevils' freedom is not wasted for pensions, higher dividends and rocking chairs.

Is it not these bright occasions in a man's life that separates him from the crowd, when he can propose a law aimed at putting himself right and not at somebody else? When I become a good wise king and do not vote just for that rascal, my dear little ego, all things I touch become happier. My conversations and my campaigning get happier; even anger and punishment then becomes medicines. What a mishap for a man to get locked into one system of justice for life and not to be able to let his sense of justice progress through his seasons.

183

How to stretch and stretch to become a hero, a miracle rice, a miracle economy, a saint and become great, so we can jump over the stretching shadow we cast? Has that not become a more defeating koan than we thought?

When I cultivate in my mind just one kind of love and make of it my darling child, all the neglected longings in me revolt. Some of these spirits I exile find new homes and do their chores from there. Others keep on itching my nerves, my stomach, my dreams, my leisure time, my patience, my health. To be heard some tirelessly pull on my sleeves, others pester me with stress. Quite behaved when allowed to thrive, these spirits, when mistreated, become demons and give me hell.

I remember an extremely deformed woman on whom all the sex spirits which a hundred puritans have driven out had to settle down. The whole psyche of this permissive woman has turned to one grotesquely glowing vagina a hundred puritans big. I remember when all the crows that every farmer in the village has chased away finally settle on the one last free cherry tree of the one last farmer still willing to share with the crows. That tree turned black with birds and hunched under the load. Every spirit—black, blue, green or white—after I drive it out, tries to settle somewhere to do his chores, who knows with whom, when and where.

When a people inbreeds itself into a high-yield farm to produce day and night and forgets the vital art of getting drunk on the Holy Spirit and of bursting out in thanks, its less ambitious compatriots who could not be made to join the production binge become outcasts. We force them to become pests, thieves, surf bums, mad dogs, hippies, druggies, welfarers, mosquitoes immune against DDT, terrorists. There seems no mischief for which this wily group of compensators could not deliver a specialist.

When I plow an acre of super spuds into free land do I not have to kill or evict its whole native community of crawlers, wrigglers, shrubs, perhaps a million obvious inhabitants in all? Do I not also provoke the modest little potato beetle to soon settle there in response and become a smart and high-yield superbug? When agriculture isolates, perverts and makes one kind of plant stand in endless rows to deliver for us alone, do we not provoke its symbiotic "lovers" to conspire and mobilize against us? We roll up our sleeves and have these little scavengers pulled out or gassed. Yet luckily, for every monopoly we impose, there seems to be an endless line of killer cells or martyrs waiting out there, ready to take their turn to heal that mishap and bring us back into the belly of God. The moment the Requiem ends for the nematodes we fumigated for also wriggling to a meal in our crop, the God of the nematodes starts to organize help. (These nifty little nibbles are now suspected to release 1/3 of all the nitrogen used by plants.) No victory goes unbemoaned and left an open wound.

It seems to be the same unnerving law of justice that behind their dressing up turns the humanistic heroes as well as the stupendously high-yield monocultures in their shadows to great neglecters and cripples. A puritan wheat field, a high-yield sycamore forest, a mind that cultivates monocultures of pity or hate, she does not let them become runaway growths for long. She counters our weakness for practicalities that soon would make us information poor. She organizes all her other troops to clean her house of such excesses. That law of compensation at work gives headaches to our moralists. True to the Bible's parable, there seems no end to Mother Nature's patience and inventiveness to bring her lost sons and daughters back home. The victors are brought back to the center. She will endlessly pester our monocultures with bad dreams. She will give these selfish fields a neurosis endlessly harassing, charming them into being tolerant, convivial and again complete. And for a welcome home, she promises music and beer for every lost critter that makes it back home and to the center again.

When an organism gets carried too far ahead and loses sight of life's symbiotic commune, also an autoimmune system seems in a self-regulating way to open in it, inviting virulent thoughts, triggering neurochemicals, natural killer cells, opioids, blisters, lame erections, roadblocks in the mind, many kinds of attacks on the ego. Outstanding success and outstanding meanness or pests might be sisters after all, never far from each other, every ready to help each other out.

Are we becoming centipedes with one or two of our hundred legs we developed much longer than the rest? Are we becoming centipedes that for their grandiose deformity limp in the dance or even lay helplessly on their backs begging to be saved in some joint venture and their two magnificent legs be put to work? I learned something from that inconspicuous Balinese dung-hill cock with nothing to show off. I saw that "worthless" cock freely promenading between the caged fighting cocks with all the hens of the village for himself.

Deep down I have always felt shy to become outstanding at anything. I feel I am made to remain round and a generalist. It is this spoiler of fame that kept in check Theo's fondness for extremes. Are the dressed up songbirds not put in cages while the toads go free?

Dominance and personal success, notions that became so attractive on the level of the individual, have remained warts for my deeper self.

Maybe life likes those unheroic heroes best who work from within and simply on themselves until with the least of turbulence and fear, they cheerfully blend in so they may never have to be punished with fame. And it's up to them to sing finally that simple song of the street: "Darling, it's all right . . . "

184

"The right to a job for everybody!" he shouted and swung his sledgehammer furiously through paradise.

When the economy worshiper promised his crowd to create work, customers and jobs, I wondered whether or not he talked about vandalism. He was seeding frightful pictures into my leisure time. He talked arson, divorce, bombings that were meant to ravage a peacefully resting heart. He seemed expert in hanging scarecrow, preoccupations, black omens in a lucid sky. He kindled mistrust in my camp. I saw him slyly blow out the lamp in a fellow man to sneak into his confused mind worms of envy, outrage, fear, fire crackers and pride. He taught me how to sue and countersue. He talked an itch into our amicable trust and soon we moved a million loads of cement and sand, built a Berlin Wall and he advertised a thousand jobs for watchmen and watch dogs to stand guard. He poured more ink over the shadow in my mind making the phantoms look blacker than they were. He defamed my desire to become in my possessions ingeniously lean and made me sing at school that to be barefooted is a shame. And he tried to make me wear a tie. I thought here is one more professional vandal ravaging through my leisure and my good faith in you and her so to create consumers and work. Yet this trickster also seriously believes he is a missionary for a better world. And he just might be right and paid by God to testingly kick in our dear old homes and routine, to sift for the unhappy would-like-to-be pioneers needed for life's arduous expeditions into what never has been tried out.

To create more jobs one first has to create disharmony, deeper footprints, more friction, new itches, fear and waste. Kick into a termite's nest and ask any termite whether this is not so. It is a simple law that to make good the catchy slogan, "We create more work," we have to ever more kick in first the eyes of our soul so, blind in our wits, we stumble and kick up work on the living earth. No wonder that no other generation was more productive at producing more gadgets and waste so every woman and man could exchange their leisure time for a job. Reading up on the economics of the Tlingit Indians here in harsh Alaska of a century ago, I note that these people "worked" an average of five and a half hours a day and enjoyed the leftovers with leisures like gambling, gossiping, flirting, walkabouts, storytelling and dance.

When each Friday at the whistle of five the labor force, a billion strong, streams from the gate of work, guess what the rivers, the woods, the tranquil ponds, all the dreams swarming gaily in and around the soul of a woman and a man then murmur and chirp about. In this temporary exodus into freedom, many of us are angered with a sense of oppression and a loss of freedom that we think we can exercise and make good in a sport in which we can command, trample over, three-wheel, shoot, swear and bully nature around. And are not sport and exercise just repair work and not leisure time. Is it not the old battered urge to simply be one's own king and to have no middleman to God, that when degraded, becomes such a terrorist? The trees, the neighbor's dog, the dunes and paddle ducks, the stillness of a pleasing evening sky settling down, our tender capacity to wish others well, our spouses, our lazy dream time that comes from a well spent day, all our subtle highs, even children, they all stifle with fear when frustrated workers finally can boss around to please their battered pride.

Ah, the power to consume, to waste, and, at least, to play king in a Hilton, to lordly steer the fastest wheels in town, the luxuries! These substitutes may be the only shingles of power a woman or man that feels degraded in his work has left to hang out.

Vandalism seems to me less the occasional revenge of a mom-and-dad-forsaken youth kicking at or spray painting his "fuck you's" on our wealth, for being left bankrupt and to have suffered castration of his soul for being left impotent to act out his dreams because we loved our toys more than him. Vandalism seems more often the last revengeful spasms of all our wonderfully impractical longings we strangle to become eligible for the safety and comfort of a nicely equipped niche in a high-tech society's bowels. It seems not so much our own oeuvre that is vandalized but the more innocent nature in and around us that has no rights to sue. It is also our latest birthday gift from life, Miss Muse and creative unemployment, giver of radar eyes and good advice—that entertainment shuts up and vandalizes.

Work has its own built-in miraculous multiplication. It produces ultimately always a little more work than what it actually is intended to accomplish. In nature work seems the most experimental and wasteful way to get things done. Work has much of its biological roots in slavery that has been practiced for a billion years. Finally the domineer becomes helplessly dependent on his workers—and democracy is the winner. There are slave hunting ant species where the whole species lost all their capacities but to hunt slaves. And it is the slaves that got inspired and took over their government.

327

No, the solution to unemployment needn't be simple vandalism. Partial creative unemployment through job-sharing distributed more evenly among all seems more fruitful to me.

In life's playful tag of war between tradition and evolution one is soon out or one gets busy with reorientation. I wish myself the luck of never getting so blind that I forget that things can be done without work. And I wish us all the gold of the dandelions celebrating spring.

185

When in the mind the sun comes out, pity and hate should get more difficult and less needed.

On a long sunny summer day more of life's wonderful happenings occur in the light; less remains shady and wrong or ghosts of fear in me.

I imagine that while my viewpoint slowly multiplies, taking sides should get more difficult and less needed. I will have fewer weed plants then, fewer weed animals, shady men and shady ladies and character traits that seem to need persecution or reform. Less life surrounding me will appear in need of being showered with privileges. There will be fewer happenings in my and in our history that I prefer not to have occurred. My mental trash should drastically reduce. I become more inclined to applause and to forgive and less a missionary for some meeker world. The great canyons in me between yin and yang, pity and hate, friends and enemies might get their bridges built. To get accustomed to multiple viewpoints I might have to wrap myself in the bark of a spruce or walk in your slippers for a week and exchange identity. I know of no other trick to make of this wonderful world a better place.

To fatten a man with goodness can bring him down, pervert him, as surely as starving him with hate. When this one hand reaches out with pity, does not the other hand in the dark unnoticed clench into a menacing fist? And while I shake your hand on whom should I turn my back? While napping under an aspen tree, a hunch occurred to me that serenity has absolutely nothing to do with abolishing suffering. And so when common sense tells me to be sad I now sometimes have my doubts.

There are many things in nature we do not see. Take a really long deer, a deer 30 generations long. We do not see it this way with our fractured vision. Yet it exists. If we could see this really long deer we would understand why one deer can die so peacefully. If we could see ourselves this long, what could fear do to us? A mother with her baby may get a taste of this long vision and become fearlessly strong although she may see herself as only two generations long.

To become multiple and more tolerant I like to bum around in the free land, be king of what I want to see, drink in its unbiased advice through my eyes, hands, ears, toes, the skin and the nose, be a hunter entering the thicket, hunting for ideas thirty generations tall. I like to interview Rapalla, the giant spruce at the head of Deep Inlet, and ask her what she thinks. I like to ask a dandelion, "Where are your good deeds?" And life shows me there that all acts in some circumstances are allowable. When I am lazy I simply sit at home and learn from what somebody killed, cooked, interpreted, regurgitated into symbols and served in books and I am nicely told then what I should see. But a book is just a carcass, isn't it? Is there not an intuitive pull into the free land when a man truly wants to instruct himself?

186
Neptune and all the fishes in his oceans probably now love surf bums better than fishermen.

No, I should not fume and revolt, should God whisper a little laziness into my children and give them that wonderful talent of modesty in work, in drilling, blasting, usefullizing and flattening further the Earth. Has not such gentleness become needed in my time, where my overkill needs mending? Is an "unproductive" existence not just another medicine that life dispenses, healing its sores by antidotes and by switching our morals around, turning the light on here and off there in our inherited memory that keeps spitfires and firefighters for every occasion.

Take anything dead or alive, slimy or clean, hyper or lazy, a swindle or a truth; there seems always somebody, something, somewhere to be found that jumps to its defense and jubilates, "Thanks for the help."

And here, another sip of hope; choose any perversion, pick your choice of misdemeanors or crimes; for each such "misbehavior" I bet there is some among the 20,000 different kinds of ant species that could make a virtue out of it and have been nicely thriving on it for quite a few million years. They even found a respectable job for their gluttons. They expanded those potbellies even more. Now these "super-hogs" are serving them nicely as their living storage tanks for honey dew. It's just unbelievable what marvelous things those little folks learned to do with our sins.

187

In that special time we lay away for daydreaming to compose inner rhymes, do we not build more fantastic bridges than the Golden Gate?

The humming and numbing activity nicely filling every nook in a man's day is suspect. A dominantly rational mind that is always seriously at work and never allowed to wonder about the follies of the soul, that mind seems to be mildly panicked and running circles around itself when I view it from a balcony higher up. It's a mind that is grounded, with a broken wing and condemned to staying in one world alone. And are the mental sports not also just repair work so a man can better work? Yet dream time is dinner time for the long-range mind: my soul.

Work, that grandiose rebellion of our smartness against our wisdom, provides spectacular short-term benefits for our dear ego. The duration of every kind of pregnancy is hurried and cut in half, and these crafty short-cuts may turn into long-term losses for those after us.

A species can only handle so much apartheid, mistrust in neighboring life and living on a pedestal. The grim uninterrupted need to patrol borders and to ponder about fitting ever better defenses, vaccines, safety measures, sanitation and pesticides into the Wall in defense of the ego to lick the presumed devils and enemies can make a man so breathless he forgets to keep breathing his soul. The way I see it, it is in creating better vision and trust in the hidden goodwill of all life and better long-distance communication with life at large, it is in this that an organism shows its fitness and creativeness. For me in a high standard of living nothing counts more than little work and a light backpack filled with all kinds of warm, tall and exotic relationships.

Yes, mankind is only my right leg. So much has been done for its betterment and growth. I realize that the more that is now done for it, the more I will limp. Would it not be a sad misunderstanding to simply create more work in an epoch in which every leaf, wriggler and strider, every Mr. Whiskers and every living fiber in and around me nearly bursts with hope that I will finally also become a happy spectator, that I too will add a third Sunday to my week? I feel it is from the additional street lights I light in my mind on these Sundays, my new goodies for comfort, my better safety belts and high adventures can come. Such a revolution in work attitude will name full-time work and the lust for even more power a sickness. It will kindle in us again a weakness for all things alive and will take place entirely in the mind, an eruption into our consciousness of a vision larger than man, the empire builder, and his inflated egotism expressed in work. An overexpressed ego seems a kind of mental cancer caused by a cataclysmic mental weather front that violently mutates and modulates our archetypical roadsigns.

In our mental epic this is a historic molting time. More of us are timidly tiptoeing out of the magic circle in which we short-circuited our love to produce a miracle economy and a miracle love for the exclusive betterment of mankind. We are starting an intellectual romance with wildness. The courage to think in paradoxes and to reason on the same line when reasoning about a man or a tree seems the hottest item life is after now. All these exclusively human attributes, like compassion, evil, perversion, illumination, sin, crime, have to undress to stand up with their biological names. All are qualities that have been successfully used by those critters that for being the most sacred in God's menagerie have survived. My stripped intellect cries out in such shivering nakedness.

I like to think that every man is busy summing up all the good in the world he can at least dimly figure out or has heard about, forming and reforming an ever larger poem of it all and taking it as his personal model of God. Some more hasty than others quickly threw away into some kind of hell whatever did not readily fit into their shell.

I like to see a man's philosophy as his shell—a little like the one in which the hermit crab temporarily houses itself. Stepping again and again

331

out of her old models of the world and of God that became too small, is that not how a person makes her ascent leaving her old knowledge behind, adding newly discovered needs and friends to a mostly inexplored symbiosis, adding to her poem slowly every imaginable word, leaving philosophies that turned out to be soap operas behind?

Maybe that's how I get to love our wonderfully profuse belief systems as I got to love a meadow in pink, yellow and blue. Aren't our religions the blossoms of our minds that are of many perfumes, forms and hues?

To find myself wrong is a triumph—not my brilliantly successful defense of yesterday's truth. That I endlessly can become wrong, is that not life's promise never to run out of new tricks and treats?

188

To balance across the highest tightrope of being soft, leaky and friendly toward all things alive, to acquire the highest degree of vulnerability and the biggest armful of dangers without falling to death—such tests may be nature's finest population controls.

It was a long festive free-for-all to love, to multiply, to possess every born human life. We jailed the dangers and the inspectors that would have enjoyed testing our quality. We paid the least of taxes with our biomass to Mother Nature, goddess of fertility, who gives food and breath to all. No generous gifts in our name were offered at the great banquet where every species is the other's guest. On the contrary, we heroically held on in a joint venture to every human life pulling it through with whatever fraud that was needed, and applauded old age as the only glorious cause of death. It is with this kind of a selfish attitude my feelings have been tattooed.

In the deluge of our huge extravagant needs to keep this feast up, we simply allowed ourselves to plow under more of God's wildflower fields. We allowed ourselves to be deadly strong—like the berserk lion with a deadly hunger who does not act the part in his script of give-aways, gentleness and play, but wants always to use his strength and claws. He wants to stand on top of a kill in every hunt.

Mr. Porcupine with his mean quills might be a wise slowpoke, after all, for never having developed speed, concluding that enough is enough! With such an extra defense, Porky might well have outbalanced himself away from his needed foes that ultimately proved the best of his friends. Such a loss of vulnerability could have made the Porky family grow and grow until it would have canned itself alive in its allotted niche. Greed for advantages can become a mortal flaw as we experience with the human population explosion right now.

We have tried to become that ungiving apple tree who decided that each of its blossoms is precious beyond price. We cold not take the whining when the wind shook the tree and knocked some apples onto the ground. And now we watch in disbelief that ambitious tree groaning under a ton of apples go down on his knees.

I feel unprepared to watch how life now takes away from many the beautiful season when our seeds catch fire. Old feelings kick me and revolt when our children are now given a music of mental IUD's so to speak, irritating, panicking their mysterious chemistry of fecundity into a strike, diverting their potency. Many among us seem now invited to make a gift of "sterility" that has become precious and needed. Widowed, they seem invited to become a new kind of dancers, yet seem often to be awkwardly whirling around themselves still looking for new partners.

More love songs are turned upside down to help abortion and birth control. At times, the wording of this new music seems a simple contraceptive invocation to me and meant to sour the honey that lures us to have children. Yet I am shown that with a new imagination, this needed change of heart can offer more than simple mutilation, deafening wealth, sports of sex with vibrators, grim abstinence. How many new adventures, what creativity can start from here!

This new music seems to speak about a worldwide need of a new kind of relationship that does not further multiply the colossal family of man. This is birth control in-depth. This is also bitter medicine for all that has merely turned humanistic in me and more so where population control grows into a cult not only to abort our seeds but also the whole psyche that knelt, like the three legendary kings, around these motherly chores. Abortions and contraceptives may be the most practical of population controls. But in the long run they might prove, among all the options in

333

nature's arsenal, the less imaginative and fruitful, the more egocentric and meeker of a people's weight controls. Look how ennobling danger can be—to invite risk, to stand up to a personality test, to get lit up and high on risking death, to be very, very careful with and less proud of help, to wake our instinctive friendliness toward death—and the simple pleasure to give in when called and say yes! Our cultivated hypersensitivity to danger and pain has made us as a species far less giving and therefore far more numerous. In the continuous interchange of biomass needed between species, attitude toward danger and pain seems one of the major population modulators. The further away from her species' secure norm an organism can survive, the more she can contribute to life.

I feel that this new cult of contraception is meant to ultimately hatch us from the egg in which humanism protected our mind, to free more of our relations to beyond those turning around our reproduction. Out of the psychosynthesis of our dear love story for two biophilia may evolve. It is the lucky chance for good old provider minds to be promoted above their haggling for ever sharper teeth, bigger reactors, a more sterile habitat and tougher Levi's pants. It is the door for those scientists who unsuspiciously got recruited by the most formidable Cosa Nostra—a worldwide syndicate producing and peddling knowledge for ego-boosters and for raping the world. Freed, some of us, from the chores to recycle ourselves; free to tease out that faint capacity to spot in the world-wide system of thought—cooked, distilled and cooked again for three billion years—the answers to our questions all perfectly acted out and with good results. We are invited to hear the magic flute.

Abortion remains heavy for me to digest when a woman or a man seems asked not just to cut their buds and divert their love to creatures more in need than mankind, but when, on the altar of ungiving selfishness, they totally abort their own lives; when they extinguish in a solitary dance everyone of their acts that were to be their children, leaving the mere fertile ashes of their love behind them. More and more of us seem to be asked for this shocking gift.

Uneasily, I ask myself whether the many kinds of self-satisfaction, the sports, the drug culture, sex by phone, the booming industries for voyeurism, the video games, single lives, anything that quiets these deadly efficient provider hands and minds, can be seen as welcome sacrifices. Could it be an emergency love which life presently cherishes more than the life of a woman in a child-bearing career or a hard-killing professional fisherman?

For me the highest price to pay so we can heal from our crowdedness comes when I have to rearrange my whole emotional upbringing; for I have to learn not to overly whine when we are thinned out.

In her steep evolutionary ascent nature is not a brute. She invites our unneeded capacities, which are to be slowly retired and left behind, to whirl in that soothing Dance Macabre composed of all our many sports: the good-bye dance of the muscle men and their macho braveries in the age when great nerds may become our needed braves.

189
Dear God, thanks for my good legs.

Dear God, thanks for making me blind to minor dangers and numb to mosquitoe bites. Thanks that I still can mostly do without a car to visit your show and be thrilled at every step by what I see. This simpleminded work-vehicle seems made to rush and not to be neighborly and to leisurely promenade into the future and the past. I have found also that a car is quite a delicate dame. She likes only to go where everything in her way has been shot, felled, whitewashed and paved. It seems that I never move as violently as when my foot is on the gas. Did you realize that in Germany about fifteen thousand square kilometers of its greenest land had to be rolled flat and paved to accommodate this demanding dame?

I am glad I do not need to move only on roads. They seem the deadest deserts conceived by the genius in boredom for the soul. Even their shoulders seem mostly emptied of diverting soul-seeking thoughts. On the road I have a one-track mind and am loaded with practical thoughts. I am a load of bread. I am there in a bullet full of workers and sportsmen with their minds armed and loaded rushing to one spot; I am pushing for hours through mute land to an oasis of friends, maybe, a hundred miles away. To not end up in a ditch my mind needs to be aimed and controlled.

Doesn't our obsession with speed tell us that we have fewer and fewer friends further and further apart—that between the few rendezvous we look forward to, we have to eat up more and more competitors and mute enemy land that leave us indifferent and cold? Should we haughtily keep on tearing up the holy spirit's traffic tickets for speeding in paradise? How would Alice want to speed through Wonderland? That race to be ahead of the others is the wonderful multiplication of our need for energy and of our viciousness.

How strictly do freeways socialize my movements, cruising me blindfolded, cushioned and safe from the high adventures of wilderness from one confinement to the next. In a car my mind feeds mostly on junk food, so to speak. The wheel might still turn out to be the form with the most friction in space-time mechanics. After all, life didn't approve its application for three billion years. The wheel might be the truest symbol of man hounded by an obsession to become the axle of the cosmic merry-go-round.

Here a fingerful of like-minded poetry: My deeper love seldom moves conveniently straight from me to you or from one generation to the next. Often its trails curl head over heels while love is playing hide and seek. It's the gravitational pull of the zillion stars that bend and zig-zag a star's light before it reaches me. It seems to be this gravitational pull not only of our egos but of the zillion egos that people the forests, the oceans, the constellations of the people and those of the hemlocks and the oaks that give our freeways of love their "amoral" curves, loops, humps, stop signs and curls.

190
You deserve better than niceness from me.

Polished people do not easily unite. Niceness may be their cover-up and skin to avoid coming dangerously close and grow together.

When a surgeon wants to make two surfaces grow together, he scrapes them, making them bleed a little and raw. A grafter unites a shoot with a plant by scraping off its bark. Open and raw, the partners can press together their bloodlines, mix, and become one.

Don't be angry with me when I am blunt with you and you whimper in pain. Scraping off skins of politeness and fig leaves I may want to grow together with you. When we are in love, becoming emperors with no clothes on, nature wants us to do these scraping-and-press-together things. In such raw openness we may merge more than in the coit.

191
Do you realize that when you talk to her or to me, you can be Columbus, landing in America?

When we converse together and stand back uncommitted, we might just be a good circus; you, a good, shameless clown trying to entertain; I, an acrobat or storyteller, a show-off muscleman. We might be two pufferfish competing to puff ourselves up, becoming vain.

I am fond of a conversation that is more than a soap opera or a nice charity fair gossiping our nagging guardian angels, our questions and doubts to sleep. When there is polite talk and copal burned, I prefer to sit quietly on an airy windowsill. Yet this gentle and mannerly flow of swindles and distractions not only seems a pacifier as old as man; soothing small talk is also our dear and needed identification hum.

I like a festival of thoughts—a kind of mental potlatch—where we make each other gifts which we might have woven out of dangerously exciting dreams. Perhaps you fashioned a metaphor into a bench for my worried mind to rest in trust and find its breath. Maybe your mind twined for me a hanging bridge to an unknown friend who remained cut off by an abyss opened up by an empty slogan. Maybe you give me an idea in which you hid for me a firestone—or a therapeutic metaphor. Better still, you might kneel down and gently, very gently blow life into my stunned heart, making a frozen talent in me stir and bud a leaf. When we do not cover up but converse, do we not mix our blood?

Are we not comets that spit fire and light up the firmament when we meet? You refuel my questions and I plant fresh adventurous seeds of doubt in your mind; you, another spring approaching, breathing life onto dormant love; I, a little frightened from the crack in my shell when you teased a mole out of me; you, a little seasick when your center of gravity becomes disturbed and you are not so sure of your resting place anymore; I, a little scared of you when you were generous and brushed my polite twitter out of your way. You took time to step down into the profuse and messy basement of my mind looking for spark plugs, tinder, dreams, for rare longings I might not have dared to recall. You blew again good mischievous life into my waste, then you asked the questions that help us to heal.

Are you a good stout midwife? You must be able to stand my fits and stinks—no narcosis, no abortion, no cowardly excusing and defusing words allowed. Maybe you just hold my hand to spellbind my hurt a little. Aren't we all full of pregnancies that we can never deliver without a storm shaking them loose, without someone's mind to reach out to us? You could be my solid ground in tormented times. You could be that mirror that can hold very still, so I could finally see myself. When in a hair-raising nap I drift against the rapids, you might yell and risk my wrath when I wake up and shower you with nasty complaints.

Talk that gives new life comes to me a little like an erection. I let it happen with no motives and prudence standing in its way. When I tell myself, "Now!", it might not happen. Whenever two link in love or hate, talk bears offspring and results.

Do you know a better opportunity for a gift than a good conversation, to spend a dime helping me to figure myself out? Who needs psychoanalysis when he cultivates good company, good conversation, brave friends? Is this not what falling from lust into love is all about? Don't stuff my holes, don't plug my whining and leaks. In my moments of great vulnerability, great things can happen to me. I often think about lucky people who do not kill such pains, but day after day save each other from sinking into a routine.

192

A man's capacity to dream can be worth a thousand years at serious work and research.

Does not a woman or a man inch a step up on their sky-ladder with every new viewpoint they add to their left and their right eye's point of view? Is not our capacity to dream walk and to visualize the gift to catapult our minds into the space-time world and watch ourselves from balconies of other species and other times? We can increase the two inch distance between our left and right eyes point of views to vistas with viewpoints many years, miles or generations apart. When using this fantastic optical tool, watching an act from viewpoints four miles or four years apart may become the same. With such witchy eyeglasses we can look around corners and explore life's goodness as no binoculars can do. Who knows? We might want to declare three Sundays per week to play with this fantastic gift. Dreamtime can do so much more walking for us than the yellow pages in the telephone books.

In that greater many-dimensional world, my common sense mind sometimes becomes puzzled about how goodness and how justice appear in other slightly incomprehensible forms and how the heroes I selected from just the viewpoint of mankind alone look rather out of step and might be indicted by the rivers, the animals, the trees for bending goodness our way. And higher up on this sky-ladder my acts that you cheer or you boo assemble differently and may trade places. There the good news and the bad news in the morning paper can change their colors and produce a sad mind amidst an enthusiastic crowd of flatlanders and also the other way around. What a relief to get out for a treat from under the dome of humanistic thought under which I was counseled to safely make my intellectual home. What a trip! That credo tattooed into me turned out to be quite an impenetrable immunity system for my mind. It spared me those creative fevers that can make of a man more than a man.

There are other forms of sunflowers that compose their petals also in perfect circles of luminous yellow flames yet group around beautiful ideas in the garden of time. Every petal in these flowers is the flaming noon of another spring eager to bloom. They are wonderful firewheels rising from between rolling hills of time into the sky. There are prairie flowers with shades of orange and yellow that vibrate so slowly they can only be seen with an eye that is focused on the colors of time. There are other forms of warm friendly wheels of love that are of man, woman and child holding hands, linking their affectionate thoughts through unrecorded generations past and to come. There are brotherhoods whose initiates can live ten miles, ten thoughts, ten generations, even ten species apart; yet in that multiple sight united they hold hands. There are good neighbors in time all dressed up just waiting for us to be each other's guest.

It is these forms of flowers one might see in dreams.

"Now shut up, Theo—remember your mouth is your biggest leak. It's the silence that gives answers and the listener who gets filled."

193
When I impatiently slashed his pride, I was startled: his mind started to bleed.

When my criticism provoked him to angrily fell a tree across my path, he must have figured I came to take something away from him. He guessed right. I wanted a trophy and to walk away with his pride. Now looking back, his meanness seems to have been just another hat, maybe a hard-hat of an awkward man with which he protects his bundle of what he thinks are the best joys he can afford with what talents he received.

If you come with the gun of the law in hand and you can make me change my course, this is also not a good victory that gives you good sleep. Ah, but with a change of heart! A man can light up my inside and make his argument kneeling in front of me so not to make my pride bleed. He may clutch my hand with strong kindness, so it will not hurt so much or sink my boat when he lets his conflict-creating thoughts sink into my anguished mind.

When she gave me a glowing ember of her soul and started a fire in me, I remember her blowing coolly on my hand so not to blister my pride.

194
Slowly more of us may note a mutual pruning and grooming between the species and applaud: "How wonderful!"

The theory of the survival of the fittest first led me into a dead end. I could only wriggle out of this trap when I realized that the fish and the kelp did not simply compete and went separate ways but evolved with each other as friends competing to better and better recycling each other's waste. Evidence becomes strong that only organisms that are productive enough so that they can make themselves also useful to others will survive for long. We also get new hints that life sifts for those imaginative critters who are the fittest to chemically and physically till and alter the earth so that it becomes a better breeding ground. And this elevates the theory favoring survival from the fittest iron fists to one favoring the survival of the fittest symbiosis an organism can compose with its habitat using also the "Fitter Gardener" or cooperation principle for defense. Yet a symbiosis is seldom as conveniently obvious as a tennis match. It's more often "the peanut man's effect." When old Santiago sells his freshly roasted peanuts he may produce a slight increase in flatulence at the village square as the only measurable "benefit."

Darwin's insights turned into powerful catalysts in focusing our intellectual effort and centering it into that hurricane of sciences now milling around the destiny of man alone boosting technology; hence our imbalance between our macho science of aggression and the feminine science of beautifully living together so fond of compassionately giving. Later Marx and Henry Ford became the stout patron saints for these sciences of better sickles, powerful fists, practical logic, tighter dams and rounder wheels and are still lobbying for those idealistic causes. Those sciences are doing more to the living earth in fifty years than an ice age has done in 10,000 years.

That impenetrable and self-contained fitness of an individual or of a species has now become suspect. Is it not ultimately the weaknesses that give an organism the opportunity to greater strength—all its nooks, openings, cracks and footholds for fellow life and fellow thoughts, inviting the whole of God's zoo to weave in their needs and their symbiotic gifts? It seems not the tree that is mightily strong and standing alone but the one weak and vulnerable enough to let other roots penetrate its system of support which finally weathers the storms. This koan echoed long back and forth in my mind. I think I see its exit now.

One might also get help in this riddle when considering why the ant peoples in all their millions of years have never eradicated the anteater but have instead begged that neighbor to be their dear devil's advocate and guest. As flowers produce and offer pollinating insects nectar so that these mini flyers will fly them in exotic genes for brighter blues and pinks, so do the ant people shower their nosy guest with gifts of some of their own biomass as nectar to lure that witty guest to come in, so they may be stream-lined, thinned and can learn from him.

So the anteater might not after all be that dull brute, but a wise old artist presenting his work "Ladies and Gentlemen, my Oeuvre d'art: the people of the ants." The teeth, the claws, the wiggling tongue may be more than tools to catch, crush and mill. Seen from above, these tools and all aggression lose their meanness to become the artist's chisels, always prob-ing for soft spots, excess, and imperfections in another organism's wits; endlessly trimming off what does less to cooperate and rhyme, or what is falling behind; always engaged in quality control in that ant and anteater's partnership.

And look how much the hares give the foxes—mind you, they could have developed quills, but they made an arms agreement and didn't. And look how small and far apart the considerate foxes keep their litters. I swear to you that compassion isn't some nice luxury we lately invented. It is the first law of nature and mostly genetically determined. And what do you think? Are we the most compassionate species of all?

For daring minds this idea can be an even more challenging hint. The same benevolent relationship might be true between mankind and its profiteers and parasites, its illnesses, its droughts, its lice, pests and tse-tse flies. "Please do not kill all the lice in our hair with pesticides," my Eskimo friend had said. "So we do not lose the sweet, warm feeling of sitting in each other's lap to groom each other and get hugged." (—and get flooded with endorphins, our "homemade" morphines, to glue and sweeten our social bonds.)

A further hint on how to enter that mystery may lie in our faint capac-ity to wish others well. That capacity dwells beyond my rational spirits which ultimately seem to hold lower functions as bodyguards and chauf-feur of my soul. It lives beyond the fisherman in me who sighs, a little relieved, when another boat does not come in with a bigger load. It lives beyond the rule that only the fittest should survive and leaves virtue and sin behind. To uncover this source of light and to listen to this wonderful soul song "que te vaya bien," to fall in love with the world leads also beyond the gods who applaud and condemn.

342

195

Basics for a shaman's initiation.

While the freeway travellers are all imprinted with the same scenic viewpoints, a man takes off from this safe merry-go-round. He tiptoes to viewpoints the crowd addicted to the communication nets does not have the nerves to try out. Daring viewpoints from unaccustomed or humiliating situations is his shaman's initiation.

The shipwrecked Spanish bookkeeper Cabeza de Vaca trekked as the first white man during eight years from Florida to Central Mexico. Haggling for his life through a hundred different tribes, languages, through as many ways of healing and cursing, through pangs of hunger, solitude, and night vigil, tasting each tribe's unique manipulations of the mind, that sober bookkeeper emerged as the feared and venerated healer and hechicero. His portfolio: an awe-inspiring collection of life's tricks to heal or curse which the good boys, who on their safe cruiseship of opulence never risked to shipwreck, had missed.

The Athabascans consider an infant born abnormal as a special gift of God. A special lad who is hypersensitive or frail or with a liking for being alone, a woman who is lopsided, mute, ugly or blind, or is swayed by the lunar tides, has entrancing fits, or has her sex both ways, aren't they predisposed to live and explore on the perifery of our routine a different reality than ours? These misfits become our satellites, meteors, creators of rites. They collect vistas the healthy million-crowd is cautioned not to meddle about. And they may run into medicines, helper spirits, poisons where others failed.

And so, while I gossip with Bill or feed on the calories of formal school, that mute or solitary woman may enter the spirit of the mountains and of your enemies, the spirit of the raven, the wind, the daimons you exiled and they hybridize together their collections of strange ideas. Maybe a blind man missed our advertisers' advise to sell his difficulties, his solitude and hypersensitivity, the pigeons roosting in his attic, his guardian spirits and the other trillion of God's "useless" patent holders. Trustingly, he invites these resourceful rascals to be also teachers to him. In such solitude or on such an island of the Galapagos a new species of viewpoints may form. And has not every new viewpoint its separate helpers and reality?

Ah, the gusto to keep one's distance and remain multiple, to live differently at the perifery of a crowd!

A shaman outsees and outhears the crowd. He does talk with the stars, the weedflowers and unbelievers and with all the many voices with which my inside is crowded, yet, with which I was discouraged to exchange advise. He devines the useful in my useless. He invites my exiled daimons to cooperate with him.

There is nothing supernatural in a shaman's initiation—after I accepted that it comes natural to us to freely play with our natural gift and crossbreed our spirits with those of the forests, the sicknesses, the heavenly constellations, the owls. We are all born as shamans. But how can this kinky birthday gift squeeze through the mills of formal school without being flattened?

In a brave moment I may dare to taste one of God's many entrancing gifts and let it break my stare on my dear common sense. And lo! I see options and helpers I had unlearned to see.

196

How does a man wriggle out of a career in egotism and spare his woman and his children the trauma of living in an environment where the sexes are in civil war?

When a woman is invaded and hurt by a man and he becomes a tumor in her soul, I feel that the cure lies beyond the distinction of the sexes. That malignant wart of machismo seems to me rather a symptom of a spiritual epidemic produced by the women and the men of many generations dedicated to the arrogance of humanism.

When a woman is stepped on and she points a finger at a man, I feel her pain and I feel with anguish my own loss of gentleness stirring again. I then also wish that finger could point less accusingly, but would rather warn us of our shared addiction to boss all the fellow-life around and indulge together in the profit from that machismo. Have we not plundered and shared between the sexes the sweet fruit of that forbidden apple tree that knows the sciences of bossing Mother Nature around for quite some time? Consider: a man who, dumb as a triumphant gladiator, steps on a woman's life, how much must he have silently already suffered under the wars of humanistic haughtiness against Mama Nature, for which society drafted him when he was still very young? Consider: has not this harsh man already as a toddler been cheered to batter and step on the warm motherly anima of his own soul and not to cry?

Here is a generation of males that has been raised so superbly practical that we can drive our crummies into the forest and completely unceremoniously clear-cut non-stop a square mile of it and then in our greasy workjeans simply walk away from that graveyard of a thousand stamps completely unimpressed. But then, were our parents not also the greatest ghost busters in the trees and in our souls and so cleared us the way?

Would not pitting now simply the sexes against each other for a cure finally cause divorce and become the most agonizing civil war, grinding us, mistrust against mistrust, down to neutered souls? More of us now take ourselves to court. We want to avert a looming siege between the sexes where women and men would have to go to night care centers and their semi-orphaned toddler to day care centers to buy professional love.

To give each other freedom in our relationships, even encouragement, to act out what we daydream about, to let no one who can be his or her own belong to another, and be loved for this reinforcement, is a wedding gift I feel no official, no law, but a better imagination may hand out.

197

Our love life is in revolution. I see millions of young people being coaxed into cradling in their minds or arms any creature in need and to find that doing so makes them feel as good as having a child.

It is not in his brilliant study of human relations that Freud has failed me. He confused me when he impatiently framed his glimpses of insight and made a separate poem of them, divorcing our seeds in heat from our deeper passions rather indiscriminately into a love with the growth of the whole rowdy crowd that homesteads with us the earth. He lets me so forget that our zest is fundamentally green, that our anima courts not only our maleness but also the whole of God's farm and not just for its bread and meat, but for the sweet high of being there in the morning to help planting a crop and in the afternoon to sit on the porch watching the sun and the rain dance and how everything underneath grows. In this great man's theorem it is our psychic relationship with all plant, animal and prokaryotic life and our innocence or guilt toward it that I miss.

I am now shown as never before that our love life is intimately part of nature's will to continue and to add new colors to its quilt. I observe that nature now well-meaningly blindfolds the spicy old sex drive of many women and men with a different mask and makes us cross the border of our species, rendering people barren here and fertile there while dancing to new roles. The trees start slowly to canonize their heroes among us like tree-spikers and Johnny Appleseeds, the senators who created the Endangered Species Act and other Ark Builders.

Slowly our drive for creation may even widen beyond seals, rivers, rain forests and whales. Who knows, after we have now over procreated ourselves, what the Great Spirit will trigger our zest to do next?

198
Why shouldn't this be said, although it may cost me your respect?

The Creator or her minister responsible for a thousand years of health filled a corner of my mind with all kinds of mischievous advice. I have entered a trauma unlike anything I have known before. In the promiscuous corner of my mind I hope for setbacks: in our population, in our excessive use of physical energy for solutions, in our productivity, in the tremendously aggressive section of our sciences that enlisted us as spies for our war to world domination, in our mania to quickly intervene when we hear whining among us, everywhere we have tumbled into excess.

I hope for alternatives to the "sustainable" fattening of the GNP that can make our relations with life more beautiful. What is a sustainable growth for a balloon ready to pop, for an economy running amok? I wish we would not eradicate danger, hunger, and discomfort but allow these tests to temper us and remain part of the wise, old and invigorating population controls. I wish that in our school system the fission of wisdom into its components, releasing it as raw cunning, will not prevail. I wish we will blush with intellectual shame when we waste ourselves simply remaining good workers for a more practical world and never become creative and make our world more beautiful.

Think: we could learn to converse with the rivers, the yucca, the mosquitoes dancing to a setting sun, with all of nature's lawyers who practice the same law sustaining us but apply it to all their neighbors, that may be crawlers, flyers, rabbits and grasses. I wish us the challenge that comes from welcoming personal risks. I wish before all for a change in attitude toward death among us.

I hope such sacrifices as abortion, creative laziness, arms reduction in our minds, and the reduction of the personal gross product can be voluntary. They seem to me benevolent gifts. Yet it's getting late.

Slowly this shady mischievous compassion large than man in me, which I was persuaded to jail, gets the upper hand in my intellect again. I begin to realize that a woman, a man, a tree—they are never what I learned them to be. I rub my eyes and look again.

Still snorting, I am drawn to read the morning news and make out its good news and its discouraging news with a new arbiter in mind who does not simply take sides for man. Slowly this crack in the egg gives me a promiscuous personality with quite different feelings, with unaccustomed reasons to be sad or to shout approval. Am I alone in this metamorphosis of feelings? Did everybody else move to town? Am I being fooled?

199

I suspect that the macho-man is a victim, yet with more deeply hidden hurts than others; a victim that is trained not to heal himself but to hide his wounds, to forget and to play dead in his soul. He seems a casualty of our megalomania—the substitute for our lost faith—who is not granted relief in tears.

When a man becomes obsessed to boss others who wilt under his inflated zest, I have learned to shake my fist accusingly at this macho pest. I have also learned to extend the other hand with pity to that person who suffers and buckles under such misguided ambitions.

When our practical world of tanks, chain saws, Mickey Mouse, humanistic laws and of ever increasing production to trap the world drafts a man for leadership, this call asks much of him. He is asked to lay down much of his tenderness. He is asked to sacrifice a bundle of joys, his dream time and all his curiosity that does not pay when he is chosen as foreman to bully nature. He is taught to mimic pride, to feel privileged bossing others around, to put his foot down on the soft expectant springs whispering in him and to crow happily about what a good player he has become. His wingless mind, sure of itself and solid on the ground as a safeguard against daydreaming, is a precious degeneration for him who is engaged in such highly responsible social function. Yet I should watch out, my accusing fist may be a simple envy frowning up to the glitter that goes with such ranks.

In a society that seems to have sworn before its Gods to subdue all other life for its own glory, has the macho-man not been the first victim of technomania—a science that promises us fantastic success as long as we do not read its clauses and strings attached for the birds and for our kids. Did he not become the first slave drafted for a power trip and a man deprived of one of his most wonderful old talents: to sit leisurely on a bench for a friendly talk with a woman, with a sky blooming with clouds, with birds full of exotic songs—but is given a clean, sober camaraderie instead? Yet is this splendid worrier for our GNP not the fulfillment of what most of our moms and dads dearly prayed for, worked for and fantasized about? Ah, the grave duty with the mask of perpetual hurrahs—a duty that does not allow its player to be tender, weak and shed tears but commands even his soul to sleep at attention and in uniform. Does this man not also need to be forgiven?

When in the tundra I am followed by a million mosquitoes, am I not their leader, and are they not after my energy and blood? Yet I like a leader who may follow behind—a man I admire who makes me look over my shoulder watching him closely for his changes of course.

200

Yesterday a community of banyan trees called long distance. They were in tears that we are so far behind with the payments of our debts to them.

I wonder: will the World Bank and its competitors do to the land what the Jesuits have done to the western mind? Will their financial high priests keep on missionizing our planet's infidel jungles of unsellable wonders and in naive good naturedness spread our overproduction and overpopulation—help that is a deadly virus with a thousand charming masks? After our forbearers and we have converted the impractical cultures and the souls that didn't venerate a Godman as symbol for their Almighty, will this new Rome do so for all pagan flora and fauna that seems unfit for human love or consumption?

These shy creatures of God still holding out in the wild shudder with fear when they are discovered by our economists who preach digital love, wonder rice, consumer binges, eucalyptus seedlings, spreading barbed wire and a practical world that may soon become unfit for happy cows. Yet it could be just one flash and boom of an insight away that this blind elephant of an institution swings around and to the help of the battered civilizations of trees and mosses, the family of grasses, the communities of the octopi and centipedes, the citizens living in ponds, the little people we have evicted from their homes so we can plant our tobacco and corn. This financial benefactor can turn into nature's first savings account and clearing house that settles claims of all native life to which we are now so enormously indebted. It can become the financial backer, PR agent, and lobbyist for all these "fourth class" citizens of the earth who are still free from our control. What a creative stroke of nonsense that could be.

Why is it that we are so slow to spend a minute of courage or invest a dime for our "sisters and brothers" in the wild who may have leaves or feathers and wear no shoes; yet in their presence we may get the highest highs? Why is there no Red Cross when we go to war with the woods? Why is it that we veterans never went to war and bombed our excesses in defense of our muse and source of wisdom, the Woman Wilderness?

Some of us wish that more Arks of happy excitement are kept afloat for our children cooking in boredom two generations ahead, although this would mean less Coke, loans, grainships and life preservers sent to the hordes of people 2,000 miles to the south whom we also taught to whine when going through purgatory to wash off excess.

Others are still puzzled why some among our young should spike trees to give these gentle and trusting creatures a thorn of steel to defend themselves against our armies of chain saws and who risk getting jailed for it by their dads.

Can you think of a more spirited gift for our kids than to give also social status to all these fourth world citizens, to provide them with their advocates when decisions are made? Think of the murmur creeks, the moors and rolling steppes, the mysterious forests and fjords, the kingdoms of the insect world, a maddening surf, the land that's still wild and mystic, all happy to populate the lonely corners of our soul yet do not talk in the language of our Internet. Think of the jungle in our minds with it's own kind of crocodiles. Think of all these great enterprises that do not produce micro chips, food, and faster wheels but rather solitude, excitement, visions, trust, rainbows, DNA, photosynthesis, dreams, yeast for our imagination and remedial metaphors. Aren't they also wise citizens and teachers worthy to be asked for advice? Would it not benefit us to treat them as such?

This first World Bank Account for the fourth world could be filled and spent so that the wild and mystic can remain our source of inspiration and mental joy, so that our kids can also bask in uneducated land, nibble on its enormous wealth of delightful ideas, get drunk on its beauty, dive into wisdom, get their daily curiosity filled.

201
Did you ever read a newspaper with the eyes of a tree? Wrap yourself in the bark of a spruce and try it. Sad news might bring you a smile.

When you shock me and I fume, remind me that your act, any act, is not a dead monument; it is a lively, wandering donkey loaded with gifts. She will always finally halt in front of a door, often not mine or a close friend's and often beyond humanism's garden fence. Often she will unload the gifts of your acts in a world and a time I barely know. Why then worry? Have faith, Theo. There might always be a receiver and a smile. Ah, to be able to fly with my mind to where that donkey unloads what she may have carried off from me, or my neighbor, or what she may have packed away from the whole so fabulously rich tribe of man; to be less bogged down just in blind faith that all things follow a law that means well, what a wonder drug such a taller vision could be. What's more, it is our sweet privilege to start making these surveillance flights into high mentality where the dance that all the ripples of our acts together perform comes into view.

Our dear good/bad complex that made us build The Wall right through the middle of our souls has during the last 2,000 years become enormously fruitful in distractions, armaments and arts, in psychology, in creating jobs, Berlin Walls and garbage piles. Keeping us busy, that fixation stole much of our Sunday time. It gave us also a closet full of fancy philosophies to dress up our minds. Few seem anxious to leave this refuge for the mind. Yet one thing I know; the assumption that daring to leave this complex, thought by scary thought, makes monsters of us, that theory is wrong.

The little cause of my little ill was not rigorously exposed and taken care of but simply being painted over and the repair postponed. The cause is now so removed from the effect and so hidden by a life-like cover-up that since long I have taken the bandage for my skin.

Nothing had tied my arms more together than this insisting lesson that man is better than all the rest of nature and for this should never be allowed to stand in the shade. Now, after hatching from humanism, anguish has turned into relief. Free I can now curiously walk all around an act. I can, when needed, walk out from its shade it may cast on us and celebrate with the squirrel and spruce who may be sunny-side-up. I can fearlessly listen to what someone has to say on the side we ignored. Might it be for such intellectual generosity that some religions need to be less preoccupied with sin, the disposal of bad men and hell? When I discount anything as crime, perversion, weed or sin do I not shoot down an option, a monkey, an unpleasant wind, a parasitic orchid in the Amazons of my mind? I can think of no other takeoff as disturbing and potentially creative as when a mind becomes fledged and it leaves humanism with its rules for non-flyers that served it nicely as a nest. It's a "get up and fly" for the mind. There is so much adventure and joy of mind, there are so many new options for forgiveness opening when I stop insisting that the mirror-mirror on the wall tells me we are the most beautiful, most deserving and wisest of all. There is so much therapeutic knowledge waiting that would readily seep in, were it not for old protective slogans that still stoically stand guard making it difficult for these messengers from other worlds to be heard. My mind starts to salivate in this sexy and free, new reality it finds. It starts to eat and digest wholesome food. Apart from thinking of rice, cassava or bread and of my tinkerings of the day, my mind can climb also way up a giraffe's neck and watch an act from its south to its north. Maybe even acts that simply produce yummy manure can from up there be loved. This break-out may be the only medicine that can cure me from my angry disputes with God.

202

At times I wish there were no man watching what I do. Not to be cheered or booed by a crowd that's drunk with too much man, might well be the sobering effect solitude has on me.

The champion logger, the prized bull, the best preacher, the highest paid life preserver for egos, the deadliest fisherman or butcher, the foxiest fox in town, the man who's left leg is the longest of all, these are titles for which I learned to compete. My mind is full of such tattoos, some more idiotic than slogans tattooed into restrooms. I try to purge myself of that learned need to be the darling of some local crowd—even if such a crowd is one whole generation of man. A crowd can be such an impatient, worthless spectator for a woman or man who compete so that they are also good to the fish, to children five generations ahead, to our sisters the trees, to the holy air that gives breath to all.

Why should I compete with you in professions that can make us even more powerful, tyrannical and numerous—that can render us even less cosmological and even more practical? Why should I combat for the higher IQ, to stand triumphantly over my soul, to get an iron cross for battling mother wilderness? What after all is a man who is nothing more than a man?

The whisper of awe and the hurrahs of a crowd, they might tell me how feared or imposing a performer is but do they tell me how much he is loved? At times I am ashamed of what foolish compliments I provoke and my dear ego eagerly laps up. Yet the thoughts or acts I make up just by myself may still give me stage-fright in a crowd, as a boy in homemade pants. A crowd can be quite harmful to me.

I am never as sharp as when I do not compete. How could I do a thing well when half of my mind is busy with what effect I am having on an onlooking crowd? Can I jump far when I waste myself thinking about the prize? And do not such competitive side glances open the same slits in our masks and breed sameness among us in what we see? Yet how intellectually comfortable it is to lower oneself to one measuring stick for all. It takes so much resolve to refuse to compare and compete, to remain different from others and to love to refine this wealth of differences. Competition is the grand seductress of my unique and thoroughly impractical way to bring my own thoughts and flowers out. Competitive education seems to have trained my generation to become the superb fighting hens and cocks for the rest of our lives. Do we not smile when our competitors fail? Competing and being mean might be close to being synonyms. With anguish I now realize that my competitive education has extinguished much of my tender capacity to wish others well.

All this wrestling for attention happens in the coliseums in Moscow, the pageants on Wall Street, on the village square, in Nobel's give-aways in Stockholm where every seat seems now taken by our kin—no paddle-frogs, no centipedes, no baobab tree, no coyote, no nightingale, no undisciplined creeks, not even the gods and goddesses in our souls are asked in to boo or cheer; no snow geese to honk a foul, just our own serious venerable crowd seems to arbitrate these games.

Deep down I have always felt slightly uncomfortable with applause. Do we applaud the weather, the earthworms and the other decomposers that give us a yummy soil? Yet they are as vital as the peacocks to life. Does not a free landscape seem so wonderfully harmonious just because there is nothing in particular to applaud?

How differently I fish and keep house when I do not remain an eter-

353

nal minor nicely following the script our hardworking parents and politicians have chosen for us. I can take off on my own vision quest. I can seek for myself the role the Great Spirit has printed into me as others seek for gold. I can step in my own costume into that arena where not all the benches are reserved for our folks. Here every named and unnamed critter is welcomed to yell, giggle, swear, vote and throw hat or tail in the air in applause. Here everything gets its turn to show off its own idea on how to fly, sing, chirp, move, clown, cheat, lubricate, quilt a society or recombine genes. Here a wise old fir can wonder with me: how does Theo do? How differently my feelings are boiled or made to shiver when also the kids three generations downstream can shout foul or simply yell from too much joy or hold their bellies from laughing at what serious clowns their grandpas have been. And my notion of rich and poor gets a little seasick with all the new options of wealth I see.

To become a less biased spectator in that show, I think I know now what I have to do. I am to relearn how to compete. I am to plunge with my thoughts willingly into life's yeasty insecurity with no middleman to God. I am to plunge into that wild mental undertaking to purge my personal mythology of all those neat old heroes, champions and saints who stubbornly and successfully competed to do the best for the empire of man, assuming we were life's only darling daughters and sons. I want to get out from under the greenhouse in which mass-media synthesizers create a sterile reality where they cultivate their docile, unimaginative voters, clients and labor force. Outside I can observe this great bunch of arbiters who transmit their points of view from above, from the left and right, from below the rotting leaves, or from seven generations away, whose assortment defies my common sense, yet seem to watch over me that there is moderation in whatever I do. I still might get tuned in.

Each has his case. In my case, there will be many worried fishes and the pristine ocean winds that do not like my engine's smoke. There are the last laughing melt-waters about to be leashed to the turbine of my plug-ins who will be among the most attentive spectators I will have to ask: How did my energy consumption do?

203
Seasons of the mind.

In times of smiles, of rosy peaches, sun and ample elbowroom, lazy leisure, watching from the porch the rain watering the corn, the soul's religious intuition may crack its husk. That divine seed wriggles out of hibernation to bring feelers out. It is time that the humus falls in love with the sun and interacts with the great general field. Reactions and decisions become bewilderingly large scale, promiscuous, diversified and flamboyant in such sunny openings. It is a grandiose time.

In times of grim competitive crowdedness, a mind shivers in stress and fear. In such congestions it initiates crisis-alert and cold reasoning. Ultimately a mind might enter hypothermia and retreat to this last stand to protect its most immediately vital parts. It follows the law which in grim times commands the snake to hibernate, the lizard to throw away its tail, the flowers to curl up in seeds. Hence that retreat into the ego to dispute just with the closest special fields. Hence that epidemic to castrate wisdom and strengthen rationality, that mania for safety, that loss of generosity. Hence, our shutting down the luxury of being diverse. Ask any farmer whether this is not so. Don't our minds tend to become sober virgins when we are so numerous that we step on each other's toes? In such emergencies neurochemicals may retract the whole intellect into one armored think tank for a technology of immediate aggression and defense, as on the sea adrenaline, our supreme egotism-booster, may shrink for one danger loaded moment my whole world to that one superb egotism of "Theo fighting the big fish." Science shelves contemplation and the art of beautiful relationships and becomes recklessly possessive. It mothballs its long-range planning-commission—its soul. Take our own harsh and competitive time; are we not becoming more and more creative in laws that benefit our contemporary adult society alone? Are we not down to five year plans and schemes within presidential terms, a generation continuously drunk and whipped on by adrenaline? We become addicts to the telecom of man and manmade information and call it a revolution. We become illiterate in the mysterious communication system that arranges good relations among all times, species and worlds.

When a grasshopper has absolutely no sensible way left to outma-
neuver a bat, it falls into a completely chaotic flight pattern to try to confuse the bat's common sense. As the last survival strategy, when cornered,
we do the same and call it panic.

Egotism seems to have its place in the seasons of the mind. It gives us
great career people, great ink-fishes, analyzers and decomposers, lock-
smiths, psychologists, clinical physicians, farmers and researchers,
builders of great monuments, business empires, and dams, and super-
providers. It shelves in us the poet and brings out the inventor. And it
gives us a love for details.

When in a cataclysm, like population explosion, the whole intellect is
overrun and plunged into a crisis-alert of "save what little you can," one is
helped to soothe the loss with deliriums, amnesiac drugs, with endorphins, soap operas, Prozac, sports, TV-lullabies and store-bought ecstasies.
As animals, so man, we all seem to behave according to biologically self-
regulating morals.

Maybe our mind with its practical side and its cosmological side, its
obvious and its mysterious, its composing and composting functions close
to Lovelock's theory of the self-regulating Daisyland.

Who knows, after we became endangered by our own monstrous
growth and had to shed part of our vitality using our own kind of autotomy to shed excessive strength and virility to get in harmony again, we
still might later eclipse the lizard's power to restore its discarded tail.

204
I tell myself: "Make a gift to nature and to your soul—
dare to think a little riskier and wilder—live kinder."

What could trigger that global renaissance that may turn on the whole
tribe of us, even our school and manufacturing boards of directors, to compete in answering that question that rewards the right answer with a zillion friends before a catastrophe screams at us: You are out—you failed!
What can make us fall in love with the holy land we are all standing on as
our western religions tried for 2,000 years to make us fall in love with just
our neighbors? The inner rumbling of this neglected need still without a

messiah and a name has become to me more nagging than other political concerns. It mocks the joys that come from smarter gadgets on my boat or a Jacuzzi tub in the home. To explore a materialistically leaner and spiritually wealthier life might well become the great adventure for today's spirited young women and men.

Our time could be remembered as the end of a dark age of missionaries and pioneers and when from a long state of war against "silent" nature, we came to an understanding even neighborly love for our amazingly talkative habitat, an epoch when not only a weed people or a weed culture but also the merry "flowers of evil" still cheering up the monotony of our fields achieve some social status in our minds. The earth—our companion!

A few ideas: In our own version of the old Chinese Examination System persons could pass a maturity test, showing that their minds can leap beyond a career and beyond the humanistic sphere into a reality larger than man. This could lead to an initiation into a new kind of statesmanship—people trained for decisions seven generations tall. Psychology could deepen and gently persuade corporate politics of the psychic health value of the Noah's arks and other refuges that keep our Muse, Miss Wilderness, afloat in the great flood of our parent's practicalities. There could be a Nobel Prize or grades for producers and nations for how well they are loved by our grandchildren, by the great people of trees, by the oceans and the fleets of beetles and butterflies, as we now give stars to hotels and grades to our students. In the science curricula, the art of transmuting physical solutions into mental solutions—the art of relationships—can become the highest discipline and more exciting than trying to transmute lead into gold. We can go for high mental adventure, scrutinize our religions for those beliefs that serve an all too humanistic prudence and free our minds from such protective confinement. We may be strong enough to dream up an ethic so daringly inclusive that the populations swaying in the wash of the tides, the tse-tse fly, people in jail, may remain children of the Holy Spirit that in yet unknown ways may all be great contributors and inventors.

In this high-flying mentality, our industry is also asked for some abortions—to slowly phase out efforts which aim at simply producing higher stock prices for the money championships.

Why not promote individual risk and bravery as virtues and as detergents for the mind instead of glorifying those whom fear buried in wealth? We can become personally brave again and kick our addiction to safety with its enormous cost to our fellow life. Rediscovering the mind altering properties of danger, hunger, risk, mind quakes, slick poverty, even of sicknesses or abstinence from sex, can win the war against the more brutal drugs. One might even start to doubt the wisdom of begging God for a master bedroom in one's home. Before all, in an understanding of our evolution it could benefit us to upgrade Darwin's theory of the survival of the best provider. From the tragedies of our own supreme fitness and power, we can learn that it may after all not simply be the strongest and fittest, but the organism capable of entering the fittest symbiosis with its habitat, the organism that loves best, that survives. The sea teaches me now that it will not be the children of the best equipped generation of fishermen that survive. Evidence insists that we are becoming blind to the law of moderation and much too fit, overpowering and over equipped. Did we fabricate a tooth bigger than the mouth?

To admit to and then fight the sickening obsession for physical world domination we could inaugurate an international gift pool in which inspired world citizens could pledge to replace a one kilowatt year with a mental solution or to set free again one hundred continuous RPMs of the enormous energy we now drive into war against our fellow life and free it as our forebears freed their slaves. Such a conversion to mental solutions might be more rewarding than to naively look for alternative energies and slaves.

To bait also our dear pride to come to our rescue, we could inaugurate a foundation that brings us a new kind of beauty pageant or Olympic Games between nations where the best keepers of the earth compete. Prizes could go to the caretakers of the most lively rivers with the merriest assortment of guests dwelling in their banks, to those soulful nations that tiptoe through their flora and fauna leaving the fewest footprints, prizes for the multinations best loved by all the creatures not under the yoke of man, prizes for the peoples who contribute the least per capita to acid rain and greenhouse problems, a nobility award for those beautiful nations who become the supreme dancers to our planet's pastoral and a thanksgiving turkey stuffed with applause for the nation that has the most effective education to this effect, a trophy for those gay countries whose children enjoy the most leisure time, freedom, inspiration, giggle, hugging and fun. And to top it all off, a jumbo thanksgiving cake to the religion that hangs the brightest lamps over our kinship with the whole rowdy crowd that peoples the earth with us.

There seems to be neglected messengers in my genes that obstinately bubble up pictures of a beautiful interspecific relationship. They whisper rules of a long-range health to me that are so long and tall they wouldn't fit into the short logic that I learned to spin around health at school. By breaking my stare simply on a career, I can discover many bridges that tease me to walk across to make trees, rivers, dangers, goofers, even my inner daimons to become my benefactors.

Did you notice, I try persuading myself to give back to Mother Nature one more of my working days a week where I leave the driving strictly to my magic spirit to take off on trips that do not kill or pollute and I do not need the oil of Iraq.

I like to see my life as my work of art. I chisel away on how I interact and express myself.

Did you notice, I am brewing for myself a special brand of medicine?

205

Paved roads are for the blind. The better roads are those laid by the mind.

When one loves to dig for the symbiosis among all living things as others eagerly dig for gold, one soon realizes that to solve a problem and reach an outstretched hand, one needs not necessarily hack another bleeding road through the countryside. The mind can stretch, worm, leap, wriggle its way to a solution. Gentler roads can be discovered, roads of thoughts winding and tiptoeing through time that do not need cobblestones, roads that do not need to roar with a thousand hps and elbow harshly through the living room of our fellow life.

To me exploring The Way is science enjoying itself—science at its best. Here is visionary science that can make me forgiving, tolerant, serene, and help my mind to digest well. Is not a great scientist a light-maker, a man or woman not cursed to prostitute their minds to spy for pay or keep their insights boxed in a patent? He is allotted the lucky chores of sniffing out for us all the well-meaning of what I presumed to be simply brute, shady, diabolic, maybe a slug in my salad bowl. I see a woman who knows to breathe confidence on me when I am confused and have a fit. I see a poet who puts in pictures and words what's inside us. Somebody is mapping the Tao's Way. Ah! here are joys finally that do not need to devour.

Medical science at its best synthesizes thought pictures that can be visualized to heal fear, gloom, aching anticipation, hate, desperation, stress, high temper, motion sickness, love with a running nose, cold feet, a grouch, congested roads and a mind that has the runs. Surprise, surprise, here is medicine which may well turn out to be a kinder drug than those the pharmaceutical industry and the drug lords are selling us. Or do you think that science does not have its saints?

You gave me a metaphor. You never made me a better gift. It has become the rope with which I pull myself out of depressions, pitch-dark tunnels, fits, contradictions and caves; may I swing with it from cliff to cliff, or to land in upper rooms.

Stop for a minute your surveyors and earth movers, Theo, stop in you the fisher. Let's take our binoculars that magnify time. We might zoom in on help that's swiftly gliding toward us on flowing freeways woven into the land of time only generations away. These roads seem laid into the intuitive mind as part of a universal communication system keeping the tenants in its orbiting family home in cheerful gossip, counseling, and in unity. Let's turn off for a moment the synthesized reality tubed in by the media and wriggle out of its spell; let's tune into a superbly communicating community called wilderness. There, we need know no English or Japanese, no grammar yet we are spoken to quite comprehensively in many kinds of languages at one time—subtle conversations flow in and out through every of our ten senses. Messages even seep through the skin. Language, nay, all messages are chemistry. I greet you—and all your muscles relax. I shout at you and I synthesize neurochemicals that make your "quills" poke up. I synthesize your yells that soon are homing in on me.

A community that needs fewer roads blazed through the land tells me, "Here lives a hospitable clan that enjoys chattering with its fellow life." It is for this that at today's morning news the earth bounced ten feet with joy when a nation in Europe announced, "Let our minds do more of our driving. We will build no new roads."

Some like art to be a beauty contest. I prefer it when art is a good road crew that clears slides, opens up new trails, viewpoints and feelers in my mind.

The pursuit of better love seems to me less the burning of copal and holding hands than to set one's heart to mine all sciences without allowing the ego to set the goals. You may profess that this world must be improved. Theo says his vision can be improved.

206

I suspect Mother Nature is wiser than to let herself be prayed into pouring even more sun, more water, more security, muscle, life preservers, tricks, loans and endurance onto that one grandiose organism that has already invaded most of her lands. Why should she want to let us become too prosperous on the account of all her other tribes?

Now that our unchecked growth and egocentric health care make us creep all over our fellow life, would God really want to give us ten billion vigorous people, stronger arms, sharper machetes, a fatter GNP, a stouter health and more acres of rice? How could it be that God would want to unite us to ten billion hardworking "saints" laboring heroically for mankind and plunge us so into even deeper debt to the planet's life? I look around and note that this naive wish is not fulfilled.

How could more ambitious, more productive women and men adding to our excesses now serve as this planet's cure and so our cure? How could this be the remedy for bringing equilibrium to the community of all things alive?

In my rather idealistic mental life, it was a wild day when I dared to realize that for a "better," richer world, we now do not need an even healthier or stronger mankind with smarter smartness and sharper teeth. To retain our creative strength and the maximum of our genetic options, a more inactive, weaker, more bleeding and giving, more divided, vulnerable, endangered and death-accepting mankind might, for our time, be a better remedy and a blessing for global life. This is a rebellious thought when seen standing alone. It not only begs me to improve on Darwin's elegantly and so conveniently rounded theory but to abandon the enormously popular mentality which stubbornly and abusively glorifies man above all. In a humanist's eyes it may make me one possessed of evil spirits.

The dear assumption that to erase diseases betters life makes sense in a society of egoists. Here the interplay between sickness and the long-range health and the creativity of a species is of little interest and poorly understood. Yet does this mischievous spoon not stir up into the orderly surface ever new situations and options? Does it not feed our mental evolution? Or was I fooled when I noted that most creative people are below average in peacefulness, wealth, common sense or health?

When I press my ear against the ground I hear most of nature pray to God not to give mankind more health but more perversion and options, more adversaries and leeches, more mentality altering drugs and creative divisions and blisters on our shamelessly ever busy fingers, more risks and tests—ah! and in our pockets more holes, so we may never rise to that fabled deluge. Such might well be the hidden good luck we are being wished by the trees, the kangaroos and the fishes.

The trees, the octopi, the woodpeckers doing their drumming, they might welcome and love our TV and drug addiction, our imitative adventures, the playboy love, the gadgets keeping us immobilized in happy house arrest. They might love our junk food habits; they even thank the Coke empire for rotting a few of our hundred billion teeth munching away at the global green. Some of life's associates might even beg God for more nuclear disasters. They figure that they can do better in radioactive and man-forsaken land than in "clean" land that is hot with our activities. Look what wonderful things the nuclear bomb tests did to the reef population at Bikini under the protection of Cesium 137 and the absence of fishermen for fifty years. Imagine, just for teasing your dear common sense, how we "bomb" a free and lively commune of life to all rubble and no wriggle before we force one of our monocultures on that wasteland. And again and again we send our exterminators in as soon as this commune starts to rebuild. Yet not even on my Sundays have I learned to see it this

362

way. How these shy creatures must appreciate also non-aggressive homo-sexual love or any love that's not monopolized by our fecundity anymore. Might not the mutations in our mentality that drain our reckless fertility, our monstrous fitness, our obsessive zest to till, calculate, whack and hack, be God's outrageous help to our battered muse, Miss Wilderness? What a timely gift from our scientists to show us just now how organisms do not always spontaneously mutate but that mutations seem also to be caused by needs. It is such thoughts that make me feel less offended by the disre-gard the creator of evolution has for our ethics.

Maybe it is these terrible kinds of thought pictures which finally will become the rope that gets me out of the well into which I fell. How many hot thoughts and painfully simple answers had a serene woman first to dream up and tame; how many open-armed "yeahs" must she have replied to Mother Grace's invitations with no other rope to hold on than faith before she could light up.

It will be the adventure of my mind to leave "l'homme révolté" with his "better world" behind. I wish there was a chef who could cook these unaccustomed ideas better and serve them more attractively than I.

207

How does the organism of a people take care of its health? How does it purge itself of diseases of degeneration and mediocre elements, freely throw up and wash itself?

Macromedicine—the wisdom how species purge, cure and invigorate themselves and live mannerly together—no longer has a faculty. Where do we learn about the anatomy of a species? Try to draw its form and its looks. Clinical medicine catering to the temporary knows a million fixes for the individual and more fixes are in demand. Society bears the cost of this nearsighted pity.

When the lifesaving industry proudly publishes its breakthroughs I feel now a little less jubilant and more pensive. In a world where we already overflow into every niche as no other weed ever did. I wonder: what will over-personalized healthcare in the long run do for our children and to the other populations that also made the earth their home? God's menagerie and botanical gardens have already paid much for underwriting our exclusive, standardized and quite virginal health for which we are ready to kill our brother death. Is there hypochondria among us which we applaud? Is clinical medicine cooking more pork for a mankind who is already obese? How to be all jubilant about reproductive medicine now that the option of physical infertility has obviously come forward as one of nature's gifts and remedies to population control which should not be lightly turned back? I can see no wisdom in the pursuit of knowledge that turns into a science for bigger warts. And how does clinical medicine pay for its success?

I look around and note that our noble professional health support industries have also gradually made the majority of us into individuals who become handicapped in our active self-maintenance. We become less alive, but more kept alive. Our learned pity that often tries to save the parents by taking from our children's world, that often loves a troubled neighbor more than a future child seems to promote many interesting disabilities and deviations in our bowels, minds and genes. Take wonderful gene therapy. Will it not also be the great helper of inherited diseases, helping them not to die out but to multiply through the coming generations? This system stands for: individuals keepers, our species the weeper.

To have more dangers jailed with laws; to have more and more sicknesses shot; to have more of these little buggers put under arrest which life provides us for inspectors to help a person over his generations to autonomous health and to pinch dormant capacities in him to wake up; to defame the high of risking death and to have more and more dull and supported old-age as the main form of death looming over us, would not all this cause a loss of courage, of daredevils, rebels, youth, sex and colors?

Nature loves the next generation more than it loves its neighbors and a father often loves his son more than the son loves in return. Is it against this unrewarding generosity the western mind teaches the world to rebel?

I live now among a native people who not long ago, when they gathered to make decisions, kept silent afterward for twenty-four hours. They thought out an impact statement. They considered how their decisions would affect the next seven generations, so they would not regret what

364

they did. They seem to have understood that healing for pay invokes its curse; that healing works best when done free of charge as a mother gives birth to a child.

A cultivated addiction to the practical blinded me to my built-in long-range system for health which does not deal in one-generation fixes. These cures, seven generations long, which freely recycle bits and pieces of life, are not appreciated by Theo, my dear ego. Being superbly practical seems to imply being superbly functional on only one level of understanding. To become so is greatly helped by a loss of soul. And so, many people now participate only in one world. It might be for this that a highly practical society is the paradise for technology, that an impractical society is a paradise for poets and children. When I think with my seven lives, to be practical and to be prodigiously nearsighted seems to become synonymous.

Endlessly, the organism of a people seems to replace old and defective cells with young cells, producing, when needed to control manias and overgrowth, all kinds of "suicide" genes and killer cells. In a shortage or drought it seems to shed many of its clan. Without much whining, it wisely withdraws, bringing those it withdrew to light again in times of abundance and when the peaches are ripe.

When I accept that nature does not want our health to conveniently sit down, standardize and repeat itself and does not like me to remain forever a healthy worm, that moment becomes to my mind the magic "stand up and walk." I become Theo at large and take part in the greatest seminar—life in action, exploration, evolution. I might get to love its many forms of health. Who said that Theo is not healthy because he has now been fighting for two months to hold onto his left leg that a stingray pierced and started to kill. Who said that a deaf person, a gay, a one-legged man, Alice lost in Wonderland, even a person who dies, are not healthy women and men?

208

I am pressed to join our revolution in communication that promises to take me out of the jungle of dialogues between all species and to wire me neatly into the worldwide nerve system of the "brave new hive of man."

I am trained to make my curiosity sit down; I am trained not to curiously, merrily fool around but to swiftly learn and communicate through the radio, the screen, the school, the alphabet, the cable, the Internet, the telephone and leave the useless talk with trees and grasses alone. When still very young I was persuaded to go safely underground into the warm bowels of the union of contemporary men and the simple world of the ABCs and to focus my attention on chores to keep those bowels working and full. Mass media offers me that nipple gushing with censored, predigested, highly simplified and usefullized information. Mass media bewitches me to come in from the multidisciplinary world of wilderness so overwhelmingly productive in options and ideas to the simple world of the numbers and words and to become one of the crowd. TV seems to turn into the most efficient feedlot for our minds.

In that cozy bunker for the mind, presumed to be self-sufficient, no alien news, no complaint from a baobab tree will interfere; no rustling wings of dragon flies frolicking in the reed will be heard. Here no equal time is allowed for that other reality that talks to me in hunches, pictures, mosquito bites, dreams, perfumes, tree language and with the silence of the night. The windows to daydreaming are closed. Slowly, softly I am to be wrapped in a closed system of communication that continuously feeds me whitewashed and proven information carefully selected, controlled, sanitized and programmed to beautify and fortify our island: the Empire of Man. I am served an oversupply of mental calories! Yet there is much unalphabetic information and signs from the free world I do not receive and interpret anymore.

When dangerously submerged in the heat of life's hottest market places for ideas, yet plugged into these earphones, I can then still do my chores undisturbed as an enzyme in the bowels of man. How tempting to just sit back and suck from the nipples of man-made information and remain a babe for life.

Yet I do not want to end up in a hundred years of solitude. I am not afraid to communicate with the outside world. I'm not afraid to decipher the picture writing of a churning sea, the ethics of a wise old tree, the wings writings of kittiwakes frolicking beyond the reach of words. I don't want my mind to simply graze on the Internet—to become a super brain that fattens on that worldwide feedlot from Oxford to Tokyo. Yesterday I didn't dance with mankind alone but took a lesson from a tidal flat and had fun. Winged with excitement a day before I walked through the scriptures published in a taiga bursting to bloom through the ice. My mind was close to indigestion from so many tricks seen acted out. What a treat for the mind when I allow it to be imprecise and to become a satellite dish by which the messages from every nook of life are fished. What a treat to leave our information freeways and dart like hummingbirds sipping the information firsthand and not, after it has been sifted and adulterated with motives, blindly gulping that witchy brew down as feedlot cows do. This free, permissive land grows more connections between my neurons than educational TV shows. Have you noticed that free, innocent information among us has become as rare a gift as free barbecued chicken at a shopping mall? By listening to the voices of other free worlds not occupied by us, are we not promised that our minds will never become simply exploited, barren and banal?

In this raging revolution of information and informers, in this meltdown of personalities within the billions bowing down in front of screens, I need a new strategy for privacy. How am I not to become composted and fodder for our economy?

209

That a people should intuitively protect their individuality and pass up the huge immediate gain they could rake in by freely trading away their unique know-how heritage is one of the hottest arguments nature presents to the economist I learned to be.

Minds everywhere are feverish with unionitis. One feeds on diversity, on the wealth of capacities that each individual and each nation keeps up just for its emergencies. The fires roar. A simple world with all Adams and no Eves. In this burn-down we become powerful beyond our dreams. Our children may find ashes where before there were feasts of blues, pinks and greens.

At first sight, I am perplexed how a species keeps its lavish variety in knowledge such as recipes, lifestyles and genes; its profusions of oddities, freaks, side-steppers and downers in its soul. Why does a species intuitively protect this bewildering profusion of expensive differences with all kinds of built in fences, with apartheid, shynesses, racism; with language barriers, shame, custom agents, segregation, subspecies, lies, trademarks and skins? Could that deeply built in contempt for a monoculture be a species' preventive medicine guarding it from becoming excessively one-sided? Could it be one of its safety measures—its options and odd remedies kept in store for all kinds of emergencies?

At second sight, our species' diversity might turn out to be a lavish gift of nature to us, and we should not make a stink of it when this capacity to be so "wastefully" different and unequal does not surrender to our obsession to become practical, global and informative but preserves itself with healthy enmities. Apartheid among its clans is not necessarily negative and offers a species an ever gushing resource of experiences, options and a wide range of tricks for adaptation. It keeps alive a thousand different recipes for cooking fish.

At third sight, we might not want to lightly squander this privilege for a single generation's gain, pushing a takeover of western thought to its one-sided end. Who knows, later on we might be glad that someone is used to washing by hand, to thinking in paradoxes, to walking on his hands, to carry water on her head.

For an imagination as neat and flat as a map, two bashful clans playing their hide and seek might seem desperately separate. For magic eyes that see into time, these two clans might be firestones and nicely united with loops of mutual stimulation and spying that criss-cross each other along the journey of the generations and when banging together they light up our horizon. Theirs might be a relationship as lasting and successful as the one between the people of honey bears and those of the bees.

A brave people may sacrifice a thousand of its own to defend its unique culture. A meek people may deny its culture just to be spared a personality test and the risk of losing a thousand of its clan. To which of the two fighters will our grandchildren give integrity's Nobel Prize?

When considering this, it might become less astonishing that some of our forebears have let themselves be skinned alive and still did not spill what they knew, thus protecting their unique kind of ballgames, truths, and songs, their own lovers' games, feathers and perfumes that made up their subspecies or tribe. Did you ever wonder why God did not have the common sense to make the woods out of just two kinds of super trees, one for lumber and one for pulp?

The wizard who dreamed up the fable about the tower of Babel (and the tower of the United Nations) confuses the economist in me and made me think a lot. I fear if there would be ten billion united women and men with one kind of business ethic imprinted in all, then the one immense grey flock of the United Mankind would have been achieved.

210

Beyond the psyche theorized by Freud, our hierarchical minds may well broaden to that gigantic stage on which an advocate for every creature on earth argues its case and offers advice.

I'm still shivering with a realization that puts my thoughts further out in the cold than the vista Galileo opened up. I suspect that, among all the clans, the clan of man is not the axle around which all the other species turn, but just one great servant among many, all players to a common will. This simple acceptance that we are not the center involves the revision of all the gigantic rest of my values to make them fit.

I'm awed and thrilled by how much can be understood, forgiven, justified and celebrated when one allows that in her deepest, most generous mind, a person does not want to become a hero for mankind alone. Yet from this loftier point of view, don't our awards, our heroes and saints, our titles, my side glances to find out how much better I am than my fellow man, the great fisherman with his bigger loads, our mythology mostly become obsolete values from a mostly obsolete earth that had been orbited by the sun?

In a cheerful moment ask Mr. Willow, ask Miss Skunk, ask anybody who doesn't have a human name which they like better; a hardworking man with his ax or calculator in hand, St. Paul, any great organizer in the empire of man, maybe the hero on your village monument, or a gentle loafer, curiously wandering and happily nibbling on crumbs of the wisdom that "uneducated" nature is proudly presenting to us. Who knows? They might just choose as their darlings, women and men whose ax chopping for humanism is now rather dull.

To fish, to help, to write, to think, as if there would be present every creature on earth as a citizen peeking over my shoulder watching me and commenting; to be as impartial as a pregnant raincloud opening up over the sea, your strawberry field, the enemy's land; to become less of an actor craving the applause of humanity alone; such advice I give myself. Here I read your thoughts. Yes, you are right. I am still an amusing beginner at not taking sides. I still slide down into pity and hate without much of a fight.

A word, an object, an act, are they not always also part of a larger system or idea which I did not follow up but did prematurely frame? I sided with the leaf and did not hear out the song of the woods.

The more time, species and names I dare to integrate into my self, making of it an ever wider hoop, the more I lose the chance to stand on a village monument. It might be this unacademic quest for multiple vision that can lead me to better understand the ingeniously instructive medicine wheel of some native American tribes and how the script not only of every man but of every critter fits in and becomes somewhere for others a pill. That wheel teaches me how to feel less surprised or threatened by other's decisions and acts.

In this wider spread mind with many scenic points of view, might it not be the completely unheroic day that becomes for me a good and serene day? Maybe the heroine is she who dares to be no heroine. Even better, maybe each of us is a saint; and absolutely nothing needs change. Each one needs only to know what he or she is doing and how we fit in.

May I linger on that thought of a serene woman or man and add that there must have been many terrible words when they were teaching themselves all that seemingly unacceptable forgiveness needed to make of themselves among the chorus of whiners the serene people they have become. Now, after they have loudly said to themselves all those things we pretend not to know and the terrible lesson has dissipated, I can naively enjoy their solid goodnaturedness. I can forget their anvil, their fits and fires, the bangs of their forging hammers. I can be puzzled by their love which seems as impartial as the dances of the rain.

211

A new lusher religion without yet a name transcends humanism and adds to the human relation stories of the Bible, the animals, and the greens.

What has happened to the sons of Newton's followers, I see now also happening to the sons and daughters of our western missionaries. Many see the Holy Spirit's new handwriting on the screen which that spirit has built into our souls. We feel encouraged to expand the theorems of early Christianity which, it seems, over cautiously led its civilization into intellectual quarantine. That spirit seems now ready to join the whole rowdy crowd of nature's other children with Miss Christianity who has been living as a good virgin on her island—protected, intellectually chaste and alone.

That spirit now teases our minds into daring this mental leap and landing on the next level in the hierarchy of societies. We are promised that this space-jump will be a joyride which will also make every creature on earth stamp their tails and feet and wave their branches with great joy and relief. We are promised that this jump will be the push button that makes our picky little humane kindness into a whale of a goodness with a belly as big as God and that it multiplies our options a thousand times.

In becoming siblings all over the earth by sharing a passionate concern to keep the bush of life lush with excitement, riddles, songs and wonders, we animate each other to scrutinize our daily routines, minute by minute, mile by mile, dollar by dollar for what can be chiseled away, and turned free, as our grandmothers, lock by lock, used to search in our hair for fleas. We wonder how we can make a gift per man per day to our good neighbors the forests, the grassland, the sea. Do they not now need nurses more urgently than we do? Even a few rpms, a roll of paper towels, one fishing day I turn loose are welcome alms to this battered fourth world. We form conspiracies to lick our consumer addiction as others join Alcoholics Anonymous. We are not so puzzled anymore by the Maya for having themselves pierced yearly, sacrificing some of their blood or for sacrificing infants to invoke the earth's fertility. Some of us ready ourselves to cut off, with this aim in mind, so to speak, one of our little fingers.

We are dumbfounded by the stupendous generosity of the lemmings who built into their genes a huge periodical giveaway of their biomass to other species. Here is perhaps one of nature's fertility rites beside which our symbolic bloodlettings, child sacrifices, seed scatterings, tree spikings, potlatches and thanksgivings seem mere petty gifts to the goddess of fertility.

The enormous mental undertaking to assemble together a green consciousness for us including wilderness will soon steal the show of the humanistic humanities that flourished on the incest of our minds and made of my soul a dull diamond that reflects only that splendor that's useful to man. Life's art of living together—mother of all social arts, seems to draw from a deeper seated religious instinct than did the Christian philosophy which tamed our minds, making us the lonely chosen folk among the many tribes that settled the earth. That family of religions seems still awkward at kindling in me the sweet gift of enthusiasm for and gossiping with all species so I can go down on my knees and caress the roots of a soulful tree.

Buy your courage a hard hat. Many vestigial and virginal spirits have to go. Old virtues and proverbs are being replaced by improved models now.

212
Science dedicated to the ego.

Are we losing the one fitness that is of supreme importance—the fitness to become poets—scientists of the soul who initiate us into taller and more rewarding relationships? Look, even a slug has become a more productive composer than most of us when weaving his needs and his roads of slime gently into the woods.

To what would I amount, to what would a scientist, even a whole species, amount, that never dreams up a more accommodating relationship, but remains day and night stuck in the grim underworld of scheming a bigger tooth, more forbidding vaccines, better meanness, more food?

A squirrel, a man, take any critter with a name, are they not ultimately graduated by life for their better capacity to be fit poets and gardeners, for taking into their hoop of friends more exiles, more waste, enemies or damned, more wholesome compost for their growth, more loose ends?

It is in this quality of becoming taller poets that our applied sciences are leaving me undernourished.

213
What is good news?

Take any good news—ask yourself: is it good news for your ego? For your economy? For your people? For mankind whose population grows out of control?

Is it good news for our harmony with life's many tribes? Or for our children five generations away? Is it good news for the loggers or the forests? For the freedom-loving meadows? The laughing waters? The woodpeckers? The mallards winging south? For God's fleet of beetles? Name any critter that peeks over our shoulders when we proudly bag a good news. Is it good news for life—that glorious rebellion against uniforms?

So many different opinions, so many shades between yeses and nos in life's orchestra!

Here is mental aerobics I like. Let the moralist in me dance to these contradictions and work up a sweat. Good, tall news as well as wisdom may have tears in the eyes and be quite frightening.

214
When I think that this flicker of life, which for the last 66 years has been dressing up in the costume we call Theo, has been successfully experimenting for three billion years, I am impressed by the portfolio of wisdom it has amassed.

When a sour crabapple tree is grafted to become a good "humane" tree to grow apples huge and yummy sweet and is made resistant to any non-human guest who enjoys nibbling, we may rub our hands, pleased. Yet do you think this snobbish tree pleases the Creator more for being snobbish and "humane" now that he grows apples only for man?

I also think, as with a tree so with a man, we are all wiser and more reliable below the graft and beneath the dress-up. When hard pressed, do we not tend to revert to the proven wisdom of our roots? Zealously virtuous and moral people under stress seem not as stable and trustworthy as "amoral" people are.

Experimenting with new or civilized virtues works best in sunny, peaceful times and well-conditioned habitats or soils, also when we have a safe job and can work steadily in the sweet sweat of our brows. Yet when abandoned in a mess and crisis alert or simply in the jungle of life, do we not tend to revert to the more stable and proven laws of our roots where we are more general practitioners and a little less humane? What happens to an orchard that we cannot daily water and manicure? Soon it will come home to a more stable unity.

Let me expand:

In a highly specialized adult cell, when cell biologists starve it into breaking out of its specialization, so they can use it for cloning, all genes can regain the potential of being played. Danger, depravation, starvation, hardship, drugs, poisonous mushrooms seem the key to produce in us an analogue reverse to basics. Neurochemicals that such crisises produce can release us from the grip of retaline-like chemicals that focus us on a specialization. An unpractical, embryonic, childlike openness starts in us to again prevail.- Free again to express any of our many native capacities!

With our focusing undone we get dangerously awake and high to celebrate for a festive while our universal options and vision. Cult and drug dealers also know to play part of this "destructive" game.

And so, when the going becomes tough, let me trek with a partner who is less moralistic and cultured. She will prove to be more adaptable under stress than a goody-goody girl or boy.

215

Shame busters: the "open sesame" to new options.

In times of abundance, shame is the gentle moderator in all I do. It is my brake so I may cruise safely through life according to its law of moderation and I do not miss its stations and its curves to other generations. It is my biological system of ethics for when there is fair sailing.

Shame to grow three arms or twelve feet tall, shame to live on help, on welfare checks, to walk on hands or lean against the next. Shame to ask for a life extension for an overripe ego, shame to prematurely fornicate, to be obedient, to shamelessly work, to create waste, to step out of the norm. Shame to have a bellyful for years and keep on killing fish simply to compete. Shame also to be a whining good boy who wants to stop the rain, the brush fires, the lightnings, the thunders, and the hail. Shame helps the magnolia not to open flowers prematurely. It may also tell the cells in my body when to stop multiplying.

Shame is guidelines, alarm systems, stop signs of my deeper self. She is a good mother but definitely no explorer. She helps me to reduce the options so my love does not get lost in confusion. She orients my love toward proven compassion, so I may not turn into an elephant man, a dwarf, giant, egoist, a lost son, a reckless experimenter, or a cancer. And so she is the stern "brakeman" on my roller-coaster ride into the fantastic world of evolution.

In the overstimulation of a crisis, like an ice age or our population explosion, then shame, that gentle inhibitor, may be biologically suspended. In such emergencies everybody seems allowed to make a run for himself. In an all out effort for new options life triggers us to try ourselves shamelessly out so we may err into all possible options and solutions for our new situation. There is great tolerance for waste and losses. We are driven into the arms of competition: God's permissive minister for excesses and outlandish choices, the daimon stocking our economy, patron saint of inventors, thief of our dear conventional vision. Our economy may so recruit an army of shame-soothers rocking to sleep shame's prudent guardian angels of the old and proven. To get fast out of the bind we are encouraged to become dwarfs, elephant men, egoists, billionaires, live on credit and not to mind traffic violations, waste, excesses. Our native embarrassment to behave unnaturally or excessively is reoriented, and we become embarrassed to remain natural, conventional, moderate and simply barefooted, so technology may step unhindered on the gas and fall head over heels into the grab bag of options even when those options use up credit that was meant for our children.

How tempting again for me to simply lament and to hammer our momentary loss of shame and implicate some evil power. But do I lament hibernation, the cornered lizard's capacity to shed its tail? Should a stranded fish remain ashamed to try walking on its tail?

Maybe I can sniff out, in our momentary shutdown of shame, one of life's wonderful arrangements for special situations—such as hibernating, vomiting, borrowing, adrenalizing, running a fever or fainting. And what would be the news that shame has lately produced on the playground of evolution?

216

May the gray, severe utilitarian world never become so devilishly just that the beggar cannot remain our flower child reminding us that there is another more illuminated way to take and to give.

Does it look to you like a disgrace to live on garbage, on wisdom that others throw away; to mop up all kinds of excesses; to nibble on addictions of others, on their pride, on the lard of the fellow life; to scavenge among the ugly ducklings and other valuables that the puritans, the swingers, the delicate minds and many Christians haul to the city jail; to live on discarded tenderness and chips of paint; to salvage sunken possibilities and loves; to use the bits of grace we throw away for lack of space in our elegantly designed theorems and to sew from it all a cozy quilt; to be a gentle beggar poet who never pays, cultivates, produces, or works where there are crumbs to be picked up after a big killer fumbled for his bread and his joys?

Begging, not working, may well be the finest form of taking on earth. There is no ax, no fear, never a loser in this exchange of gifts. Look at the smiles when the baby begs for milk! Look at the cockroach; nature loves this king of beggars so well, it has been sustaining it from pole to pole ever since it greeted the arrival of the dinosaurs, one hundred seventy million years ago.

Beggars seem a people's golden eggs. Is it not from such unemployed minds that its prophets and poets often hatch? In other cultures beggars are respected as the gurus and the wise. They are seen as the guardian angels of wisdom from before we were ordered to toil in the sweat of our brows and to pay for every apple we munch. Maybe we find the great beggars of our time among the unmotivated visionary scientists begging for grants.

To live hungry and lean, to hold out as an apprentice and remain a vacuum always ready to be instructed and filled; to become a master yielder and leave the least of turbulence behind; it might be such unglamorous qualities that can make us the fittest children in the garden of the gods.

217
A king who used to brave the four winds comes shivering in.

How easily one forgets, behind the promises, the simple law that the more a man is socialized, coming in from his weather-beaten peak and from being his own king, the more he gives up his luxurious capacity to see and love the woods, the birds, the open sky, and his mistress in indigo the sea, the mysterious beauty of paradoxes, the permissive overpowering laws of the outdoors. To enter *our* society, he must give up society. His love of a generalist is discreetly focused and monopolized by the sect of mankind into whose bowels he safely retreats. His bewildering sensitivity to all things alive simplifies to a local humane kindness; his wisdom melts down to a mighty utilitarian smartness and a retarded soul.

Slowly he gives up his capacity to directly converse with his environment and with God and to excitedly watch the Holy Spirit's outdoor play in which every critter acts out a tiny scene and yell his applause. Slowly he gives up to a priesthood and an environmental protection agency's staff pieces of his soul. When he so withdraws from that United Tribes of Life which is made of the family of grasses, of the phytoplanktons, the schools of fishes, the queendoms of insects and the prairie dog towns, the peoples of the elephants and those of man, the bacteria—greatest combiners and recombiners of life—the skeins of snow geese; he can neatly shack up with his own kind. Yet Mother Nature soon worries about a lost son. She fears that when this man so used to safely circulating in the bowels of man is assigned again a job in the living outdoors, he might, estranged, stumble and fumble as does any city man, soldier or drunk. She worries that a man who lost his soul is a lost man when left without a policeman guiding him, and is likely to kick up an ecological mess. And tell me: how can a man who has lost his love for the wild really love a woman?

I encouraged myself: Theo, step up again the ladder in the hierarchy of societies. Is not each of us now as never before beseeched to step forward, brave vertigo, brave the wrath of those who cannot yet venerate a God whose hair is of grasses and trees? Leap with impeccable faith from the island of humanitarian kindness into a love as inclusive and permissive as the Amazons. What a thrill to get so close to God without a middleman taking the heat. The muse, that charming mistress, pulls me lightly by my sleeves to the cliff: "Jump, you can hang-glide on your soul. Many of my tricks I can only teach you beyond that abyss."

218

Look through the Pandora telescope that magnifies the world beyond the empire of man—if you are not afraid to be left a changed man.

Committing Galileo's "crime" one might discover that our deepest feelings do not orbit ourselves; they do not even orbit mankind, but court the whole living world. These commanding hunches are so bewilderingly great, it was decided to have them tamed.

Committing Galileo's "crime" to climb that scenic viewpoint, wasting all this courage and time, the mountain of hateful things—even our own sins—may start making awesome sense. From there many character traits on which I impatiently sneered with contempt show themselves to me finally as vital faraway friends. From there I might be urged to do things that do not directly benefit man—even more: that global mind might "curse" a courageous few to do terrible acts that truly bleed us and may only pay us in generations we do not know. Earlier cultures saw in such unpopular actors those performers of the Sun Dance who danced the parts of the Great Give-Away. And so blessed be also the composters, the fermenters, and recyclers that grace the flooding Nile each spring with the rotten, the yummy ashes and the foul.

In the heat of such a sun, the lover of mankind or moralist in me steams with sweat and wants to hatch. He must leave the safety of the egg—braving the sweet terror of a mind that metamorphoses to be truly born. Many expensive ideas in her wardrobe will not fit and they crack when later again put on. With awe and joy he grasps the implications of what he sees. She has become naked and vulnerable to bugs, options, foes, seed ideas and friends that didn't exist for her before.

219
Are you a great artist? Can you teach me to read beyond words?

When very young I learned to depend on words to read the messages from the Dream of the Earth. My parents were proud. Soon I became quite deaf to the daily news of the lively outdoor world. My mind became tender. I wanted information well-done and simplified into ABCs. I got used to having God's actors killed seven times, chewed and regurgitated into comprehensive chunks so I may be fed in a mental trophallaxis just the useful sections of what they all know. Yet usefulness proved to be a short yardstick to appreciate God's circus show.

I note that in the systems of communication beyond words, we became rather a generation of illiterates. On that huge stage where even the dung beetle acts out for me amazing seminars and we now find a simple tuft of moss to be an even more complex corporation than the worldwide tangle of IBM, the use of the alphabet is such a weak tool to catch the great ideas that the Creator prints out in every living thing. The insights that serve me best are in pictures of likenesses, not in numbers and words.

When I see a drought, should I have to wait for the news reporter to tell me what it is all about? When I see a waterfall, can I not read in it ten theses in ten different sciences at one time? I don't run home to nose for answers in books. Look how snugly a tree fits into the woods, how he adapts his slender trunk, his limbs and leaves, how he calibrates his shade, the number of his seeds, his refuse, and his perfume. All this happens without letters going back and forth, without one single word. Yet don't tell me there is no communication, no awareness in these towns of trees.

When one talks about an educated person, I wonder whether one talks about a person who processed his vivid intellect into a supermarket where all the lively things are neatly butchered, canned, and shelfed in compartments for sale.

Out on the prairies, out among the milling clouds, out in the woods humming with mysteries, I read from a wise old picture book, compared to which not even our sacred scriptures seem to be as profound. Did you ever think of all you did not see and did not do while you were sitting in formal school? And what if only what I have lived through is true?

220
The Masterbaker.

Pressing my ear against a crack in the sky I listened into what the Creator in judgment of souls back from the fabulous journey to Earth had to say. I was astonished. Virtuous law-abiding creatures presented their deeds. He barely looked up. Absent-mindedly he reminded them: "Good boys are a waste of time—why repeat a successful experiment again and again? Evolving life is no merry-go-round. Even gold I do not allow to remain gold. Well, on second thought, I need you all." He delegated this bunch to one of his quarries in paradise to hammer rock into gravel to the beat of celestial music.

A mischievous-looking bunch of souls paraded in front of him. He looked up—looked again, then pricked his ears and made them sit down. From their liquid eyes you could tell that this gang dared trespass, make mistakes and sins. They were creatures foolish enough to walk on water, wriggle with gills out of their beloved ocean into the dry land of a scorching sun, critters who gave up sweet potatoes to live on bribes, others that grew most wasteful peacock feathers instead of keeping up their hair for warmth, others that made themselves so mean that in their blistering barren desert souls new, exotic cacti came alive. There were males who experimented in loving males; the Creator praised them all. "You were on Earth to serve me with your mistakes and you did well. I dip into the zillion options to beautify the world. I want every North Pole, every one of these zillion options, every cave, every impossibility and extreme explored— never mind the losses. It is for this I give the salmon a bellyful of eggs and the fox a litter of five. I made it to your nature to be unnatural when it comes to create new rhymes."

"Who said I would let my experimenters roast in a hell? Sinners, Amundsens, phenomena, eclipses, sicknesses, weirdoes, perversions, mutations, ugly ducklings, the ooze of chaos and meteors are my yeast to which the blind may have given a thousand ugly names. They are the yeast with which I rise and evolve my world."

221

Have you noticed that in the friction of danger, a man starts to glow?

Did you note that a child is born a Columbus, yet we tend to talk it out of being brave later on? Why should we want to put the chicken back into the egg, making of a man an eternal embryo? Why send the insurance man to talk the child out of discovering his own America and to sell it a sleeping pill instead?

Danger gives a natural high. It makes our body's chemistry release into our routines all kinds of psychedelic drugs. It bubbles resources up from below the sediments of our cultures. It makes us into dragons, angels, meteors, furiously digging worms. We become explosive firestones; so much so, that when we bang together and slowly break up, the lightning that we produce lights up our horizon. Danger wakes up in us seven lives.

Do you know a better therapy than welcoming danger to free a congested mind? Its shock waves crack peepholes into other worlds. Encourage me to seek out the biggest bite of danger I can swallow; to live on the periphery of society and move to the edge of my capacities—gladly risking—not holding back; not waiting for the biological clock to announce: "your time is up, you failed the test; you never risked death." When I desert danger, that clock relentlessly runs me down and calls the executioner in. Encourage me to let an opponent get close, to plunge into such a weather front, to be hurled up, thrown down, to come out of it a changed man.

Why is it that an invitation into danger should become an outdated gift? And, tell me, do you know a fairer, more thrilling and wiser population control than danger?

222

Who are the guinea pigs of evolution that are most hypered, starved or injected with new potentially lethal ideas?

I found the bug in my eye! It's my beloved assumption that a man's life is meant to be whole, loyal to his inherited nature and innocent, that a woman be idyllic, and our lives be the crown of life, harmonious and beautiful. I learned to judge a human life or mankind by how well it plays beautifully by itself. Nearly every preacher and artist and moralist has been teaching me this, but the epic of evolution never rests to prove to me that no creature, no species is allowed to become a harmonious merry-go-round of genetics and a good boy for long.

Every man seems planted with a seed of some talent or some excess. Each is loaded with the yeast of a little craziness. We seem each periodically tested whether we are still creators or whether it's time to turn our individuality in and become again compost for life's other projects.

We are stretched and stretched some more; torn between what we are and what we are yet to be but do not know. It's unbelievable how flexible we are, in how much perversion we can deviate, how much we can err from our soul's routine without breaking up.

I am also blessed with a few moments of peace, when my thoughts, words and acts may walk hand in hand and I am allowed to be loyal to my dear old self. Ah—what a treat!

We are beautiful trees but aren't meant to end up as beautiful trees. We are violated, felled, sawed, split in two and three. We are boiled and bent. Exquisite parts of us end up as timbers in new construction sites. Lesser capacities are shed.

It's the second act in the great saga. Early life, the free-swimming bacteria, have invented the basic tricks of life. They have regrouped and redefined themselves in symbiotic colonies with the founders finally so deformed and interdependent, one now calls these colonies simply by names such as Clara or Theo.

I see us being again led away from our hearts and homes and submitted to ever more demanding life style tests. We can seldom wake up into a new morning and take for granted that what was good yesterday is still good. So much in us is tentatively suppressed, reoriented or blown up to excess. Obsessions are grafted into our souls. Some of us are whirled wildly around our egos to confuse our mentality forcing it to mutate. Some are tried out at careers in anger or in a wrecking crew. Others are hoaxed to be so false to their roots and their inborn script, they seem to me a walking grimace. Some err around with half their minds suppressed. Some are lions trained to baby-sit the lambs. Some had, one by one, so many capacities of their individuality pruned that they seem now remnants, leaners and simply magnificent tools. Some are tried out on half rations of affection. There seems to be no perversion and extreme into which we have not been plunged. No other species seems to be blessed with so many daimons tempting them into the unknown.

Many vestigial abilities remain just recognizable enough to remind me of what a woman or a man were able to do. However, I see no new role models yet that let me anxiously welcome all these trade-ins.

Am I to aim at living beautifully by myself, to become settled, locked into that carousel that endlessly turns harmoniously around what is proven good and let this goal be my lazy, wishful wish? Am I to be true to our species of poets, plunged into homelessness, neurosis, restlessness, curiosity and doubt; blown with the winds into every shade, up to the moon, into every niche and the grand opening of our genes, the scenario in which new symbioses, the greatest poetry, begins?

223

I know now what I am asked to do.

I am to make my own tallest and deepest picture of every woman and man I learned to condemn, of every unpopular act, weed, vermin, of every energy, sucker and pest I do not like; of the ugly snails, ducklings and toads, of every sin, and nail all these pictures over my bed; to choose one of them every morning and mobilize all my intellect to make peace with it, to track down its good side effects whatever it takes, day after day, until I am called out of the game or until there is none of those shocking pictures hanging anymore. To trust that this peace is possible, in spite of all the peddlers of sin, hell, pest controls, garbage cans and jails; and stick meanwhile to an archetypical soul picture of an all-forgiving justice in my deepest mind is, for me, to have faith. To let, a restless intellect freely progress toward it might reveal a soul in purgatory that's having fun.

To make peace with my shadow is to me no ghost hunt anymore. My shadow is all the terrible people, the others, my needs that do not fit under the uniform. It's the garbage and weeds along my road. It's you when you shock me with what you do.

Looking down into the peaks, hills and canyons of time, a good stout enemy may become a formidable long range friend; a cozy friend may lose his special glow; the braver opponent may become my better sharpening stone.

224

Finally, this child has grown up and can fend for itself.

I think not only am I partly possessed with "evil" spirits, I suspect every creature is blessed with them. Without these spirits, I sense a people would soon get fat. For me my bad spirits have become my spirits that give away, those spirits that do not put more layers of wealth around our waist but test us, chisel on our success and compensate for our growth or when our goodness becomes recklessly selective. They take from all of us to keep us lean, maybe to wrap up birthday gifts for our children, maybe to give back

384

some of our excessive wealth and biomass to all life that starves on the other side of our fence and asks for help. Who else would watch so that we become not too many so that the animals and plants can remain plentiful? They are assigned the unglamorous job to draft among us demolition crews that happily clear the construction sites for all the new. These devil's advocates can be the true voices of guardian angels full of thoughtful mischief who are deaf to my moaning and fearlessly engage me in acts that care for the earthlings living ten generations up the slope. They may have to ask mutilations of our generation that is so overdone, bloodlettings, contributions of inactivity, many kinds of abortions. They may be caretakers of our good long-range fortune, the working of which I do not quite understand.

After a hundred generations of great childbearing women, of unabashed farmers with glorious farms, of ever greater fishermen and loggers who have a lot to brag about, I find my historic generation singled out for which these natural acts, that are still so loved by my blood and still seem so instinctively right to my romantic mind, are now losing their glory. We are taken to court for personal and inherited excesses; and I think that each woman and man, culprit or not, is now asked to make some kind of reparation. For me this means giving up my dear addiction to fishing, which has been my pride and at which I am so good. I am aiming instead for four Sundays a week free of blood. Yet wow! this sacrifice is already turning into a treat! Even better: I have a hunch that for a mind liberated from humanism, careers in such reparations can be as enjoyable as fishing or eating apple pie.

Could not in this sense the self-mutilations that some of us are driven to and the many kinds of abortions, even people felled in battle, become rather reorientations and gifts to the fertility of all life, maybe Mother's Day gifts of elbow room to the lucky among us who are still lured into the love affair of having children? I see compassionate men and women who, sensing the catastrophic pressure, take themselves out of that competition. Here at last are human acts that the whole crowd of fauna and flora can cheer as acts of friends.

I try to make peace with these unhappy spirits in me which a puritanical civilization persuaded me to lock in a closet. I let them come out from hiding after I have damned them for so long for standing in my way to becoming the instant hero of a local crowd. When finally let out, they seem at first to growl and to flex themselves angrily. I believe I have to make peace with them. I expect a woman or man who can make that peace becomes a more serene person. As long as life wriggles, chisels and drives suckerroots, this to me is the only desirable and biologically possible peace. I do not know any expedition more bewildering, profitable, even more amusing to me than this discovery trip here to my deeper self that seems to be so shamelessly friendly with every imaginable rascal of the world. The day I can tell myself that I am ready to never again communicate harshly with any creature and make a racket; that day will mark the day I earned a birthday cake. To earn that cake I realize that thoughts are needed that are not socially acceptable yet.

I am not ready for this serenity. I should have warned you earlier that this promiscuous way of looking at things is new to me. At times I am chicken and I get seasick of what I see. It makes me once more an unsure adolescent always tempted to hide my doubts behind arrogance. Please forgive me. I hope when I can listen to these daimons not as enemies, they can turn on in me new lights.

I honestly expect that some of the unauthorized ideas I have stirred up will soon for many become common sense.

I do not feel at my best when I spin some nifty logic how things are wrong and who can be blamed. Anybody can produce garbage, can spit, complain, cuss, accuse, criticize and waste. But when I follow blindly my faith telling me all is put to good use, and finally can welcome into my guesthouse this or that from the huge pile of what I do not like, turn it into a helper, add it to my serenity, I may have found a thought worth more than a dime. No wonder my faith that all is ultimately a quality of God has also become the spicy stinger reminding me that when I criticize, I always criticize myself.